ABOUT GUIDEPOSTS MAGAZINE

Guideposts magazine, with a circulation of over
3½ million and an average monthly readership of
more than 15 million, is America's most beloved
magazine of spiritual help and encouragement. It
features true first-person stories written by people
who, with God's help, have found answers in their
most difficult crises.

Founded by Norman Vincent Peale, *Guideposts*
counts among its contributors the greatest inspirational writers of our day, including Catherine
Marshall, Marjorie Holmes, Kathryn Kuhlman
and Billy Graham.

ABOUT THE GUIDEPOSTS TREASURIES

These volumes, each one a hardcover bestseller,
have long been sold only in hardcover, and only
through the pages of *Guideposts* magazine. Now,
by special arrangement with Bantam books, all
five are available in paperback at bookstores
everywhere, or will be coming soon:
THE GUIDEPOSTS TREASURY OF HOPE •
THE GUIDEPOSTS CHRISTMAS TREASURY
• THE GUIDEPOSTS TREASURY OF FAITH
• THE GUIDEPOSTS TREASURY OF INSPI-
RATIONAL CLASSICS • THE GUIDEPOSTS
TREASURY OF LOVE

Guideposts Treasuries by Bantam Books

THE GUIDEPOSTS TREASURY OF FAITH
THE GUIDEPOSTS TREASURY OF HOPE

The
Guideposts
Treasury
of
Faith

BANTAM BOOKS · TORONTO · NEW YORK · LONDON

GUIDEPOSTS TREASURY OF FAITH

*A Bantam Book / published by arrangement with
Doubleday & Company, Inc.*

PRINTING HISTORY

The Guideposts Treasury of Faith *was originally
published by Guideposts Associates in 1970*

*Doubleday edition published August 1979
3rd printing through May 1980*

Serialized in Grit *and* National Enquirer

Bantam edition / October 1980

ACKNOWLEDGMENTS

*Permission to quote material from the following sources is
gratefully acknowledged:*

*"Thank You, Dad" by James Stewart as told to Floyd
Miller, reprinted from* McCall's, © *1964, McCall Corp., N.Y.C.
"The Host of Heaven" by Dr. S. Ralph Harlow, condensed
from* A Life After Death, © *1961, Dr. S. Ralph Harlow and
Evan Hill, Doubleday & Company, Inc., N.Y.C. "Return from
Tomorrow"* © *1963 by Dr. George C. Richie, Jr. Used by
permission.*

ISBN 0-553-14132-5

Published simultaneously in the United States and Canada

PRINTED IN THE UNITED STATES OF AMERICA

0 9 8 7 6 5 4 3 2 1

Contents

SECTION THREE
HOW FAITH CAN STRENGTHEN THE HOME

SECTION FOUR
WHEN FAITH DIRECTS YOUNG LIVES

SECTION FIVE
THE HEALING POWER OF FAITH

SECTION NINE
FAITH CAN CHANGE THE WORLD

SECTION TEN
FAITH—DOORWAY TO A NEW LIFE

The Guideposts Story—
An Impossible Dream
Come True
by Leonard E. LeSourd

It seemed pointless, this interview, because it wasn't the kind of job I wanted at all. The man I was to see was a preacher-friend of the family. I had the uncomfortable feeling that the whole business was an attempt to get me straightened out after four years of high living as a pilot in World War II. These small leaflets he was publishing—what were they called . . . Guideposts?—seemed pallid in comparison to the earthy novel I wanted to write about returning servicemen.

Nevertheless, on a windy October day in 1946 I was shown into the study of Dr. Norman Vincent Peale in his New York City church. He asked a few questions about my editorial background (editor of a college yearbook, author of a book of war experiences called *Skybent*) and then described this new publishing venture, Guideposts.

"Most people in our world don't relate their religion to their everyday life," he said. "They feel that God should be confined to church on Sundays. The pastor is expected to handle Sunday services, marry and bury and that's about it."

I nodded, remembering the chaplains I had met in the Air Corps, many of whom were self-conscious while mingling with us and overconcerned about our attending chapel services.

"There is a great hunger in people to find real meaning in life," he went on. "We can achieve success in a material way, but most of us are not able to achieve deep-down fulfillment. Have you found this to be true?"

The question took me off guard. I was 27, single, self-centered. Thoughts like this had found little ground for growth in me. I nodded an affirmation I wasn't sure I felt.

1

Doctor Peale went on to describe the dream he and Mr. Raymond Thornburg, the publisher of Guideposts, shared. It was of a new kind of publication—written mostly by laymen of all faiths, personal experiences showing faith in God transforming people and situations. "This is not a pious Sunday-school approach," he said. "Guideposts is just that—guides to better living. We want to show how prayer, the Bible, faith can have real meaning in one's business, in the factory, in the ball park, in school, in the home. People are hungry today for this kind of good news."

Doctor Peale then described how Guideposts had been launched on faith alone.

"We started by renting a small room over a drugstore in Pawling, New York," he said. "We have no assets except our enthusiasm and faith, and what we feel is a great idea."

He paused a moment to scrutinize me carefully. "I've handled all the editorial work during the first year from my office here in New York. I need help. Guideposts is growing. But we have no money to hire an editor."

I felt a momentary sense of relief: There was no job here for me after all.

"But I have one idea that may interest you," Doctor Peale continued. "It would be a venture of faith for you too. Help us out on a trial basis as a kind of writer-editor. I think we can find twenty-five dollars a week as a starting salary."

I left Doctor Peale's office a short time later, wondering what I had gotten myself into—a job in a field where I had no interest—and for a salary on which I could not live. Yet something long buried in my life had been touched during this interview. It was more than the challenge to adventure: It was the challenge to give something of myself.

The next afternoon I drove 75 miles north to Pawling to meet Raymond Thornburg, the man who had conceived the idea of Guideposts, and to look over the publishing offices. These were in a large frame house on Quaker Hill which had been loaned to Guideposts by an interested neighbor. When I walked inside I was struck by the bare floors, the lack of furnishings. In the living room were a series of long tables behind which sat three elderly women. Piled on top of the tables were stacks of small four-page leaflets. These were Guideposts. There were no regular mailings of these leaflets to subscribers; a group of four leaflets was printed and mailed out as a unit only when enough money had been raised to pay the costs.

I introduced myself to the women and then watched them with some fascination. One was tying bundles of Guideposts with string and brown paper for mailing to bulk subscribers. The other two were checking through the list of subscribers which were on three by five cards in cigar boxes. I asked how many subscribers Guideposts had. None of the women knew.

Raymond Thornburg, president of the Pawling Rubber Corporation, was a hearty, enthusiastic man. He gave me a quick tour of the house (a few tables, chairs, files, boxes of leaflets, etc.) and then took me to dinner. Called "Pinky" because of his red hair and occasional flashes of temper, Mr. Thornburg had nothing but optimism for the future of Guideposts.

"We originally thought of it as a kind of spiritual Kiplinger letter which would arrive on the desk of a businessman every Monday morning to help guide his thinking through the week. But we found it too expensive to mail one leaflet each week, so we try to mail four a month."

Also at dinner was Fred Decker, a man in his thirties with ten years experience in advertising who had just been hired—also on faith—to direct the business operations. Fred was warm, articulate and, like me, short on spiritual knowledge.

One upstairs room of the Guideposts house had been equipped with a cot. This was where I spent the night. As I listened to the furnace pounding away, I put my hand against the wall. It was hot. Uneasily, I lay on the cot, sleepless, thinking that all this was totally unreal.

A minister, a rubber manufacturer, an advertising man and an ex-Air Corps pilot, banding together to get out a religious booklet. Elderly ladies tying together leaflets with string. An old firetrap as a publishing center. Although my parents were active Methodists and I had joined the church at age 15, it had been years since I had prayed or thought about God. What did I really feel about religion? Why had I accepted this impossible situation? How could any publishing venture succeed on such a shoestring and when the people running it knew so little about how to proceed?

Less than three months later—on Sunday afternoon, January 13, 1947—a fire started in the hot walls of the Guideposts publishing house. Before fire engines arrived, the blaze was out of control. Raymond Thornburg and other nearby residents watched helplessly as the building burned completely to the ground.

Doctor Peale, Fred Decker and I gathered together the next day in Mr. Thornburg's living room. The assessment of the situation was grim. There was no duplicate list of subscribers. All records and files had been burned except for the miscellaneous correspondence we had in our briefcases or homes. "No one will ever know how many subscribers we really did have," I thought to myself.

As Mr. Thornburg and Mr. Decker reviewed the facts, Doctor Peale sat in reflective silence. It would have been easy to fold up the project at that low point. My mind was already turning to other possibilities. Fred Decker had left a good job and could easily go back to it. For Doctor Peale and Raymond Thornburg, Guideposts was only a side project.

Then Doctor Peale spoke: "I realize the situation looks pretty hopeless," he began. "Yet I have the strangest feeling that the Lord is really in this situation trying to tell us something. For a little over a year now we have been telling our subscribers in the pages of Guideposts that faith can overcome obstacles. Perhaps the time has come for us to practice what we have been preaching."

With the decision to start all over again, people were moved to come to our aid. Lowell Thomas, a resident of Pawling and a supporter of Guideposts from the beginning, went on his radio news program that Monday night and told the story of the small struggling publication whose building had burned down. "Everything was lost," Lowell said to his coast-to-coast audience. "All records, the names and addresses of all subscribers. Everything is gone but their faith that God can bring good out of a calamity like this. If you were a subscriber to Guideposts, send in your name and address so that a new and better Guideposts can emerge from the ashes."

And people responded. The mail poured in. Some from subscribers, most from listeners who had not previously known about us. Temporary office space was obtained in the basement of the Pawling Methodist Church. "The fire may have been the best thing that could have happened to us," Fred Decker said one day as the postman delivered a huge bag of mail. "It burned up all our mistakes."

Well—not exactly.

Four months later Guideposts mailed out its first post-fire issue from another temporary office on Quaker Hill—a ski lodge filled with field mice. During the day the mice kept their distance, but when working on manuscripts there at night I could see them scurrying in and out of desk drawers, over and under the desks and even up the side of the walls.

Each day Fred Decker and I would thumb through the daily mail, anxiously looking for contributions large enough to assure that the next payroll could be met. Fred had a wife and two children to support, so it was a question of survival for him. I was single and still had a few thousand dollars of poker winnings from my days in the Air Corps to draw upon. Without this questionable resource I could not have remained with Guideposts—which went to confirm what I had begun to suspect about God's sense of humor.

DeWitt Wallace of the *Reader's Digest* was another who came to the aid of Guideposts in this time of need. Through him we met Fulton and Grace Oursler. Fulton Oursler, a senior editor at the *Digest* and author of the famous bestseller, *The Greatest Story Ever Told*, wrote a short item telling millions of *Digest* readers about the tribulations of our small publication with the big mission. More mail poured in.

Meanwhile, Grace Oursler, a writer of many books and articles herself, accepted—also on faith—the position of executive editor of Guideposts. Grace urged us to change the format to a monthly magazine and include helpful short material along with the personal experience stories. Doctor Peale and Mr. Thornburg were reluctant to abandon the original four-page leaflet idea. The compromise worked out was to commit Guideposts to a monthly delivery, double its number of pages, but with the new short material ("methodology" Grace called it) on separate four-page leaflets loosely inserted in the story leaflets.

The result was a more interesting and helpful magazine, but an unwieldly package.

Guideposts' second big crisis came to a head in the summer of 1948. Debts had reached $30,000. The New York City printer carried us for two mailings, then refused to print another issue until his bill of $5000 was paid. Regular operations in the editoral and business office ceased while we searched for an angel to help us with our financial crisis.

My father—Dr. Howard LeSourd, a dean at Boston University at the time—had an idea. "Go and see Mrs. Milton Durlach," he suggested. "She's a wealthy Jewish lady with a great passion for world peace."

A few days later Fred Decker and I were ushered into

the high-ceilinged living room of Mrs. Durlach's Park Avenue apartment. When white-haired Mrs. Durlach appeared, we saw at once that the peace she wanted for the world she had achieved in herself—she radiated tranquility. "Please call me Tessie," she said as we introduced ourselves. "Everyone does."

As we began to talk about Guideposts, Tessie Durlach went over to her desk and collected paper and three pencils. "Go on talking," she said. "I'm just preparing us to have 'written guidance' about your problem."

Fred and I looked at each other a bit uncertainly, then continued to present Guideposts' dilemma in the best possible light.

"Do you know about the old Oxford Group?" she asked when we both paused in our presentation.

We shook our heads.

"I won't go into details," she said. "Years ago some men and women in England started this movement. They learned to pray together and to share their problems with each other with great honesty. The Oxford Group taught me a great method of receiving guidance from God. It is done with paper and pencil. Don't let this throw you. We will simply have a prayer together in which we will ask God to guide us into the right course of action for your Guideposts."

Tessie handed us paper and pencils while Fred and I looked on in some dismay. "I'll pray first; you both join in too if you feel like it," she told us. "Then simply write down every thought which comes to you, even if it seems irrelevant. You may have to clear away some of the debris in your mind before God's wisdom can flow through."

This white-haired lady prayed softly but eloquently. Fred and I followed with a few halting, self-conscious words. Then we started writing. I jotted down the fact that I needed a haircut, that I needed to know more about prayer, that Guideposts had many needs, and so on.

Fred and I were finished long before Tessie was. She wrote and wrote. Finally she looked up. "Let's read what we have."

This was also rather embarrassing for Fred and myself, but we struggled through it. Tessie had a lot to read, most of which did not encourage me that she might be willing to make a financial contribution to Guideposts.

She finished, then was silent in deep thought. "The guidance I get now is that we must get together with Doctor

Peale and Mr. Thornburg so that we can all seek God's will together for Guideposts. Let's have their wives join us too. And Mr. and Mrs. Oursler."

This now-historic meeting took place on the porch of Doctor Peale's Quaker Hill farmhouse in July of 1948. There were eight of us: Doctor and Mrs. Peale, Mr. and Mrs. Thornburg, Grace Oursler, Fred Decker, Tessie and myself. We talked for a while, then Tessie once again presented her written guidance suggestion. Paper was passed out. Doctor Peale prayed, and then there was total quiet except for scratching of pencil on paper.

Fred and I had prepared the others for the reading aloud that was to follow. Even so, the atmosphere was awkward, strained. Six Protestants and one Roman Catholic felt strangely defensive while confronted with this quiet but deeply committed Jewish lady.

Each of us read our "written guidance." The same comments were made over and over. Guideposts was in deep trouble; survival was at stake; all operations had stopped until we paid the $5000 debt to the printer; we needed more equipment, more creative people, and more financial contributions.

Then it was Tessie's turn. Her face was serene but serious. "It is a curious thing . . . I wonder if anyone else here feels the same way . . . but everything that has been said so far makes one impression on me."

There was a long pause.

"Instead of revealing to me what a marvelous project you have, you all are thinking *lack*."

It took a long moment for the meaning of the word lack to sink in. Then Doctor Peale broke the silence. "Tessie, you are dead right. You are absolutely right. We have been sitting here feeling sorry for ourselves, complaining about our lack of resources when we should be thanking God for the great idea and the tremendous opportunity He gave us in Guideposts."

Suddenly the atmosphere on the porch began to change. "You know, Tessie, we should be honest with you," Doctor Peale continued. "Not one of us was looking forward to this meeting because we weren't really open to your idea of written guidance. We were simply hopeful that you would give us five thousand dollars to pay our printer. But you have given us something much better; you have shown us that our approach is wrong. We have got to see clearly the infinite resources God has for Guideposts. Instead of complaining about how few subscribers we have, we need to picture Guideposts reaching fifty thousand subscribers—yes, even a hundred thousand. Now that's a real vision for us. One hundred thousand subscribers!"

A happy smile spread across Tessie's face. "That's it—positive thinking. Believe you can do it and you will. Thank God in advance for His resources and they will be made available to you."

The atmosphere around the porch was now electric with excitement. "We need to be much more businesslike with Guideposts," said Raymond Thornburg. "We have had too much of a begging posture. If we really believe in Guideposts, we should put our faith on the line at the bank. Norman, we may have to stick our necks out a bit, but I'm willing to go to the bank tomorrow and seek a loan if you are."

Doctor Peale nodded, only half hearing. "Positive thinking," he said, rolling the words over his tongue with delight. "What a wonderful phrase. Tessie, you'll never know how much the Lord has used you today."

The meeting broke up with much warmth of feeling. Doctor and Mrs. Peale walked with Tessie to her car, thanking her profusely for coming, the idea of her financial contribution forgotten. Tessie got in her car, reached for the ignition key, paused. "Norman, I feel guided to do something I really had no intention of doing while I was here. I feel that I'm supposed to write you a check for five thousand dollars."

She took out her checkbook, wrote out the check, handed it to the astonished Doctor Peale and drove off.

This guidance meeting on the Peale porch was significant in many ways. It enabled Guideposts to resume publication. It encouraged Pinky Thornburg and Doctor Peale to borrow the money for equipment needed to streamline the business operations, signifying a more professional approach in this area. It helped bring about an important change in the format of the magazine itself. The leaflet idea was thrown out, and Guideposts became a 24-page magazine (later 32 pages) as of the August, 1948, issue. And it was soon after this "porch meeting" that Doctor Peale began writing a book that was to become a long-term best seller and create publishing history. Its title: *The Power of Positive Thinking*.

In May, 1950, Guideposts celebrated its Fifth Anniversary with a remarkable dinner at the Hotel Astor in New

York City. Not only did some 2000 friends and subscribers jam every bit of space in the hotel ballroom, but the dais included 50 of America's top names and leaders, representing every faith, color, occupation and section of the country. Early supporters were there—Lowell Thomas (toastmaster), Branch Rickey, Eddie Rickenbacker, Conrad Hilton, De Witt Wallace, Stanley S. Kresge—plus leaders from the arts, entertainment, business and government, many of whom had written their own personal stories for Guideposts.

It was an evening I could not have dreamed of that night on the cot in Pawling. Fulton Oursler really startled me when he told the audience: "That same year—Nineteen-forty-five—saw the inception of two new forces: the atomic bomb and Guideposts—one for the purpose of destruction, the other for the purpose of creating a better climate of faith and brotherhood in the world."

He's putting *us* on a par with the bomb, I thought! He thinks we can generate that kind of power!

The Fifth Anniversary marked the end of an era of groping. The combination of a great publication idea, the dauntless vitality of a few people, and the grace of God overcame our inexperience and inefficiency. And that impossible circulation dream of 100,000 subscribers, which seemed so far away that day on Doctor Peale's porch in the summer of 1948, was reached three years later in 1951!

A new era began in the early Fifties with the purchase—also on faith—of a 52-acre site in Carmel, New York, property which for nearly 100 years had housed Drew Seminary for Girls. Classrooms, bedrooms and gymnasium were converted into offices and publication facilities. Gradually our editorial skills increased, and our business methods improved.

As Guideposts continued to grow steadily—some years spectacularly—every now and then I would pick up a copy of the magazine and look objectively at it. Pocket-size, two colors, never more than 32 pages, I would say to myself in some amazement, "What is your secret?"

I asked this question when we reached a million paid subscribers in 1961. I asked it again the other day when circulation figures showed us approaching the two-million mark. I have asked it of Doctor and Mrs. Peale, Raymond Thornburg and his wife Pherbia (both on the Board of Directors from the beginning) and many others who have been important to the project.

All agree that Guideposts' unique format—no advertising, interfaith, inspirational, nonprofit—has given us a great opportunity for distribution into many areas. In the early days when Guideposts' survival was a day-to-day drama, Doctor Peale and Mr. Thornburg went from city to city holding luncheons for businessmen in hopes of getting bulk subscriptions. The breakthrough came one day in Winston-Salem, North Carolina. After a meeting with some of the top business leaders of that city, John C. Whitaker, president of the Reynolds Tobacco Company, announced that his company was subscribing for its 14,000 employees.

This not only gave our subscription drive a shot of adrenaline at a critical moment, but it set an example for other companies. Today some 2000 firms subscribe for over 300,000 employees, thanks to the work of Guideposts men in the field like Charles Kennard, Nelson Rector and Irving Granville. In 1951 Conrad Hilton ordered copies of Guideposts for the rooms of every Hilton Hotel (later to include Statler Hotels). Other hotels and motels (including many of the Holiday Inns) have followed this plan so that today over 50,000 copies each month are made available to travelers.

But important as industrial subscriptions have been, this is not the real reason behind the Guideposts success story.

Could the answer lie in the basic principle we who work at Guideposts have tried to follow ever since the fire in 1947—"Practice what you preach"?

This means that if we publish stories in Guideposts about having right relationships with other people, about the power of prayer, about putting God first in our lives, then we as employees had better live this way on the job.

The truth is, of course, that while we try to do this, we have often failed. Sometimes we haven't even tried. Sometimes we have succeeded in spite of ourselves.

We needed an associate editor during one period of our growth. In prayer one morning I asked God to send us a young man who had a combination of writing skills and spiritual dedication. By the time I arrived at the office, however, my request was completely gone from my mind.

But God was already working on it. A young man with these exact requirements was in New York seeking an editorial position. In this Hilton hotel room he picked up a copy of Guideposts and read through it with growing interest. Below the masthead he noted the address of the New York editorial office of Guideposts. Without bothering to ask for an appointment, he strolled into our office.

"There's a young man outside who would like to talk to one of the editors," the receptionist reported to me over the intercom.

I was deeply involved in editing an article. "In a few minutes," I said.

Fifteen minutes later the young man decided to leave and told the receptionist that he might be back again later that day. The receptionist buzzed me again and somewhat grumpily I asked her to show the young man into my office.

At first as the young man began talking, I was still thinking about interrupted work. Then he said he was seeking God's will for his life in the editorial field. Something clicked. From then on he had my total interest and attention. Within a month Fred Bauer, who served as Managing Editor for a while and is now a Roving Editor, was added to our staff.

"Forgive me, Lord, for my lack of faith and for getting in the way of Your answer to prayer," I said contritely sometime later when I saw the experience in perspective.

We have tried to practice what we preach at the regular editorial meetings where the unique factor is the diversity of staff representation: Protestant, Catholic, Jew, liberal and conservative, male and female, high- and low-income earner, evangelical and social-gospel advocate, young protester and senior citizen.

Each meeting starts with a prayer offered by one member of the group. It takes many forms, this prayer, but in essence it is a request for God's guidance, for open minds and receptive hearts, for honesty and sincerity, for the wisdom and insights that will enable Guideposts Magazine to help those who read it.

Sometimes the prayer is totally urgent. In 1959 Senior Editor John Sherrill went in for a routine physical examination. Melanoma cancer—a particularly virulent form of the disease—was discovered in his neck.

While John began getting his affairs in order, the rest of us at Guideposts began marshaling the best resource we had. There was staff prayer for John; Doctor Peale had congregational prayer for John in the Marble Collegiate Church; a wire went off to the Silent Unity Prayer Tower; and we enlisted the support of every prayer group we could think of. It was a period of total, concentrated effort.

When John went in for his operation several days later,

there was no sign of the cancer that a biopsy had previously exposed! Guideposts, which for many years had reported miracles in the lives of others, was blessed by a miracle to one of its own editors.

And so among the Guideposts family deep friendships have formed, lives have been changed, even dramatically saved—all of which makes an exciting and unique story in itself. But is this the secret that has made Guideposts what it is today?

I don't really think so.

Let's look at the editorial content of Guideposts. Some years ago, a letter came on plain white paper from a woman in New Jersey. She told us that she had decided to end her life, had checked into a hotel with this purpose in mind, and then happened to see a copy of Guideposts on the dresser. "It was almost as if God was guiding my hand to your article about the National Save a Life League," she wrote us. "The article spoke so directly to me that I soon found myself on my knees by the bed, weeping uncontrollably and asking God's forgiveness for what I had almost done."

The letter meant a lot to me because I had worked hard on this story about suicides when it was in manuscript form. I had come up with the article's title, "Now They Want to Live." I felt a part of a team effort that had saved the life of this woman; it gave me a thrill the like of which I had never experienced before.

From then on I became fascinated by the letters we receive on how Guideposts has influenced lives. A businessman wrote that an article on honesty checked him from making a shady deal. Another man told us how a Guideposts story on family prayer made him so ashamed of an affair he was having that he stopped it cold. A teen-ager wrote that she had decided to stop cheating in school and requested us to "please pray for my father and mother, that they will stop fighting all the time and make our home a happy place."

At editorial meetings one question is now always asked: "What is the *take-away* for the reader?" The criteria for selecting nearly every item in each issue became its spiritual helpfulness. And not just giving the reader something to think about—but something he could *do* about his problem, or his friend's, or a community need.

During the past decade, newspapers, television, movies, magazines, books, have become increasingly fascinated by the negatives of our society. Violence, immorality, shocking behavior make news and get wide coverage in all these media. Yet most people yearn deep down for good news!

From the beginning, Guideposts has attempted to offer hope and enlightenment for people who want to know of the good in our world. For while bad news receives most of the publicity, the nobility of man is still at work today; sometimes it comes forth in an exciting way. When this occurs, Guideposts is there to capture the story. While evil seems to be sweeping over our world, there have never been so many exciting stories of God working through people to achieve His miracles.

And so I am convinced the real secret of Guideposts' amazing growth and impact does not lie in circulation techniques, no matter how well executed, nor in the remarkable ministry of Doctor Peale, although this has certainly helped. It does not lie in staff creativity, nor in the high quality of inspirational writers we have developed over the years. The secret goes back to 1945 and something sensed by Guideposts' founders in the yearnings of a people tired of war and confused by the growing complexity of our age.

"Find a need and fill it," they were told; that's the formula for success in almost any field. So it was for Guideposts.

Section One—

The Inner Struggle Toward Faith

Section One—
Introduction

During the past 25 years, our world has evolved from a so-called Atomic Age into a Space Age where men are probing into the further reaches of the universe. Yet, no matter how far he explores into space, the most revealing journey man will ever make is the one he takes inward into the very soul of his being. And the searching questions man has always asked are still relevant today or will be whatever the future brings: Where did I come from? Why am I here? Where am I going?

In this initial section, Guideposts presents ten widely different accounts by people who struggled to a faith which would guide them through the difficulties and frustrations of life. Each in his own way found a truth that has broad application. Babe Ruth told Guideposts readers of his discovery in 1948 shortly before he died. Stella Shepard, a one-time Communist leader, revealed the inner illumination which changed the direction of her life. Billy Graham wrote about his personal "Hour of Decision" which was to set him on a remarkable course of worldwide evangelism; Helen Keller, though deaf and blind all her years, personally typed out for Guideposts the philosophy of faith that lighted her life.

Somewhere in these stories is a truth that will reinforce your faith—or an idea which will help you build on beliefs already tested—or an insight that could start you as a beginner on a rewarding spiritual journey.

My Restless Search
by Fulton Oursler

The author of the classic, The Greatest Story
Ever Told, *writes another great story—his own*

One April morning at the beginning of the century, my
colored nurse led me to a gray stone chapel in Baltimore.
Welcoming me inside, a Sunday-school teacher awesomely informed that I was now in God's house.

"Whereabouts," I asked, "is God?" "God," the lady assured me, "is everywhere."

But I wanted Him to be *somewhere*. That was why I refused to sit still on my little oaken chair, but ran about the
room during the singing of "Little Drops of Water." I peeked
under the pew and in a broom closet, only to be rescued finally, breathless and dusty, from behind the pipe organ,
weeping because I had not found God.

Thus my quest began, and through half a century I
never entirely abandoned it. Even in childhood the reality or
nonreality of the Creator seemed to me the most important
matter in life; nor can I understand today how any intelligent
person can think otherwise. It is the one supreme matter on
which a man has to be sure, for every decision he makes
hinges upon it.

In my search for truth I explored many different fields.
A study of comparative religions over a decade of years led
me from Buddhism, all the way to Bahaism and Zoroastrian-
ism. As a reporter for the Baltimore American, I attended
many religious conferences, and covered evangelistic meetings
of Billy Sunday. I even waited for spectres in darkroom
seances of spiritualistic mediums.

Out of all this I emerged, at the age of thirty, a self-
styled agnostic. In those days I considered myself a liberal
person, emancipated from superstition, although still genially

17

loyal to ethical values—when they did not interfere too much with what I wanted to do.

Such tolerance and emancipation, and what I considered common sense and goodwill, should have brought me happiness but did not. Nor did they bring happiness to anyone I knew. Most of my friends felt as I did; none of us better or worse than the other, I suppose; all very independent and self-reliant and disdainful of the old-fashioned faith of our fathers. We all had a great deal of fun, too, but somehow our hilarities left us dispirited.

With our freedom, we should have known a high sense of contented integrity. Not one of us knew any such security. Instead we all had an inner restlessness of disappointment and discontent.

This inner sulkiness and depression had nothing to do with material success. Among my friends were many who had achieved fame and riches, or, at least, a lot of money in the bank. But no matter how much more wealth they piled up, how often their pictures were on the front page, their new possessions, their new wives—nothing was ever enough. After they got what they wanted, they didn't want it. Without avail, they haunted doctors and psychiatrists and yogis.

The world in which I lived was a world of self-pity, self-justification, alibis, envies, jealousies, greeds, fears, resentments, grudges, and hatreds. Today was never good enough, but tomorrow they hoped to be glad. I say they, but I mean we. Today, 1950, there are eight million men and women, quite like us, who are under mental care. There will be, psychiatrists tell us, ten million in a year or so.

I shall be forever grateful that in the midst of mental bleakness I found the way out. It is not easy to tell how this happened; I cannot bring myself to open old wounds to public gaze. But you may remember the true story of the illustrious refugee at Lourdes, a famous liberal writer who, with his wife, had slipped through the Nazi frontier. They were working their way southward from Germany through France. The Gestapo was after them, and capture meant the concentration camp or worse. Their hope was to cross the Spanish border and sail for the United States. But they were stopped by Spanish officials. Bribes and entreaty alike failed; they were turned back and found a lodging in the little town in the Pyrenees called Lourdes. On his first night there the fugitive writer stood in front of the famous shrine and made a prayer, a cry from the heart.

"I do not believe in you," he said, in effect, "and I must be honest and say so. But my danger is great, and in my extremity, on the chance that you might after all be real, I ask your help. See my wife and me safely across the barrier, and when I get to the United States I will write the story of this place for all the world to read."

Strange as it sounds, Franz Werfel and his wife got safely through, within the week. The first thing he did, once safe in our land, was to write The Song of Bernadette. In our day no more popular tribute to faith was ever penned than the story written by the refugee novelist. Before he died he told me that in the terror of plight he had come to know God and thereafter had never lost the sense of His presence.

Now something akin to that happened to me. It was nothing so spectacular as a flight from Hitler's agents, but within my own modest sphere I, too, felt surrounded and in danger and afraid. My agnostic self-reliance was no longer helpful; trouble came and littered my doorstep. Not only I but those nearest and dearest to me were in trouble with me, until I felt I really needed God's help. Yet even then I could not, as an intelligent man, command myself to believe, or pretend to obey—for a man is a fool who tries to deceive either God or himself. The most—the best that I could manage was to admit to myself that I wished I could believe. And that was enough!

Faith is a gift—but you can ask for it! "O Lord," prayed a man in the Bible, "I believe; help Thou mine unbelief." As he laid his situation before God, and as Werfel did, so did I. Not in Palestine, nor in the Pyrenees, but close to the fashionable parade on Fifth Avenue. On a blustery day, with dark clouds lowering, I entered a house of God and asked for faith. And in the chapel, I took one more vital step.

"In ten minutes or less I may change my mind," I prayed. "I may scoff at all this—and love error again. Pay no attention to me then. For this little time I am in my right mind and heart. This is my best. Take it and forget the rest; and, if You are really there, help me."

It was a striking omen to me that when I came out on the steps the sun had crashed through the dark skies and the lordly avenue was full of color and light.

Merely for the record, the perplexities of my problem were most remarkably and swiftly disposed of. The complication dissolved itself by the oncoming of a series of what the rationalist would call beautiful coincidences. In two weeks I no longer had a serious problem.

But for me the real knowing of God was just beginning on that day. Only incidentally is prayer asking for help. Prayer is not a slot machine, where you drop in a request and a boon comes tumbling out of the bottom. We do pray for help, but oftener we pray for help for others, and even oftener we pray our thanks for blessings already received. Above everything else, we pray daily in sheer felicity, in communion, in close contact with the Father, asking nothing whatever but the joy of knowing Him.

It is through prayer that we know there is a God, that God is there; through prayer that we know Him—as Father and friend.

Even with this new feeling of profound tranquillity, nevertheless, you want to be active. Your kind instincts will no longer be satisfied with sending checks to worthy charities; you will be ashamed to buy yourself off. Such gifts to charity are necessary, but never enough. We have to do the corporal works of mercy ourselves; and, as we come to know God, the urge to serve Him personally becomes overpowering. We must feed the hungry, visit the sick, comfort the widow and orphan, clothe the naked, shelter the shelterless—under our own roof, with our own bare hands.

That is when a human being comes closest to God and knows Him best.

Isn't it strange that it should have taken me so many years to find that simple key to the mystery? Ten thousand times in a half century, God walked with me to school, rode with me in the bus, held out a beggar's hand at the corner alley, roared at me in the very blasphemy of a reeling old sot from whom all had fled. So many times He was at my elbow, and I pushed on, unaware. Fifty years of never noticing! I have much lost time to make up for.

Occasionally I meet someone who seems to have a secret, some special knowledge that sets that person apart. Such a person was Ruby Free. I met her when she was conducting our Holy Land tour.

"She must have a secret," I said to myself enviously. "How else can she accomplish so much, so easily?" She was a good listener, a troubleshooter, an organizer, a mother hen to all 72 of us plus her own two little children; yet she was never tired, never out of sorts.

Then, back home again, I visited Ruby. And I think I discovered her secret. There it was, a two-word motto over her sink:

"YES, LORD."

ROSA CORNELIA VEAL
Spartanburg, South Carolina

My Luminous Universe
by Helen Keller

A beautiful story by a beautiful woman.

It is difficult for me to answer when I am asked what are the main lessons life has taught me. Looking deeply into my inner self, I feel that ultimately I have not been influenced by any particular "lessons," but rather by forces working on my subconsciousness that have borne me on an unseen current.

The tendencies which my teacher* divined and developed were the making of the ship that has carried me far out into the ocean of public life. Joy in adventure, travel and love of service to my fellow men were stronger than physical handicaps.

Instinctively I found my greatest satisfaction in working with men and women everywhere who ask not, "Shall I labor among Christians or Jews or Buddhists?" but say rather, "God, in Thy wisdom help me to decrease the sorrows of Thy children and increase their advantages and joys." Blindness and deafness were simply the banks that guided the course of my life-ship until the stream joined the sea.

But there is one lesson I have consciously learned—that, although in Ecclesiastes it is said *There is no new thing under the sun***, yet history is full of new meanings in every age and nation, which continually blossom and bear fruit. To my surprise I discovered in my Greek sayings, "There is no force so mighty in the world as perseverance." It never occurred to the writer of that rich sentence in ancient times that it would sow new seeds of significance until a day would come when the blind, the deaf, and the crippled would rise up in the might of purpose, compel their obstacles aside, and press onward to creative accomplishment.

---

* *Anne Sullivan, who began teaching Helen Keller at the age of seven.*
** *Eccl. 1:9*

I have caught rays of light from different thinkers—Socrates, Plato, Bacon, Kant, and Emanuel Swedenborg, the Swedish seer. With Socrates I believe in thinking out the meaning of words before committing them to speech. Plato's theory of the Absolute strengthens me because it gives truth to what I know is true, beauty to the beautiful, music to what I cannot hear, and light to what I cannot see. Swedenborg has shaken down the barriers of time and space in my life and supplied me with likenesses or correspondences between the world within and the world without, which give me courage and imagination beyond my three senses.

Thus I move from one philosophy to another, constructing out of a fragmentary outward environment a luminous, resonant universe.

These varied thoughts convince me that, blind or seeing, one is not happy unless one's heart is filled with the sun which never dissolves into gloom. God is that sun, and if one's faith in Him is only strong, He will somehow or other reveal one's powers and brighten the darkest days with His divine beams.

Since my 17th year I have tried to live according to the teachings of Emanuel Swedenborg. By "church" he did not mean an ecclesiastical organization, but a spiritual fellowship of thoughtful men and women who spend their lives for a service to mankind which outlasts them. He called it a civilization that was to be born of a healthy, universal religion—goodwill, mutual understanding, service from all to each and each to all, regardless of dogma or ritual.

Swedenborg's religious works are in many long volumes, but their sum and substance are in three main ideas—God as Divine Love, God as Divine Wisdom, and God as Power for use. These ideas come as waves from an ocean which floods every bay and harbor of life with new potency of will, of faith, of effort.

By love I do not mean a vague, aimless sentiment, but a desire for good united with wisdom and fulfilled in work and deed. Because God is infinite, He puts resources into each human being that outrun the possibilities of evil. He is always creating in us new forms of self-development and channels through which, even if unaware, we may quicken new impulses towards civilization, art, or humanitarianism.

My confidence in the final triumph of idealism over materialism does not spring from closing my mental eyes to the suffering or the evil-doing of men, but rather from a steadfast belief that goodwill climbs upward in human nature while the meanness and hatred drop into their native nothingness, and life goes on with unabated vigor to its new earth and heaven.

With me optimism has changed from the hard bud of girlhood to a fuller knowledge of human affairs and the tragedies and horrors that often seem to pervert men from God's Plan of Good. But my faith in progress has not wavered.

In my travels around the world I have witnessed here and there wonderful awakenings to spiritual truth and a sense of responsibility for the welfare of the blind, the deaf and other unfortunate human beings, which would be impossible if there were not a growing desire for the common good among mankind.

There are two ways to look at destiny, one from below and the other from above. In one view we are being pushed by irresistible forces, obsessed by the fear that war, ignorance, poverty, and barbarism will never be abolished. But looking up to the clock of Truth, I see that man has been civilized only a few minutes, and I rest in the assurance that out of the problems and tensions which disturb thinking minds and warm hearts there shall break the morning star of universal peace.

In this world full of perplexities, shuttling creeds and philosophies, I have struggled like everybody else to find myself and enter a field of usefulness. I believe that we begin heaven now and here if we do our work for others faithfully. There is no useful work that is not part of the welfare of mankind. Even the humblest occupation is "skilled labor" if it contains an effort above mere self-support to serve a spiritual or social need.

During many years of work for the handicapped, I have been braced by the happy consciousness that I can be "an architect of fate" and I never need to stop growing until the after-life.

I have never let myself be bothered by the idea of a supernatural heaven, but I have a joyous sense of personal immortality. Life in the other world is just as real and full of change and wonder as on earth, but one is given eyes and ears to perceive far more clearly the varieties of good and constructive thought which the flesh conceals on earth.

In a sense souls transmigrate, not from place to place, but through endless phases of personality. Angels and demons are all from the human race, and each chooses his dwelling either in the light or in the shadows. All peoples and kindreds who believe in God, yes, even those who worship idols from a desire to do good, are taught new concepts of Him and how to live for the peace and happiness of those around them.

Love and brotherhood and harmonious thoughts send fragrance and music into the atmosphere as they are wrought into service. Life in heaven is free from the clogs of time and the burdens of weight.

I do not believe that anyone ever attains perfection because that attribute belongs to the infinite alone. But the longing for perfection, which is one way of loving God, causes one to grow nobler and to taste innumerable delights through eternity.

The Kids Can't Take It If We Don't Give It

by Babe Ruth

A parting word from baseball's unforgettable home-run hero.

Bad boy Ruth—that was me.

Don't get the idea that I'm proud of my harum-scarum youth. I'm not. I simply had a rotten start in life, and it took me a long time to get my bearings.

Looking back to my youth, I honestly don't think I knew the difference between right and wrong. I spent much of my early boyhood living over my father's saloon, in Baltimore—and when I wasn't living over it, I was in it, soaking up the atmosphere. I hardly knew my parents.

St. Mary's Industrial School in Baltimore, where I was finally taken, has been called an orphanage and a reform school. It was, in fact, a training school for orphans, incorrigibles, delinquents and runaways picked up on the streets of the city. I was listed as an incorrigible. I guess I was. Perhaps I would always have been but for Brother Matthias, the greatest man I have ever known, and for the religious training I received there which has since been so important to me.

I doubt if any appeal could have straightened me out except a Power over and above man—the appeal of God. Iron-rod discipline couldn't have done it. Nor all the punishment and reward systems that could have been devised. God had an eye out for me, just as He has for you, and He was pulling for me to make the grade.

As I look back now, I realize that knowledge of God was a big crossroads with me. I got one thing straight (and I wish all kids did)—that God was Boss. He was not only my Boss but Boss of all my bosses. Up till then, like all bad kids,

26

I hated most of the people who had control over me and could punish me. I began to see that I had a higher Person to reckon with who never changed, whereas my earthly authorities changed from year to year. Those who bossed me had the same self-battles—they, like me, had to account to God. I also realized that God was not only just, but merciful. He knew we were weak and that we all found it easier to be stinkers than good sons of God, not only as kids but all through our lives.

That clear picture, I'm sure, would be important to any kid who hates a teacher, or resents a person in charge. This picture of my relationship to man and God was what helped relieve me of bitterness and rancor and a desire to get even.

I've seen a great number of "hemen" in my baseball career, but never one equal to Brother Matthias. He stood six feet six and weighed 250 pounds. It was all muscle. He could have been successful at anything he wanted to in life—and he chose the church.

It was he who introduced me to baseball. Very early he noticed that I had some natural talent for throwing and catching. He used to back me in a corner of the big yard at St. Mary's and bunt a ball to me by the hour, correcting the mistakes I made with my hands and feet. I never will forget the first time I saw him hit a ball. The baseball in 1902 was a lump of mush, but Brother Matthias would stand at the end of the yard, throw the ball up with his left hand, and give it a terrific belt with the bat he held in his right hand. The ball would carry 350 feet, a tremendous knock in those days. I would watch him bugeyed.

Thanks to Brother Matthias I was able to leave St. Mary's in 1914 and begin my professional career with the famous Baltimore Orioles. Out on my own . . . free from the rigid rules of a religious school . . . boy, did it go to my head. I began really to cut capers.

I strayed from the church, but don't think I forgot my religious training. I just overlooked it. I prayed often and hard, but like many irrepressible young fellows, the swift tempo of living shoved religion into the background.

So what good was all the hard work and ceaseless interest of the Brothers, people would argue? You can't make kids religious, they say, because it just won't take. Send kids to Sunday school and they too often end up hating it and the church.

Don't you believe it. As far as I'm concerned, and I

think as far as most kids go, once religion sinks in, it stays there—deep down. The lads who get religious training, get it where it counts—in the roots. They may fail it, but it never fails them. When the score is against them, or they get a bum pitch, that unfailing Something inside will be there to draw on.

I've seen it with kids. I know from the letters they write me.

The more I think of it, the more important I feel it is to give kids "the works" as far as religion is concerned. They'll never want to be holy—they'll act like tough monkeys in contrast, but somewhere inside will be a solid little chapel. It may get dusty from neglect, but the time will come when the door will be opened with much relief. But the kids can't take it, if we don't give it to them.

I've been criticized as often as I've been praised for my activities with kids on the grounds that what I did was for publicity. Well, criticism doesn't matter. I never forgot where I came from. Every dirtyfaced kid I see is another useful citizen. No one knew better than I what it meant not to have your own home, a back yard, your own kitchen and ice box. That's why all through the years, even when the big money was rolling in, I'd never forget St. Mary's, Brother Matthias and the boys I left behind. I kept going back.

As I look back, those moments when I let the kids down—they were my worst. I guess I was so anxious to enjoy life to the fullest that I forgot the rules—or ignored them. Once in a while you can get away with it, but not for long. When I broke training, the effects were felt by myself and by the ball team—and even by the fans.

While I drifted away from the church, I did have my own "altar," a big window of my New York apartment overlooking the city lights. Often I would kneel before that window and say my prayers. I would feel quite humble then. I'd ask God to help me not make such a big fool of myself and pray that I'd measure up to what He expected of me.

In December, 1946, I was in French Hospital, New York, facing a serious operation. Paul Carey, one of my oldest and closest friends, was by my bed one night.

"They're going to operate in the morning, Babe," Paul said. "Don't you think you ought to put your house in order?"

I didn't dodge the long, challenging look in his eyes. I knew what he meant. For the first time I realized that death might strike me out. I nodded, and Paul got up, called in a Chaplain, and I made a full confession.

"I'll return in the morning and give you Holy Communion," the chaplain said. "But you don't have to fast."

"I'll fast," I said. I didn't have even a drop of water.

As I lay in bed that evening I thought to myself what a comfortable feeling to be free from fear and worries. I now could simply turn them over to God. Later on, my wife brought in a letter from a little kid in Jersey City.

"Dear Babe," he wrote, "Everybody in the seventh grade class is pulling and praying for you. I am enclosing a medal which if you wear will make you better. Your pal—Mike Quinlan.

"P.S. I know this will be your 61st homer. You'll hit it."

I asked them to pin the Miraculous Medal to my pajama coat. I've worn the medal constantly ever since. I'll wear it to my grave.

In One Blinding Moment
by Max Ellerbusch

"I cannot explain it. I can only describe how a man can change from hate to love."

It was a busy Friday, six days before Christmas, 1958. I was in my instrument-repair shop, working feverishly so that I could have all of the Christmas holiday at home with my family. Then the phone rang and a voice was saying that our five-year-old, Craig, had been hit by a car.

There was a crowd standing around him by the time I got there, but they stepped back for me. Craig was lying in the middle of the road; his curly blond hair was not even rumpled.

He died at Children's Hospital that afternoon.

There were many witnesses. It had happened at the school crossing. They told us that Craig had waited on the curb until the safety-patrol boy signaled him to cross. Craig, how well you remembered! How often your mother called after you as you started off for kindergarten, "Don't cross till you get the signal!" You didn't forget!

The signal came, Craig stepped into the street. The car came so fast no one had seen it. The patrol boy shouted, waved, had to jump for his own life. The car never stopped.

Grace and I drove home from the hospital through the Christmas-lighted streets, not believing what had happened to us. It wasn't until night, passing the unused bed, that I knew. Suddenly I was crying, not just for that empty bed but for the emptiness, the senselessness of life itself. All night long, with Grace awake beside me, I searched what I knew of life for some hint of a loving God at work in it, and found none.

As a child I certainly had been led to expect none. My father used to say that in all his childhood he did not experience one act of charity or Christian kindness. Father was an orphan, growing up in 19th century Germany, a supposedly

30

Christian land. Orphans were rented out to farmers as machines are rented today, and treated with far less consideration. He grew into a stern, brooding man who looked upon life as an unassisted journey to the grave.

He married another orphan and, as their own children started to come, they decided to emigrate to America. Father got a job aboard a ship; in New York harbor he went ashore and simply kept going. He stopped in Cincinnati where so many Germans were then settling. He took every job he could find, and in a year and a half had saved enough money to send for his family.

On the boat coming over, two of my sisters contracted scarlet fever; they died on Ellis Island. Something in Mother died with them, for from that day on she showed no affection for any living being. I grew up in a silent house, without laughter, without faith.

Later, in my own married life, I was determined not to allow these grim shadows to fall on our own children. Grace and I had four: Diane, Michael, Craig and Ruth Carol. It was Craig, even more than the others, who seemed to lay low my childhood pessimism, to tell me that the world was a wonderful and purposeful place. As a baby he would smile so delightedly at everyone he saw that there was always a little group around his carriage. When we went visiting it was Craig, three years old, who would run to the hostess to say, "You have a lovely house." If he received a gift he was touched to tears, and then gave it away to the first child who envied it. Sunday morning when Grace dressed to sing in the choir, Craig never forgot to say, "You're beautiful."

And if such a child can die, I thought as I fought my bed that Friday night, if such a life can be snuffed out in a minute, then life is meaningless and faith in God is self-delusion. By morning my hopelessness and helplessness had found a target, a blinding hatred for the person who had done this to us. That morning police picked him up in Tennessee: George Williams. Fifteen years old.

He came from a broken home, the police learned. His mother worked a night shift and slept during the day. Friday he had cut school, taken her car keys while she was asleep, sped down a street. All my rage at a senseless universe seemed to focus on the name George Williams. I phoned our lawyer and begged him to prosecute Williams to the limit. "Get him tried as an adult, juvenile court's not tough enough."

So this was my frame of mind when the thing occurred which changed my life. I cannot explain it, I can only describe it.

It happened in the space of time that it takes to walk two steps. It was late Saturday night. I was pacing the hall outside our bedroom, my head in my hands. I felt sick and dizzy, and tired, so tired. "Oh God," I prayed, "show me why!"

Right then, between that step and the next, my life was changed. The breath went out of me in a great sigh—and with it all the sickness. In its place was a feeling of love and joy so strong it was almost pain.

Other men have called it "the presence of Christ." I'd known the phrase, of course, but I'd thought it was some abstract, theological idea. I never dreamed it was Someone, an actual Person, filling that narrow hall with love.

It was the suddenness of it that dazed me. It was like a lightning stroke that turned out to be the dawn. I stood blinking in an unfamiliar light. Vengefulness, grief, hate, anger—it was not that I struggled to be rid of them—like goblins imagined in the dark, in morning's light they simply were not there.

And all the while I had the extraordinary feeling that I was two people. I had another self, a self that was millions of miles from that hall, learning things men don't yet have words to express. I have tried so often to remember the things I knew then, but the learning seemed to take place in a mind apart from the one I ordinarily think with, as though the answer to my question was too vast for my small intellect. But, in that mind beyond logic, that question was answered. In that instant I *knew* why Craig had to leave us. Though I had no visual sensation, I knew afterward that I had met him, and he was wiser than I, so that I was the little boy and he the man. And he was so busy. Craig had so much to do, unimaginably important things into which I must not inquire. My concerns were still on earth.

In the clarity of that moment it came to me: This life is a simple thing! I remember the very words in which the thought came. "Life is a grade in school; in this grade we must learn only one lesson: We must establish relationships of love."

"Oh, Craig," I thought. "Little Craig, in your five short years how fast you learned, how quickly you progressed, how soon you graduated!"

I don't know how long I stood there in the hall. Perhaps it was no time at all as we ordinarily measure things. Grace was sitting up in bed when I reached the door of our room. Not reading, not doing anything, just looking straight ahead of her as she had much of the time since Friday afternoon.

Even my appearance must have changed because as she turned her eyes slowly to me she gave a little gasp and sat up straighter. I started to talk, words tumbling over each other, laughing, eager, trying to say that the world was not an accident, that life meant something, that earthly tragedy was not the end, that all around our incompleteness was a universe of purpose, that the purpose was good beyond our furthest hopes.

"Tonight," I told her, "Craig is beyond needing us. Someone else needs us. George Williams. It's almost Christmas. Maybe, at the Juvenile Detention Home, there'll be no Christmas gift for him unless we send it."

Grace listened, silent, unmoving, staring at me. Suddenly she burst into tears.

"Yes," she said. "That's right, that's right. It's the first thing that's been right since Craig died."

And it has been right. George turned out to be an intelligent, confused, desperately lonely boy, needing a father as much as I needed a son. He got his gift, Christmas Day, and his mother got a box of Grace's good Christmas cookies. We asked for and got his release, a few days later, and this house became his second home. He works with me in the shop after school, joins us for meals around the kitchen table, is a big brother for Diane and Michael and Ruth Carol.

But more than just my feeling about George was changed, in that moment when I met Christ. That meeting has affected every phase of my life, my approach to business, to friends, to strangers. I don't mean I've been able to sustain the ecstacy of that moment; I doubt that the human body could contain such joy for very many days.

But I now know with infinite sureness that no matter what life does to us in the future, I will never again touch the rock-bottom of despair. No matter how ultimate the blow seems, I glimpsed an even more ultimate joy that blinding moment when the door swung wide.

Your Hour of Decision
by Billy Graham,
as told to Leonard E. LeSourd

Though written in 1951, the message of this evangelist has not changed.

People come up to me and say: "Why should I make a decision about God? I'm happy doing what I'm doing. You call it sin—I call it fun. Live and let live."

If they don't say it in these words, the thought's there unspoken, in their faces.

There's pleasure in sin—but only for a season. Deep down there is a gnawing, dull dissatisfaction.

I sat down with a 69-year-old business executive in a large Eastern city recently who told me, "I have fifty million dollars and everything I could ever want—and I am the most miserable man in this city."

One of the biggest names in Hollywood, a tall, strapping, swash-buckling type, revealed the same thing in different words. His life, he admitted, was lonely and empty.

These are two prominent people who have discovered that wealth and fame aren't enough in life. Millions more feel the same way. Telling lies and dodging the facts cannot shield them from the real truth—that because their consciences are black with acts against God, they can find no inner peace. To cleanse out this dirt, they need the injection of a driving spiritual force in their lives.

Jim Vaus came out of World War II a master of electronics. Within a few years he was in the employ of big gamblers on the West Coast, drawing down huge fees for his craftmanship at wire tapping and communications.

One night Jim dropped in on one of our meetings in Los Angeles to kill time before he was to take off by plane for a very important deal in St. Louis. Outwardly indifferent, he stood at the rear of the hall. Then the call came for those in the audience to come forward and make a decision for

34

Christ, a quiet man next to big Jim tapped him on the shoulder.

"Will you go forward with me?"

Jim whirled on him. "Lay off me or I'll knock your head off."

The other man didn't retreat. "You can do anything you like to me," he said gently, "but that won't right things between you and God."

Something clicked inside of Jim Vaus at that moment. His face twisted with emotion, he started walking to the front of the hall. Jim then made a decision to break clean with his old life and contacts. Today, he is one of the Lord's hardest workers.

Jim Vaus found out later that the plane he didn't catch that night of decision was met in St. Louis by gunmen *who had instructions to kill him.*

This is a spectacular example of what God can do with a person. Hundreds of men and women are reborn, less dramatically at every meeting.

"But, Billy," some people say, "what do you mean by being born again?"

To be born again means that the Divine Life has entered the human soul. God's objective then is to have that person start life anew, living in the image of His Son, Jesus Christ. The two conditions of this rebirth are repentance toward God and faith toward Christ.

At our meetings emphasizing the family and home, whole families have come forward to make their decision together.

Once a husband and wife, who had parted, came to the meeting separately. He started forward at the end. So did she. Startled, they met face to face, then joined hands with tears in their eyes.

We hold these meetings over periods of four to eight weeks in cities and towns, usually where we have received a joint invitation from the churches in the community. The effectiveness of our meetings, we have found, depends on working with local churches and giving them the responsibility of following up our efforts with their own program.

The results so far have been heartening—for which we give God the glory. Our continuing prayer in these days is that we can remain in a position of usefulness to God and play a part in calling the world back to Him before it is too late.

If you are a disbeliever, a skeptic or just indifferent, I know what you're going through. I've gone through it all myself. If you feel that you are just naturally weak, let me assure you that many persons who once were weak, today are the strongest workers for God. The Scripture says that strength comes from weakness.

When I wandered into my first revival meeting back in 1934 in Charlotte, North Carolina, I was a gangling kid of 16 with a consuming ambition to be a major-league ball player. The last thing I wanted to be was a preacher. From our worldly crowd, two of us, Grady Wilson and I, went to the meeting to see what the shouting was about.

The first night I hid behind a stout lady's big hat. I recall vividly the smell of pine shavings in my nostrils . . . also the strange stirrings that churned up inside me to know more about Christ. Although my family had reared me in a fine religious background, I had shrugged much of it off during this particular period of teen-age restlessness.

The second night I sat up closer and battled with the questions everyone asks. Was it sissified to embrace Christ? Could you be religious and still have fun? Who would be looking if I were to go forward at the end of the meeting? Why couldn't I make a decision without walking all the way to the front?

All these questions are rooted in man's pride and egotism. God didn't come through to me as a real Presence until I publicly made the decision to be living, breathing worker for God. Not an evangelist, though, I said to myself.

Months later, after some of the most exhaustive prayer sessions I have ever had, I decided to make religion my career.

To earn enough money to pay my way through Bible school, I spent one summer selling brushes. This experience taught me that regardless of whether I offered brushes or faith in God, without personal convictions and enthusiasm I was wasting my time.

Being jilted at 18 made a terrific impact on me. The fact that the girl in question said she didn't think I would amount to anything helped light a fire under me. After a long session of self-analysis, I decided I did want to amount to something—not for myself but for God.

While attending the Florida Bible Institute, I began to practice preaching in a nearby woods. Almost daily I would slip into the swampland, lay my notes on a stump and offer my sermon to the birds, alligators, frogs and all who would listen.

Then came the question that nags many who start out doing God's work. "How do I know God wants me to do this?"

The only way I knew I could get an answer was through prayer. "God," I said, "if you want me to preach, help me locate a pulpit."

That same day a man came up to me, said he had heard me preaching and asked if I would give a sermon at a gospel meeting that night down the road. This—my first real answer to prayer—started my career for the Lord.

Today when a cynic asks me—"How does giving your life to God pay off?" or, "If I change, what will God do for me?"—I can answer by telling him what He has done for me.

He forgave my sins; He gave me peace of mind; He took away my fear of death. He stirred up creative powers within me that I never realized existed. But more important than what I received from God are the efforts I have since been able to make for Him.

"Grace Before Greatness"
by Marian Anderson

A famous singer recalls a blessed gift from her mother.

Failure and frustration are in the unwritten pages of everyone's record. I have had my share of them. But if my mother's gentle hands were not there to guide me, perhaps my life in music would have ended long ago.

The faith my mother taught me is my foundation. It is the only ground on which I stand. With it I have a freedom in life I could not have in any other way. Whatever is in my voice, my faith has put it there.

Her presence runs through everything I ever wanted to be. The particular religion a child echoes is an accident of birth. But I was converted to my mother's faith and patient understanding long before I could define either.

We were poor folk. But there was a wealth in our poverty, a wealth of music, and love and faith. My two sisters, Alice and Ethel, and I were all in the church choir—the junior, not the senior one. There is still a vivid memory of our mother and father, their faces shining with pride, watching us from the front pews. And when I was six I was once fortunate enough to be selected to step out in front of the choir and sing "The Lord Is My Shepherd."

It was a Baptist Church we attended in Philadelphia. But my mother taught us early that the form of one's faith is less important than what's in one's heart.

"When you come to Him," she said, "He never asks what you are."

We children never heard her complain about her lot; or criticize those who offended her. One of her guiding precepts has always been: "Never abuse those who abuse you. Bear them no malice, and theirs will disappear."

My sisters still attend the Baptist Church in Philadelphia. It is a church and a congregation I hold most fondly in my heart for many reasons. These were the people who, years ago, pooled their pennies into what they grandly called "The Fund for Marian Anderson's Future," a gesture of love and confidence impossible to forget in a lifetime. When I come to Philadelphia, I always try to see some of these people who have been so important to me, and though it seldom is possible these days, I love to sing in their choir.

My father died when I was twelve, and my mother's burden became heavier. Before she became a housewife, and the mother of three daughters, she was a schoolteacher. Now she became a father to us as well as a mother and earned our whole livelihood by taking in washing. It was terribly difficult for her, I know, but she would not even hear of any of us children leaving school for work.

During these years I began to have my first opportunity to earn a little money by singing. Almost entirely they were Sunday evening concerts for the church, or for the YWCA and the YMCA. At these affairs I could sing, perhaps, two or three songs, and my fee was a very grand 50 cents, or once in a great while, $1.00. Sometimes I would dash to four or five of these concerts in one evening.

Many people were kind to me: teachers who took no fees, those who urged me forward when I was discouraged. Gradually I began to sing with glee clubs and churches in other cities. After one minor effort in Harlem, I was hastily sponsored for a concert in Town Hall in New York by a group of well-meaning people.

It seemed at once incredible and wonderful. But I wasn't ready: Indeed, I was far from it either in experience or maturity. On the exciting night of my first real concert I was told Town Hall was sold out. While waiting in a dazed delight to go on, my sponsor said there would be a slight delay. I waited five, ten, fifteen minutes. Then peeked through the curtain.

The house was half empty! I died inside. But when the curtain went up I sang my heart out. And when the concert was over, I knew I had failed. The critics next day agreed with me, but what they said was really not so important. I was shattered because within me I felt I had let down all those people who had had faith and confidence in me. It seemed irrevocable.

"I'd better forget all about singing and do something else," I told my mother.

"Why don't you think about it a little, and pray a lot, first?" she cautioned.

She had taught me to make my own decisions when I could, and pray for the right ones when I could not. But I did not heed her now. I refused a few offers to sing at other concerts. I avoided my music teacher. For a whole year I brooded in silence. My mother suffered because I was not expressing myself in the only way I knew happiness. But she knew I had to find my own way back alone. From time to time she just prodded me, gently:

"Have you prayed, Marian? Have you prayed?"

No, I hadn't. Nothing would help. I embraced my grief. It was sufficient. But in those tearful hours there slowly came the thought that there is a time when even the most self-sufficient cannot find enough strength to stand alone. Then, one prays with a fervor one never had before. From my torment I prayed with the sure knowledge there was Someone to Whom I could pour out the greatest need of my heart and soul. It did not matter if He answered. It was enough to pray.

Slowly I came out of my despair. My mind began to clear. No one was to blame for my failure. Self-pity left me. In a burst of exuberance I told my mother, "I want to study again. I want to be the best, and be loved by everyone, and be perfect in everything."

"That's a wonderful goal," she chided. "But our dear Lord walked this earth as the most perfect of all beings, yet not everybody loved Him."

Subdued, I decided to return to my music to seek humbleness before perfection.

One day I came home from my teacher unaware that I was humming. It was the first music I had uttered at home in a whole year. My mother heard it, and she rushed to meet me, and put her arms around me and kissed me. It was her way of saying, "Your prayers have been answered, and mine have too."

For a brief moment we stood there silently. Then my mother defined the sweet spell of our gratitude, "Prayer begins where human capacity ends," she said.

The golden echo of that moment has always been with me through the years of struggle that followed. Today I am blessed with an active career, and the worldly goods that come with it. If sometimes I do not hear the echo and listen only to the applause, my mother reminds me quickly of what should come first, "Grace must always come before greatness," she says.

Out of Prison Darkness
by Starr Daily

In solitary confinement, this ex-convict turned writer found the answer for which he had been searching.

Picture, if you can, a man who lives exclusively for the execution and planning of crime. Picture a man whose health was broken by the incessant hammer-blows of dissipation and prison rebellion . . . a man completely incapable of cooperating with any save fellow-criminals, and then only out of selfish motives.

This man was myself over 40 years ago.

I'll never forget the words of the judge who sentenced me to prison for the third and final time.

"I know you are sick," he said to me. "And I know that more punishment is not the remedy. I don't know what else to do. Our helplessness is your hopelessness."

My earliest childhood memory is that of fear: fear of death, fear of sin and a fear of being locked in. Yet I did have beautiful spiritual dreams about Jesus Christ.

My mother, a lovely and sensitive woman, died shortly after my birth. My hardworking father could not cope with my boyhood conflicts. I developed a sense of self-pity and false pride, and started to run away from difficult situations.

I began to dislike boys of my own age and seek the society of older boys, whose fellowship I won by copying their vices: chiefly gambling, pool-playing, and drinking. At 12 came my first drink. Then came stealing.

I began fraternizing with thieves and fugitives whose deeds were black as Stygian Hell. With eagerness I looked forward to the day when my record, too, would be long and black; when the police would refer to me with a shudder.

The picture of my patient father will always remain. His

42

was a splendid indulgent love, a love that stood the severest possible test, since he saw me through my complete degradation.

For years he spent time, energy and money trying to keep me out of jail. Because of me he lost his reputation for being a man of sound judgment; he forfeited friends; he became an object of pity. It didn't seem to make a great deal of difference.

Yet how frustrated he must have been because his persistence in helping always seemed to be rewarded by the increase of my weakness.

Once, having arranged for the premature end of my sentence, he came all the way to the prison to meet me and share the joy of my freedom. As we rode away together, he spoke quietly of his faith in me. There was no preachment in his tones.

"You see, son, I want you to make good," he said. "Not for my sake, but to realize your mother's faith in you."

While he talked I was meditating upon my next crime. It seems almost a sacrilege, but I went to the little town of my birth to commit this act. In this village I was caught burglarizing a store.

The next morning my father heard the news. It broke his heart, but not his faith. He came immediately to the jail, put his hand through the bars and held mine. He suffered in silence. When the jailer told him his time was up, he spoke briefly, "It's all right, son. Somehow, in some way it will all be made right." With that he left. Soon after I was sentenced to prison. I never saw my father again.

Strange how prisons, penal farms, chain gangs, the third degree of the police world—the whole futile program of punishment had tried to straighten out my twisted character and failed. How, also, good men, reaching to me with selfless hands, had tried to help to no avail. All for the simple reason that I didn't want to be corrected. Only God can help the man who has no desire to help himself.

I reentered prison for the third time with sinister ideas. Three times I tried to fight my way to freedom. The first two times were of the "lone wolf" variety; the third involved group action, destruction and physical violence. Our plan was to cause a mob riot and during its height to seize the deputy warden as a shield and hostage, then under threats of death force him to give the order that would open the gates.

The plot was discovered and I was sentenced to the dungeon.

The average time for a strong man in "the hole" is 15 days, at the end of which time the doctor ends the sentence. This time came and went. Finally, I collapsed. I seemed to be sustained by hate alone as I lay mired in the lowest hell earth had to offer.

Yet as I lay near death on the icy floor of the cell, a strange new thought came to me. I realized that I had been a dynamo of energy in everything I had done. I began to wonder what would have happened if I had used my powers for something other than destruction. It was a completely revolutionary thought!

What then followed is difficult to describe. I first began to dream disconnected dreams; then they took on meaning. These dreams were the same I had as a child—beautiful dreams of Jesus Christ, the Man I had tried to avoid for many years. He paused near my side and looked down deep into my eyes as though He were trying to penetrate my soul. In all my life I had never seen or felt such love.

Then I seemed to see all the people I had injured directly or indirectly, or who had injured me. I poured out love to them which seemed to heal their hurts. Then we were in a great auditorium and I spoke to all the people concerning love. I seemed to be assuring myself at the same time that I was awake and that I would never forget these words flowing over my lips.

When I consciously returned to my dungeon environment, the state of my mind had completely changed. The cell was illuminated with a new kind of light—the light of my own redeemed eye. Before that experience I was a calloused criminal; after it I was completely healed of my criminal tendencies! As a result, the prison doors swung open five years in advance of the time set for my release.

Often I've thought of my father and his faith in me. He had died before it was justified. Or perhaps it was my father's and mother's faith in me, which, with God's help, brought my transformation in that cold, foul prison cell.

I'd like to think so.

———————————

"I've gossiped about my neighbor," the woman confessed to her minister. "One day I saw her stagger about the yard, so I told a few friends that she had been drunk. Now I find her staggering was caused by a leg injury. How can I undo this gossip I started?"

The minister excused himself for a moment, returned with a pillow and asked the woman to follow him to the side porch. He took out a knife, cut a hole in the pillow and emptied the feathers over the porch railing.

A small breeze soon scattered tiny feathers all about the yard, among shrubs, flowers, even up in the trees. A few feathers floated across the street, heading for unknown destinations.

The minister turned to the woman. "Will you go out now and gather up every one of the feathers?"

The woman looked stunned. "Why that would be impossible!"

"Exactly," replied the minister sorrowfully. "So it is with your gossip."

SOURCE UNKNOWN

The Deception
by Stella Shepard

She became a zealous Communist and rose high in the party, but then her life took a new course.

You and I live in an unbalanced world, a world of hunger next to feasting, slums not far from mansions. What do you do when inequality wrings your heart?

I know what I did: I joined the Communist Party.

I grew up one of nine children of an often-unemployed factory worker in Cleveland. Father was a skilled tool blacksmith, but steel was coming in and blacksmiths waited many weeks between jobs.

My eight brothers and sisters though knew hardship without becoming Communists. I seem to have been one of those children who for some reason took things hard.

There was a Polish immigrant community in Cleveland then which was looked down upon by older residents. In the school yard the "Poles" played in one section, "Americans" in another. At recess each day I would play with the Polish children. Soon, too, I was avoided.

And so I grew up, idealistic, resentful, lonely. In 1925, when I was 20 years old, I went to Chicago to look for work and the job I happened to find was on the *Daily Worker*. Here were others who felt as I did about low wages, hungry children, discrimination. With a heart full of hope I set out to work for a perfect world.

We started with the premise that the great mass of men—common, workingmen—were essentially good, high-principled, generous. It was only the greedy few, rich capitalists and selfish employers, who kept them from being happy.

Passionately believing this, we could not understand why the workingmen were so slow to revolt. We read them page after page from the Communist text: economics as the basis of history, the struggle of classes, overproduction as the cause of war. People were bored. They walked away from our street meetings; they fell asleep at our rallies. So we fell back on an age-old technique for moving people in a hurry: Hate.

I will never forget the funeral for Harry Simms. I'd known him slightly, a skinny 17-year-old who went down to Kentucky to address some striking coal miners and was shot to death by a company policeman. Now I watched a master strategist make use of his death. Harry's funeral was held in a 12,000-seat fight arena in the Bronx, New York. Every seat was taken and 2,000 people stood. From my seat near the back I saw William Z. Foster stride to where the coffin lay. He raised his fist, his voice boomed out over the crowd, "Someone will pay for this!"

An angry roar came from the crowd, I had seen the secret of moving masses. I became Bill Foster's secretary and for years watched the efficiency of this Communist leader, beside whose bier in Moscow Khrushchev eventually stood.

I learned that hate is the easiest of human emotions to arouse. Find a sore subject: magnify a hurt, fan a fear, threaten a self-interest—then name an enemy. Fighting words, angry gestures and a thousand people howl for action.

On the whirlwind of hate the Communist cause advanced. I advanced with it. I became president of the Office Workers' Union; helped with the hunger marches on Washington, worked on the legal machinery which put the Communist party on the ballot. And the extraordinary thing was that at no time did I feel a conflict between the goal of human happiness and the means which were to bring it about.

In 1933 I married a member of the Party's national committee. Our apartment in Buffalo, New York, where he was western state organizer, was always filled with the homeless and the unemployed. For many years I lived in this strange no-world of Communism: believing love and preaching hate, yearning for brotherhood and sowing division.

Looking back, I believe my disillusionment began in the early forties, though at first I refused to acknowledge what my eyes saw. But the fact was that, as I moved higher and higher in the Party, I began to encounter corruption: leaders who had lost sight of the people's struggles in a thirst for personal power, a cynical disregard in practice for the principles they preached, outright financial swindling.

People to whom I have told my story often do not understand why this discovery of corruption should have had such a shattering effect on me. "It can happen in any group," is a typical reaction. "What do you expect of human nature?"

Yet here is the very heart of the error which is Communism: I had *not* expected these things. The whole Communist superstructure is built on the supposition that man is nobly-inclined, fair, unselfish— or will be, when the purely external causes of his evil-doing are removed. Then, when man is revealed as weak, when workingman of the proletariat, lifted to a position of power, exhibits the very same symptons of selfishness which Communists teach us belong solely to bourgeois-man, when in other words man's problem is suspected to be man himself, the whole card-house comes tumbling down. For in all Communist heavens, there is no one else but man: If he is evil then all is hopeless.

By the late forties I had seen too much betrayal and greed to pretend belief even to myself. I left the Party. This is easily done: Any year that one does not renew the oaths and pay the steep dues, he is out forever from this inner circle of the Communist movement. At 48 my life was a void. This was the person I was when the miracle happened in my life.

In January, 1953, I went to New York's Bellevue Hospital with a diaphragmatic hernia. A city law provides that before a patient is given anesthesia his chart must be signed by a clergyman. To Arthur Elcombe, Protestant chaplain in the hospital, was assigned all patients who were neither Jewish nor Catholic. I am sure I was not his first atheist.

I was in the curiously detached, loose-tongued state that sedatives induce when I saw him approaching down the hall.

"If there was a God," I cried brazenly, "there would be no such thing as hunger and poverty and discrim—discrim—" my relaxed tongue refused the effort. "Race trouble," I finished lamely.

The minister's head was directly over me now, warm brown eyes smiling into mine. "So true," he said gently. "We do tend to keep Him out of our affairs, don't we?" He stood looking down at me. "I'd like to ask a blessing for you."

"Go ahead," I said giddily. "It won't do any good."

Mr. Elcombe laid his hands on my head and prayed. Then the ceiling slid by and I was under the bright lights of the operating room.

The next day he was at my bedside. "You can help me," he said.

As chaplain at Bellevue, he explained, he was in charge

of ministerial students who came there for training. Some were Negroes and occasionally encountered race feeling among the patients. He was Canadian and unfamiliar with such problems. Could I give him advice?

And I, who thought I knew something about strategy, swallowed the bait whole. For an hour we talked about the church's problems in Bellevue. His thanks rang so loud in my ears that it was a minute or two before I detached his parting remark, "Service in the chapel Sunday. I'll look for you!"

I spent the rest of the week telling myself that he would not find me. Every fiber in my body yearned to go to the chapel and every ounce of conviction resisted it. Down there lay the destruction of the mind, the opiate of the people. Conviction won. I did not go down.

Into the ward next week was moved a 15-year-old Ukrainian girl dying of spinal tuberculosis. I did a few simple things for her and won her pathetic devotion. She told me in halting English that she got through the week only because of Sunday when a volunteer church worker would wheel her down to the chapel.

That Sunday, however, no church worker came. Why that day, of all times? I seized the wheelchair and pushed it out to the elevator and into the chapel.

I intended to wait for her in the hall, but her thin little hand gripped my arm and I dropped into a chair beside her. Mr. Elcombe was there but the guest preacher was a Negro. His sermon was a stirring and eloquent plea for brotherhood. He did not minimize the difficulties in the way of a just society. "With man," he finished, "it is impossible. But with God, all things are possible."*

The congregation rose and began to sing, but I hardly heard. For something frightening was happening to me. First I began to shake, then came great choking gasps I could not control. When the hymn ended I buried my face in my hands, sure that I was dying or going insane. Mr. Elcombe walked back and laid a reassuring hand on my shoulder. He had seen conversions before. "Would you like to come to my office and talk about it?" he said.

And so when I had got my little girl back upstairs, I went to his office. I came back the next day and for many weeks, long after I had left the hospital. "Man cannot save

---

* Matthew 19:26

himself," he would tell me. "That's why there had to be Jesus."

To accept Jesus meant to lose my husband, my friends of 25 years, my job. Yet His pull on me had a strangely physical quality. Going to the grocery store, I would walk blocks out of my way just to see the name "Jesus" on a church.

I had found the only real answer to the world's sorrows. I saw now that men could devise a perfect society, achieve an absolutely equal distribution of wealth, and still brother would take unfair advantage of brother, the strong would prey upon the weak. For the seeds of unfairness and cruelty and greed lay in man himself. What was needed was not a political revolution, but a revolution in the hearts of men—the revolution Christians call conversion.

Sunday mornings I began to feel an immense hunger to attend a church service. My husband was mystified: Why would anyone leave the house Sunday morning? But it was on one of these secretive visits that I asked Jesus to complete the revolution in my life. I was sitting in the darkened church after the service was over, a small Episcopal church on Henry Street, when quite suddenly I prayed, "Lord Jesus, change *me*." The wonder of that moment, the joy and peace and sureness of Him thrills me still.

But change comes hard. When I admitted that I was a Christian, my husband and I split up. I took an apartment alone. My friends would not answer my letters or return my phone calls. I met one of them on the street. I had nursed her through influenza three winters before. She spit in my face.

I joined St. Augustine's Chapel on Henry Street, and with the help of the pastor, the Reverend C. Kilmer Myers, began the adventure of getting to know Jesus. Gradually He revealed His Mission for me: it is to preach His transforming power to anyone who will hear it.

Some of the people I have since witnessed to have been Communists. Accepting Christ has meant for them rejecting Communism. But this is not the chief thing for me: it is the sense of working in Christ's Kingdom that makes my life rewarding beyond all words.

Yet for a long time there was something about this kind of personal mission which bothered me.

I had been used to the swift, mass-movement techniques of Communism: the hatred that can charge a rally and sway a mob. But Jesus' way is love, and love is slow. I had thought in terms of groups, nations, classes, now I thought in terms of a single man or woman. Sometimes as I sat night after night in a living room somewhere, watching the slow birth of belief in some heart I would wonder, "At this rate how will love ever win the world?"

It took me a long time to learn that love is also power. That it changes lives, deep down where food and clothing and increased wages cannot reach: that it wants to redeem the nature that brought hunger into the world. That because it works when two or three are gathered, it does not need a rally to start its slow, sure process.

Today, when I hear Christians say, "What can *I* do— just one person?" I want to laugh for sheer joy. Because the single human being is the vehicle God has chosen. With you or me, right now, wherever we are, He can begin the redemption of the world.

When I Leveled With God
by Keith Miller

A best-selling author explains how he found the
path to a vital personal prayer life.

Until that day on the highway in East Texas I had said only
mechanical little prayers whenever the occasion demanded.
From Christian parents I had inherited the standard kind of
faith that included church attendance, grace at meals and the
acceptance of a shadowy Father who would help me be good.

The trouble was much of me was pulled toward things
that I knew He wouldn't consider good at all: self-centered-
ness, pride, lust, greed.

This conflict went on until I was 28 years old. I had a
wife whom I loved very much and two small children, yet I
was empty in my soul and filled with incompleteness and
despair. On this particular day I got into the company car (I
worked for an oil firm) and took off on a field trip. While
driving through the tall pine woods of East Texas, I suddenly
pulled off to the side of the road.

I had a feeling of total desolation. Usually an optimistic
person who could always say "there is one more bounce in
the ball," I told myself that a couple of martinis and a good
night's sleep would fix me up. It was no good. I seemed to be
a man on a treadmill going no place in a world that was
made up of black clouds.

To my surprise tears filled my eyes and ran down my
cheeks. I looked up in the sky. "God," I said, "if there is anything You want in this stinking soul, take it."

Something came into my life that day 15 years ago
which has never left. There wasn't any ringing of bells or
flashing of lights, but there was a deep, intuitive realization of
what it is that God wants from a man, which I had never
known before. And the peace that came with this understanding was not an experience in itself, but was a cessation of the

conflict of a lifetime. I realized then that God is not so much interested in having my money nor my time, as much as my will. When I offered Him my will, He began to show me life as I had never seen it.

The process of change that began in my life after that experience has covered every area, but I want to dwell on just one—prayer. For when I set out to live my life for Jesus Christ, I realized I did not know how to find His will for me. I guess I had naively assumed that making a total commitment automatically ushered one into a vital prayer life (whatever that meant). But it didn't happen this way to me. Prayers such as "Dear God, forgive me for all the bad things I do," seemed to cover everything, but nothing much happened in my life. Then I began trying to find times during the day for specific private prayer.

I can remember the alarm going off very early. Groggily I would force myself to my feet to grope about in the dark for slippers, robe and my Bible. Many times I would tell God sleepily, "Lord, You know it's not fair for me to wake up my family just to satisfy my selfish desire to have a time of prayer. Deliver me from that kind of legalism." And I'd go back to bed.

Nothing seemed to be working until I posed my problem to a Christian layman who had a dynamic ministry with people. "For me, there is nothing more important than to read the Scriptures every day and to have a specific time of prayer for developing a close relationship with Christ," he told me.

Seeing a man's life with which I could identify did for me what all my "trying" could not. I began getting up again in the morning, using this one specific period each day for prayer and reading Scripture. This prayer time has become the center from which I live the rest of my life.

Soon things began to happen. Since my closest relationships with people were with those who knew the most about me and loved me anyway, to find such a relationship with Jesus Christ, I began to reveal my inner life to Him, *even though I knew He knew already.*

This experience taught me the strange power in prayer of being specific with the Lord. In trying to be totally honest with Him I found a new freedom and sense of being accepted. Instead of saying, "Lord, today I exaggerated a little on my expense account, but You know that everybody does,"

I was able to say, "Lord, I cheated on my expense account today. Help me not to be a dirty thief."

For a long time I had been disturbed about the problem of my mind wandering during prayer. I would be trying to pray and suddenly my mind would jump to a business appointment I needed to make. For years I forced these things out of my mind to get back to "spiritual things." Then I learned to keep note paper by my side so that when these thoughts came, I would jot them down and then get back to God. Such thoughts during prayer might be His way of telling me of significant people to see or things to do.

The more honest I was in my prayers, the more real He became. I used to start out by saying, "God, I love You" (whether I really did or not that morning). Now I can say (when it is true) "Lord, I'm sorry but I'm tired of You today." But now I can also continue, "You must be sick of me, too, Lord, but forgive me and help me get back on the beam." I discovered that this was a real act of faith because there was no religious feeling involved.

Looking back now, I see that for years I had been a kind of spiritual sensualist, always wanting to have goose pimples in prayer and being depressed when I didn't. I began to feel very tender toward God on those mornings when I would pray on raw faith. I felt this way because at last I was giving back to Him the gift of faith.

The discipline of regular prayer resulted in other changes. I didn't get rid of my problems; I simply began to get a new set of problems. God didn't take things out of my life; instead He brought in a great many new positive things. For example, He filled me with a desire to tell people that life was not a hopeless rat race—that there is the Good News. This led to my teaching an adult Sunday-school class, then participation in a prayer group.

As my wife and I began to fill our lives with these new activities, certain old practices seemed to just fall off. God didn't force us to give up anything; He just made the life we were finding such an adventure that many of the activities we had been so busy with now seemed unreal and unimportant.

In conclusion, I have realized that prayer is not a series of requests to get God to help me do the things I think need to be done. Prayer is a direction of life, a focusing of one's most personal and deepest attention Godward. The purpose is to love God and learn to know Him so well, that our wills and our actions will be more and more aligned with His, until even our unconscious reactions and purposes will have the mark of His love and His life.

Prayer no longer seems like an activity to me; it has become the continuing language of the relationship I believe God designed to fulfill a human life.

The Joyous Way
by Gert Behanna

---

*She found her problems could not be solved with
a bottle.*

I was 53 years old when I found out there was a God. The
shock and wonder of that discovery have never worn off in
the more than 20 years since. But I've had another shock in
my life, almost as great as the first. In fact, it happened the
very next Sunday: It was meeting my first churchgoers.

I'd never been to church in my life and I remember how
eagerly I awaited that first Sunday. I'd just had a glimpse of
God Almighty—me, an alcoholic, a drug addict, rich, lonely,
and miserable—and already I was beginning to know what
joy really was. And now on Sunday I was going to meet
people who had known Him for years! What ecstatic people
these long-time Christians would be! I was shy about going. I
was afraid they would embarrass me with their love and enthusiasm.

Well, Sunday came, and I went to church, and of course
you know what I found. Bowed heads, long faces, and fu-
nereal whispers. Far from alarming me with the warmth of
their welcome, nobody spoke to me at all.

At first I was sure this was just one isolated experience.
But as time went on and I attended other churches in various
parts of the country, I made a bewildering discovery. These
long-faced, listless people were present in every congregation.
How could they come into God's presence Sunday after Sunday without breathing in the joy that danced in the very air?

I know the answer now, although it took me many years
to confirm it. The answer is that these people never learned
the simple directions to Christian joy. During those years, you
see, I also came to know true Christians—many, many of
them—the kind of glowing, giving personalities I had expected in every pew that first Sunday. And every one of these ra-

diant people, whatever his background, had come into joy by taking three distinct steps.

The steps, I learned from them, are the same, whether for the decent citizen or the reformed drunk. In fact, after years of watching far better people than I struggle far longer, I've come to the conclusion that in this matter of step-taking there's only one difference between the responsible citizen and the drunk: For the drunk the process is probably easier.

Take the very first step: *Ask God to forgive you.*

The catch is that to ask Him, you have to know you need forgiveness. Now for me that was no problem at all. I'd had three marriages and wrecked them all. I'd never learned to do anything, neither cook nor sew nor iron a blouse. Even the raising of my two sons I'd left to household help. For years I'd taken stimulants in the morning to get me up, alcohol to keep me going and sleeping pills to put me down again.

When I realized what a bore life was to me and to everyone else, I'd tried to kill myself and bungled even that. Oh, I knew I needed forgiveness all right, and the minute I knew there was a God, it was the first thing I told Him.

And He—the splendor of it stuns me still—He forgave me! For my soiled life He gave me His clean one. Right then I knew I would never again take a pill or a drink. Not through willpower—I didn't have any—but through discovering the bliss I'd been seeking all along.

The advantage to *my* sins, you see, was that they were gaudy, blaring ones. It's our quiet sins, like self-satisfaction or stinginess or pride, that can tiptoe along for years unnoticed—and therefore unforgiven.

Or take the second step: *Ask God to love you.*

Again, the surprise is that we have to ask. Doesn't He love us anyhow, all the time, whether or not we ask Him? Doubtless, but it's equally clear that we can shut out even such love as His by our inattention and our haste. Especially, it seems to me, by our haste to get out and do good.

Love thy neighbor as thyself, Christ tells us. But somehow the very best-intentioned people, the hardest workers in so many churches, hear only half His commandment. They skip over their own need for love and rush out to roll bandages and teach Sunday school. Unchanged, untransformed, unhealed, they try to give to others what they themselves have never received.

God's order is different. He wants to love us first: so

unconditionally, so life-changingly that His love overflows, almost without our knowing it, into the world around us. And here again I was lucky, because once I stopped drinking, I found I had a lot of empty hours on my hands, time to take in His love. For that's what it takes—as in any relationship—enough simple minutes, days and weeks together.

For me it meant giving up a bad habit; for the harried church worker it may mean a far harder relinquishment. It may mean giving up that Sunday-school class or a used-clothing drive—things that in themselves are good. But I am convinced that this is sometimes what God wants. He wants us to lie fallow, like empty fields in the sun and the wind and the rain, not forcing some pretty plant of our own choosing, but just waiting to see what God will bring forth.

There are two sure ways of asking for God's love, and both need this kind of fallow time. One is to talk to everyone we can find—no matter how far we have to travel—who knows anything about this love of God.

The other is to read the Bible. Not to plod through it, yawning over it, but to pick it up eagerly as though we'd never before read it.

For me this was easy: I never had. Occasionally, in museums, I'd seen a huge, illuminated Bible in a glass case, and I'd often seen a Bible in hotel rooms, But incredibly enough, until the week following my conversion, I had never held a Bible in my hand.

And then I couldn't put it down. Every time I read it I burst into tears. I, who'd been seeking love in a thousand sick and mistaken ways, knew that I had suddenly touched the Source of love. I'd been an empty cup, empty because my heart was upside down. Now I let Him set me upright and fill my emptiness with Himself.

If the first two steps came easily for me, the last came with difficulty. The third step is: *Ask God to take away your fear.*

Fear takes different shapes. For some it's death, for some it's snakes, for some it's high places, or pain, or old age—but whatever form it takes it's always a door closed on some part of life. And for me the fear was public speaking.

All my life the very thought of standing up before a group of people and giving a talk had turned my heart to jelly. I used to go around announcing, though no one had asked me, that the one thing I would never, never do was to give a speech. And so, of course, when God undertook to make me whole, this was the first area He went to work on.

It was Dr. Sam Shoemaker who passed on the message. He was one of the fine Christians to whom I had gone for instruction, and one Tuesday afternoon he informed me, "You're to be the speaker at Calvary Episcopal Church Thursday night. We expect about 500 people."

Thursday evening, after two hideous nights and 48 hours without a bite of food, I crawled onto the speaker's platform and gasped out the story of my life—B.C,A.D.

Then I was asked to speak again! People must have decided I looked too miserable to be making it up. The second speech was, if possible, harder than the first; the third one was worse yet. And this went on for 11 terrible years! All that time I spoke as though we could earn salvation by the amount of our suffering. I spoke in churches, prisons, colleges, to psychiatric groups—thousands of speeches—and every one pure agony. I'd arrive at the designated location at the precise moment the speech was scheduled and run for the platform, in terror lest someone speak to me and drive the memorized words from my head.

I know now that when God asks us to do what we fear, it is to free us from the fear itself. But I didn't know it then, and so instead of giving the fear to Him, I hung onto it. I persisted in the infantile idea that these were my just deserts. I'd led a bad life: it was fitting that I spend the rest of it doing what I'd always dreaded. I still hadn't understood that He'd paid the whole price long ago, that all debts were cancelled on that cross, that every commandment of His is to our joy.

As long as I could crawl to a lectern I did, dragging my fear along. And I might be dragging it still, except that at last came a speech that I couldn't manage, not even on my hands and knees.

I was invited to Battell Chapel, at Yale University, the first woman ever to be asked to speak there. I knew people at Yale, knew from my "socialite days" how demanding, how critical, how perfectionist they could be. And this time my fear put me to bed, literally paralyzed: my stomach in knots, my neck too rigid to move.

And so at last I had to give it all up! I relinquished everything: the fear, the mental block, the lifelong aversion. "I'll speak, Lord." I whispered. "You can have the terror."

And He did take it. Because at last I let Him. Then and

there the pain went, the constricted neck, the trembling hands. To seal the pact I threw away the speech I'd memorized so painstakingly, word for word. And so the next day I stepped into that pulpit without even a mental note.

And, of course, it was the best talk I ever gave—and I even enjoyed it. When we let God take away our fear, He gives delight, eagerness, concern for people—all those qualities of His that fear had blocked out. I have spoken 1000 times in a single year and only regret that a year is but 365 days long.

Ask God to forgive you. Ask God to love you. Ask God to take away your fear. Three steps, and every one sheer joy, because each step brings you closer to Him.

Section Two—

The Art of Living Your Faith

Section Two—
Introduction

One of the regular features in Guideposts magazine is the kind of article editors label "art of living." And it is well named, for these highly personal experiences relate some encounters with life that actually taught the author how to cope with some frustrating everyday problem. These stories have wide appeal because in each there is a focal point of universality with which everyone can identify.

It isn't necessary to be black to understand the problems Jackie Robinson faced when he broke baseball's race barrier. Guideposts told that story when Jackie's fight was still going on in 1948.

Arthur Gordon wrote an article which has been quoted over and over for the past 12 years: "Be Bold and Mighty Forces Will Come to Your Aid."

Also, in this section you'll want to read the David Wilkerson story that led to his extraordinary work with teen-agers; Bob Hope's article on laughter and astronaut Ed White's testimony "What I Took Into Space"—an article which has special significance when one remembers that the story appeared in October, 1965—just a few months before a launching-pad tragedy at Cape Kennedy took his life.

Faith is not very relevant unless it is lived. Here are stories which show *how*.

Trouble Ahead Needn't Bother You

by Jackie Robinson

---

*For nearly a century major-league baseball had
excluded the Negro. Here is the story of how this
barrier was broken down—and of the men responsible for cracking it.*

I'll never forget the day Branch Rickey, president of the
Brooklyn Dodgers, asked me to join his baseball organization.
I would be the first Negro to play in organized baseball—that
is, if I were good enough to make the grade.

Mr. Rickey's office was large and simply furnished.
There were four framed pictures on the wall. One was a
kodachrome snapshot of Leo Durocher, the field manager of
the Dodgers. Another was a portrait of the late Charlie Bar-
rett, one of the greatest scouts in the game. A third was of
General Chennault. And the fourth and largest smiled down
on me with calm reassurance, the portrait of the sad, trusting Abraham Lincoln who had pleaded for malice toward
none . . .

This was the never-to-be-forgotten day when our Marines landed on the soil of Japan, August 29, 1945. It was a
hot day with venetian blinds shutting out the sun, and the
Brooklyn clamor of Montague Street mingled with the noisy
traffic around Boro Hall.

From behind his desk the big, powerful, bushy-browed
Branch Rickey, who seemed a combination of father and
boss, mapped out to me his daring strategy to break the color
line in major-league baseball.

I was excited at the opportunity. It was a tremendous
challenge. But was I good enough?

"Mr. Rickey," I said, "it sounds like a dream come true—for me and for my race. For seventy years there has been racial exclusion in big-league baseball. There will be trouble ahead—for you, for me, for my people and for baseball."

"Trouble ahead," Rickey rolled the phrase over his lips as though he liked the sound. "You know, Jackie, I was a small boy when I took my first train ride. On the same train was an old couple, also riding for the first time. We were going through the Rocky Mountains. The old man sitting by the window looked forward and said to his wife, 'Trouble ahead, Ma! We're high up over a precipice and we're gonna run right off.'

"To my boyish ears the noise of the wheels repeated 'Trouble-ahead-trouble-ahead . . .' I never hear train wheels to this day but what I think of this. But our train course bent into a tunnel right after the old man spoke, and we came out on the other side of the mountain. That's the way it is with most trouble ahead in this world, Jackie—if we use the common sense and courage God gave us. But you've got to study the hazards and build wisely."

I've never forgotten that little story. It helped me through many of the rough moments I was to face in the future. I signed my contract that day with a humble feeling of great responsibility. I prayed that I would be equal to the test.

"God is with us in this, Jackie," Mr. Rickey said quietly. "You know your Bible. It's good, simple Christianity for us to face realities and to recognize what we're up against. We can't go out and preach and crusade and bust our heads against a wall. We've got to fight out our problems together with tact and common sense."

To give me experience and seasoning, Mr. Rickey sent me the first year to play with the Montreal Royals, a farm club for the Brooklyn organization. I was the cause of trouble from the start—but we expected it. Pre-season exhibition games were cancelled because of "mixed athletes," although the official reason was always different.

Some of my teammates may have resented me. If so, I didn't blame them. They had problems enough playing ball without being a part of a racial issue. I tried hard not to develop "rabbit ears," a malady picked up by all athletes who are sensitive to abuse and criticism shouted from the fans.

One of my top thrills was my opening game for Montreal at Jersey City. The pressure was on and I was very nervous. But during that contest I slapped out four hits, including a home run. I couldn't have dreamed up a better start.

But as the season began to unroll game after game, my play grew erratic. I was trying too hard. I knew I had to keep my temper bridled at every turn. Guarding so carefully against outbursts can put a damper on one's competitive spirit.

Every athlete at some time or other likes "to blow his top." It seldom does any harm and acts like a safety valve. A hitter in a slump may drive the ball deep to the infield, then leg it to first sure that he has beaten the throw. The umpire calls him out. With this the frustrated athlete jerks off his cap, slams it on the ground and thunders all his pent-up irritations at the umpire. The crowd roars its approval or dislike depending on whether the player is on the home or visiting team. The umpire merely turns his back, and the ball player after giving vent to his unhappiness, trots back to the bench feeling much better. It's all a part of the game.

But I didn't dare let loose this way. Many would have dubbed me a "hothead" and point to my outburst as a reason why Negroes should not play in organized baseball. This was one of the hardest problems I had to face.

As the season rolled along, however, the players became accustomed to me. My play improved. When the season ended, Montreal had won the Junior World Series. I admit proudly to winning the batting championship of the league with an average .349.

On April 10, 1947, Branch Rickey made the announcement that gave me my greatest thrill. I was to join the Brooklyn Dodgers and become the first Negro to compete in the Major Leagues.

To add to my regular problems of bucking the expected publicity and criticism from the usual quarters, I was placed at a strange position—first base. At Montreal I had played second base.

It was Montreal all over again, only this time the pressure was much greater, the competition keener, and the stakes tremendous. It wasn't a question so much of a colored athlete making good as a big leaguer, but whether the whole racial question would be advanced or retarded.

I prayed as I never had before.

As a first baseman I had many fielding shortcomings. I

worked hard to iron them out and both fans and players by and large were rooting for me. This encouragement was a big factor in helping me improve my game.

Again I faced the same problems. An opposing player drove a hard grounder to the infield. When he crossed first base his spikes bit painfully into my foot. Accident or deliberate? Who can tell? But the first reaction of a competitive ball player is to double up fists and lash out. I saw a blinding red. It took every bit of my discipline to bridle my temper. But when my teammates rushed to my support in white hot anger, it gave me the warmest feeling I've ever felt. At that moment I belonged.

That year the Dodgers won the pennant. I was thrilled to know that my efforts were considered an important factor in winning. But I also cherished another triumph. Baseball as a whole had come to accept the Negro. From now on the colored ball player, to make the grade, will simply have to be a good enough player. As Mr. Rickey says, a champion is a champion in America, black or white.

Why Should I Get Involved
by Sal F. Lazzerotti

A bystander faces a dilemma when he witnesses a strange conflict on a New York subway train.

One way to avoid involvement in other people's problems is to play the monkey game—hear no evil, speak no evil, see no evil. It's a simple matter of withdrawing yourself from a situation where you might be asked to give something like time or money or talent.

Most of us are 50 percenters, I suppose. That's about the category in which I fall. Sometimes I act when I see a need, other times I just "pass by on the other side."

Not too long ago I stood face-to-face with a tough decision. The choice I made taught me a lesson I won't soon forget.

It was such a refreshing, bright spring day—the day that I tried to cover my eyes, ears and mouth—that I lingered at the top of the subway steps to catch a couple of extra breaths of air. But finally the sound of an approaching train sent me scurrying into the cavern below. Aboard the train, I took a seat beside the door and began reading the morning paper, a regular ritual for the 45-minute ride to our Guideposts office in New York City.

As an artist I like to study people—their faces, their actions. That day a graying grandmother-type sat across from me sleeping. Her head sagged to the left in a 45-degree list. A lanky, dark-haired boy of about 18 stood holding the center post, a brown paper sack under his arm. Directly across from me, an attractive young lady—brunette, maybe 25—was a portrait of poise as she sat erectly reading a paperback book.

As we pulled into the 57th Street stop, "Grandma" rubbed her eyes, ran her fingers through her hair, jumped to her feet and bounded out the door.

67

Next was the 50th Street stop near Rockefeller Center. People were standing, but it was nowhere near the usual jam.

As the train lurched to a stop, she rose and walked to the door, passing the dark-haired boy. Suddenly, the young lady whirled and screamed:

"You fresh punk! Don't look so innocent! I know you touched me!" Her pretty face was now contorted in anger.

Then the girl began flailing the astonished boy, who in defense, threw his arms up and tried to push her away. In doing so he must have hit her in the face because suddenly her mouth was all bloody.

At last the boy broke free and made a dash down the platform. The girl pursued—her high heels clicking as she ran.

"Police, police!" she shrieked.

With the sound of her voice and the noise of her shoes still echoing through the station, the doors of the train closed and we continued on our way. I sat staring at the door not sure that I wasn't dreaming. When it came shut, it was something like the curtain closing on the first act of a play.

Inside the car, passengers smiled, amused, and then almost in unison, they shrugged their shoulders and returned to papers and books. I smiled rather smugly myself until the full impact of the incident hit me.

I had seen that boy standing, and had detected no move to touch the girl. I wondered what would happen to the boy if he were caught. The girl's story would carry more weight, I told myself.

He might be taken to a police station and be charged with molesting her. Was it fair for me—a witness—to remain silent?

"It's not your battle . . . don't stick your nose in someone else's business . . . he probably ran away and nothing will come of it." These thoughts turned cartwheels in my mind as I left the subway and headed for the office.

Still I felt a compulsion to help the boy. At the office, I got some coffee, made a couple of phone calls and worked on a rough sketch, but I could not forget the sound of that girl's voice and those high heels echoing through the subway, "Police . . . clickety click, clickety click . . . police!"

What was the right thing to do? As I thought about it, I remembered Christ's parable of the Good Samaritan who helped a man he didn't know. I knew I should do the same.

It took four calls to locate the right police precinct. The

desk sergeant listened to my story. "You saw it all, huh? Well, the boy has been sent to Juvenile Court, downtown."

I called Juvenile Court and obtained the boy's name, Steven Larsen, and his parent's address. By the time I got in touch with Mrs. Larsen she knew the details. There was a quiver in her voice and I could tell she was fighting tears.

"We don't have any money to help Steve, Mr. Lazzarotti."

Through a girl in our office I learned of a lawyer named George Fleary. He was contacted and agreed to represent the boy without charge. Later, he called back and asked me to meet him in court the following Monday. I was to testify.

When I arrived Monday at the courtroom, Mr. Fleary took me aside and briefed me on what he had learned: Steve had been in trouble once before when he was 15. Police picked him up on suspicion of stealing a car with some other boys, but he had not been charged. Then Mr. Fleary outlined the accusations that would be brought by the girl's attorney.

"If Steve's found guilty of these charges, he could receive a sentence from six months to a year," he said.

Steve's mother arrived, her face was painted with worry. Steve now entered the courtroom, accompanied by an officer and was seated at a table with Mr. Fleary.

"Is Steve still in school?" I asked Mrs. Larsen.

"No, he quit when he was a junior," she answered. "He works in the mail room of an advertising agency. He wants to be a copywriter some day. My husband is a longshoreman. He wanted to come today, but he couldn't afford to take the day off."

The judge came into the room and proceedings began. Counsel for the girl presented charges that seemed a mile long to me. Then the judge began questioning the girl. Without inhibition, she described what Steve supposedly had done. I shook my head in disbelief. Nothing she said possibly could have happened. Steve flushed with embarrassment and squirmed in his seat.

The judge interrupted, asking her to be more specific:

"There is a witness to the incident present, so be sure of what you say."

The girl's eyes searched the room and then came to rest on me. She looked at me incredulously. Then a strange reaction came over her. She started fumbling with words, qualifying previous statements, and contradicting herself. Within five minutes, the judge called the two lawyers forward. They huddled, whispered, nodded. Then Mr. Fleary came back to where we were sitting and said:

"The case has been dismissed. The judge feels the girl needs psychiatric help."

Steve grabbed my hand firmly to show his gratitude, but he was too choked up to speak. Through tears of joy, his mother thanked us over and over.

After Steve and his mother left, I talked with Mr. Fleary and told him how much I admired him for giving his time to the case.

"Our job is made easy when witnesses will come forward and testify," he said. "Too many people say 'It's none of my business.' "

On my way home that night, I thought how close I had come to saying, "It's none of my business." How close I had come to playing the monkey game.

"Thank You, God," I said. "Thank You for giving me the courage to act. Help me be more sensitive to others in need. Open my eyes and ears and mouth—and heart."

Too Strange to be Coincidence
by John L. Sherrill

How does the Holy Spirit work through people?
Here is the dramatic story of Dave Wilkerson,
who calls himself "just a skinny country preacher."

One winter morning in 1958, Dave Wilkerson, a skinny country preacher, was sitting in his living room, reading *Life* magazine. He turned a page and saw a picture of seven boys. That picture was to change his life.

Dave was the pastor of the small Assemblies of God Church in Philipsburg, Pennsylvania. He was at home in the slow-paced rural community; life for him, his wife and three small children was comfortably routine and it probably would have remained that way except for one thing. Dave Wilkerson had turned over his life to God. He had simply handed over his feet and his hands and his heart and asked the Holy Spirit to use them.

For Dave the Holy Spirit was no vague theological term; He was the Spirit of Christ, a living personality to be listened to and obeyed. On that particular morning, looking at the picture in the magazine, Dave Wilkerson began to weep.

It showed seven teen-age defendants on trial in New York City for the death of Michael Farmer, the young polio victim, who was brutally beaten by members of a teen-age gang. But it wasn't the story of the murder itself which especially gripped Dave. It was the faces of the defendants. In their eyes he saw an anger and loneliness he had never known existed. All that day he was drawn to the picture. And during the next week he felt the conviction growing that he himself—David Wilkerson—should take a toothbrush, get into his car, drive to New York where he had never been in his life, and try to help these boys.

At last Dave told his wife. "I don't understand why," he

said, "but I must go." It was the boldest step of obedience to the Holy Spirit that he had yet taken. Almost before he knew how it happened, Dave and Miles Hoover, the youth director of his small church, were driving across the George Washington Bridge. It was the afternoon of February 28, 1958.

In New York he parked in front of a drugstore and telephoned the office of the District Attorney named in the article.

"If you want to see the defendants," he was told, "the judge himself will have to give you permission." So Dave tried to telephone the judge. He was unsuccessful. But he was not discouraged.

The next day David and Miles went to the trial. All morning they sat quietly, watching the seven young defendants. Toward the end of the court session, Dave popped to his feet, ran down the aisle and stood before the bench. He knew that if he were going to see the judge at all he would have to do it then and there.

"Your honor? Would you do me the courtesy of talking with me for a few s. . . ."

"Get him out of here," the judge interrupted brusquely.

Two guards swept down on Dave, picked him up by his elbows and rushed him toward the rear of the courtroom. Reporters and photographers jumped to their feet. Flashbulbs popped.

Later it was learned that the judge had been threatened by gang members and had thought the skinny preacher was one of them.

That evening the newspapers carried stories about the Reverend David Wilkerson being ejected bodily from the courtroom. As Dave and his youth director drove home, they were both depressed and confused. What kind of guidance had this been? David remembered Biblical accounts of men who were guided by the Holy Spirit. He'd started his own grand experiment assuming that Christ's Spirit would guide people today, just as it did in New Testament times. Why, then, was he in trouble?

At home, he and Miles faced a disgruntled congregation, annoyed that their minister had made a public spectacle of himself. And as the days passed, Dave's confusion increased. Not only was it difficult to explain why he had gotten into such a mess; it was still more difficult to explain why, as soon as possible, he was going back to New York.

But that's where he was, the next week. When he telephoned the District Attorney's office a second time he was told that if he wanted to see the boys he needed written permission from each of the parents.

"Fine," said Dave. "Could you give me their names?"

The line went dead. Dave stepped out of the phone booth. He smoothed out the now crumpled page from *Life* and scanned the caption. The leader of the boys was named Luis Alvarez. He began to call all the Alvarezes in the telephone book.

In each case the answer was indignant. No, of course they didn't have a son Luis who was a defendant in the Farmer trial!

Dave was running out of dimes and there were still more than 150 Alvarezes to go. He gave up and stepped outside, praying, "All right, Lord. I just don't know what to do next. If this is Your business I'm on, then Your Spirit will have to show me the way."

Dave got into his car and began to drive aimlessly through the strange streets. Eventually he found himself in the heart of Spanish Harlem. Tired of driving, he parked in the first empty space he found. He got out and asked a boy if he knew where a Luis Alvarez lived.

"Luis Alvarez?" said the boy. "You parked in front of his house." He pointed to a brownstone building. "Fourth floor."

"Thank you, Lord," said Dave.

"What you say?"

Dave put his hands on the boy's shoulder. "Thank you. Thank you *very* much."

Dave climbed to the fourth floor, found the Alvarez' apartment and knocked on the door.

"Come in."

He pushed the door open and saw a tired-looking man sitting on an overstuffed chair. Señor Alvarez barely looked up. "Ah, here you are, Preacher. I been expecting you. I see your picture in the paper. I say my prayers that you will come." At last Dave seemed to be getting his go-ahead sign.

Early the next morning he was back at the city jail with seven written permissions to visit the seven boys on trial.

Again he failed.

The jail chaplain, feeling that the boys were in his own spiritual care, refused to allow him entrance. David was crushed. "What are you trying to say to me, Lord?" Dave asked. "Show me where my vision is too small." He had no way of knowing that this door had to be closed in order for another—much larger—to be opened.

Suddenly a jolting idea occurred to him. Perhaps his vision *was* too small. Perhaps the Holy Spirit didn't intend him to work just for the seven defendants in the Michael Farmer trial *but for all the lonely, angry kids on the New York streets.*

Two weeks later Dave Wilkerson was back in New York. On this trip he brought with him no preconceived ideas of whom he was to help or how. He simply walked the streets, and everywhere he walked he made the same discovery: the picture of him in a New York tabloid that had seemed to Dave like a mockery of his guidance—was his entree to the street gangs of New York. Wherever he went he was recognized, "Hi ya, Preach!" from a cluster of kids on a street corner. "You're one of us, Davey!" from a tenement stoop.

Soon the churches were asking questions about this man who was "in" where they'd never even had a toe hold. Fifty parishes got together and asked him to conduct a two-week youth revival in St. Nicholas Arena. Five thousand teen-agers flocked to hear him. A few months later Dave had a weekly television show where teen-age drug addicts, adolescent alcoholics, and 14-year-old prostitutes told the stories of their conversions. Eleven years ago Dave moved his family to New York so that he could minister full time to these young people. Today he directs Teen Challenge Center in Brooklyn, a home where boys and girls in trouble can come for a new start—and where the fresh paint, the curtains in the windows, and the new flower beds are largely the work of the kids themselves.

As for the seven defendants in the Michael Farmer trial, three were acquitted; four sent to prison. When Dave visits them at the penitentiary it is no longer as an unknown country preacher begging admission. It is as the man whose results among teen-age hoodlums have people in New York shaking their heads in wonder.

As they say, it's amazing what can happen when the average man—any average man—lets the Holy Spirit be his guide.

As I was walking along one of the busy streets of my home town today I heard someone singing above the noise of the traffic. It wasn't noisy singing—almost like someone singing to himself—but I heard it. Then I located the singer. He was pushing himself along through the crowd in a wheelchair by the power of his two arms, the only useful limbs he had left.

As I caught up with him I said, "A man in a wheelchair singing gives everyone who hears him a lift."

He answered, "When I stopped looking at what I had lost, and began looking at all I had left, I could sing again."

ROBERT E. BRUCE
Redlands, California

Why Laughter Has Power
by Bob Hope

"A merry heart doeth good like medicine," says the Scriptures, and this great comedian attests to its truth.

Once when I was in Shreveport, Louisiana, a minister offered me his pulpit for a sermon on "God and Hollywood."

Hastily I explained that in my business, success was measured by "yocks" versus "boffs." When that just confused him I said, "You know, yocks . . . little laughs . . . and boffs . . . great big ones. And if I got up there in your church I might still, unconsciously, be trying for those boffs."

We let the matter drop. But afterward, during a nightmare, I found myself in a pulpit and the laughs were rolling down the aisle shaking the dignified old rafters. I told a friend of this dream.

"And what would be so wrong about that?" he wanted to know. "Laughter has a spiritual value. An Englishman named John Donne had that pegged over 400 years ago. He said, 'Religion is not a melancholy, the spirit of God is not a dampe.' "

He had a point. Certainly I knew that laughter has a constructive power. I have seen what a laugh can do. It can transform almost unbearable tears into something bearable, even hopeful.

Overseas in 1944 with USO Camp Shows, Frances Langford and I saw it lift a whole ward at the service hospital in Pearl Harbor. We were working our way up a long aisle when a nurse touched my arm.

"That boy near the end in the very high bed. They pulled him out of a B-17. Herbert hasn't spoken a word for weeks. If there's anything you can do . . ."

As we got to that end of the ward I winked at Frances. "Okay, boys," I said. "Frances Langford is going to sing you a song . . . and Herbert," I pointed to the bed where we could just see a white face, bandages covering the eyes, "Herbert, this is for you."

Frances approached the bed slowly, beginning her song . . . "Embrace me, my sweet embraceable you." An unnatural stillness settled over the entire ward. One of those that doesn't feel right, too hushed and breathless. All you could hear was Frances' low plaintive song:

"Embrace me, you irreplaceable you . . ." And then, just as she reached him, her voice broke off.

In two steps I was beside her looking down at Herbert. Where his arms had been there were only short stumps.

For several seconds we all just stood there stunned. No one moved. But the part of the mind where habit and involuntary reaction holds sway provided me with a diversion.

A couple of guys laughed, bless 'em. On I rushed trying to build that chain of laughter while Frances regained her composure. But the miracle was Herbert. Herbert spoke, *for the first time in weeks.*

"It's all right, Miss Langford," he said. "Don't worry about it."

Laughter binds men together in a kind of secret free masonry.

Hear it sometime travel around a circle . . . then notice that, however large that circle may be, it is a closed one.

For a brief few hours in 1944 I met 15,000 Marines of the 21st Division at Pavuvu. They were on their way to the invasion of Peleliu. We were doing a routine series of camp shows on the Pacific Islands.

When an officer suggested the unscheduled stop he said, "We'll have to fly you over, a few at a time in small planes, and land you on a road. There's no airport. But it'll be worth it to them."

As we circled for our landing such a shout arose from 15,000 throats that we could actually *feel* it like a cushion of sound under our wings. We were from home! We were the promise of laughter . . . today. Tomorrow, and they knew it, wouldn't come back.

We laughed and clowned as we landed. But looking at those faces I knew how Charles Lamb must have felt when he "jested that he might not weep."

Later back in the States, my wife and I at the dedication of Oak Knoll Hospital, walked into a ward to be greeted with that same laughter. One of those explosions that happen between old friends.

Voices kept yelling, "Pavuvu! Pavuvu!" Dolores was a bewildered outsider. But I was in. It was the 1st Marines . . . or what was left of them.

Laughter can sometimes appeal beyond reason, prejudice and cynicism.

In a jungle I heard the jokes of padres lift G.I.'s spirits into wanting the fearlessness and gaiety of the men of God, where no amount of solemn approach would have inspired them.

And I have heard a minister devastate a profane agnostic with quiet wit.

It happened at a very swank club one night. After a pointless and slightly blasphemous story the comedian noticed that all eyes were suddenly fastened on the collar insignia of a big, silent man at the end of the table.

"F'r crissakes," blustered the story-teller. "Are you a chaplain?"

With a light smile and deliberate emphasis the chaplain replied. "Yes, for *Christ's* sake, I am."

Laughter can return a sense of proportion to a troubled mind, for it erases self-pity, self-justification, self-importance.

But perhaps the most important thing laughter can do is to bring back the will to live—and, when the times comes, give us the courage to go with good cheer.

I've seen the ones who aren't going to make it—boys smiling their way right up to St. Peter's gate, and I've got a hunch they're holding a sure pass. Like one youngster who was stretched out on the ground getting a blood transfusion. "I see they're giving you the old raspberry, son," I said.

"It sure feels good," he laughed. "The guy who gave this must have been tax exempt or raised his own beef. It's strong stuff."

Before I had gotten 20 yards he had gone his way, smiling.

My young brother Sydney passed on a number of years ago and, for quite a while, he knew he was going. Someone with a very long face and a "religion of melancholy" had urged him to "prepare to meet his Maker" . . . to "petition Providence to provide for his poor little orphans."

It took the whole family and his five kids to convince him that "the spirit of God is not a dampe," here or hereafter, except for those who choose to have it so.

Every gay thing, every joyous or humorous or good thing that came to our attention we offered to my brother as proof of the infinite wisdom and kindness of God. When he went, he went smiling—and trusting. And, we had done such a good job for him that we had healed ourselves of much of our grief.

A comedian can't take much credit either, because people insist they are funny. You become a habit—a laugh habit. Sometimes people laugh at me before I open my mouth—even when they can't see me. Mention the arrival of someone they've laughed at before and they relax. They drop their strain. They expect to laugh and so they do.

They depend, too, on the laughmaker to stay the same. They want new jokes but not too much change. I don't think they've ever forgiven Charlie Chaplin for abandoning his big shoes, cane and derby hat. When I go into a service hospital they expect me to louse up the joint. To go on being me. No sympathy. They want me to walk into a ward filled with guys harnessed to torturous contraptions and say, "Don't get up fellows."

When I come to a Christmas party if I notice the lone star atop a pathetic Christmas tree I'm supposed to say, "Don't tell me a Brigadier General is running this show too."

So I say it. And when people wonder how a guy can go on and on like that . . . well, the answer is that the results themselves keep you up. You can't possibly not do it. The power works both ways. You are sustained by *their* laughter.

Nor does the power belong exclusively to the professional funnyman. There is a kind of geniality that brings mirth, and confidence. Bing Crosby had that. If there are two kinds of people, people who lift and people who lean, Bing was a lifter. Geniality might be defined as strength to spare.

The power of laughter lies in its ability to lift the spirit. For laughter cannot exist with clipped wings. It cannot be dictated to. It must be spontaneous and free as the air you breathe. Thus it is a special property of free men in a free land who are able to laugh at anything . . . or anyone . . . especially themselves.

Because of a little piece of paper today is a very special day. This world suddenly belongs to me in a way it never did before. I also belong to it in a new way.

That child pedaling his bicycle along the road—I see the

years of love and sacrifice that brought him to this place. I realize the incalculable heartbreak if some accident should befall this child.

The man approaching me in the pick-up truck is a very ordinary looking man. But doubtless he is the heart and mainstay of some nearby home.

The old lady glancing about hesitantly before crossing the street is elderly and slightly stooped, walking with studied care. How precious these late September days must be to her.

God, make me alert that no action of mine may darken or shorten the life of one of Your people.

Today is a very special day for me. I hold in my hand a little piece of paper that is a passport to a broader world of freedom and discovery. God, grant that I use it only for good.

Today I received my driver's license.

JULIA C. MAHON
North Grosvenor Dale, Connecticut

Thank You, Dad

by James Stewart,
(as told to Floyd Miller)

A famous movie star reminisces about a time, a place and a man—all gone but very much alive in his heart.

When I was a boy in the town of Indiana, Pennsylvania, Stewart's Hardware Store seemed the center of the universe. It was a three-story structure filled with everything needed to build a house, hunt a deer, plant a garden, repair a car or make a scrapbook.

Even after I moved away and saw larger sights, the store remained with me. But then I realized that what was central to my life was not just the store but the man who presided over it—my father.

Alexander Stewart was a muscular Irishman whose talk was as blunt as his face. The store not only provided his family a living but also was a forum where he pronounced opinions seldom tailored to the popular style. If he ever heard the slogan about the customer always being right, he would have scorned it as toadyism as well as a falsehood. And yet his tone was never harsh, and he was never vindictive. If a man failed to follow his advice, Father merely made allowance for human frailty and felt no ill will.

Dad was a Presbyterian, strong in his religion as he was in all beliefs. He sang in the choir with a true but penetrating tenor voice, and someone once described the hymns as "solos by Mr. Stewart, with accompanying voices."

Strangely, Dad never sang very loudly at home. We lived in a rambling house with a large front porch loaded with wicker furniture. The living room, high ceilinged and trimmed with dark woodwork, held a grand piano, around which we gathered for family sings. My sister Virginia played the piano, my other sister Mary played the violin and I played the accordion—after a fashion.

During these sessions, Dad sang very softly, so as not to cover up Mother's clear, sweet voice. Her name was Elizabeth, and he called her Bessie and adored her. Though small and gentle and not given to contention, she frequently had her way over him because she possessed patience and endurance.

Doing things with my father was always fun, for his imagination added a dimension to events. When, at 10, I announced that I was going to Africa to bring back wild animals, my mother and sisters pointed out my age, the problems of transportation and all such mundane and inconsequential facts.

But not Dad. He brought home books about Africa, train and boat schedules for us to study, and even some iron bars which we used to build cages for the animals I was to bring back. When the departure day approached and I was becoming apprehensive, my father brought home a newspaper that told of a wreck on the railroad that was to take me to Baltimore. This postponed my trip and, by the time the train tracks were repaired, he and I were off on a new and more exciting project.

When President Harding died, the funeral train was scheduled to pass through a town about 20 miles from ours. I wanted desperately to go and see this train, but Mother pointed out that there would be school the next day and that it would be a long trip. That ended the discussion.

But Dad did not forget. When the day arrived, he came to me and, in a voice as near a whisper as his nature would allow, said, "Jim, boy, it's time to see the funeral train."

We drove along without talking much, bound together by the comradeship of our adventure. When we came to the railroad station, a half dozen people were talking in hushed tones and looking down the tracks. Suddenly the tracks gave off a low hum—the funeral train was coming!

Dad shoved two pennies into my hand and said, "Run, put them on the rails. Quick!"

I did as directed and jumped back to hold his hand as the engine thundered past, pulling a glass-windowed observation car in which we saw the flag-draped casket, guarded by two Marines, their glistening bayonets at attention. I could hardly breathe, so overwhelming were the sight and sound.

After the train had roared off, I retrieved the two flattened pennies from the track. Dad put one in his pocket and I kept the other.

As we drove home, I examined mine and found that the two feathers of the Indian headdress had become a great plume. On the other side two slender stalks of wheat had grown and burst, as if the seed had ripened and scattered.

For years, Dad and I carried those coins flattened by the weight of history. And the knowledge of what we shared made me feel very close to him.

With his temperament, it was amazing how patient Dad could be, how subtle his discipline. I don't recall a time when he stood across my path; he always walked beside, guiding me with his own steps. When a neighbor's dog killed my dog Bounce, I vowed to kill that dog in revenge. I vowed it day after day in the most bloodthirsty terms, almost making myself ill with my own hate.

"You are determined to kill the dog," my father stated abruptly one evening after dinner. "All right, let's get it done. Come on."

I followed him to the store, to discover that he had tied the dog in the alley. He got a deer rifle out of stock, loaded it, handed it to me, then stepped back for me to do my bloody work. The dog and I looked at each other. He wagged his tail in a tentative offer of friendship and his large brown eyes were innocent and trusting. Suddenly the gun was too heavy for me to hold and it dropped to the ground. The dog came up and licked my hand.

The three of us walked home together, the dog gamboling in front. No word was ever said about what had happened. None was needed.

During World War II, I enlisted in the Air Corps and became part of a bomber squadron. When we were ready to fly overseas, Dad came to the farewell ceremonies in Sioux City, Iowa. We were very self-conscious with each other, talking in generalities, trying to conceal our awareness that, starting tomorrow, he could no longer walk with me. At the time of the greatest crisis in my life, he would have to stand aside. We were both afraid.

At the moment of parting, he studied his shoes a moment, then looked at the sky. I knew he was searching for a final word to sustain me, but he couldn't find it. He opened his mouth, then shut it hard, almost in anger. We embraced, then he turned and walked quickly away. Only after he had gone did I realize that he had put a small envelope in my pocket.

That night alone in my bunk, I opened it and read, "My dear Jim, soon after you read this letter, you will be on your way to the worst sort of danger. I have had this in mind for a long time and I am very concerned. . . . But Jim, I am banking on the enclosed copy of the 91st Psalm. The thing that takes the place of fear and worry is the promise in these words. I am staking my faith in these words. I feel sure that God will lead you through this mad experience . . . I can say no more. I only continue to pray. God bless you and keep you. I love you more than I can tell you. Dad."

Never before had he said he loved me. I always knew he did but he had never said it until now. I wept. In the envelope there was also a small booklet bearing the title *The Secret Place—A Key to the 91st Psalm*. I began to read it. From that day, the little booklet was always with me. Before every bombing raid over Europe, I read some of it, and with each reading the meaning deepened for me.

I will say of the Lord, He is my refuge and my fortress. . . . His truth shall be thy shield and buckler. Thou shalt not be afraid for the terror by night; nor for the arrow that flieth by day. . . . For He shall give His angels charge over thee, to keep thee in all thy ways. They shall bear thee up in their hands, lest thou dash thy foot against a stone.

And I was borne up.

Dad had committed me to God, but I felt the presence of both throughout the war.

When Mother died in 1956, we buried her in the family plot in Indiana, Pennsylvania. With his wife gone, Dad could work up no new enthusiasms. Her quiet strength had sustained him, and with her gone he quickly withered away.

It was a bleak January day when I saw him placed beside his ancestors, men who had lived longer than he had but who were perhaps less demanding of life. Most of the town came to the funeral with respect and grief.

After it was all over, I went to the hardware store and let myself in with a key I hadn't touched for 30 years. The interior smelled of metal, leather, oil and fertilizer, the odors of my childhood.

I sat at his scarred oak desk and idly pulled open the middle drawer. It held a clutter of pencils and paper clips and bolts and paint samples. Something glinted dully among them. I picked up the funeral-train penny with the flattened Indian face and the burst grain.

For a long time I sat there at his desk, fingering the Indian head penny and thinking. Then I put it in my pocket, took a last look at familiar and loved objects, and walked out of the store, locking the door behind me.

Confidence is Contagious
by Bart Starr

An all-pro quarterback for the Green Bay Pack-
ers tells about the man who saved him from
mediocrity.

This is the story of how a small city in Wisconsin—and a team of football players—were hit by lightning. The lightning I'm referring to is Vincent Lombardi, a stocky Italian-American whom many consider the best football coach in the world. The city happened to be the town where I live, Green Bay, where the Packers come from.

In case you are not a sports' fan, the Green Bay Packers are a professional football team. They are one of the fabled teams of the game with a history of excellence going back to 1919. In that post-World War I year the first players trotted out on the gridiron wearing jerseys that said "Packers" on them, and this was for the nearby meat packing plant which put up the money for the jerseys. The Packers won 10 games out of 11 that season and started on their way towards making themselves one of the resounding stories of sports.

When my wife, Cherry, and I came up from the University of Alabama in 1956, all eager and dazzled by the prospects of my being quarterback on so illustrious a team, the Green Bay Packers had fallen upon some dismal days.

My first year in Green Bay we lost twice as many games as we won, and in 1957 we lost three times as many. In pro ball, records like those are something you don't joke about. Winning with us is a serious business, our bread and butter.

Pro football is a sport—and a clean one—but it is very much a money-making venture. Not winning, therefore, is like not selling the product you've manufactured. It's a science, too, involving hundreds of plays, intricate formations both for offense and defense.

For a player like me, who wanted to be in pro ball more than anything else in the world, the season of 1958 was frightening. In all that long "history of excellence" the Packers' '58 season was absolutely the bottom. Out of 12 games on our schedule, we tied one game and won—just one. Ten losses: sheer disaster.

In December our coach resigned. The danger signals were up for me and I knew it. I hadn't exactly sparkled out there on the field.

And then the lightning struck!

We were a squeamish group who gathered to meet our new coach and general manager that day in 1959.

"Gentlemen," Coach Lombardi said that day, "we're going to have a football team. We are going to win some games. Do you know why? Because you are going to have confidence in me and my system. By being alert you are going to make fewer mistakes than your opponents. By working harder you are going to out-execute, out-block, out-tackle every team that comes your way."

As the coach talked, you could see the guys straightening up to take a closer look at this intense man.

"But first of all," he went on, "you are going to prepare yourself up here." He put his finger to his temple. "You can't win if you're not ready to win mentally. Therefore, I expect you to think about only three things while you are part of this organization: your family, your religion and the Green Bay Packers."

I for one walked out of that meeting feeling 10 feet tall—and I hadn't played a lick for him!

All of us caught his enthusiasm. Just as he said we would, we started working harder on the field.

I know I worked harder too. It reminded me of the summer I was waiting for my try-out with the Packers. Cherry's folks had a big yard around their house and there I set up a large A-frame. Day in, day out, from morning to night I threw passes into the opening of the A-frame. High, low, on the run, standing still, I worked away at those passes from every conceivable motion and angle. I believe that that total concentration helped get me the job. And that same spirit of hard work was re-ignited by Coach Lombardi.

We started our pre-season games. The tempo rose. Suddenly we won a game and our spirits soared. They kept on soaring. By the end of the 1959 season, we had won seven out of 12 games with virtually the same players who had lost

10 games the year before. In 1960 we won a Division title, then in 1961 a World title, and after that the sky always seemed to be our limit.

How had Coach Lombardi accomplished these things?

You can say, of course, that he did it with his particular genius. But that's not an explanation. Having played for him for nine seasons, I think I have reason to say that his "genius" consists of some very simple things. These are ideas available to all of us and useful in any undertaking if we but have the mental toughness to weld them together into a way of living.

Coach Lombardi doesn't make a secret of those principles. Wherever he is they come out in the way he lives his own life and in the way he thinks. We get plenty of his thoughts. Not only verbally, but in writing. Every week he tacks up fragments of home-grown advice on the locker room bulletin board.

At the start of the training season one year we found this typewritten notice, "Fatigue makes cowards of us all. High physical condition is vital to victory."

This was supplanted the next week by, "The harder a man works, the harder it is to surrender;" followed by, "Pride is what causes a winning team's performance." And so it went week after week.

I can never forget, nor will I ever stop being grateful for, what Coach Lombardi did for me. As I look back to that first question mark of a year under him, I am quite sure he had never seen a three-year veteran who knew less than I did. But he was a patient teacher and he brought out something in me that changed my career and my life. Confidence.

Mind you, I was always sure of my talent. I never really doubted that I could play good football, but I lacked the kind of confidence that Coach Lombardi himself had, the kind that oozes out to others. A quarterback is in a position of command; it is he who calls the plays. He must be alert and ready to adjust to the sudden and the unexpected. He has got to have a high boiling point because opponents are going to try to rattle him and he's going to get a lot of whacking around.

Coach Lombardi started building my confidence by first giving me the enthusiasm to work harder, the way I had done with the A-frame. He spent a lot of time just talking to me, examining the "hows" and "whys" of the game. Then he began to bear down on my thinking.

"Treat mistakes with a vengeance!" he'd pound at me. "Don't brood over them, profit from them. If you think about mistakes, you'll make more mistakes. Just come back wiser and harder."

Through it all, the coach repeated his theory that winning is a habit. "It's contagious," he'd say, "and so is losing."

Coach Lombardi won't permit losing thoughts. He contends that pro football has reached a point of such sophistication, that the opposing forces are now in such complicated balance, that on any given afternoon any team can defeat any other. To him there are only two or three plays in a game that decide who wins or loses and if you are not ready for them at all times, you're in serious trouble.

In 1966 we won the Western Division championship even before we had played our last game with the Los Angeles Rams. We were riding high and jubilant. But Coach Lombardi was not. He worried about the last game, even though it didn't affect our league standing. He didn't want us to get out of the winning habit—and we didn't that day!

"If you give anything less than the best of yourselves today," he said to us before the game that Sunday, "you're not just cheating yourselves, or the team, or the millions of fans who are expecting a top-grade Packer performance. No, beyond all others, you are cheating your Maker, the God who gave you your special talent for ball-playing. Such waste is the worst cheating of all."

This was strong and unusual stuff from him and though you may think it a corny, God-in-the-locker-room tactic, you wouldn't think that for long if you really knew Vincent Lombardi. He is a sincere and believing man who goes to church every day of the week, who seldom talks in religious tones, but whose religion is as natural and as integral a part of him as are the prayers we say together before and after every Packer game.

Those prayers are something else I have learned from Coach Lombardi's example. After the week's preparations are over, after the sweat of the practice field and after the groggy hours examining movies and of note-making and of drawing diagrams, after all these things have been completed, the Lord's Prayer said in unison becomes a unifying force pulling all our efforts together. And I have yet to come up from my knees without feeling personally that we were going to do all the things that Coach Lombardi had prepared us to do.

Be Bold . . .
and mighty forces will come to your aid
by Arthur Gordon

A powerful principle is discovered that could change your life, too.

Once when I was facing a decision that involved (I thought) considerable risk, I took the problem to a friend much older and wiser than myself. "I'd go ahead," I said unhappily, "if I were *sure* I could swing it. But . . ."

He looked at me for a moment, then scribbled ten words on a piece of paper and pushed it across the desk. I picked it up and read, in a single sentence, the best advice I ever had: *Be Bold—and mighty forces will come to your aid.*

It's amazing how even a fragment of truth will illuminate things. The words my friend had written were from a quotation, I discovered later, in a book by Basil King.* They made me see clearly that in the past, whenever I had fallen short in almost any undertaking, it was seldom because I had tried and failed. It was because I had let fear of failure stop me from trying at all.

On the other hand, whenever I *had* plunged into deep water, impelled by a momentary flash of courage or just plain pushed by the rude hand of circumstance, I had always been able to swim until I got my feet on the ground again.

Be bold—that was no exhortation to be reckless or foolhardy. Boldness meant a deliberate decision, from time to time, to bite off more than you were sure you could chew. And there was nothing vague or mysterious about the mighty

---

* The Conquest of Fear by Basil King (Doubleday)

forces referred to. They were the latent powers that all of us possess: energy, skill, sound judgment, creative ideas—yes, even physical strength and endurance in far greater measure than most of us realize.

Boldness, in other words, creates a state of emergency to which the organism will respond. I once heard a famous British mountaineer say that occasionally a climber will get himself into a position where he can't back down, he can only go up. He added that sometimes he put himself into such a spot on purpose. "When there's nowhere to go but up," he said, "you jolly well go up!"

The same principle works, less dramatically but just as surely, in something as commonplace as accepting the chairmanship of some civic committee, or even seeking a more responsible job. In either case, you know you'll have to deliver—or else. And unless you're hopelessly unqualified, you *will* deliver. Your pride, your competitive instinct, and your sense of obligation will see to it that you do.

These are some of the mighty forces that will come to your aid. They are, admittedly, psychic forces. But they are more important than physical ones. It was centrifugal force, in a hurtling pebble, that killed Goliath. But it was courage that enabled David to face the champion of the Philistines in the first place.

It's curious, actually, how spiritual laws often have their counterpart in the physical world. A college classmate of mine was a crack football player, noted particularly for his fierce tackling although he was much lighter than the average varsity player. Someone remarked that it was surprising that he didn't get hurt.

"Well," he said, "I think it goes back to something I discovered when I was a somewhat timid youngster playing sandlot football. In one game, playing safety-man, I suddenly found myself confronting the opposing fullback, who had nothing but me between him and our goal line. He looked absolutely gigantic! I was so frightened that I closed my eyes and hurled myself at him like a panicky bullet . . . and stopped him cold. Right there I learned that the harder you tackle a bigger player, the less likely you are to be hurt. The reason is simple: Momentum equals weight times velocity."

In other words, if you are bold enough, even the laws of motion will come to your aid.

This personality trait—a willingness to put yourself in a position where you will have to extend yourself to the utmost—is not one that can be acquired overnight. But it can be taught to children and developed in adults. Confidence is a cumulative thing.

To be sure, there will be setbacks and disappointments in any program of expanded living; boldness in itself is no guarantee of success. But, as someone said, the man who tries to do something and fails is a lot better off than the man who tries to do nothing and succeeds.

Boldness, of course, like any other virtue, can be pushed too far. Once, in my more impulsive days, I jumped out of an airplane just to see what it was like. I had a parachute, naturally—two, in fact—but I promptly wound up in a hospital with a broken ankle. I suppose I did achieve my main objective, which was to write a story about paratroopers with a certain amount of realism. But it was hardly worth it.

Still, for every time you thus overshoot your target, there are a hundred times that you undershoot it. In the famous Parable of the Talents, the servant who buries his master's money in the ground is severely reprimanded for failing to do anything with it or take any risk. And the servant's answer is very significant. It could be summarized in three words: *I was afraid . . .* *

Fear, the opposite of boldness, is the most paralyzing of all emotions. It can literally stiffen the muscles, as anyone knows who has ever been really scared. And (again the psychic-physical parallel holds) it can also stupefy the mind and the will. Most of us free-lance writers know this very well. When you are blessed—or cursed—with a vivid imagination, it's all too easy to become convinced that your energy is dwindling, that the flow of ideas is drying up, that your latest effort is also your last. Such thoughts are dangerous. Fears, like hopes and dreams, have a way of clothing themselves ultimately with reality. As Job said, reviewing his troubles (and anticipating the psychiatrists by a couple of millenia), *The thing which I greatly feared is come upon me. . . .* **

Almost from the beginning of recorded history, mankind has recognized that the surest antidote for fear is religious faith. Belief—and trust—in a personal God makes a man bigger than himself and stronger than himself. Washington bore witness to this repeatedly; so did Lincoln. Joan of Arc was a

---

* *Matthew 25:25*
** *Job 3:25*

shining example of the power of faith to transform an individual, and through an individual a whole nation.

This source of power is just as available to the rank and file as to the leaders. The man who believes firmly that the Creator of the universe loves him and cares infinitely what he does with his life—this man is automatically freed from much of the self-distrust that afflicts less certain men. Fear, guilt, hostility, anger—these are the emotions that stifle thought and impede action. By reducing or eliminating them, religious faith makes boldness possible, and boldness makes achievement possible. Over and over again, in both the Old and New Testaments, the Bible hammers this message home: *The Lord is my light and my salvation; whom shall I fear?** *... According to your faith be it unto you.***

Boldness is not always spectacular; there is also a quiet kind. I knew a city-dwelling family once that wanted to move to the country. They had no financial resources, but plenty of spiritual ones. Instead of counting the pennies and deciding the move was impossible, they calmly drew up a list of six requirements that they considered essential (actually, they agreed they would settle for five of the six). The place, they decided, would have to have a pleasant view, some shade trees, a stream or brook, some arable land to grow things, some pasture for animals, and it had to be near enough to the city for the father to milk the cows every morning and still commute to his job.

They finally found such a place, borrowed the money to make a down payment, and have been living there happily (and boldly, although no doubt the word would astonish them) ever since.

This sort of self-confidence and decisiveness often marks a leader in the business world. The best executive I ever worked for was a man who made almost instantaneous decisions. "At least," he used to say wryly, "I make my mistakes quickly." On one occasion someone asked this man if he didn't believe in the old adage, "Look before you leap."

"No," he said cheerfully, "I don't." He thought for a minute, then added, "The trouble with that axiom is that if you look too long, or too often, you never leap at all."

A willingness to take chances, a solid faith in the ability of the individual to cope, God helping him, with just about

---

* *Psalms 27:1*
** *Matthew 9:29*

any problem—these characteristics are part of the traditional American heritage. Is that spirit dying out? Some observers claim that our preoccupation with security is weakening it. Initiative, they say, is the instinctive response to lack. Security is the absence of lack. Can the two really exist, side by side?

I think they can, simply because there are always new and more challenging worlds to conquer. We may be remembered as the generation that sought, and provided, material security for many. But we are also the generation that dared to pick the lock of the universe, the generation that invaded the heart of the atom. The risks were, and still are, appalling. But the mighty forces unleashed by our boldness will come to our aid some day in the form of unlimited light and heat and power for all mankind.

One of the best speeches I ever heard was made by a little man who came into our schoolroom one day and was invited to say a few words to us. I don't remember who he was, and probably I am not quoting him verbatim, but what he said was very close to this:

Love life. Be grateful for it always. And show your gratitude by not shying away from its challenges. Try always to live a little bit beyond your capacities. You'll find that you never succeed.

What I Took Into Space
by Edward H. White II

An astronaut whose faith still lives.

At the first public briefing Jim McDivitt and I held after the completion of our Gemini-4 flight, one reporter asked if we had taken personal items on the mission. I wouldn't have remembered my exact words except that they were taped. I said:

"There were three personal objects I'd like to mention. They are things that were very important to me, kind of a philosophy that I had on the flight. I'll try to express it to you as well as I can.

"I took along a St. Christopher medal, a gold Cross, and a Star of David. I took these things to express, a bit, the great faith I had in the people and the equipment we were using for the mission. I had faith in myself, and in Jim and especially in my God. Faith was the most important thing I had going for me on the flight. I couldn't take something for every religion in the country, but I took the three with which I was most familiar."

I have been absolutely amazed at the response to these few sentences when they were quoted in the newspapers. All over the country people have asked me to explain a little more about this philosophy. The requests have come, often from young people who seemed surprised that an astronaut could be so interested in religion.

When I was a boy I don't suppose I had a more lively interest in faith than most youngsters. I was interested in football and track and in camping in the woods.

But I had parents who knew how to communicate their own beliefs in terms I could understand. My brother Jim and my sister Jean and I never doubted where our parents stood on the question of religion. The Bible in our home was not a book to sit on the shelf; it was out where it could be used.

95

Church was not a seasonal affair; going to church on Sunday was as much a part of the rhythm of life as washing clothes on Monday.

My mother knew that the best way to communicate her faith was not through words alone, but through her life. Dad was an experienced aviator in the Army and Air Force, and I suppose there is no job anywhere that is harder on a wife. Dad was in a serious aircraft accident when I was a young boy. He was at Wright Patterson Air Base when his plane's engines cut out just after takeoff. My father barely survived but we kids never knew how badly he was hurt until much later.

Mother moved through the experience with the calm, quiet assurance that can come only from a deep faith. When she finally told us what a close call it had been, she listed the ingredients that had helped bring him back to us. Right at the top of the list was prayer.

Dad like Mother, did a large part of his communicating through action rather than through words. I remember, for instance, when Dad was assigned to a base located 12 miles outside Tokyo, that the chapel there was a dreary little quonset hut. One of the first things Dad did when he assumed his command was to get together with the base chaplain and make the chapel as attractive as possible. He wanted it to be a place he and his men would like to visit.

My father believed that the way to teach his children about faith was to talk in terms of day-to-day experience. One of his favorite Bible verses is, *Ask, and it shall be given you; seek, and ye shall find; knock, and it shall be opened unto you.* Dad loved to illustrate the power of this verse by telling stories of times he had asked, or sought or knocked.

When he was a boy he wanted more than anything else to get into West Point. He got his appointment, on his own initiative, when he was 16 years old by boldly accosting the most influential man he knew—the editor of the *Sentinel*, in Fort Wayne, Indiana—and asking his assistance. He got the help, and he won the appointment.

"If you want something, ask for it," Dad would tell us time and again. And then, later, in his own special quiet way he would encourage us to ask for things in our prayers. He was not shy about this because he believed that the best way to introduce a young person to the reality of prayer was through the reality of his own needs and desires.

As we grew older, though, Dad pointed out that an

asking-prayer was not always appropriate. Faith was not some kind of magic. At times we would need to pray a *seeking-prayer* which required a long, sustained effort.

I had a chance to discover this for myself when I first formed the dream of becoming an astronaut. I had gone through West Point and was stationed in Germany when, in 1957, the astronaut program was first being discussed. I could see that this was to be the future of aviation in our generation and I knew it was something in which I wanted to take part. From that day on I had a dream: to become an astronaut, and perhaps some day to be the first man to set foot on the moon.

The only difficulty was that I wasn't qualified. I needed test pilot flight training. So I began my long search by going back to school. I enrolled at the University of Michigan, and it was there that I met Jim McDivitt and learned that he, too, had many of the same goals. After school came training to be a test pilot. While working as a test pilot at Wright Patterson AFB, Ohio, I had the opportunity to apply to NASA for their manned spaceflight program. After six months of screening I was selected. It had taken five years of seeking, but I knew I was close to my goal of becoming an astronaut.

I moved with my wife, Pat, and our two children, Eddie and Bonnie, to the Manned Spacecraft Center in Houston where we bought a home, transferred our church membership, rolled up our sleeves and prepared to get involved with PTA and Little League.

It was shortly after our arrival in Houston that I and the other men in the program each received a very special gift. It was a medal of St. Christopher, the patron saint of travelers. The medal was given to us by Pope John.

"On February 22, 1963," the accompanying letter read, "in an audience with Pope John XXIII, the Pope presented an American emissary with a specially blessed St. Christopher medal for each of the sixteen American astronauts. The Pope volunteered, during this audience, that whenever he learned that there was a man orbiting in space he said the prayer, 'May God protect this brave man and bring him safely home to earth.' "

Even though Pat and I are active Methodists, this medal meant as much to us, I feel sure, as it did to the McDivitts who are Catholic. I brought it home in its small red box and placed it on a shelf above the desk in my study. It was sitting there at the moment I made my final decision about what personal items to carry aboard Gemini-4.

I had given the question considerable thought over a long period of time. Whatever I chose had to be made of material that would space-qualifiy: certain materials will out-gas—give off gases due to the extremes of pressure and temperature which we encounter in space, and could even dissolve. Gold, I knew, would qualify, and my first thought was to take along a small gold Cross as a symbol of my faith. Then one day my eye fell on the St. Christopher medal the Pope had given us—why not take that along too? And as a logical next idea: Why not a Star of David?

At breakfast the next morning I explained my idea to Pat. She thought it was fine. Pat offered to let me take along her own gold Cross, but it was too small. So while I was making the final preparations for the flight, Pat shopped for a gold Cross and gold Star of David to accompany St. Christopher. They were just right.

As a final symbol of the meaning of this gesture, I wrapped the three symbols in two small flags: An American one, indicating that in our country we live in brotherhood under one flag, differing yet united, and a United Nations flag representing my hope that someday all the world will live in brotherhood.

When Jim McDivitt and I arrived at Launch Pad 19 on Cape Kennedy, June 3, 1965, I was carrying the three symbols, sewn into a special pouch on the left leg of my space suit. Interestingly, Jim had chosen to bring along his own St. Christopher medal which he had fastened to his instrument panel. Once we were in orbit, and weightless, it floated lazily on the end of its short chain, reminding us constantly not only of the prayer Pope John had said for astronauts, but of the prayers of our fellow Americans. It's hard to describe the feeling that comes with the knowledge that 190 million people are praying for you and wishing you well: You have the sensation of not being yourself at all. It makes you feel very, very small and humble.

During the fourth hour of our flight an incident occurred which brought to mind the reality behind the symbols we were carrying. The time arrived for our EVA (extravehicular activity). It was our first step into space, so we wanted to be sure the procedures were done thoroughly and correctly. Finally we were ready to go. We opened the hatch and I departed the spacecraft, carrying the three symbols with me.

Twenty minutes later I got word from the flight director a hundred miles below me in Houston that I was to come back into the spacecraft. It was as I was preparing to close the hatch that I discovered we had a malfunction. The closing lever was turning free without ratcheting the hatch down.

If we had not been properly prepared, this could have been a most serious mishap. But our training had anticipated just exactly this possibility. Using the procedure we had practiced together, Jim and I forced the hatch down. The interesting thing is that, aside from a slight increase in pulse rate, the doctors' monitoring instruments down on earth registered no signals of alarm as might have been expected in such a situation. I am convinced that this was not the result of any strength of our own. It was that the faith we had in our training, in each other, and in our God didn't leave room for negative thoughts.

When I returned home after our flight, Eddie and Bonnie were very anxious to see the tokens. I was amused. The trip into space had given these medals a new significance and they just wanted to see if the trip had changed them.

To me this is the best possible illustration of the use to which these tokens can be put. When the kids asked questions about what they stood for it gave me a chance to tell them how, as Jim and I sped past the continents at 17,500 miles per hour, it was obvious to us that man was being drawn closer together as never before. The space program is progressively decreasing the size of the world. Eventually, if we are to survive, people will just have to get along better and settle their differences like good neighbors.

We in America have learned to set an example of how this can be attempted. Even with all our troubles, we know our understanding of brotherhood can work. When I wrapped the Cross and the St. Christopher medal and the Star of David in those little flags, I was saying, in an action, a prayer that is on so many of our lips today; the seeking-prayer that pleads for a true brotherhood for all mankind.

COLONEL WHITE'S FAVORITE PRAYER

O God, our Father, Thou searcher of men's hearts,
help us to draw nearer to Thee in sincerity and truth . . .
Make us to choose the harder right instead of the
easier wrong, and never to be content with a half
truth when the whole can be won.

*Endow us with courage that is born of loyalty to all that is
noble and worthy, that scorns to compromise with vice and
injustice, and knows no fear when truth and right are
in jeopardy . . .*
*Kindle our hearts in fellowship with those of a cheerful
countenance, and soften our hearts with sympathy for
those who sorrow and suffer . . .*
*Help us, in our work and in our play, to keep ourselves
physically strong, mentally awake and morally straight,
that we may better maintain the honor of the Corps
untarnished . . . to realize the ideals of West Point
in doing our duty to Thee and to our Country.*

from the West Point Cadet's Prayer

The Angry Ones
by Eleanor Armstrong

---

*A young teacher puts her faith to work and trans-
forms a classroom.*

People used to wonder why I always walked to my teaching
job at the big central grade school two miles out of town. I
walked because I needed the solitude to prepare myself for
the day ahead—and the two miles often weren't far enough.

I'd come from my home state to a poverty-stricken area
of Appalachia to try to set up an art program. But it went so
slow! Scissors, for instance; it had taken me two years to get
together enough for even one small group. For paint brushes
I took cotton swabs from the health-supply closet.

But it wasn't the lack of supplies that really worried me;
it was the children. Belligerent, restless, seething with anger, I
couldn't keep their attention long enough to teach them. The
anger didn't seem directed at me especially. It turned on each
other: scuffles, kicks, stealing, senseless destructivness, foul
language. It was as though each child arrived at school at the
bursting point from some terrible unseen pressure.

I knew that most of their families were poor, but it took
me a long time to understand what "poor" means in this part
of the country. In my classes were children whose winter
clothes went on in October and didn't come off until the following April. There was a family of brothers and sisters who
fought each other for the old car seats that served as beds. "I
get the blanket when Ma don't come home," one little girl
told me proudly.

When the children gradually got the idea that the pictures they drew did not have to be exact copies of what I had
on the blackboard, but could come from inside themselves, I
gave them the subject "My Family" to draw. The results were
a revelation. Perhaps one in four showed a normal family

group: two large figures, several smaller ones, a dog or a cat. The rest had one striking feature in common: there was no father. Or if there was a father he was a tiny figure, drawn always at the very bottom of the page. Often neither parent was shown. And inevitably the small artist had drawn himself standing alone, as far away from the other figures as the little piece of paper would allow.

I sat for a long time after the last bus had gone that afternoon, holding those drawings, thinking of the card filed for each child in the office. "Father unknown. . . . Mother in jail. . . . Mother alcoholic. . . ." and so on. Those had been words only, but now I held in my hands the pictures of these things.

Obviously what these children needed was a large dose of love. But where was such love to come from? I was only one person and I taught 600 children a week.

Oh, there were little things I could do. An arm around a shoulder or, for the littlest ones, five minutes on my lap did more to improve their work than 20 lessons. But the need was so much greater than the supply!

More might have been done if the teachers had been willing to work together. But the hostility among the children seemed to infect the staff as well. So each morning on the way to school I used the solitude to talk over my problems with God.

And it was one of these walks, during my fourth year at school, which changed everything. I was moving even slower than usual because today was Thursday. Thursdays my first class was 4C, the one I dreaded above all others. Since there was no art room in the school I moved from classroom to classroom giving my lessons, and I had come to recognize a special mood for each room.

Room 4C had a sound of its own: an undercurrent of stinging, jeering words that never ceased. In four months this class had learned less about art than any other.

The school came in sight. "Dear Jesus," I prayed, "let 4C pay attention today! Let them stop quarreling just for a little while! Help me to have patience with them."

"I can't do any of these things"—the answer came as clear as if a voice had spoken—"if you leave Me at the door of the school."

I was used to these prayer dialogues; they had kept me going for three and a half years. But this time the thoughts came so completely from outside myself that I listened with a thumping heart.

"Look for Me in the classroom," the incredible suggestion went on. "Look into the children's eyes and you will see Me. And when you see Me, call Me by My Name. You must no longer keep Me to yourself. If you want to change people you must talk to them about Me."

Far down the hall I could hear the sound of 4C, the jeers, the catcalls. I walked in and propped up along the blackboard the newest of my efforts to bring beautiful things into these lives: a set of reproductions of famous paintings on which I had spent my last week's salary. The home-room teacher finished calling the roll and left. The next moment a tall boy named Johnny strode to the front of the room, grabbed a ruler and slashed the first picture in half. I jumped between him and the others.

"Can I find You in Johnny, Lord?" I wondered. I looked into his eyes as Jesus told me to do though I had to tilt my head back to do it. Johnny, 13, had been in the fourth grade so long he was a fixture like the map of Europe. Six feet tall, he was a hero to the small, picked-on children. Nobody picked on Johnny. And suddenly looking up into Johnny's face, I knew that in his very strength there was something Christlike, if only I chose to see it. He was strong, Johnny was. Like Jesus.

What was there in this recognition that made Johnny lower the ruler, never taking his eyes off mine, and place it on the desk?

As he walked back to his seat I looked into another pair of eyes. Sarah and her four sisters had been brought up to steal. Their mother would send them into a store with paper bags, then stage a fainting fit while the girls filled the bags. The children had been placed in the county home three years ago, and all but Sarah had stopped stealing.

She'd been whipped, lectured, locked up—she never changed and no one had ever seen Sarah cry. Like Jesus, Sarah could not be frightened.

Mary was almost a stranger in class, she'd been out sick so much. Her blue eyes glowed nearly black against skin white as eggshell; her hands looked almost transparent. Like Jesus, she bore suffering without a murmur.

Up and down the aisles I walked, silently looking deep into each pair of eyes. And every time it was Jesus who looked back at me.

Since I entered the room I had not spoken a single word. But gradually that restless roomful of children quieted down and a hush settled over us all.

I went back to the front of the room on tiptoe, for I felt suddenly that I was in a church instead of a classroom. A kind of glow seemed to shimmer in the air, brightening the daylight.

"Jesus is here," I whispered. "Jesus loves you. Jesus wants you. He cares for you. He will not leave you alone."

In the third row a girl was crying, tears streaming down her cheeks. I looked twice to make sure. It was Sarah who had never cried. In the back row Johnny put his head on his arms and began to sob.

And all the while we were wrapped in that brilliant light. Ordinarily in that first period the hall outside the open door was noisy with traffic. Messengers popped in and out with notes, announcements came over the loudspeaker. Not today. It was as if we had been lifted for a while outside of ordinary time and space. I don't know how long the moment lasted.

Now if I were to tell you that I never again heard a cruel or hurting word in 4C, that Sarah stopped stealing right then and forever, that Mary's cheeks grew red and she didn't miss another day of school all year, that Johnny became one of the most cheerful boys in school instead of the surliest, I would not blame you for not believing me.

And yet these things are precisely what did happen, and not only in 4C but in every other class when I looked there for Jesus. From that day on the art was only a means to Him. Every lesson became an excuse to talk about Him. If we painted a tree it was because He had made it; if we worked with clay, it was to understand the Master Potter.

Once I got over the idea that I must have solitude to seek Him, I found Him everywhere. And wherever I found Him I talked about Him: in the classroom, on the playground, in the teachers' room. Some of the teachers who had been coolest to me responded the most warmly when I spoke to the Jesus in them.

For wherever I saw Him and showed Him to others, there was healing. Healing of bodies, of minds, above all healing of hatred and mistrust and friction between people.

One little boy put it best of all. I had been trying to tell his first grade class how Jesus felt about them. "You know how you feel when you draw a picture," I said. "You want everybody to see it and admire it because you made it. That's how Jesus feels about you. You're the picture He draws."

Henry thought about this a long time, then his small blond towhead appeared at my desk. "Is *everybody* Jesus' picture?" he asked.

"That's right."

"Even Annie?"

"Even Annie."

A scrap of brown paper fluttered into my wastebasket. "I was going to put flypaper in Annie's milk," he said sadly, "only Jesus drew her, so I better not."

The Healing in Solitude
by Mary Martin

This celebrated Broadway star reveals a secret she discovered about hearing God's voice.

When I was very young I remember going by a large estate, hidden by trees, and being told that the road behind the huge iron gates led to a mysterious building called The Retreat, where nuns lived in solitude.

Alone? I wondered. *Away from everyone and everything? How terrible!*

Many years later my husband, Richard Halliday, and I were having dinner in a restaurant when a friend stopped to talk to us. "I heard you spent two months on a freighter," he said, "just the two of you as the only passengers. And now I hear you've bought a farm where you can retreat whenever you need to. I guess you two really value your solitude."

I forget what I answered. Before my eyes was a picture of dark trees and high iron railings and the road that led to that mysterious building. For he had used those words, "solitude" and "retreat"—words that for me still evoked the gloom and terror of that childhood scene. Not once had I applied them to what Richard and I did. Days gazing out over the endless sea, not another passenger aboard; the farm where the phone never rang because there was none to ring—were these in some sense "retreats"? Was it to be alone that we chose them?

We have traveled on many freighters and spent much time on that isolated farm. I know now that these are indeed retreats, and that solitude is their essence. And I have discovered that the real thing is utterly different from what I imagined, peering through that iron fence. To my child's mind, solitude meant loneliness—that fearful state of lovelessness and separation—and retreat meant to run away. But solitude, I know now, is the very opposite, not a loss of love, but a deliberate embrace of silence and uncluttered living in order to become more capable of love.

Nor have we ever run away from anything—or anyone. Rather, we have instinctively run to a change in the rhythm of life: to refuel, to gather fresh air and sun, to rest the mind and body, to feel the blood surge as a small ship creaks and groans through plunging waves; or to hear the wind whistling from a mountaintop climbed on foot.

At the farm, up at sunrise, to bed soon after 9 p.m. To know the joy of being hungry and taking the time to savor each bite of freshly picked fruit and vegetable. To rest, to read, to listen to the music of the night. And suddenly the mind is alive with new ideas, new thoughts, new hopes, new knowledge of ourselves and where we fit into the world of other people.

Such solitude, like all things of value, has its price. If I am to be alone, I must do without many of the conveniences of life—because they depend on other people. When the sleek and ultra-automatic refrigerator in our New York apartment breaks down (as it has three times in the past 14 months), I phone the serviceman, who finally comes and tells me the job needs a specialist—who finally comes and tells me I must order a part from the factory. And I spend my time phoning and writing letters and waiting for the experts and the part that never comes. Interdependence is the condition of technology.

But the old white icebox on our farm, like the lamps there, runs on kerosene and an old-fashioned wick. When it stops making ice, I turn it upside down to get rid of the air pocket—like burping a baby—and then it makes ice again. It doesn't deposit symmetrical cubes into a pretty container, but it does let me breathe the air of privacy.

Six years ago Richard and I decided that instead of waiting until we were at the conventional retirement age of 65, we would live that 65th year now—and live it alone, on our farm. We made many discoveries, that year of preview-retirement, but the chief one was that there wasn't one dull, boring moment. The 52 weeks sped by like four. We both spent more hours "together" and more hours "apart" than we had ever thought possible. We knew a stillness, a quietness; we had lived with ourselves and had no fears. We felt more eager to plunge into our next undertaking than ever before. We had learned the strengths that come naturally from those moments of solitude which nature needs from us all. We had not been alone, nor known loneliness.

Nature leads the bear to hibernate. But we human beings, especially we women, have to work to learn what riches we can gain in only a few moments of drawing aside—because, of course, solitude does not have to be taken in great hunks of a year, or even a week. These are the "big solitudes" in response to big weariness and confusion. But the frictions and frustrations of every day need healing too, and for those there are "small solitudes." Just a door to shut for ten minutes between ourselves and the demands upon us, giving time for prayer and contemplation. A walk in the park. The time to hear a favorite record all the way through, with the window shades down and the phone off the hook. All those can be retreats-in-miniature, part of the ancient wisdom of life's ebb and flow.

For like the land, we have to lie fallow from time to time—whether short or long; like the land, we must renew our strength in emptiness. For the human spirit this means solitude in order to soar again.

I learned that truth in an unforgettable manner not long ago. After doing *The Sound of Music*, I was part of a group preparing a show called *Jenny*. The author said he was writing a serious play. The composer and lyricists insisted they were writing a light, entertaining score. It was my conceit at the time that I could bring their opposing purposes together to make a successful whole. What followed was my most torturous and frightening experience.

When we opened in Boston, the critics and audiences were disappointed. New material had to be written; cast changes made, requiring rehearsals before and after performances. My body grew weary, my vocal cords strained. I needed a doctor daily and soon required a throat specialist.

Our next stop in Detroit was equally disappointing, and with a second attempt at new material and additional rehearsals, I was near exhaustion. After six weeks we announced we would close the show and not bring it to New York.

A few hours later we were told we would be sued for $2 million if I did not open with the show in New York. I had 48 hours to decide whether to continue to perform and ask the audiences to share my disappointment or go to court and be forced to work the rest of my life to pay out an enormous sum of money.

I decided that I would not spend the future in lawyers'

offices and courts. I would not work to pay all my earnings to men with whom I was in total disagreement.

We opened in New York, and the critics and audiences liked the show no more than they did in Boston and Detroit. I doubted at the time that I would ever want, or be able, to appear on the stage again.

Richard and I retreated to our farm. I saw the sunny days through a haze. I slept 10, 12, even 13 hours a night. I was not thinking of the past or the future. I was very much living in the present. I discovered I could still be pleased with the rolls and bread I baked. I got out the ancient treadle sewing machine and made a flower-print dress. Another day I found my oil paints and started painting again.

Gradually I became aware of the world about me. A baby on the farm next to ours died, and the distraught father asked our help to arrange the burial. Two babies were born to couples living on our land. They had no milk for them. I found myself on horseback riding over the mountains as Richard and I went to buy milk cows.

And all at once I knew that I was anxious to get back to work. I was still not sure that I would ever sing again. For the first time in my life I had heard no music for three months. I had not whistled or hummed or sung a note. I think I was frightened to hear the sound that would come out of my abused voice. What was more terrifying was that I felt no music within me. I could not even recall the joy of singing.

But I was scheduled to make recordings with a group of gifted child singers soon after we returned to New York. For the first time in my life, I went to the studio without working on the music. I was strangely calm. The children were gay and beautiful to look at. The moment came for us to blend our voices together.

There was a silence in the studio. The music began. The children's voices rose.

And to my joy I felt that glorious life-giving force from within and I sang.

Like the fallow earth, my voice had rested, and I sang clearly and fervently. Like the fallow earth, the spirit within me soared.

I understand better now that building called The Retreat, hidden behind its forest. It is in solitude that we hear the voice of God.

Section Three—

How Faith Can Strengthen the Home

Section Three—
Introduction

Never in the history of our young country has the American home ever been so awash, so buffeted, so endangered than it is today. Believing that the strength of this basic unit is an accurate barometer of our society's health, Guideposts has over the years devoted many articles to the subjects of family, children and marriage.

In this section, we present a selected few of them. Such well-known homemakers as Mrs. Billy Graham, Dale Evans Rogers, Mrs. Jerry Lewis, Colleen Townsend Evans and Mrs. Norman Vincent Peale share some of their time-tested secrets. Other articles deal with some common marital problems: infidelity, alcoholism, money and use of time. The section also includes some wise advice from Dr. David Mace, family counselor, on the subject of sex and its proper role in marriage.

In each article, the common ingredient for solution is the bringing of spiritual truths into practice. The uncommon ingredient is the specific way each author has found to achieve a better, fuller, more complete relationship.

Inside Our Home
by Mrs. Billy Graham

The wife of the famous evangelist gives her philosophy for a Christ-centered home.

One of the peculiar things about living in a preacher's family is the way strangers expect to see halos shining from all our heads. I say strangers. Our friends know better. They've seen little Franklin bite his sisters; they've seen Virginia and Anne and Ruth shouting or perhaps scrapping out on the front lawn. Our friends are fully aware that, for all our striving to make God the center of our home, life in the Billy Graham household is not a matter of uninterrupted sweetness and light.

And it's not just the children. Our friends might very well have heard me moan to my husband, Bill, about how I can never muster enthusiasm for doing dishes three times a day for a family of six. I love being a wife, mother, and homemaker. To me it is the nicest, most rewarding job in the world, second in importance to none, not even preaching.

But I don't like washing dishes.

To me there is no future in doing the dishes, nothing creative. And they are always there after each meal. I've even tried placing a little motto on the window sill above my sink. It's a motto I've had ever since high school, and it says: Praise and Pray and Peg Away. I made my dissatisfaction with the dishes a definite prayer concern and still I couldn't seem to dig up much enthusiasm.

But, as so often happens, my prayers were answered in an unusual way. I took sick at Christmas time. It was Bill, then, who had to take over and do the dishes.

What did Bill give me for Christmas?

An electric dishwasher.

That's not the end of the story. When Dr. James Stewart of Edinburgh was in Montreal one summer, we were discussing housekeeping as a divinely appointed task, and he told of visiting a Scottish kitchen. Over the sink were these words:

"Divine service will be conducted here three times daily."

Bill and I do try to make our daily duties a divine service. Take, for instance, the job of disciplining the children. We try whenever possible to deal with our children's waywardness in terms of the Bible. I remember one time when Virginia, our eldest, had to be disciplined. I've forgotten what the trouble was now. But that day I took heed of the proverb: Spare the rod and spoil the child.* Virginia was sweet as sugar for three days after that, and then she came to me and asked:

"Mother, why'd God ever create the devil and make me bad?"

It was a good question, although actually it's not too hard to answer. We talked about temptation. We talked about how if there was no devil, there'd be no test of our love for God. And we talked about the best ways to fight back, with prayer and with long talks with Christ.

The question of our relation to Christ is, of course, a very serious one in our house. When I say serious, I don't mean long-faced. You aren't long-faced when you talk over a problem with a good friend. But from the time they were first able to talk, we have tried very hard to teach our children that Christ is their personal Friend as well as their Savior. And then, having prepared the soil, we let them grown in their own relationship to Him.

We try to start this relationship with the children's first nightly prayers. One time Franklin, at age three, was disciplined for continuing to pick the cat up by its tail, and that night he said in his prayers: "Please help Mommy to be a good Mommy and not shut me in my room anymore."

These first prayers aren't ridiculous in the sight of a child, nor in the sight of the Lord. They are a fine beginning. In time, we try to show our children, by our own example, the different ways to live close to God throughout the day.

With four children, the unexpected is always happening, like the time I heard Ruth, when she was four, break into a scream outside. I ran to see what the matter was and found her older sister smacking her first on one side of the face and then on the other.

---

* *Proverbs 13:24*

"What on earth's going on?" I asked the older child.

"I'm just teaching her the Bible, Mommy, to turn the other cheek when she gets slapped."

It took quite some time to straighten that out.

Nothing is ever rigid around our house. For one thing, Bill's away so much of the time. Then, we always seem to be having visitors, both expected and unexpected. We even have a small zoo to keep track of. We don't count the temporary boarders like minnows and frogs and lame birds. As permanent guests we have a canary and a "budgie"; two patient and long-suffering cats, one of whom is so ugly we call her Moldy; and a dog, an enormous Great Pyrenees called Belshazzar. Because he eats so much he reminds us of Belshazzar's Feast in the Old Testament.

Anyhow, with the four children and the animals, with guests coming and going, with travel, with Bill's work, and just the normal household emergencies, a regularly scheduled time for worship is a bit difficult. Of course, we try hard to have morning family devotions and evening prayers, and always we have grace before meals. But I've long wished for a regularly scheduled private devotion period that makes a person feel he is living in the presence of God.

For years now I've found two substitutes:

One is day-long Bible reading which seems as natural to the kids as my preparing meals. The Bible stays open in the kitchen or around the house all day, and whenever there is a spare moment, I enjoy a few minutes with it. When Bill is away and there is a problem, I find a lot of help in Proverbs. Proverbs has more practical help in it than any ten child psychology books put together. The 31 chapters in Proverbs and the 31 days of the month fit hand-in-glove.

Then there is prayer. Since we can't always seem to find one set-aside time, both Bill and I have learned what Paul meant when he wrote: *Pray without ceasing.** I heard of a lady once who had six children and a very small home. She had no place for privacy. Whenever life got too hectic, she just pulled her apron over her head and the children knew she was praying and quieted down.

I don't do that myself, although I think it's a fine idea. Instead, as I'm busy around the house, dusting, making beds, cooking, sewing—whatever has to be done—I think of Christ as standing beside me. I talk to Him as to a visible friend.

---

* *I Thessalonians 5:17*

This is part and parcel of our daily lives so that keeping close to God becomes as much a part of our children's training as keeping clean.

Sunday, we feel, should be a day set apart. It is a family day for us, but even more it's a day when we try to learn to know God better. It can be the most interesting experience in a child's life. We don't allow our children to play with their other playmates on Sunday, preferring it to be a family day. But we do have story books and coloring books, puzzles and games, all about the Bible. And we have special treats, like candy and soda, which they're not allowed to have on the other days. And we go up to our mountain cabin for the afternoon and sometimes for the night.

All in all, we have a wonderful time with no one but the family around, and somehow on Sunday there is a minimum of bedeviling and a maximum of very enjoyable companionship.

It seems to Bill and me that the word "enjoyable" would somehow be missing if we tried to go too fast with the spiritual growth of our children, with their halo-growing as it were. We believe spiritual growth can't be forced without raising a brood of little hypocrites. We prepare the soil and plant the seed, and water and weed and tend the plant faithfully. But it is "God that giveth the increase."* We're willing to take our time and let growth come from the inside, through Christ; not merely from the outside, through our puny efforts.

Yet, even if the motto I have out in the kitchen doesn't apply too well to dishes, it does apply to children and the problem of growing halos. Maybe the best thing, after all, is to Praise and Pray and Peg Away. The halos will take care of themselves.

Dear Lord,—before I take my place
Today behind the wheel,
Please let me come with humble heart
Before Thy throne to kneel—
And pray, that I am fit to drive
Each busy thoroughfare,
And that I keep a watchful eye
Lest some small child be there.

----

* *1 Corinthians 3:7*

And keep me thinking constantly
About the Golden Rule
When driving past the playground zones
Or by some busy school.
Then, when I stop to give someone
His right to cross the street,
Let me—my brother's keeper be
And spare a life that's sweet.
Please make me feel this car I drive
You gave me to enjoy,
And that its purpose is to serve
Mankind—but not destroy.

It didn't even occur to me until later. Jerry to change his religion. My mother may not have taught me much theology, but she had taught me the essentials of married life: to cook

Two Faiths One Love
by Mrs. Jerry Lewis

The wife of the famous comedian, tells, with wit and tenderness, her story of their 25 years together.

I am a Roman Catholic; my husband is a Jew. When people ask if such a marriage didn't take courage I have to tell them, "No, only ignorance."

You see, when Jerry and I met I had no idea he was a Jew. My parents were Italian immigrants, and so was everyone else I knew.

I had a singing job in a theater near our home in Detroit. Jerry had a pantomime act in the same show. One look at that mop of black hair and, well, I just assumed he was Italian too.

Nowadays it's hard to remember the kind of superstitious terror our little old-country community felt for Jews. There was only one Jew in our neighborhood, the man who kept the corner grocery store. As a little girl I used to run past his open door, as though the devil himself lurked inside.

My religious education was lacking in every way. Papa was a coal miner who was away most of the time. Mama worked in a factory and had no time for abstract ideas. There was always St. Anthony, of course, for whom my mother felt a warm devotion. He was Mama's special saint and she kept a little statue of him in our apartment. But aside from St. Anthony there were only two religious certainties in my life: you went to Mass on Sunday and you ran when you saw a Jew.

But you see, by the time I knew about Jerry, it was too late to run. We'd had two dates and already I'd discovered that life without him was not worth living. One afternoon I found a pair of soap baby shoes on my table in the theater dressing room. On the makeup mirror above it he'd scrawled in lipstick, "Let's fill these."

118

It didn't even cross my mind to ask Jerry to change his religion. My mother may not have taught me much theology, but she had taught me the essentials of married life: to cook, wash, sew and to obey your husband. There was no question in Mama's mind as to who made the decisions in a family.

Both still in our teens, we were married in the fall, under the *huppah* in the synagogue. Jerry's parents and two of his aunts were our witnesses, holding the four posts of the *huppah*, which is a kind of canopy under which the bride and groom stand. I understood nothing of the long Hebrew service. Above us the canopy sagged and drooped as the witnesses, too, grew weary. Then Jerry nudged me and I said, "I do." A wine cup was passed to us and we both drank, to symbolize drinking together from the cup of life.

And now for me began the realization of something so unexpected, and yet so obvious, that I wonder how I could not have known it. Jews were as frightened of Christians as we were of them! I began to realize how deeply Jerry's family mistrusted the *shiksa*, the Gentile girl, in their midst.

I think the hardest time for me was when our first child, Gary, was born. We were living in New Jersey, too far for my own family to come, and that week Jerry had a much-needed job at a theater in Baltimore. He did get up to the hospital for the *bris,* the circumcision ceremony. In fact his whole family turned out for it, for the birth of a boy in a Jewish family is a great event. But when the day came for me to go home from the hospital, although they knew Jerry was in Baltimore, not one of my new family appeared. I called a taxi to take me home, feeling as lonely—as lonely as the old Jewish grocer in Detroit must have felt when his Christian neighbors froze him out of their lives.

The one in Jerry's family whose disapproval I feared most was his grandfather, the rabbi. This tiny old man was the last of a line of rabbis going back many generations. Jerry's father, and now Jerry, too, had broken the tradition by going into show business. But one of the old man's daughters still kept a kosher home for him, two sets of dishes and strict rules for every phase of life. From sundown Friday until sundown Saturday he would carry no money, nor ride in any kind of vehicle. Saturday he would pray in the synagogue.

Jerry adored him, and so—shyly, not daring to say so— did I. I used to gaze at the wrinkled face between the skull cap and the beard, and think he was the saintliest man I had ever seen. I lived in terror that he would find me out. They had never dared to tell him that his favorite grandson had married a Gentile, so I had been presented to him as a good Jewish girl, and coached before each visit as to what to do.

One day when Gary was still a baby, we were visiting his grandfather in his little apartment in Brooklyn. Other relatives were there too. Suddenly Grandfather slapped the arm of his chair.

"You think you're fooling me, don't you?" he said glaring around at the roomful of children and grandchildren. He pointed a finger at me. "I know she's a *shiksa*. I've known it from the first day."

I held my breath. The finger moved to Jerry. "Now look at my grandson. She loves him. She takes care of him. He is happy. All this . . ." with a sweep of his arm he seemed to demolish candlesticks, prayer shawl, dietary vessels, "all this is small before God. Love like theirs is big."

As the old man spoke, something small dropped from my eyes too. Behind the *huppah* and the *bris* I caught a glimpse of the God Jews worship, and He was the God St. Anthony worshipped too.

My own first glimpse of the truth which was bigger than our differences came from his grandfather; Jerry's came through my mother.

Mama had tried to be shocked about our marriage, but Jerry would always get her laughing and before long she loved him too. Still, she never stopped praying that I could be a good wife to him and a good Catholic. She gave me the little statue of St. Anthony to take with me into my new home.

We'd been married 10 years when Mama died. I'd gone to Mass, of course, all those years, and occasionally I'd asked Jerry just to step into the church with me to see that there was nothing to fear. But something always held him back.

Loving Mama as he did, however, I was sure he would go with me to her funeral. And so he did. I don't know for whom I prayed harder that day, Mama or Jerry—that some hurt deep inside him would be healed, as it had been for me in his grandfather's home so many years before.

I had my answer as we reached the sidewalk. "I," he said slowly, "have been three times a blind, bigoted fool. Did you hear them talk about the children of Israel? Did you hear that about the Son of David and Jerusalem? And they have candles, and vestments, and psalms—like in a temple!"

Oh, I don't mean that all our prejudices vanished then

and there, but it was the beginning. A few months later an enormous crate arrived from Italy. It was a beautiful marble St. Anthony to stand in our garden in memory of Mama. Soon afterward I ordered a marble Moses to stand nearby him. In the joyous months and years that followed, Jerry and I tried to outdo one another in appreciating each other's faith. I bought a child's book of Jewish history and read it aloud in the evenings. I got a Hebrew dictionary and the boys and I would surprise Jerry at the dinner table with the new words we'd learned. But Jerry eclipsed all my efforts with a single sentence.

"I believe," he said one day a couple of years after Mama's funeral, "it would make you happy to have the children baptized."

Happy? The happiest day of my life. And Jerry's too, I think, though he pretended great terror of the holy water and kept warning the priest not to get any on him by mistake. To this day he makes a show of indignation at every Christian innovation. If I make the sign of the cross at the table he'll retaliate with an elaborate gesture that he claims is the Star of David. He keeps a jealous eye on Moses, too, to be sure his flower bed gets as much attention as St. Anthony's.

"Don't lose him in the bullrushes!" he'll cry when the weeds get high.

But the fact is that both of our faiths have been strengthened by knowing and loving the other one. Jerry's joy and pride in being a Jew, his love of his own traditions, his unceasing work for Israel—all of it has a new dimension now that he sees the place of all these things not only in his tradition but in mine. As for me, I know I am a better Christian after 25 years of marriage to Jerry than I could ever have been by growing only in my own faith.

Often in the evening when I'm hearing the younger children's prayers, he will come and stand in the doorway. First the boys will say Jewish prayers and then Christian ones. That's the secret, you see, in our two-faith family, not to take anything away, but to love God twice as much as before.

On the front door of our home today are two symbols: a *mezzuzah* and a cross, and above them are two mottoes: "Shalom," and "Love One Another." The children still open their gifts as they light the Hanukkah candles, but now we keep the candlestick in front of the portrait of the Blessed Virgin. Jerry says it helps to have a Jewish mother keeping an eye on me.

When Married to an Alcoholic
by Mary Fred Bond

---

*A patient, forgiving woman makes a surprise
discovery about her husband—and herself.*

Why did I stay with my husband through those 17 years of
disillusionment?

Was it his plea when he'd stumble home after midnight,
muttering drunkenly, "Honey, don't ever leave me?"

Was it the admonition in the Bible which I had carried
with me everywhere, even on our honeymoon, *Let not the
wife depart from the husband,** which made me feel that
marriage—even a poor one—was for keeps?

Or was it a word engraved in two golden circles: our
wedding bands, each bearing the message, *Mizpah*. We'd
been married only a few months when I'd taken the rings
back to the jeweler to have that word added. I remember the
old man's curious gaze as I'd come to pick them up. "Lady, I
sure had a time engraving that word in your rings. What does
Mizpah mean anyway?"

And I had answered, "It is from the Bible and means,
*May the Lord watch between me and thee while we are ab-
sent one from the other."***

This inscription was intended to give us courage during
our months apart while George was overseas in the war.
Little did I know how I was to need this courage, not only
during the war, but even more in the long years following it.

For George came home, as did many soldiers, with a
kind of haunted restlessness that seemed to be quieted only
when he drank. But for George, once he started drinking,
there was no stopping point. Living with an alcoholic is indescribable to anyone who has not experienced it. The

---

* I Corinthians 7:10
** Genesis 31:49

122

promises broken repeatedly, the shame and humiliation, the daily heartaches etch little inroads of anguish into the soul.

Over and over George would promise to quit drinking, but each time he found a new excuse for not doing so. Over and over, humble and penitent, he would seek my forgiveness. And I would always give it, sincerely believing that next time would be different.

On one rare occasion when he attended church with me, he actually went forward to the altar and rededicated his life to God in sight of the whole congregation. This time I was certain the change was real and for days I was in heaven. Then he slipped back into the usual pattern and heaven crashed down around me. I continued my daily prayers for him, but they were hollow and heartless.

Increasingly my prayers became ones of bitterness and self-pity. "Why me?" I would cry out. "My faith is strong and I try so hard. Why can't I find peace within and solutions to the problems around me?"

The answer was the one I least expected. One day I read a small devotional article which drove home the thought that we are wrong to pray for the perfect situation in our lives. *The situation we are in,* the article said, *can be God's perfect place for us.* But we cannot discover this until we surrender ourselves totally—our wills, our preconceptions, our pet ideas—and earnestly let God use us in these real circumstances.

Had I, this brand-new thought startled me, ever actually made such a surrender? And suddenly, for the first time in 17 years, I was looking with a critical eye not at my husband but at myself. I saw a Christian, yes, and it was true, one who was not committing the more obvious physical sins. But what about the equally deadly spiritual sins? Had I felt superior to my husband's struggles, smug in my martyrdom, self-righteous, scornful of his weakness? Had I, perhaps, even added to it by my attitude?

Almost without knowing it I found myself on my knees, begging God's forgiveness in the first genuine prayer in many years. "And oh, Lord," I finished, "if this is where You want me to be, take my life and use it here, and give me strength to face each day."

I remained on my knees a long time, feeling the animosity, the anguish and the tension that had plagued me so long slip quietly away. My husband's problem was his—his and God's—and I realized now it was not up to me to solve it nor to condemn him for it. Instead I realized that my own self-righteousness had made me unfit for use in God's real work.

I shall never understand the events that followed this moment of truth. Something had changed inside me but I was not conscious of any outer change in my behavior toward George. But within two weeks my husband stopped drinking, this time for good. Why a prayer for myself should so have affected someone else, I could not guess; I didn't question God, I just rejoiced.

But God was not through; Clearly He was going to test the sincerity of my prayer of surrender. Through all of these years I had been active in my church, a leader in women's groups, never missing Sunday worship. One night my niece came for the weekend. To her my husband confided that he would like to start attending church again if only I would go with him to the church he had attended as a child.

My heart sank when I heard this from my niece. George had made so many promises before—and now the thought of giving up my church to go to a strange one was almost too much. Not that I would have to change my faith (both churches were Protestant), but it meant a wrenching adjustment of practices and associations.

The pastor of George's church told me of the requirements for membership, necessary regardless of how many years I had been a communicant in good standing elsewhere. A few weeks before, I know that the wound to my pride would have been too painful. I had seen myself as the upright citizen, counseling the fallen, working for the Lord week by week. Now it seemed I was being asked to join the sinners again before I could be accepted. All George would have to do was move his membership to the church of his childhood.

How marvelously God leads each of us to the step we most need; how graciously He lends us the necessary strength. I fulfilled the requirements for membership into George's church and then began an adventure in happiness—a family united in God's will and prepared for His guidance.

The sermon that very first Sunday was on a plan of witnessing to others. The next week my husband began talking to two of his old buddies who were already astounded at the change in him. He spoke so convincingly that they decided there really was a Power that could help them too. In a few days one of them committed his life to God, the other several weeks later.

George's friends continued to gravitate to our home, but what used to end up as beery brawls now became ice-tea suppers. When new neighbors moved in across the street a friend remarked, "Poor people, they don't know it yet, but they've had the last rest they'll get until George hears them say they love God!"

Thirteen years have passed since that day when I stopped feeling sorry for myself and my marriage and let God pour His light into our home. How easy it is for us housewives to block out these rays, thinking we are doing all we can in difficult situations, unaware of the real power of His love.

Today George is a deacon in the church, and I am the happiest and proudest wife in town. How faithfully the promise of *Mizpah* has been kept in our lives. Indeed we were "absent" many years from the place at each other's side that God had prepared for us. But He watched over us when we both were blind; He drew us together when we placed our hands in His.

My Family Comes First
by Colleen Townsend Evans

What this former actress learned about running a household.

Jamie had wakened and cried during the night. I had comforted him, fed, and cuddled him and then tucked him back into his crib. Then I'd just got back to sleep myself when Tim had fallen out of bed, so I'd had to dash to pick him up.

As I sought sleep once more I thought to myself that being the wife of a busy young minister, mother to four youngsters, cook, maid, chauffeur, as well as hostess to our entire church was altogether different from the life I had had as an actress.

Deliberately, happily I had given up my own career to marry Lou. Yet now sheer physical weariness, the sense of being burdened with more than one woman could handle was beginning to take away the glow.

I loved Lou dearly. I reached out a finger now to touch him for reassurance. He needed that sleep. Day by day he was giving all of himself to other people in the name of Christ. I would not have exchanged my happiness with him and my children for any career in the world.

"No, Lord, a career outside my home is not what I want," I found myself praying. "It's just that I don't want the glow to go. I want to be able to handle this. But I'm desperate. I've too much work to do. Please show me how to do all that's expected and still keep my health and the right attitudes."

Right then I discovered an important truth about prayer: It had to be honest—or it isn't even prayer. Yes, even if we have to let resentment spill out. God honors honest anger and then can dissolve it for us, but He can't honor bottled-up feelings and unreal piety.

I also discovered that though God heard my cry for

help, He was not going to give me all my answers that first night nor ever in any simple, neat package. The answers were to come slowly, painfully, over a matter of weeks. Looking ... seeing ... asking ... receiving. They were given to me in a variety of ways too: through insight; through Scripture; through a relationship, a living relationship with the Person of Jesus Christ. And because I think that many women—and men too—have the problem I did—that of feeling burdened with more than they can handle—I'd like to share some of the help that I received.

The first insight was that I was harassed because I did not know how to say "No." One morning as I was reading a verse from Deuteronomy, it had leapt out at me from the page: *As thy days, so shall thy strength be.**

But then that inner voice, which I have gradually come to recognize as one of God's valid ways of speaking to us today, had added firmly, "But that is true only if you will let Me tell you when to say 'Yes' and when to say 'No.' "

Experimenting with this, I soon found that some of my tasks were motivated by my ambition, my hunger for unnecessary praise, or my insistence on doing things my way. But the things that were really necessary to keep my family healthy and happy and spiritually whole, yes, for these I did have strength.

And I found God's directives fascinating. One day it might be that reading aloud to my children was more important than scrubbing the kitchen floor. Or that a cake from the bakery would do as well as a home-baked one, so that I could take the children to the beach. I began to realize that the children wanted *me* and my attention more than they wanted my cake. And out of a feeling of rightness about these times with them, new joy flooded into our reading-aloud times or our romps on California's beautiful beaches.

I also had to learn to say "No" to some other people in order to say "Yes" to my family.

For example, there was the time I was asked to be the speaker at a religious conference. It would have taken me away from my home and family for two weeks. The theme, ironically enough, was the role of the Christian wife and mother.

At first, I was puzzled about whether or not I should go. My conscience reminded me of the need to share Christian

---

* *Deuteronomy 33:25*

experience with other wives. "But what about leaving my family that long?" I reasoned. "They're my greatest opportunity to serve God. If I miss the mark with them, will anything else matter?" So I turned down the invitation.

Shortly after that I was reading Paul Tournier's book *Guilt and Grace,** and came across the passage, "False guilt comes from saying no to people. . . . The only true guilt comes from saying no to God."

This was it! False guilt had too often robbed me of energy and joy that rightfully belonged to our family. From then on, saying "No" became easier and one of the secrets of released time for me.

The second answer to my sense of being overburdened was the "how" of acquiring that inner quietness and poise without which our life flies to pieces in busyness. In the beginning of our marriage, a time of quiet meditation and prayer had been a part of my daily schedule.

But then had come the busy years. Ours was such a new church that for four years our home was the center for board meetings, Bible studies, Sunday-school planning, prayer meetings. The house always had to be clean and often cookies baked.

Although all these activities brought a real sense of joy and love, I found it hard to adjust to all the pressure. But with four active preschool children to be taken care of—and the doorbell and telephone to be answered over and over again—there were no quiet times. Gradually I came to feel spiritually famished.

Perhaps at that time I was feeling a bit sorry for myself because God's truth was jolting. . . . "You think you're too busy. Your real problem is that you have allowed Me to be pushed from the center of your life." My heart told me suddenly that this was so. My burning desire to spend some time alone with that living Presence had gradually cooled. So the real problem was not with my activity but with my affection for God.

And when I asked, "But *when* do I have a quiet time. . . ?" His answer was, "You don't, not as you have understood a quiet time. For a few years, until the children are older, you're going to have to learn to pray on the run, in the car, in any odd place. Try this new way."

So I did, and found that the chinks of time—in a den-

* *Harper and Row, New York City*

tist's waiting room, before the PTA meeting, or while baking a pie—could be blessed times of communion.

How real some of these times have been is shown by their fruits. For out of this "on the run" communion I have learned much about human relationships. And so many creative ideas have come—like the substitute for expensive toys for our children. Lou fills up the trunk of our car with scraps of all shapes from a woodworking shop. We keep them in the garage in large plastic tubs—bright red, yellow, blue. Then we turn the boys and their friends loose with hammer and nails to make whatever they can. The only requirement: tools back in place and garage cleaned up when they finish.

Or that idea for our vacation one year in the High Sierras . . . books were carefully selected ahead of time such as—*Cry, The Beloved Country* and *To Kill A Mockingbird*. As the children lay snugly in their warm sleeping bags, looking up at the stars, Lou and I would take turns reading to them. I think that all their lives our children will remember that summer, for never have we felt more closely knit as a family. And every so often, one of them will quote something from one of the books, "Remember the summer when. . . ."

The Role of Sex in Marriage
by David R. Mace, Ph.D.

An eminent counselor on family problems brings
wisdom and insight to bear on the so-called
"sexual revolution."

After decades of research and the counseling of hundreds of
couples, it is quite obvious to me that within the holy bonds
of matrimony sex is still too often misunderstood. Nearly everyone agrees that sex is a vital, important part of marriage.
Too frequently, though, couples are unaware of the subtleties
of that challenging relationship.

Every sexual partnership is different; one cannot use the
experience of one couple as an absolute guide for another.
Yet basic concepts are available to all of us and specific help
for those willing to seek it.

To begin with, there are two factors which make a good
marriage: cultural similarity and emotional complementarity.
One of the fallacies most couples labor under, especially the
romantic ones, is the belief that marriage is a merging, a co-
alescing. This is ridiculous. A true union of two distinct, indi-
vidualistic persons would result only in the annihilation of
both.

The Bible says: *And they . . . shall be one flesh.**
Not "one," but "one flesh." There is sexual union, yes, but
the remainder of the successful marriage is a subtle equilibrium—a balance between two opposing forces, male and female. Every marriage must find its equilibrium, or fail. Most
often this is a struggle involving some hostility, open fighting,
pain. In a sense, love is tragic; it is something which is never
to be fully achieved.

I have seen couples achieve marital equilibrium in surprising ways, often through sheer luck. Sometimes it is be-

* Matthew 19:5

130

cause of, and sometimes despite, sex. I have known couples whose sex methods were so awkward and unrewarding that their marriage defied the rules of the textbook—and yet, so compatible were they in every other way that their sexual naïveté was overwhelmed. Conversely, I have known couples whose life in bed was so meaningful that their day-to-day antagonisms were subjugated. Such cases are related somewhat to those uncomplicated people for whom sex is merely an animal function. But with more sensitive persons—more finely tuned and spiritual ones—there is a greater chance that sex will become a problem.

Consider the case history of Tyler and Josie Caldwell.* Josie, a hesitant, rather plain young woman, came to me for counseling. She was about to divorce her husband. What had begun as a rather beautiful marriage seven years earlier had disintegrated into something ugly. Yet once Josie and Tyler had been deeply in love. They shared similar backgrounds and had many of the same interests; they had even met in church and both considered religion an important part of their lives.

Unfortunately, Tyler proved to be weak in character. Before the first year was out, he started gambling, and in time he had gambled away nearly everything. He had lost his job, taken Josie's money and, finally, after one irresponsible action followed another, Josie's outraged parents persuaded her that there was nothing to do but leave her husband. The couple had been separated for some months when Josie came to me.

"Tyler killed my love for him," Josie told me tragically.

"If your marriage is as dead as you say it is," I asked her, "why did you come to see me?"

Josie had trouble formulating her thoughts. "I married this man," she said finally, "and I tried to work things out with him until I think I have finished trying. Yet, somehow or other I have a feeling that, as a Christian, I should not give up."

Then she became intense. "Dr. Mace, is it possible that a marriage like this could be made to work? What about a man who is so utterly irresponsible and deplorable? Should I forgive him as it says in the Bible, seventy times seven?"

I didn't answer her because I wanted her to find the answer for herself. Yet I knew well the important fact that

---

* Names have been changed.

where love has once existed, including sexual love, it can exist again.

From what Josie told me, I suspected the root of this couple's problem immediately. "Tell me about your relationship. Your sex life, for instance. Was it good?"

Josie shrugged her shoulders. "It was at first. It didn't work out after a while."

"Why?"

She became flustered. "I'd really rather not talk about it. I don't know how I feel about this."

I didn't press her then, but I told her I wanted her to return and that she must be prepared to talk about her feelings on such intimate subjects. Over the weeks, she did begin to talk; we discussed what she told me and I gave her books to read. Gradually she came to have a different view of her marriage.

And what was the real story of Josie and Tyler? It began with Josie. She had been reared with no sex education. She was one of those remnants of an earlier era, one of those people who grew up believing that sex is basically sinful. Yet, before her wedding, Josie had come to accept the principle that sex in marriage was indeed permissible. And so, in the first months of her marriage the act of sex was satisfying to both her and her husband.

Gradually, though, something changed. Something was wrong. Josie would lie awake at night after Tyler had gone to sleep. The old feelings of the wickedness of sex began to return and she became progressively evasive. She would put Tyler off. The relationship deteriorated.

"Have you any idea what it means to a man to be rebuffed?" I asked Josie. She did not, really. I tried to explain how sexual gratification undergirds a man's role as head of the house. By refusing her husband or diminishing his role as lover, the wife shakes the fabric of his masculinity.

In time, Josie came to understand what this had meant to her husband. He was a sensitive man, though weak and non-assertive. Tyler could not combat his wife's refusals or the frustration which ensued. Some men's response to their wife's neglect is to find another woman. Yet other men can't do that. Instead, they drink, they bury themselves in work. Tyler took to gambling.

When Josie gained this new insight, she wept. "Then, all this time it's been my fault?"

Not really. Tyler, too, was responsible. He had yet to

learn that the function of the wife is to respond and that her ability to perform lies in her capacity for response. All wives have difficulty in being responsive at some time or another. But if that difficulty becomes habitual, the husband might well look to himself and question whether his approach to his wife is the right one.

Tyler's approach to Josie was wrought with confusion. It caused her anguish. Neither she nor he realized it, but Josie simply didn't want sex on his terms. An adjustment was necessary, but before that could be made, Josie had slipped back into her old feelings that sex was sinful.

When at last Josie had become aware of the full story, she was in despair. "What am I to do?" she asked me helplessly.

"What do you think you ought to do?"

"Tell him," Josie said. "I think I ought to tell him what I've learned." And she did. Josie sat down and wrote Tyler a long letter.

I am still amused at the response. It was a telegram. "Coming to you at once," Tyler cabled to Josie.

The couple went back together and they are still together. Today Tyler and Josie do not have a perfect marriage, but it is a good one, a working one, and it is reasonable to say that they are happier together than if they were apart. Now, at last, they have children.

Josie and Tyler are a good example of what delicate creatures we are, at the mercy of pride and misunderstanding. The couple also point up how religion can both hinder and help a marriage. In the final analysis though, it was Josie's persevering religious faith, her unwillingness to give up, that saved her marriage.

This case history reminds me of the corollary to "Thou shalt not commit adultery." It is: "Thou shalt not keep thy partner without." I've counseled more than one ardently religious woman who was sexually cold. Frequently it is such a woman who complains because her "infidel" husband will not go to church with her. Invariably the husband has identified his wife's avoidance of him with her spirituality. He refuses, therefore, to go to church or have anything to do with "her" God.

I believe that the act of sex demands the ethics of religion. Why? Because there is always a strong relationship between sexual behavior and personal integrity. What we do sexually is a dramatic manifestation of our total attitude towards others. If one is a selfish person, he will take advantage of his sexual partner. If one is gentle and considerate in sex, he is gentle and considerate as a person. If one has idealism, one brings those qualities to the act of sex. I believe that sex needs the qualities of religion—human virtues, loving thy neighbor as thyself and enduring love.

I hope that it is not necessary to state that sex is a beautiful gift from God; that our bodies are temples of the Holy Spirit, made in the likeness of God, and that it is our responsibility to preserve that likeness. Yet I also hope that people regard this thinking as something other than a collection of clichés. For if they have become clichés, it is because the experience of the ages has made them true.

The Case of the Too-Busy Husband

by Lydia Johnson

A matter of time—and how it is spent.

Strange as it may seem, it is difficult to be married to a good man, one who is busily involved with his fellowman. My husband, Bill, a lawyer with his own private practice, also worked as legal counsel for the Police Department, served on the local Draft Board as a Government appeals agent, and was active in church and community affairs.

For the first years of our marriage I worked as a secretary, and Bill's busyness was just a cause of annoyance, and inconvenience. Then as the late hours, meetings, and missed dinners increased, so did my irritation. I felt as if I were a part-time wife who shared just a few hours of my husband's attention—hours when he could squeeze me into his busy life. I was lonely.

A close friend offered little sympathy. "What if Bill drank or gambled or ran after women?" she said. "Then you'd have something real to complain about."

Yet this response was of no help to me. My marriage was threatened for seemingly trivial reasons—I knew it. Bill and I were drawing farther apart.

A telephone call from Father Finnerty, a priest at our church, would turn me blue with anger, knowing that it meant Bill was needed to be a lector in a Mass or perhaps to supervise a teen-agers' dance. A friend's dropping in meant that the few minutes that I had with Bill were now to be shared with one more intruder. Bill was often late for dinner. Waiting for him infuriated me. Inevitably I ended up fighting with him.

"How can you love me?" I upbraided Bill one night. "If

you did, you wouldn't rush away from me every time someone asked you to do something."

"Loving you has nothing to do with it, dear. We don't have to spend all our time together to prove our love. I have a responsibility to others, too." Then he smiled and reminded me of something we had often discussed. "Those who have been given much, have to give much."

Well, it was true that Bill and I were fortunate—we had a lovely home, were prospering, had many friends, were both healthy. But despite that awareness, I still didn't like sharing Bill with many people—and spending all those lonely hours.

One night Father Finnerty dropped in after dinner. He began talking about how much easier it was to reach young people through athletics and that young people needed to relate to adults who set good examples. My heart sank.

"Bill, we've decided to start a track team," he continued. "You were a top man in this sport. How about coaching the team?"

Before Bill could answer, I blurted out, "Someone told me recently that Bill was a pillar of the church, but it looks like he *is* the church, with all the extra jobs he is doing there."

There was a strained silence for a moment, and I felt uncomfortable. Then our priest began talking again about the critical needs of teen-agers. I finally agreed that having a track team was one good answer. So it meant more lonely hours for me.

Then there was the dinner dance of our bowling league. I had a new dress and hairdo and eagerly looked forward to the evening. Another couple came to our house so that we could all go together. We waited and waited, but Bill never came nor phoned. Finally my friends insisted we leave without him. I went, but the party was spoiled for me. Bill finally arrived at 11 p.m. when the dinner was almost over. He'd become involved and couldn't get to a phone.

Our relationship was slowly deteriorating. I loved Bill and knew he loved me. What was happening to us? I tried prayer, but my words didn't seem to rise out of the room. Finally I went to see Father Finnerty.

The priest, wise and compassionate, listened to me quietly for a while, then spoke. "First of all, let me make it clear that I cannot solve your problem; you must do that through a spirit of hope and trust in God. However, some of those defects you see in Bill are really virtues, like his service to others."

I had to admit that Father Finnerty was right. I went home and tried prayer again. This time I prayed not for Bill to change, but that I might be understanding and patient.

The change came about almost in spite of myself and also as an answer to my prayer. For some time Father Finnerty had been asking Bill and me to attend a three-day Cursillo—a concentrated period of fellowship for Christian growth and development, held separately for men and women. Bill had been too busy to go and I, frankly, just hadn't wanted to go.

Now suddenly I did.

For three days I lived with about 35 other women in the Cursillo Center in Brooklyn. There were no luxuries—the four-story red brick building, a former hospital, was almost dingy. I slept in a large room with four other women. There were no curtains on the windows, and the furniture was sparse: cots and a few bedside tables. But scribbled all over the walls were messages from former occupants—messages of faith. They were from teen-agers who had come to the Cursillo Center to hold their own "encounter."

We women met in small groups for talks, spiritual delving and exchange of experiences, led by a priest and a team of women who had already made a Cursillo. At one of the discussions, someone said something that hit my heart as if it were meant for me: "To be a Christian, you have to *really* love and be patient—you have to let a lot of things go, to accept things as they are." I realized I had certainly not been doing that. After that remark, I listened attentively to all that was said.

The zeal and love of those people literally woke me up. They were all doers, as Bill was, and I felt apart from them. When a 21-year-old ex-member of a street gang told of going back to the gang members to help them find Christ, when a nurse shared her experiences in Africa among the natives, or a teacher spoke of her involvement with parents in her slum school distinct, they spoke not as just "busy people" but as people with a purpose. One of them explained the force which motivated all they did: "You have to look for Christ in your brothers and sisters."

And that was what Bill always did—that explained his devotion to his fellowman. Suddenly I was ashamed. I realized that I was responsible for much of the trouble in our marriage. I was the classic example of the nagging wife. At that moment I knew I had to change. I was standing still—worse, backsliding—in my Christian growth, while Bill was moving ahead. This was perhaps the biggest reason for our drawing apart.

Later, at our evening Mass at the Cursillo, when it came time to pray, each of us gathered around the altar to voice our personal prayer out loud. I prayed, "Dear God, help me to look for You in others." At that time I felt God's presence in a way I never had before.

Then began a tremendous effort on my part to be a loving wife, a more understanding one.

Sometimes when I grow impatient or angry, I say, "Oh, I'm not living it right," and I start over again.

In reaching out into the community, I have since discovered what Bill already knew—in loving people, you love God. Together Bill and I share this concern—it brings us closer to each other. Since Bill made his Cursillo a month after I did, we also have another common bond of interest.

My relationship with people has improved too. In the office where I formerly worked as a secretary, there was a typist who had many problems and felt defeated and unable to cope with life. As I got closer to Christ, I decided to try to help her. Mostly I listened. To my surprise she became more relaxed, more at peace. One day she thanked me for helping her. But all I had done was listen, I thought. It was then that I recalled some words from a Rodgers and Hammerstein song in *The Sound of Music* . . . *love isn't love until you give it.*

Since I discovered the reason for action, I am able to accept Bill's work for others—not in terms of inconvenience, but others' needs. And sometimes it is Bill who has to wait for me to come home from an evening meeting.

I had to smile the first time I heard Bill refuse to attend a civic meeting.

"Sorry, my wife and I have special plans tonight." Bill was trying just as I was.

We're far from perfect, Bill and I. He is still late for dinner, and I still get annoyed. But our home life is altogether different since I changed my thinking about Bill's accepting calls for service.

When friends call, I remember that they need him. I'm willing to accept and share now, knowing that by giving ourselves more to others, we have so much more love for each other.

Bedlam Can Be Beautiful
by Dale Evans Rogers

A three-day retreat taught her something about home and children.

The front door slammed as Cheryl ran for the high-school bus. "Three children off," I made a mental note. "Four to go."

In the bedroom I had finished the first braid in Dodie's hair and was reaching for the rubber band when a shriek from the bathroom sent me running there. Debbie had cut her lip against the washstand.

I was still dabbing with a wad of cotton when Sandy appeared in the doorway in his pajama pants.

"Mama, make Dusty stop throwing my socks!" he demanded.

"Dale!" This was Roy from our bedroom. "The recording session's at ten, you know!"

I dashed for the kitchen and started cracking eggs into a bowl. "After the kids are off, I'll just have time to get that laundry sorted," I promised myself. For two days my washing machine had been out of order and the soiled-clothes heap was now a mountain.

The phone rang and I jerked the skillet of eggs off the fire.

"Mrs. Rogers?" The lady's voice was apologetic. "Could you and Mr. Rogers be at the studio at nine instead of ten this morning?"

An especially hectic beginning to a day? No—just a very average morning at the Rogers' house.

If you have children and a busy husband, it probably sounds a little like mornings at your house, too. And not only the mornings, but all day long the noise and the rush and the thousand *little* crises go on. Most of us can rise to the really big emergencies; the problem we mothers share is how to get through a normal day.

And actually, I sometimes think my day is easier than other mothers'. I do have Mrs. Ordono to get most of our meals and to be with the children while I'm working. And a lady comes in to do the laundry. People ask me how I manage to raise a family and at the same time keep up with the fast pace of Hollywood. I tell them the pace of Hollywood is a vacation after the pace of a home with seven children in it.

I'll never forget one perfectly run-of-the-mill Saturday when Mrs. Ordono was away for the weekend and the children had been yelling since dawn. If I can't get off by myself for a moment, I thought, I'm going to be yelling too. I needed to sit down, compose myself, and ask God for a little patience. But to talk to God, I believed, you needed silence—and there certainly wasn't any of that in the house.

So I ducked a small plastic plane that was sailing through the air and headed for the big rocks in back of the barn. And there, I tried to concentrate on a prayer for strength. But all I could think about was the children. Why didn't Linda finish her lunch? Should I have left the boys alone with that rope? What was Dodie getting into? . . .

"It's no use," I said aloud. Prayer wouldn't come and I walked slowly back to the mayhem in the house with the feeling that not even God had any help for mothers.

I felt the same sense of failure when I tried to read the Bible. I had the feeling that Bible reading had to be a thing set apart. So I put aside a special time for it: half an hour first thing in the morning.

But if your house is anything like ours, there isn't really any "first thing" in the morning. You open your eyes, and the next thing you know, one child feels sick, another has lost his homework, and you're snatched up into the whirl of the day. Then I wondered why I didn't get my Bible read!

At last I decided I had to get away for a few days of peace. And so, with four other women from our church, I joined a three-day retreat at an Episcopal convent high in the hills near here. For three days none of us was allowed to speak a word.

And up there in the silence, I learned something about our noisy home in the valley. It was such a simple discovery I am almost ashamed to repeat it, but it's made all the difference to me. I learned that our home is not a convent!

The orderly life that those holy women lead up there is

the most beautiful and selfless in the world, but I suddenly knew it was not my life. I was a wife and a mother, and my religion had to be like my life—as spontaneous and spur of the moment as the little crises that keep me jumping.

I still think Bible-reading is the best way to start the day. But now in my kitchen I keep a little box shaped like a loaf of bread. It's called the "Bread of Life" and in it are tiny cards with scripture verses on them. Now, instead of trying to find an imaginary free hour, I need only a free second. While I'm waiting for the cereal water to boil, I have time to pick up one of the cards and learn it by heart.

The Bible itself I save not till the end of the day when the children are in bed and there are no—well, not so many—interruptions.

And I've found a wonderful place to pray, once I realized I didn't need total silence in which to do it. It's my car. Our ranch is so far from everything that I have lots of driving to do. It's a long way to the grocery store or the dry cleaner's, and when one of the children makes a friend at school, he's sure to live at the other end of the valley.

I used to fret over the wasted time I spent at the wheel. Now I drive just as slowly as I dare. I have time to think about each child and to pray for understanding and patience with him.

Bible lessons are different now too. We have a family altar in our living room—actually an old radio cabinet with a dresser scarf and candles on it—and our original plan was to gather around it each evening for prayers and a brief lesson. But it was club night for one child or choir practice for another and somehow we didn't get the lessons in very often.

Today, instead of having a set hour for religious teaching, I try to introduce my children to Jesus Christ in the little day-to-day things that happen all the time. Dodie has always been painfully afraid of the dark. One night she began to cry as I tucked her into bed.

"Don't turn the light out, Mama," she begged.

"Would you be afraid if *I* were here with you?" I asked.

"Of course not," said Dodie.

"Well, I can't always be with you, of course. But, Dodie—the Lord can."

Dodie was silent, so I tiptoed out, leaving the light on. In a few minutes—oh miracle of miracles—I heard the light click off. And, just audible, I heard Dodie's little voice speak two words. She said to the dark, "Hello, Jesus."

A week of lessons couldn't have taught her—or me—as much!

Another time I was walking with Debbie on a lonely corner of the ranch when two vicious-looking dogs rushed at us. The little girl screamed. Debbie had come to us from Korea where dogs were trained to kill during the war. She wouldn't even come near our gentle old Bullet, and these dogs were really savage.

Then I remembered the lesson I'd read to the children about love casting out fear. I held out my hands to the dogs and put every bit of love I could into my "Nice dog!" The dogs slowed down, puzzled. I kept on telling them what good dogs they were until they stopped growling and started sniffing my hands instead. Then suddenly they both tried to lick my face!

Never was a lesson in love so swiftly taught!

So I'm not trying to get away anymore to ask God's help. I'm inviting God right in, to the most commonplace, troublesome times of the day—and finding that He makes them brighter.

Take bickering at the dinnertable, for instance. The children used to come clamoring to the table bringing the afternoon's quarrels with them and Roy and I would spend mealtime as an unwilling court of appeals.

Then a while ago I had an idea. During meals at the convent, the Mother Superior read aloud from the Bible. What if I read aloud at the dinner table, just long enough for the ruckus to quiet down?

The Bible itself, of course, was a little difficult for the five-year-olds. Then I discovered *The Moody Bible Story Book*, simple enough for Dodie and Debbie but complete enough for our teen-agers.

Each chapter takes about ten minutes to read, long enough for quarrels to be forgotten. And if my own potatoes are a little cold by then—why, the Bible has help for that too:

> *Better a morsel of dry bread, and peace with it,*
> *Than a house full of feasting, with strife.*[*]

One evening during the latter part of his life, John Ruskin sat at a window in his home watching a lamplighter, with torch in hand, ignite the street lamps on a distant hill. Since it was

---

[*] Proverbs *17:1 (Goodspeed Bible)*

dark the lamplighter himself could not be seen, but his progress up the hill could be observed as successive lamps were lighted.

After a few minutes Ruskin turned to a friend and said, "That illustrates what I mean by a genuine Christian. You may not know him or ever see him, but his way has been marked by the lights he leaves burning."

RALPH L. WOODS
Ramsey, New Jersey

One Million Reasons My Marriage Went Wrong

by Millard Fuller

Money is often the problem, but not quite the same way it was for this couple.

How much is a marriage worth? In November, 1965, I gave a million dollars for mine.

Giving away that money was the end of a dream. For I can remember how early I set my heart on becoming a millionaire. I used to go out with my father, delivering groceries for his little country store in Lanett, Alabama. "See that farm, Millard?" Dad would say. "That man's on his way to a million."

Or, as a customer pushed open the screen door of the store, Dad might whisper, "Here's one who made it, Son. Worth a million."

Dad himself was the son of a sharecropper, and money was important to him in the way it is only to the poor. I began looking for ways to get rich while I was still at the University of Alabama.

One day I met another student there named Morris Dees. We got to talking and discovered that we were as alike as dollar bills. "We ought to make a team," I said, and as casually as that began the partnership which was to last eight very profitable years.

While we were still undergraduates we sold mistletoe, campus telephone directories and birthday cakes to the other students, parlaying our profits so that when we graduated, instead of owing money for our education, we had $25,000 in the bank.

How well I remember the day we opened our mail order business in Montgomery—Fuller and Dees Marketing Group.

As soon as I got home I took our my diary and in it wrote, "A million dollars before I'm thirty."

And I made it too—with a year to spare. But in the process of gaining the million I nearly lost everything else—including my wife.

Linda and I had married while we were still in college. After graduation I did a short term of military service at Fort Sill, Oklahoma, where we determined to live within my soldier's pay. We drove an old jalopy, rented a two-room efficiency, and for six months had a wonderful marriage. The very day we got back to Montgomery I deserted my wife.

Oh, it didn't look like a desertion to our family and friends. But it was, all the same. I left Linda for the mail order business.

The day we moved back to Montgomery I plunged into moneymaking with such compulsion that there was time for nothing else. Many days Morris and I were at the office before dawn and home after midnight. Three years after we opened the office we were the largest publishers of cookbooks in the United States. As far as we could tell there was no limit to how far we could go—provided only that we worked hard enough.

Sure, there were trouble signs at home, but I didn't read them. I remember one evening coming home for supper.

"Oh, Daddy!" my son, Chris, shouted, jumping up to hug me, "I'm so glad you're *home*."

Home? I hadn't been anywhere!

Then abruptly, within just two weeks, I received both the best news and the worst news of my life.

One fall day in 1964 the treasurer of our company walked through the door with a smile on her face. She spread out papers on my desk and said, "Congratulations, Mr. Fuller. As of today, you're a millionaire."

I stared at those columns of figures, awaiting the feeling of a job well done that I had expected along with them. Instead I was aware of a different emotion. As soon as the treasurer left I took out a piece of paper, as I'd done a few years earlier, and on it wrote, "Ten million next."

It was just two weeks later that Linda walked through the same door. I was busy planning a strategy meeting with the staff and didn't glance up.

"It's all over," Linda said.

She had to repeat it before I heard. Then I got up and came over to put my arms around her and try to get her to tell me what the trouble was. She could only reply that our marriage was dead.

We got into our Lincoln Continental and drove slowly through the Alabama countryside for an hour trying to communicate. But we'd lost the art. Linda could only stammer and I could only ask her what had gone wrong.

Linda announced later that she was going to New York. Once when I had taken her along on a business trip there we'd attended the Broadway United Church of Christ and heard Dr. Lawrence Durgin. "I'm going to ask for an appointment with Dr. Durgin," Linda said, "and I'm going to do some thinking. I'll call you if I have anything to say."

And the next day she was gone.

Though I had spent so little time with her it was amazing what an emptiness her leaving created. At home I began spending more time with the children, but they were only confused by my sudden attention and grew shy. At the office I called a week-long meeting of all department heads. But I couldn't fill the night hours and eventually I had to start thinking. I began to see that the sickness in our marriage was just one symptom of a still deeper disease. At home, or visiting friends, or even at church it was always the same: my mind was elsewhere, reviewing sales charts, analyzing trends, phrasing letters.

To attain a future goal I had cut myself off from today. What would happen, I asked myself one sleepless night, if I chucked the whole thing. Suppose Linda and I were to start over again in another efficiency, driving another jalopy, getting to know each other once more? The thought was so frightening I never did get to sleep.

And then at last Linda called from New York. She asked, "Can you come up on Tuesday?"

And that was how one evening the following week I was sitting in a hotel room in Manhattan. Linda and I were embarrassed being with each other, like high school kids on a first date. We decided to go to a movie and, perhaps symbolically, Linda chose "Never Too Late." Standing in the lobby she suddenly began to cry.

"Let's get out of here," I said.

We walked up Fifth Avenue, our coat collars pulled high against the bite of a November wind. Linda was still crying so we stepped into a doorway. We talked for more than an hour, sharing all that was wrong in our lives. When it got too cold I hailed a taxi and we started back to the hotel.

And there in that cab came the moment which was to change our lives. For as we were riding through the streets of New York I suddenly felt God's presence. He was closer than I had ever known Him. He spoke directly to me. "Millard, why don't you let Me direct your life?"

Up in the hotel room I told Linda what had happened. "I know what we've got to do to set our lives straight. The trouble is, we've never put God first. We've got to get out of the business and start all over."

I picked up the phone and called Dr. Durgin. It was after midnight.

"Sorry, Dr. Durgin, but I just had to make the promise to someone besides Linda. I've made a decision. I'm going to sell the business and give away the money—all of it."

"Millard . . ." Linda's eyes were bright with excitement.

"And I'm going to turn over my life to Christ. Altogether. I'm going to put God first."

"Oh yes, Millard," Linda said. "That's what I want too."

That night was indeed the turning point. I sold my half of the business to my partner, Morris. We sold our personal possessions too—the cars and the house and the cabin on the lake and the speedboats and the horses and the beautiful plot of land where we were planning to build a $150,000 house. We gave the money to various charitable projects.

That was more than four years ago, and we have never been so happy. We have another child and Linda is busy in our little apartment while I'm busy at my new job. But what a difference. Problems in my work are Linda's, too, and I share her problems with the children. I'm still doing what I like best, working on projects to make money, but I'm doing it for nonprofit causes now.

I'm still busy, but I'm strangely free. Free to grow into Linda's life. Free to invite her into mine. Free for the first time to be really married, which means to put Christ in charge.

The question friends ask is, "Yes, but did you have to give away so much? Surely you don't suggest this to others?"

No, I don't. It isn't necessary for every man with a compulsive desire for money or power to give up all that he possesses. It isn't necessary for anyone to get rid of whatever chains are binding him. But I can report what happened to one person who did: the day I gave away a million was the day, at last, that I became truly rich.

How To Have a "Good" Argument
by Mrs. Norman Vincent Peale

A realistic approach to husband-wife disagreements.

I looked at our friends in astonishment and wondered if I had heard correctly. But yes, the wife *was* saying, "In twenty-two years of marriage we've never had a disagreement."

All I could think was, *How dull!*

I wouldn't think of agreeing with my husband about everything, because he is not always right. By the same token he often thoroughly disagrees with me. But these differences of opinion—far from being disadvantages—are among the most stimulating and rewarding aspects of our marriage. They mean that the two of us, just because we are so different, can explore the most diverse paths in solving problems.

The secret of such constructive disagreement—and a skill every marriage needs—is to keep these differences in the mind where they can be put to work, and out of the emotions where they can hurt.

I learned my first "don't" in this area even before we were married. On a date once, Norman asked what I thought of the sermon I had just heard him preach. And I, a novice in man-woman relationships, did not hear the need for encouragement but thought he wanted my critical opinion. "It starts well," I said, "but the ending's weak." And on I went, making suggestions, never seeing the disappointment in his eyes until at last he burst out:

"Ruth, what you say convinces me of something I've suspected for a long time—I'll never make a preacher."

Alarmed, I changed my tone to one of reassurance, and had my first practical experience in how not to have an argument. Criticism of the other one's ability to do his life's work is an unrewarding area for verbal give-and-take. Where your partner's creativity is concerned, support and appreciation are more valuable than critical prowess.

I can't believe, for instance, that in 40 years Norman has liked every lamp and slipcover I've picked out. But he doesn't criticize my decorating efforts; he knows that the joy and confidence I feel in fixing up a home are more important than his preventing an occasional mistake.

An area, on the other hand, where there's probably too little frank exchange in many marriages is the matter of in-laws. Before Norman marries a couple, he and I like to sit down and talk with them as a foursome, and this is a piece of advice we often give: "Share your real feelings about your in-laws."

The Bible tells us: "For this cause shall a man leave father and mother"—and that means leaving behind our larger-than-life notions about our parents too. It isn't easy. It wasn't easy for Norman to hear me talk about his mother's fearfulness. It wasn't easy for me to see my mother through his eyes as an ultraconservative, judgmental person. But because we could discuss these things together, they never became sore points in our marriage.

How can husband and wife pursue such topics without stirring up a bee's nest of emotion? Here are some techniques Norman and I have discovered:

Take it in stages. "Let's get this decided here and now" ignores the psyche's natural tempo for making changes and adjustments. Norman and I have discovered that the best discussions are conducted in slow motion. We're having such a one now over where to go on our vacation this year. This is always a potential source of arguments because while Norman enjoys returning year after year to the same spot, I like trying new places.

"I'd like to go to the big island of Hawaii," I told him. "That's a place I've always wanted to see."

And then I dropped it. We'll come back to it in a couple of days, I'm sure, and have a reasonable exchange of opinions about it. And while I don't know where we'll end up going, I know we'll both be happy with the choice.

I'm also sure that I could have precipitated a quarrel if I'd been in a hurry or even been too positive in my desire about Hawaii. I could have smothered him with arguments: he's had the flu and needs sun, friends are going, there's no fuss with passports—each of which would have provoked a counterargument and left us defending positions instead of communicating.

Emphasize the positive. When our children were little, we resisted the temptation of moving to the suburbs, far from Norman's work, and instead brought them up in New York City. But I said, "We must find a little place in the country where they can have some grass and fresh air and normal living occasionally."

We finally found such a house, built in 1796, and it was all I had desired. But there was a big barn across the road, and this Norman did not like. Why should he go to the country and have a big barn cut off his view of the hills?

Now, I disagreed with him. I thought the barn was lovely—part of the whole setting. But I didn't argue about the barn. Instead I drew his attention to the 24-pane windows in the old house and talked about all the writing he could do in front of the antique fireplace. And soon Norman fell in love with the house, and for 21 years we were very happy there.

But do you know, he never was reconciled to that barn!

Five years ago, only half a mile up the road, a house on a hill with a commanding view in three directions—and no barn in the way—came on the market. By that time, of course, I'd put a bit of myself into every corner and cranny of our old house and loved it more than ever. But after 21 years of "my" barn, it was only fair to try "his" view, and today we are both extremely happy at our new place, the Hill Farm.

That decision to move, of course, involved the most basic principle of all: *compromise.* Not only when you disagree, but all the time, marriage is that middle road where two people who respect as well as love each other can walk side by side. And so often it's a better road than either could have found alone!

But if compromise can resolve many conflicts, there are a few in every marriage that are handled best by another great principle: *silence.* These are the areas—and every married person recognizes them—where your partner is not really talking about the issue at hand but something different and emotion-charged. I don't know at what moments Norman keeps silent for me, but for him the area is money.

It has always been my responsibility in our household to pay the bills and do the juggling when it seemed there couldn't possibly be enough to cover everything. This isn't because Norman couldn't do it, but because we discovered early in our life together that the minute he began to think about money, his creativity simply dried up. So I took over the checkbook and accounts and learned never even to discuss them with him.

But sometimes Norman gets on the subject. And his ideas of how to balance the budget are either too radical or plain impossible. That is when I have to keep silent. I count to ten. I tell myself how much I love him, what great abilities he has in other areas.

And when Norman has talked himself out, he is satisfied, I go ahead with my usual juggling, and we have avoided an emotional argument. I remember one time when the children were small, Norman decided we needed a station wagon. I had to tell him there wasn't enough money.

He came home that night after a day of staring at his desk, unable to work, and said, "Ruth, we're going to have to retrench all down the line." He wouldn't get the overcoat he'd been needing, John would wear Margaret's old boots, and so on and on.

At one time I would have argued with him, would have brought out the books and shown him how I had planned ahead for those necessary purchases. But by then, I knew that his reaction was not really to the current situation at all. It was to voices a small boy had heard long ago: "How will we pay the grocer's bill? How will we manage?" And I'd learned better than to fight phantoms.

Those, then, are the techniques Norman and I use for taking the heat out of disagreements: Take it slowly, make it positive, compromise and keep quiet. But not one of them would work—at least in our experience—if Christ were not the real head of our home. He is not only the source of love and insight and patience, which you cannot acquire without His guidance, but the example of all those things at work in the world.

When my children were born, I dedicated them to serve God. I was very sure that my first duty was to foster their faith in Him. As the children began to grow up, however, I began to realize that their trust in God was surpassing mine.

One night as Donna was going to bed, I suggested she

might pray for an end to the drought that was threatening the livelihood of everyone in the countryside.

"Well," she hesitated, looking up sleepily from her pillow, "if I do, will you bring my dolls inside? I left them in the sandbox, and I don't want them to get wet."

I remember so well the evening Robin ran downstairs to kiss some visiting relatives good night.

"Now be sure to say your prayers," her grandmother admonished.

"I will," Robin promised solemnly. Then, turning to the guests, she asked with innocent yet total assurance, "Anybody need anything?"

LUCILLE CAMPBELL
Cainesville, Missouri

Section Four—

When Faith Directs Young Lives

Section Four—
Introduction

In 1964 Guideposts' annual Youth Writing Contest was inaugurated. Since that time thousands of high-school juniors and seniors have written and submitted personal-experience stories on how faith helped them deal with their everyday-life situations. A number of these articles have appeared in Guideposts magazine, and thousands of dollars in scholarship prize money has been awarded.

Though Guideposts has from its earliest days been interested in presenting stories about and by young people, this relatively new contest has signaled an even greater emphasis on young people who are trying to find meaning in life. The stories we have presented have stressed the spiritual side, of course, and we have been gratified to learn that these examples of faith have given strength to other young men and women.

Of the stories included in this section, more than half were contest prizewinners. They range in content from Linda Lockwood's battle with a moral dilemma to Glenda Jones's internal struggle when her mother suffered a mental breakdown. From Susan Hayes's temptation toward shoplifting to Margaret Crider's inner torment brought on by classmates who didn't understand her physical problem.

Also in this section are two articles by black young people. Legson Kayira's dramatic walk across Africa in order to attend college in America is a testimony to the faith and perseverance of today's young people. Hope is the message of Linda Marshall's piece about the teacher who taught her to dream.

College protest, spiritual discovery, sexual temptation and a strange gang out to do good round out the themes of this unusual chapter about young people who too seldom make headlines.

Bird On My Shoulder
by Diane Sawyer

A former Junior Miss tells of her spiritual discovery.

The other night I was sitting alone in my room at Wellesley College trying to write on the subject, "Why I Believe in God." After hours of walking in circles—both mentally and physically—I decided to try out my ideas on some of the other students in the dorm. A lively argument began. I sensed in those girls the same confusion which I've felt so often. Yes, and the same need for answers.

Perhaps it's different in the adult world. But it seemed to me last year in high school—and now in college too—that when we young people set out to find God with our reason, we reach a dead-end every time. For me, truth is like a parakeet let out of its cage. I chase it around my room, across the campus, into the chapel itself, but it flies farther away all the time.

And then when I've stopped racing after it, perhaps when I'm not even thinking about it, it will come gently and light on my shoulder.

I had one of these inexpressible nudges from something outside myself the day before the Junior Miss Pageant began in March, 1963. I was driving into Louisville late that afternoon on some last minute errands. Suddenly a rabbit was under the wheels of the car—before I could even begin to use the brakes. I knew I had hit the animal although there was no impact. I drove on.

Then, inexplicably, I was blinded by tears. An impulse that was not my own said, "Stop. Go back. Don't leave the rabbit on the road."

"That's silly," my rational self replied. "You just don't stop to pick up a rabbit. Besides, it wasn't my fault."

But the tears blinded me so that I hardly could see

155

ahead. "I won't turn around," I repeated. Everything human in me said "drive on."

Yet that something stronger kept insisting. And finally I obeyed. I turned the car around and drove back to the spot where the rabbit had streaked from the underbrush. There it was, lying beside the pavement. It was dead. Gently I picked it up and laid it beneath a bush, well back from the road.

And with that act the tears stopped just as suddenly as they had started.

What was the truth that had touched me so compellingly? Was it a message about the oneness and importance of all God's creation? At a moment when my own plans and affairs loomed very large, hadn't a whisper come to me from the Love that included rabbits—and even the two sparrows which were sold for a farthing?

After the exciting experience in Mobile, there was a lot of travel for the Pageant. One Sunday in a large city, my chaperone and I slipped into a church near our hotel. The sanctuary was almost full—not quite. When it came time for the announcements, the pastor solemnly stood up and here is what he said as best as I can remember:

"I have witnessed the disunity resulting from recent attempts of Negroes to worship in a nearby church. In order to avoid what happened down the street, I called a special meeting of the board of directors. We have informed the ushers to tell any of these Negro agitators who come and try to attend our worship service, that we haven't room enough for our own members."

That was all. Just a simple announcement. I looked around at the people. Theirs was a routine reaction. Again, I know that the emotion I felt was larger than my own.

I am no crusader. I think I understand some of the complexity of this problem. But suddenly I knew that I could no longer take up this pew space that was so valuable.

The minister was reading some more announcements, but the words that crashed in my ears were different: *Though I speak with the tongues of men and of angels and have not charity, I am become as sounding brass. . . .** It was that other Voice impelling me to action once again. With my astonished chaperone gathering gloves and pocketbook, I got up and walked from the church—wondering if I ever would be able to explain it to her, or to myself.

---

* *1 Corinthians 13:1*

Back in the hotel room I tried to describe it. It was as though something more concerned and more dedicated than I had reached down and made a decision for me that I might not have reached by myself. For I often had wrestled in my own mind with this question of integration without reaching a very clear-cut conclusion.

A friend to whom I told this experience said he had no doubt that it was the Holy Spirit. He believes that the Spirit daily tries to reach each one of us with His perfect counsel. "The key," he said, "is our obedience. As long as we obey that subtle prompting, it will come ever clearer and more frequently. But if ever we begin to stop our ears, it will grow faint and then disappear."

That made sense to me, because nine or ten months before there had come a moment when I was sure the Holy Spirit had revealed a new truth to me. It was during a period in my life when I had pulled away from the religious training I'd received as a child.

I think most teen-agers go through a time like this, and when adults ask why, the nearest I can come is the word *embarrassment*. Teen-agers are terribly self-conscious. And Jesus represents a kind of simplicity and humility that is not at all attractive if you're primarily concerned with what people think of you.

Furthermore, I'd use the word *vulnerability*. There is something about Christ's life of sacrifice and service that made Him totally vulnerable to people. Whether we admit it or not, young people pull away from situations where we can be hurt. And so we pull away from identifying with Christ who was hurt.

I hadn't realized how far it had gone in my own case until one of the boys in high school said some things that bothered me. He, too, was reared in a Christian home, yet he had become a doubter.

"I could step on a Bible right now and not feel a thing," he said. Then he scoffed at church ritual and the idea of a divine Christ.

I tried to talk to him, but inside I was more upset than I showed. What bothered me was not as much his attitude as mine. For I'd realized suddenly as he talked that I could not counter his disbelief with a really strong faith of my own.

That night I could not sleep. A feeling of despair surrounded me. Why must I be so confused? It was nearly four a.m. before I dropped off to sleep.

The next night it was the same . . . a great feeling of depression . . . inability to sleep. I was tortured by questions about Christ. Was He a myth? Was He God? Did He really perform those miracles? My thoughts seem to start off in one direction and end up back at the starting point. There the big question was always waiting: was Jesus who He said He was?

I've wondered since why I did not turn to my parents for answers when I needed them so badly. Mother and Dad are the kind of Christians who live their faith and had tried to teach my sister and me to live it too. Perhaps that was just the trouble. What faith I had had been given to me, with no effort on my part. Perhaps it was time to earn a faith of my own.

For five nights the torment lasted . . . sleeplessness . . . emptiness . . . straining to know . . . reaching out for something. On the fifth night it happened. I can't describe it in any other way than to say that a cloud about me seemed to lift, the answer of Faith formed a pathway to light: He was! He is!

I got up and began to read the New Testament. I had read the entire Bible through twice before, but never like this. Once I'd read it as a lover of literature, once for its history. Now I read as a seeker. Words leapt at me from the page, thrilling and true. I read on and on, excited, with a feeling of great joy.

When I arose the next morning—to the same breakfast of eggs, the familiar school routine—the feeling of elation and belief was still there. But I had no idea as to how to share it or use it.

There have been other whispers from God, not as loud nor as clear as that night's revelation, but enough to keep me remembering that He seeks us even more fervently than we seek Him. Sometimes in my search for truth I feel as if I'm climbing a ladder up the side of the Empire State Building. At the 100th floor there is great vision and wisdom for the climber. Right now I'm up to the fifth floor and sometimes when I look up and see the distance to go, my heart sinks.

Then a bird lights on my shoulder and I remember that it's really not like this at all. It's not a long climb that we must accomplish alone. The distance was overcome when Truth came down to our level. Now He stands outside each separate heart, and we must only be ready to fling wide the door when we hear His gentle knock.

Barefoot to America
by Legson Kayira

The incredible story of a young man's 2000-mile walk across Africa—a modern Pilgrim's Progress.

My mother did not know where America was. I said to her, "Mother, I want to go to America to go to college. Will you give me your permission?"

"Very well," she said. "You may go. When will you leave?"

I did not want to give her time to discover from others in our village how far away America was, for fear that she would change her mind. "Tomorrow," I said.

"Very well," she said. "I will prepare some maize for you to eat along the way."

Next day, October 14, 1958, I left my home in the village of Mpale, in northern Nyasaland, East Africa. I had only the clothes I wore, a khaki shirt and shorts. I carried the two treasures I owned: a Bible and a copy of *Pilgrim's Progress*. I carried, too, the maize my mother had given me, wrapped in banana leaves, and a small ax for protection.

My goal was a continent and an ocean away, but I did not doubt that I would reach it.

I had no idea how old I was. Such things mean little in a land where time is always the same. I suppose I was 16 or 18.

My father died when I was very young. In 1952, my mother listened to the words of the missionaries of the Church of Scotland (Presbyterian), with the result that our family became Christian. From the missionaries, I learned not only to love God but also that if I was ever to be of value to my village, my people, my country, it would be necessary for me to have an education.

At Wenya, eight miles away, was a mission primary

159

school. One day when I felt I was ready to study, I walked there.

I learned many things. I learned I was not, as most Africans believed, the victim of my circumstances but the master of them. I learned that, as a Christian, I had an obligation to use the talents God had given me to make life better for others.

Later, in high school, I learned about America. I read the life of Abraham Lincoln and grew to love this man who suffered so much to help the enslaved Africans in his country. I read, too, the autobiography of Booker T. Washington, himself born in slavery in America, and who had risen in dignity and honor to become a benefactor of his people and his country.

I gradually realized that it would be only in America that I would receive the training and opportunities to prepare myself to emulate these men in my own land, to be, like them, a leader, perhaps even the president of my country.

My intention was to make my way to Cairo, where I hoped to get passage on a ship to America. Cairo was over 3,000 miles away, a distance I could not comprehend, and I foolishly thought I could walk it in four or five days. In four or five days, I was about 25 miles from home, my food was gone, I had no money, and I did not know what to do, except that I must keep going.

I developed a pattern of travel that became my life for more than a year. Villages were usually five or six miles apart, on forest paths. I would arrive at one in the afternoon and ask if I could work to earn food, water and a place to sleep. When this was possible, I would spend the night there, then move on to the next village in the morning.

It was not always possible. Tribal languages change every few miles in Africa; often I was among people with whom I could not communicate. This clearly made me a stranger to them, perhaps an enemy; they would not let me into the villages, and I had to sleep in the forests, eating herbs or wild fruit.

I soon discovered that my ax sometimes gave people the impression I had come to fight or to steal, so I bartered the ax for a knife I could carry unseen. I was actually defenseless against the forest animals I dreaded, but although I heard them at night none of them approached me. Malaria mosquitoes, however, were constant companions, and I often was sick.

But two comforts sustained me: my Bible and my *Pilgrim's Progress*. Over and over again I read my Bible, particularly finding confidence in the promise *Trust in the Lord with all thine heart, and lean not unto thine own understanding. . . . Then shalt thou walk in thy way safely, and thy foot shall not stumble.**

By the end of 1959, I had walked 1,000 miles to Uganda, where a family took me in and I found a job making bricks for government buildings. I remained there six months and I sent most of my earnings to my mother.

In *Pilgrim's Progress*, I read many times of the tribulations of the Christian who wandered through the wilderness seeking God, and I compared this to my own wanderings toward the goal I believed God had put into my heart. I could not give up, any more than the Christian had given up.

One afternoon at the USIS library in Kampala, I unexpectedly came upon a directory of American colleges. Opening it at random, I saw the name of Skagit Valley College, Mount Vernon, Washington. I had heard that American colleges sometimes gave scholarships to deserving Africans, so I wrote Dean George Hodson and applied for one. I realized that I might be refused but I was not discouraged: I would write to one school after another in the directory until I found one that would help me.

Three weeks later, Dean Hodson replied: I was granted a scholarship and the school would help me find a job. Overjoyed, I went to the American authorities, only to be told that this was not enough. I would need a passport and the round-trip fare in order to obtain a visa.

I wrote to the Nyasaland government for a passport but it was refused because I could not tell them when I was born. I then wrote to the missionaries who had taught me in my childhood, and it was through their efforts that I was granted a passport. But I still could not get the visa at Kampala because I did not have the fare.

Still determined, I left Kampala and resumed my trip northward. So strong was my faith that I used my last money to buy my first pair of shoes: I knew I could not walk into Skagit Valley College in my bare feet. I carried the shoes to save them.

Across Uganda and into the Sudan, the villages were farther apart and the people were less friendly to me. Some-

* *Proverbs 3:5, 23*

times I had to walk 20 or 30 miles in a day to find a place to sleep or to work to earn some food. At last I reached Khartoum, where I learned that there was an American consulate and I went there to try my luck.

Once again I heard about the entrance requirements, this time from Vice-Consul Emmett M. Coxson, but Mr. Coxson wrote the college about my plight. Back came a cable.

The students, hearing about me and my problems, had raised the fare of $1,700 through benefit parties.

I was thrilled and deeply grateful; overjoyed that I had judged Americans correctly for their friendship and brotherhood. I was thankful to God for His guidance and I pledged my future to His service.

News that I had walked for over two years and 2,500 miles circulated in Khartoum. The Communists came to me and offered to send me to school in Yugoslavia, all expenses paid, including travel, and a subsistence during my studies.

"I am a Christian," I told them, "and I could not be educated into the kind of man I want to be in your godless schools."

They warned me that, as an African, I would have racial difficulties in the United States, but I had read enough in American newspapers to feel this was a diminishing factor. My religion had taught me that men are not perfect, but as long as they strive to be they will be pleasing to God. The American effort, I felt, was why the land was so blessed.

In December, 1960, carrying my two books and wearing my first suit, I arrived at Skagit Valley College.

In my speech of gratitude to the student body, I disclosed my desire to become prime minister or president of my country, and I noticed some smiles. I wondered if I had said something naïve. I do not think so.

When God has put an impossible dream in your heart, He means to help you fulfill it. I believed this to be true when, as an African bush boy, I felt compelled to become an American college graduate. This is to become true in June when I will graduate from the University of Washington. And if God has given me the dream of becoming president of Nyasaland, this too, will become true.

It is when we resist God that we remain nothing. When we submit to Him, whatever the sacrifice or hardship, we can become far more than we dare dream.

WHAT DOES LOVE LOOK LIKE?

It has the hands to help others.
It has the feet to hasten to the poor and needy.
It has the eyes to see misery and want.
It has the ears to hear the sighs and sorrows of men.
That is what love looks like.

St. Augustine (354–430)

The Day My Faith Meant Most to Me

by Glenda Jones

A young girl's darkest Christmas Eve serves as a springboard for new hope.

One afternoon in December, my little sister and I bounded off the school bus and into our house. Tonight would surely be different—tonight Mom would greet us with that special exuberant spirit all her own. The Christmas Spirit was just too infectious, especially for Mom, who usually was the most susceptible one of all. Into the kitchen we trounced, bubbling over with joy. But the bubbles soon burst as we stared at the lone piece of paper lying on the table. My happy little world ended as I read Dad's familiar scrawl.

All we could see were those dreaded words looming before our eyes. "I have taken Mother to Cherokee . . . Dad." Cherokee was an accepted joke around our school. Seldom did a day go by when someone didn't make some smart remark about a certain person being bound for a strait jacket at Cherokee. How I had howled at such humor then!

Never could I feel the same way again. It was as if a door of my life had slammed shut, denying me my former carefree days. Oh, I had known that Mom had not been alert for several months, but I had refused to face the situation. Now I had no choice but to accept the fact that Mom—my own mother—was mentally ill and might not be home for months!

And who did that leave in charge as "chief cook and bottle washer?" Me—15-year-old me. Dazedly, I threw together a few meager scraps which hardly could be considered a meal. I was too stunned to care about anything except . . . what was *I* going to do? How could *I* manage a household

164

and keep my grades up at the same time? Would *I* have to sacrifice my social life?

The back door slammed and my dad came in. Time can erase every other memory, but I can never forget his face at that moment—eyes so devoid of emotion and hope as to seem transparent, his whole face frozen in an expression of despair. One look and I knew that my problems were insignificant compared with those my dad had to shoulder.

Right then and there I made up my mind that, no matter what, our family would hold the fort for Dad's sake. Although I knew I could never replace Mom (and didn't intend to try), I would do my own best to make things easier for my family.

I could end the story right here by saying that turning to God in my hour of despair gave me the needed strength and confidence. But God was the farthest from my thoughts during that next week. "After all," I reasoned bitterly, "if God let such misfortune happen to a family who didn't deserve it, then surely my prayers—if even heard—would be unwelcome and go unanswered.

As if matters weren't already bad enough, gradually I began to feel sorry for myself—for the bad stroke of fate, for the additional responsibility and work. My temper became short. I would lash out at my little sister for leaving her dirty socks on the davenport. I would argue with Dad as though it were I who ran everything in the household.

Finally December 24 arrived. But this year it was more than just Christmas Eve; it was the day at last that Dad and I could visit Mom. That morning, my bitter ways seemed sweetened somewhat by the magical effect of the day and I began to think of someone beside myself. I began to realize what a lonely Christmas Mom and many others like her would be spending. By the time we were ready to leave, I was loaded down with presents—not only for Mom, but paper plates of candy and cookies my sister and I had made for others at Cherokee.

Since my dad had an appointment with Mom's doctor before we could visit her, I waited in the lobby. While sitting in the great hallway filled with other visitors and with patients going home for the holidays, my old resentment began to tug at my conscience. Once again I began to wonder how God could be so merciless as to let such an illness strike us.

"You look very sad," said a voice that snapped me back to reality. "That's no way to be on Christmas Eve." It was the elderly lady sitting next to me. In no time I was deep in conversation with her.

My new friend was of such a sunny nature that it came as a surprise for me to learn that her son was a patient in Cherokee. Later I learned that her daughter at home was paralyzed by polio from the waist down. Accepting her handicap, this girl had made the most of her abilities and was currently writing a novel. It seems impossible that with all the heartache she had suffered, this woman could be so cheerful and optimistic, so outgoing. Before I realized it—I heard myself pouring out all my problems as if she were an old friend.

When I had finished, she grew very serious and carefully explained to me how one simple act—prayer—had relieved her of an unaccountable amount of grief and had made her reliance upon God strong and vital. So at last was unlocked the mystery of this woman's cheerful perseverance. She soon made me realize that my prayers would have to be from the heart and not of a superficial type. When she had prayed for her children, she had asked God "to take care of them as He saw fit, not as I saw." In such a manner, must I ask God for help. For only then would I feel that my burden had been lightened. At last I realized that I had been shunning the only One who could help me but, nevertheless, He had been waiting patiently by my side until I could "see the light" and put my wholehearted trust in Him.

Maybe it was God watching over me who sent such a person to teach me one of the most important lessons of life. I'd rather believe that it was also the magic of Christmas Eve and the fact that on such a day, many years ago, the greatest miracle of all mankind took place, a miracle that made possible such minor miracles as had taken place this particular day.

Yes, the day my faith meant the most to me was the day I found it on a snowy Christmas Eve in the lobby of a mental hospital. There I found faith that sustained me over the year that my mother struggled up the rocky road to recovery.

Breakthrough at City College
by Steve Frank

How one student met the protest crisis.

I shook my head to clear it, not believing what I had heard. Some militant members of the Student Council at Los Angeles City College were giving speeches. The council in theory represents the entire campus, yet these militants were taking stands which certainly did not represent me.

Now, as I sat in the lecture room, unbelieving, I heard the speaker say, "The only way to handle an enemy is to put a bullet through his skull."

I rose to my feet. "Wait a minute!" I called out. The speaker stopped, and the room fell silent. "Do you realize what you're saying! After the Kennedys! After Martin Luther King!"

Suddenly there were catcalls, hoots and shouts. "Sit down!" The speaker turned to four hefty nonstudents sitting next to him. "Get him out of here," I heard him say.

The four ran to me, picked me up by my arms and started walking me toward the door. They carried me out of the hall, down the steps and across the common.

That night I couldn't sleep. What was I going to do? The issue was especially important for me because of a decision I'd made a few months earlier.

There hadn't been many Jewish soldiers in my Army outfit, but at Passover we did get together to eat the ritual meal. I joined my friends more out of sentiment than conviction. Although I did attend synagogue, Judaism just didn't seem relevant.

But on that evening, there at the celebration of Passover, far from home, I heard the traditional question: "Wherefore is this night distinguished from all others?" This time, instead of being just a ritual, the question seemed directed to me. Why indeed is this night different?

A shiver ran down my spine. At that moment Passover became for me more than the memory of an event which happened in antiquity; it became an event happening right then. It became a current story of God liberating men from chains. Stunned, shaken, sitting there with my cup of wine before me, I knew that this called for a response on my part.

Now in my room at school, I was wrestling with the anger of being thrown off my own campus. I saw that unless we were careful at City College, even the campus revolution, which had so much that was fine in its original motivation, could become chains of a sort. People were calling for freedom with one voice, but they were denying freedom with another.

The next day I tried to get friends to join me in challenging extremism. Only a few wanted to support me. "Besides," I was often asked, "what can you do all by yourself?"

What, in fact, could I do? There was an attitude among the students, faculty and administration that militancy was proper no matter how extreme.

On January 15, 1969, students took over the public-address system of the school, confiscated food being prepared for a luncheon, broke up classes. No one got excited.

But neither did we get excited when a strike was called on March 10, and the head of the art department was beaten by three students. Worse, a math teacher who tried to open the door of his classroom was pummeled so badly he was temporarily blinded.

In spite of these events I still had only a handful of backers—20 to be precise—who agreed that militancy had gone too far. On the second day of the strike, those 20 young people and I set up a table on campus trying to score the use of violence, but a group of boys turned over our table, tore up the pamphlets we had made and built a bonfire with our posters.

Later that day strikers succeeded in closing the school altogether. Barricades were set up at approaches to the campus.

We decided that the time had come to make a dramatic appeal for support. What would happen if we walked through that barricade so that we could go to our classes? We would have to take a part of the barricade down. But we agreed that under no circumstances would we use violence. If we were attacked, we would not fight back.

Early on March 12 we moved onto campus, 20 against 200. At the barricade, in addition to the militants, there was a large group of "neutral" students who had come to watch. Just how neutral were they? Would they do nothing? Would they help the militants? Or would they—as I hoped—follow us into school?

We made our way to the main barricade. Remembering my Army training, I made a suggestion. "You," I said to five of our biggest boys, "make a show of leaving us, go around the building to that smaller barricade. Maybe you can draw some of these people away."

The boys split, making as much noise as possible, and moved off. It worked: More than half the militants followed those boys.

Now we moved in. Newspaper photographers who had come to cover the strike took pictures of us as we dismantled just enough of the barricade to allow a line of students to move through. It was perhaps the presence of the press—recording all that happened—that kept most of the militants from trying to stop us. We walked through the breached barricade unhindered.

Now came an important moment. I almost dared not turn around. But when I did, I saw the sight I'd hoped for: On our heels came a stream of neutral students who, of course, had not been neutral at all.

It was apparent that the Student Council did not represent the majority of the students. On April 17, friends and I circulated a petition for the recall of the Student Council. Almost instantly I was surrounded by boys who took my papers and tore them up. I was backed against a wall. Someone hit me in the stomach, then in the face. My lip was split open. Blood spurted over my clothes.

It was perhaps a painful way to get support; but after that beating, our petition gained signatures rapidly. All in all we got more than 4000 names. Along with friends, I put up a slate which advocated that we take a more moderate stand at City College. We won the election.

We don't really know where we go from here. Militants have as much right to be in school as we do, but they do not have the right to destroy campus democracy. I trust that we are moving toward the center, where there will be no more beatings and burnings of classrooms, and no more denying the right of free speech.

At City College the struggle for freedom had killed

freedom itself. I had no idea when I made my commitment at Passover that I was going to be plunged so quickly into relevant issues. "Why is this night different from all others?" we ask at Passover. Because this is a time when God became involved in man's struggle for freedom. And for me at least, Passover is still happening today.

I Prayed to Get Caught
by Susan Hayes

---

*An unusual petition to God from a girl with a
serious problem.*

There was a time when my life could have been said to be
synonymous with the Latin verb *aio*—present, imperfect and
having no future. If there had been a rebellious organization
in my school or community at that time, I would have probably joined simply to have a cause. I wanted to stand for
something, not fall for anything. But I did fall.

"Hey, man, what are you, a dupe or something? These
business cats are cheating you blind. Anyway, they'll never
miss this little stuff we swipe." That's how the whole shoplifting mess started, with a challenge and some illogical
reasoning.

I started my "five-finger discount" career at the age of
11. At first, only small things were taken—candy, pencils,
knickknacks. But then the dam was broken, and there was
no stopping.

Why does a child shoplift? Maybe because that's the
only way to get what he wants, or because "everyone else
does it." Or maybe just to see if it can be done. My reason, if
there can be one, would be the last one. I'd always mistrusted
adults, and as I was stubborn and rebellious anyway, this was
my chance to beat them in their world. Often I'd take something while standing right by a clerk, walk out with it, then
bring it back and put it where I'd taken it from. This was a
sport, and the more I won, the more I tried.

I involved my friends in my sport. We would walk into
a store; they'd show me what they wanted, then we'd walk
around the store. Once outside the store, they'd try to find
where I put the items I took. I could slip things in their
purses or pockets and they never knew it. I began taking

things I didn't even want. I just couldn't walk into a store without taking something.

I knew what I was doing was wrong, but the full realization didn't dawn on me until my game had me in a deadly grip. I had been attending my church all this time. In fact, I was one of the most active youths in the church. Even though I was a church member, I thought the whole church was a big farce. I watched all those pious adults and older teens say one thing and do another. I decided I was as good as they, and if they were Christians on their way to Heaven, so was I. But even then, I could sense something missing in their lives—and most of all, something was missing in mine.

By now I had been playing my game for almost four years. I now knew the penalty if I were caught and I decided it was time to stop. To my amazement, I found I couldn't stop. I couldn't control myself. This was something I couldn't handle alone.

My very best friend was a Christian of great faith. She didn't know my problem, but in her I recognized a power for which I had been searching. Her faith was so real, so relevant to her. Maybe God could become real to me, too.

I began reading my Bible, believing that the only way I would find help was through the Lord. I was desperate to break my habit, and in my desperation, I prayed. Strangely, I found myself praying to get caught.

A week later a saleslady tapped me on the shoulder and coldly said, "Take that out of your pocket, pay for it, then never come in this store again!" The Lord had answered my prayer. The game began to lose its grip. That night, February 27, 1965, the Lord took over my heart, mind, soul and body.

But my trial wasn't over yet. Something said, "Go back to that store; tell that saleslady what happened to you." I couldn't do that, I just couldn't. I didn't want to do it, especially by myself. I prayed about what I should do—and suddenly I knew I could do it, for I wouldn't be alone. I knew that the Lord would be with me.

The first Saturday in April I walked into the store and said to the saleslady, Mrs. Lollis, "Ma'am, you caught me shoplifting in here about a month ago; but I want to tell you that after that, I found the Lord and by my faith in Him which He gives me, I won't do it again. I'm sorry about the other time."

Tears came to her eyes, which told me her reply. With a heart happier than it had ever been, I walked out with the knowledge I was free now, totally free. Through faith, my Lord taught me to realize that a little wealth gained honestly is better than great wealth gained dishonestly, for a life of doing right is the wisest life there is.

My life is no longer like that Latin verb *aio*. I am still present and still imperfect. But now through faith I have a future—a lifetime with the Lord. That makes the greatest future of all.

The Day The Talking Stopped
by Margaret Crider

---

*There was something different about her all right
—she had a faith that wouldn't quit.*

Several months after my family moved to Harbor Creek
in July, 1967, I found myself in the midst of cold strangers at
the high school. The students did nothing to accept me, and
then rumors were soon all over the school. "She's a queer."
Such malicious tales and remarks made it impossible for my
brother, who was a senior, even to get a date. When I walked
down the hall, the kids would move away from me. I cried
out to God asking Him the reason for, and the solution to,
this problem.

Friday night, January 12, 1968, was very cold and
snowy, not the kind of night you would dream held the key
to your problem or the answer to your prayer. I had invited
my only girl friend, Melody, home for supper; and after the
dishes were done, we sat and talked.

At first, our conversation was casual, but gradually it
deepened. The previous week my Advanced English teacher,
Mr. Sanfilippo, had called me out of the room to ask me if I
thought Melody, being the only Negro in the class, would be
hurt if we read and discussed *To Kill a Mockingbird*. I had
offered to find out how she felt about it. After stumbling
around, I managed to ask her, and she felt we should defi-
nitely read it. Now it was her turn to hesitate about something. Finally, as we were walking back to her house, she told
me the kids at school thought I was queer because I stared.

That was the key. I have had psychomotor epilepsy for
over eight years. My seizures are generally very slight, but
during them I appear to be staring. Some of the kids had
seen me during a seizure; and holding the belief that queers
stare, they deducted that I must be one.

When I returned home, I broke down. Through many

tears, I told my father and mother what Melody had disclosed. My next move was to call my guidance counselor, Mrs. Arnold, who had been desperately trying to solve the problem. Mother and I were to be in her office at 8:15 the following Monday morning.

I had been relying very heavily upon God ever since this all began in September, and that weekend was no exception. Through much prayer and a schoolteacher friend, a plan was worked out. Monday morning, January 15, 1968, I would walk to my Advanced English class, where most of the trouble was originating. We were studying the novel *Silas Marner,* as many former high school sophomores have, and our teacher, Mr. Sanfilippo, had been pointing out the problems ignorance and superstition can create. Silas Marner had cataleptic fits very similar to my epileptic seizures. Because of them, he had been accused of being demon-possessed and was not accepted by the people of the town into which he had just moved. God's timing was perfect. I was to talk to the class about epilepsy, tying my own predicament in with Silas Marner's.

All weekend, various ways of presenting epilepsy to the class darted through my mind. But my biggest problem was keeping my mind off myself. It was naturally easy to feel sorry for myself and revengeful toward my classmates. I knew I had to love these kids and forgive them just as God continually loves and forgives me. These are the problems I face daily, not just ones I faced that weekend.

Monday morning dawned crisp and clear. Mother and I went to school together, where we went over the plan with Mrs. Arnold; then my mother returned home. I went on to my homeroom while Mrs. Arnold went to contact Mr. Sanfilippo. The first period bell rang, and off I went to my English class armed with a few pamphlets, clippings, and diagrams. Mrs. Arnold also came in and sat down. Mr. Sanfilippo started off the class by refreshing our memories about superstition and Silas Marner. Then he proceeded to say:

"Last week I called Margaret out into the hall, and after beating her over the head a few times, she consented to do some work for me. She is going to tell us about epilepsy."

I arose from my seat in the back of the room and prayed as I neared the front: "Holy Spirit, You take over and speak through me." Any plans I had flew out the window as the Holy Spirit took over. We spoke to the class for about 20 minutes and answered as many of their questions as time permitted. I found myself saying such things as: "Medication helps, but I find prayer and God help the most;" "When I feel a seizure coming on, I often pray and God helps me."

Before I knew it, the period was almost over. Mrs. Arnold arose and thanked me, and the class applauded. After Mr. Sanfilippo and I left the room, he remarked that for some time now he had wanted me to speak to the class about epilepsy, but feared it would upset me.

Mrs. Arnold talked to the students a bit more about the situation after we had left and said, "I think we had better all get down on our knees tonight and thank God for the good health He has given us."

Since that day, things have changed. There are many friendly smiles and greetings, as well as new friendships. And I have learned that my best and wisest Friend can use anything, even epilepsy, to glorify Himself. I can truly agree with the statement my mother made that evening: "Today is one day I thanked God that He hasn't yet healed you."

The Gillnet Gang Does Its Own Thing

by Spenser W. Havlick

Where will this roving band strike next?

In the late-evening shadows I stood back and watched the gang of teen-agers, armed with paint-spray cans, launch their attack. Their target: obscenities on an overpass which shouted insults at passing traffic.

Black paint hissed, and the epithets faded away.

The Gillnet Gang had struck again.

Later I heard somebody say, "Well, the railroad finally got busy. I wondered when they would get around to *that*." The youngsters got no credit. And that's the way they wanted it.

The Gillnet Gang of Ann Arbor, Michigan, gets its kicks by roaming the city at night, working swiftly and silently, leaving no calling card. Neither city authorities nor their schools know who they are.

As the local paper put it, "This gang works for society, not against it. Their goal is not money or power, but good deeds; and the enemy is not the establishment, but red tape."

As a confidant to the gang, I smiled when I read that. For in a way, a big-city ghetto gang should be thanked for the Gillnet Gang's existence.

The idea began about four years ago when my wife and I were serving as counselors to the Methodist Youth Fellowship of Ann Arbor's First United Methodist Church. Our group members had been devoting some of their vacation time to working in big-city ghettos. Some of the kids were working in Chicago's West Side. They were fascinated with the way city youths organized into powerful street gangs. When they returned home, the idea came out in one of our talk sessions.

177

"We were wondering," said one, "how we could form our own gang here—not to fight, but to *help* people."

They didn't want any personal glory, but just the fun of doing something for others. "We don't even want people to know *who* we are," they emphasized. Anonymity kept their parents out of the picture and helped them avoid the "do-gooders" stigma among their friends.

"Sounds like something out of Robin Hood," I said.

We chose the name "Gillnet" to connote the religious symbol of Peter, the fisherman, and the other early disciples who went on to become "fishers of men" for God. And, of course, our main idea is that once anyone is involved in the net of giving, for the pure sake of giving, he'll be captured by its satisfactions.

The group has never elected officers; there are no formal leaders. The member who instigates a project becomes its chief and starts the ball rolling.

Informality is the rule. They wear no emblazoned jackets, just everyday clothes. And though they prefer to work under cover of darkness, some jobs must be done during the day. Transportation is no problem: if they can't borrow the family car, it's a bicycle. And often it means a long hike on foot to complete the job.

I serve as a sounding board for projects and strategies for carrying them out. Naturally, I point out the physical or legal hazards and help them think not only of the deed but of its consequences.

But they make the final decision. If the word is "go," then their telephone message chain begins buzzing.

And their phones are busy. Perhaps it will be something one of the youngsters noticed while out driving, like the overpass. Or the kids will spot a plea in the *Ann Arbor News* "Action Please" column.

Such was the case of the too-high hedge which blinded vision at a street corner. Many accidents were blamed on it. People fired off letters to the newspaper; city officials debated what to do. Suddenly one morning the hedge was just the right size.

No one knows officially how it happened. The owner was angry, but the public good was served.

Often their target is a festering community problem bogged down in quandary. Given enough time and push by citizens, it would eventually be taken care of. The Gillnet

Gang takes pride in getting it done a little sooner and a little more surely.

When the city installed big garden planters along Main Street, they gaped empty and forlorn while the city argued with businessmen about who'd plant and care for the flowers. The Gillnetters filled one of the planters at night to give downtown a quick taste of color. Since then the businessmen and city have together taken over the task.

Several civic groups not long ago planned a Saturday-morning cleanup along a section of our Huron River's littered bank.

Friday evening about 40 Gillnetters biked out to the section. I never saw kids work so hard and fast before. Within a couple of hours they had piled all the trash into a giant heap, ready for the truck to pick it up.

Next morning the adults arrived to find all their work done. They stood around the pile in open-mouthed astonishment, but not for long. They went on to clean up *another* section of the river front.

I get a warm feeling about the way the kids keep a sharp eye out for elderly people being hospitalized so they can welcome them home with a fresh-cut lawn. We've heard that neighbors often call a former patient asking to hire "those young people working for you." And all the while the homeowner had assumed it was his neighbors who had done the yard work.

Concern for children figures in a lot of their projects. A need developed for a school-crossing sign at a certain critical intersection. While officials discussed and rediscussed proper procedures for its installation, children continued to cross the street without protection. Suddenly a temporary but completely adequate warning sign sprouted at the intersection.

Gillnetters are finding it difficult to keep their light under a bushel, no matter how hard they try. And I'm glad. Though our youngsters still want to preserve their anonymity, I know they'd like to see their idea spread to other cities.

Whether youth gangs exist for good or bad, they do fill a need among the members. Kids hunger for a close-knit group of their very own. They want to accomplish as part of it, to be where the action is.

And I've seen how a group like the Gillnet Gang fills this need—with good results.

The greatest blessing was in discovering that there are so many youngsters who want to give for the pure sake of giving. Because of this, the Gillnet Gang has outgrown its original MYF nucleus. Today, with four adult counselors, including myself, the group is not identified with any particular church or denomination. It has become a city-wide gang, composed of kids of all classes, faiths and races—white, black, Oriental—all teamed together in the great fraternity of His Spirit.

The original creed of the Gillnetters remains the same: *Your good deed must be secret, and your Father Who sees what is done in secret will reward you.**

But the reward is no secret; you see it shining in their eyes.

---

* *Matthew 6:4 (NEB)*

The Teacher Who Taught Me to Dream
by Linda Diane Marshall

A young black girl writes about the person who most helped her faith to grow.

Children, please repeat after me, 'I am only one, but I *am* one. I can't do everything, but I can do *something*. What I *can* do, I *ought* to do; and what I ought to do, by the grace of God, I *will* do!"

That was my introduction to my eighth-grade homeroom teacher—the one special person who did most to make my faith grow. She was to be my homeroom teacher for the next three years and my English teacher for the eighth and eleventh grades.

Mrs. Carolyn Long was the smallest person in the room, but she dominated it. She smiled and we all were glad we had chosen that school. She walked, talked, and even seemed to eat too fast. She seemed to feel that time would run out before she taught us anything and that if it did the fault would be hers.

Yet there was no lack of patience with us. Instead she made each of us feel that we were special people without bestowing special favor upon anyone. She always found time to give each of us "his five minute" as she called it. None was neglected.

I came to her thoroughly convinced that I was never meant to be anybody of importance. I had long ago decided that no one cared and nothing mattered, so I existed from day to day without any thought of tomorrow. The distant future was beyond my conception. Drab and unhappy circumstances had stunted my growth, killed my faith and left me floating on a directionless sea of time.

My home, I felt, was merely a place to go when school

closed. I thought it a prison. My mother provided food and
shelter for my body but really had little time for me. Separated from my father, she had full responsibility for my nine
brothers and sisters. There just were too many other things
which took her time. I never got my "five minute" with her
as with Mrs. Long. We just never talked about the things I
had on my mind.

I felt life was hopeless—and it was—until I met Mrs.
Long, who kept nudging me with remarks like, "Use your
mind, Linda, and free your body." "You can break out of the
prison of your environment if you study hard and do your
lessons every day." Or she would say, "You can be somebody
if you want to be."

The Lord knows I wanted to be somebody.

She continued to admonish us daily with that devotional
chant, "You are only one, but you are one . . ."—meaning
we ought to be proud of ourselves and if we weren't, we
ought to have guts enough to do something about it. I tried
not to listen, but I heard her. I tried to ignore what she
meant, but I got the message, loud and clear. I told myself
she was a fake, a too-good-to-be-true pretender, but she
sounded so sincere. When I was on the verge of becoming a
convert, I angrily denounced her for fussing all the time.

Then, one day she asked us to look out of the window
and to write about whatever came into our minds as we
looked. It was a dark wintry day. I wrote a little poem about
whispering leaves and the snowkissed earth. She was ecstatic.
One would have thought she had discovered another Shakespeare. I had never dared to show anyone my poetry before
lest I be ridiculed. Her enthusiastic praise melted my sorrow
and broke the dam of my resolution. I wrote all my themes
in poetry that year.

She wouldn't accept dirty, incorrect work. We had to
write it over until it was pretty and clean and errorless. Then
basking in the glory of her smile we would pin it on the bulletin board. "See! Everyone can create beauty," she'd say,
pointing to our themes, which, I must admit, did look beautiful. Sloppy work, she swore, would develop sloppy characters
in us and that would blight our futures. Heaven forbid!

I could go on forever enumerating how this little, ener-
getic, enthusiastic lady rekindled my faith in myself and my
ability to fight against the odds; how she inspired me to a
greater faith in God; how she helped me to believe in the in-
nate goodness of my fellowman.

Slowly, I believed and slowly, believing changed me. I joined the Student Council. I accepted an invitation to appear on an assembly program. She helped me, encouraged me and was waiting to praise me when it was over; but sweeter than that was the thundering applause of my schoolmates who proved that she was right.

My sprouting wings continued to grow to full strength through my high-school years. It was not always easy, but Mrs. Long was my radar, able to detect my wavering convictions, always encouraging, urging and pointing the way.

"That's good, Linda, but you can do better," she would say and I would do better. If I stumbled she'd say, "You can't stop now, Linda," and I would try again.

With her help I have achieved confidence in my ability to face the future. I understand myself and my potential. I also understand the circumstances about my home.

My determination to find a way led me into business education and a trade. My dogged "do it well, if at all" training has gotten me a part-time job in one of the school offices and the confidence of my superiors. I dare to dream of a college degree, and I have the faith to believe that somehow, someway, I shall achieve it. After all, I am only one but *I am* one. I can't do everything, but I can do *something*. What I *can* do, I *ought* to do; and what I ought to do, by the grace of God, *I will* do! My most fervent prayer is that someday Mrs. Long will have cause to be really proud of me and that I shall be able to wrap the mantle of her faith around another child like myself.

The Moment
by Shirley Tatro

How long can a girl and boy simply say, "I love you"?

Without really meaning to, I had fallen into a beautiful and innocent young love. For the first time in my life I began to give of myself unselfishly. And the boy I had come to love returned twofold any happiness that I may have given him. I guess that is the wonderful thing about true affection.

Through our moments together, our relationship continued to grow into one of deep understanding and mutual respect and trust. Each day that I wore his ring on my finger only added to the love I felt in my heart.

But a feeling of such complete devotion has a funny way of playing tricks on a person. And when you are only 17, a year becomes a long time to have been telling a guy, "I love you." So as we shared these deep feelings for each other we explored the thrills of kisses and caresses together.

I think we always knew that a moment of final decision was inevitable. Yet we pushed such serious thoughts to the back of our minds, telling ourselves, "It won't happen this time."

But tomorrow always arrives, and our time also came. After months of nights filled with dark roads and searching kisses, we encountered a brick wall that had only one door. We now had a choice to make. It would be so easy to go through that door, with the excuse, "We're doing it out of love." Yet we knew we would pay a very dear price—our innocence.

Maybe the complete unselfishness that I had thought we felt was not so complete after all, for on that night there was something in each of us that made us stop. Or perhaps we both knew we would be losing something that could never be replaced, and we just could not bring ourselves to make that sacrifice. Whatever the reason, we didn't open that door that night. But we had at least realized that we could be terribly tempted—and we knew that many nights and temptations lay before us.

We had to find some way either to change or justify the thing we were doing. We became aware of one fact—our awful misconception that love and sex are synonymous was on the verge of destroying us. We had begun to forget how to laugh and be happy just that we were together. Tears no longer eased the shame. Words became hollow and meaningless sounds. We needed a solution, but where could we turn?

It is a little ironic that the answer to our question was so simple and was there with us all the time. It came, along with one of the greatest moments in my relationship with the boy I love, when he held me and said, "Let's pray." Only two small words, but they lifted the burden from our shoulders and put it in the hands of Someone far, far stronger. The God that had given us these bodies, these emotions and these desires would now guide us in their use.

We found that the road back is not an easy one. Sometimes we stumble and fall, but there is always a firm and gentle hand to pick us up and urge us on our way.

We know now that a small part of us died that night, but at the same time a new seed of faith was planted and began to grow.

Perhaps someday, if it is His will, the God Who gave us the courage to turn back and keep that beautiful love we held will give us His blessings to return to that door, open it and really begin our lives together.

Until that day, my guy and I have an obligation to keep. We have promised to care for and nourish our young love until one day when it blooms in full glory.

How My Faith Helped Me to Make a Difficult Decision

by Linda Lockwood

Her dilemma was simple enough to solve. The question was: Did she have the courage to act?

"Trumpeting, junior feminine," the judge announced. I held my breath in the pause that followed and repeated, "Debbie Adams, Debbie Adams" over and over to myself to lessen my inevitable disappointment.

"Linda Lockwood!" came over the loudspeaker.

Waves of disbelief, amazement and excitement swept over me as my parents hugged me. "Northeastern States Champion," my father whispered with pride in his voice. My teacher, Mr. Stannard, went to get my medal.

I had been playing a trumpet for almost six years. When I was 10, I had joined a small drum corps in my community. Besides learning to play, I had the opportunity each summer to travel to drum corps contests in Massachusetts and Connecticut. Although from Vermont, our corps belongs to the Massachusetts Fife, Drum and Bugle Association and is thus eligible to compete for Massachusetts State Championship titles. Winning the championship in individual trumpeting had made me eligible for the Northeastern States title. The competition was very stiff, and I knew it. Debbie Adams, the Connecticut State champ, was very good; I had heard her play before.

Everyone I knew was thrilled to think that I had brought such an honor to our corps. Items about the contest appeared in our two local newspapers. With pride I had the medal engraved. What a thrill to wear it and realize what I had achieved.

One Monday evening about a month later, when I was waiting to have my weekly trumpet lesson, I noticed a recap of the contest. Curiosity made me look and discover that I had won by a mere 1.1 points. That same evening, Mr. Stannard showed me my score sheet, which he had just received through the mail. We went over it together, and he explained what this mark and that mark might mean in terms of my mistakes. I took the paper home to show my parents.

My mother, knowing even less about the mysteries of judging than I did, had to know just how my final mark was determined. As I was explaining, I checked the scores myself, something Mr. Stannard and I had neglected to do before. "See," I told Mom, "here the judge recorded 10 mistakes. Then he took off . . . 10 points here." At least, that was what I was going to say but couldn't because only eight had been subtracted from the total. I checked again. Ten and eight! It just couldn't be true. But it was. By mistake I had been given two extra points. I hadn't really won.

The next few days were an agony of doubt and dread. My parents and I were the only ones who knew about the mistake. They would say nothing, I knew; and if I, too, remained silent, the secret would be ours. No one else need ever know—I felt reasonably sure that Mr. Stannard would never give the sheet another glance. Yet Someone else did know. Silence seemed so easy but, because I am a Christian, my conscience would give me no peace. I cried myself to sleep nights and prayed for strength to do what I knew was right—what I knew I had to do. Somehow my faith kept me strong. The next Thursday I showed Mr. Stannard the mistake with a tiny hope in my heart that he could explain it all.

"You know what this means?"

"Yes," I replied.

"Now, when we had only the recap, you were the winner," he said kindly. "I can write to the President of the Connecticut Association and tell her, but. . . ."

"Please, Mr. Stannard," I said, "do what must be done."

Mr. Stannard took care of all the necessary details and kept me informed. He would not allow me to return the medal until we had a photostatic copy of Debbie's sheet to check for mistakes. When all my hope of more mistakes had been killed, there was just one thing to do. With the Lord's help and strength I gave Debbie the medal at a contest in Connecticut.

This might have been the end of the episode, but it wasn't. A few months later I was invited to the annual Christmas party of Debbie's corps. I was honored in many ways, but the best thing that happened was the medal that Debbie gave me. It was engraved "Linda, a true champion." That medal means more to me than all the ones I have won; it is a symbol of true friendship.

My faith helped me to make a difficult decision, but the Lord turned a mistake into a blessing.

In Pittsburgh during the last century a retired Army man, Colonel Anderson, became concerned about some underprivileged boys who had no opportunity to own or read good books. The Colonel, a man of small means, unfortunately wasn't in a position to give books to these boys.

The Colonel, however, did have a fair-sized library of his own, and so he invited these boys to come up and borrow anything they liked.

Andy, an immigrant boy who made $25 monthly as a telegraph clerk, leaped at this chance. Each week he would return one book and borrow another. Then after supper he and his mother would read aloud to each other.

The youthful borrower never forgot this kindness.

Today, thousands of Americans enjoy free libraries—the gift of that grateful man—Andrew (Andy) Carnegie.

How do you know that *you* have nothing to give?

Section Five—

The Healing Power of Faith

Section Five—
Introduction

How is a person healed?

What are the conditions for healing?

Who may be healed?

Those are questions asked often by our readers. And over the years, Guideposts has presented a great many stories illustrating both physical and mental healings. Though we don't know now or have we ever pretended to understand the process of spiritual healing, we are convinced that God is a healer who can and does cure even the most incurable diseases. We believe this because of the many case histories which have come before us testifying to the power of prayer. There are too many not to believe!

The ten stories presented here represent a myriad of experiences. As with most Guideposts articles, some are by and about the famous; others are obscure names among men. But God is no respecter of persons. He was apparently as concerned for young Karen Emmotts in Dr. William Reed's story and Juan Yepez in Dr. Howard Rusk's article as for baseball player Tony Conigliaro and actor William Gargan and Arthur Godfrey—as well as the young boy in Grace Perkins Oursler's inspiring piece, a boy who was to lead a nation one day.

Sometimes the curing of mental and emotional wounds is more difficult than the physical—as Agnes Sanford shows us in "The Healing of Memories" or as J.B. Phillips does in his personal "Dark Night of the Soul." For still other dimensions of healing, read the all-time favorite prayer-of-relinquishment article by Catherine Marshall and Doctor Tournier's poignantly provocative "A Place for You."

Whatever selection you turn to in this section, you will be thrilled again by the realization that the Lord is alive today and working miracles just as He performed them nearly 2000 years ago.

Case History of a Prayer
by William S. Reed, M.D.

---

*There is no pulse and no blood pressure. The
girl has had a cardiac arrest.*

Does a doctor ever have the right to give a patient hope
when all his medical training tells him there is no basis for it?

I had to face this question in a poignant way in 1960.

It was September. I had flown out to Oklahoma City to
give a speech on how prayer can aid a doctor in his work. I
spoke in a church saying—perhaps a little glibly—that in
God's eyes there were no hopeless cases. After the lecture, a
woman asked:

"If you really believe that, Dr. Reed, I wonder what
you'd say about Karen Emmott."

Karen, she said, was a 15-year-old girl whose brain had
been permanently damaged when her heart stopped during an
operation. "Everyone has given her up: even her father and
he's a doctor."

The same afternoon I went to see Karen in a convalescent home. I went not as a physician but as a Christian.
Dr. Emmott told me details of the story.

That July 4th, Karen had been a normal teen-age girl.
The eldest of six children, she was her mother's mainstay: a
very vivacious, attractive high school drum majorette. The
operation which brought about Karen's tragedy was itself
quite minor and routine: it consisted of draining a gynecolog-
ical infection. Surgery was scheduled for 1:00 p.m., July 5th.
Karen's father, who was on the staff of the same hospital,
continued his work in his clinic. Such a routine affair, but
then followed one of those freaks of chance that can turn the
routine into the catastrophic. The anesthetic had been ad-
ministered and the surgeon began. He had completed the
brief operation when the anesthetist announced:

"There is no pulse and no blood pressure. We have a cardiac arrest."

Cardiac arrest! From his earliest training every surgeon is conditioned to act instinctively. He must instantly incise the chest and massage the heart back to life. Any delay will cause brain damage.

As quickly as possible, Karen's chest was opened. Her heart was massaged with sure fingers. And it did respond. But did the heart beat soon enough? This was the question on everyone's mind as Karen was wheeled to the recovery room. An hour passed, two, three, four. By eight o'clock that evening it was apparent that Karen was not going to wake up.

A week later there was still no glimmer of knowing in her eyes. Six weeks later, she still was unresponsive. Karen's body was alive, but her brain was dead. It was the consensus of all the specialists called in that the girl would remain in this vegetative state indefinitely. The Emmotts were advised to place her in a nursing home and forget her.

The Emmotts did move Karen to Convalscent Children's Hospital, just outside Oklahoma City. But how could they forget her? Karen lay in a bed with side rails to keep her from falling to the floor. Her body's functions were mechanically maintained. One tube emerged from her nose, from her throat another. There was a catheter in her bladder and restraints on her arms and legs to prevent self-damage.

This was the Karen Emmott I was taken to see some months after the operation: a pathetic mindless creature whose own father told me, "I hold no hope."

The best scientific care already was being given the child. What help could I offer them here as a Christian? Against the best of man's wisdom, I could only say, " 'With men this is impossible; but with God all things are possible.'* Now let's see what we must do to get Karen better."

Dr. Emmott looked at me suspiciously. He was skeptical of hope that was not based on scientific data. I stood by Karen's bedside and suggested that although the girl was not mentally awake, she was spiritually awake, and we could contact this spiritual Karen through our prayers.

"I don't understand," said Mrs. Emmott.

I told Dr. and Mrs. Emmott of times that I had prayed aloud for an anesthetized patient who later remembered whole portions of the experience. I told of praying for a

---

* *Matthew 19:26; Mark 10:27*

young boy in a coma. Later he told his father how glad he was that someone had prayed for him.

"With Karen, too, we must not neglect this spiritual consciousness. On your part," I said to Mrs. Emmott, "bring Karen something pretty on your morning visits. Comb her hair. Talk to her about the day she will be coming home. No more despairing words in this room, Isabel." And to Dr. Emmott, I suggested, "How soon can she be free of all this?" I indicated the catheter, the feeding tube.

We enlisted the help of the nurses. "When you come in to straighten the bedclothes, say a prayer. Then talk about the signs of progress that you see. Talk to her as if she were hearing every word."

And myself? I received the parents' permission to pray for Karen then and there in the manner of the traditional Episcopal healing service. I admit that I was hoping desperately for some sign that would vindicate all I'd been saying. I reached down inside the side rails of the bed, put my hands on the tossing head and closed my eyes. "Oh Lord," I said to myself, "Jesus. Help me. . . ."

Then, aloud, I prayed that Karen be restored to perfect health.

The three of us stood intently around the bed, watching for the slightest change.

There was none. No relaxation, no hint of response.

Never have I felt so confused. Deep inside arose a question about the rightness of what I was doing.

Then I looked at the Emmotts. And suddenly, there on their faces, I saw the miracle I had been looking for, because in the eyes of these two parents was a powerful new light. The Emmotts were different. The tremendous energy of *hope* had entered their lives.

Now I knew we had a real chance.

My role in Karen's story was only that of a catalyst: the next day I had to return to my practice. How impatiently I waited for news that Karen was improving.

Then it came. The Emmotts telephoned to say that they were almost positive there was a change. Karen's ceaseless thrashing was slowing down. Within a week I heard again, she was resting more quietly.

"We're tremendously excited," Isabel said. "The next thing we're going to do is remove the catheter."

From that day on the Emmotts were rewarded with reason for the hope they had carried, at first, simply in faith. The miracle of Karen unfolded slowly, but it did unfold.

Every morning, day after day, week after week, Mrs. Emmott arrived at the convalescent home to continue her work with Karen. Every morning she met Karen with news from home, reports from school, stories of the funny things her baby brother did, messages from her friends. She reported them as if Karen could understand every word. She prayed, too, both in Karen's presence and at home.

The most pressing problem was getting Karen to take solid food. Swallowing was difficult; chewing seemed impossible. Each day Isabel tried to get a spoonful of baby food into Karen's mouth. And each day, after a heartbreaking struggle, Isabel would admit defeat and a nurse would administer tube feedings.

Karen dropped to 84 pounds. Suddenly it came to Isabel that perhaps she was not stepping out far enough on faith. Maybe Karen was not supposed to be eating strained foods.

What Isabel did next was completely unorthodox. First she got down on her knees and asked for guidance. Then she went to the kitchen and prepared one of Karen's favorites: a tuna fish sandwich.

Karen gobbled it down. She ate with better co-ordination in chewing and swallowing than Isabel had dreamed she could.

That was the end of the feeding tube: hamburgers and french fries, ice cream and hot dogs, all the foods loved by teen-agers became Karen's diet. She thrived on them.

"From now on," Dr. Emmott said, "we're going to assume that any change is a sign of progress."

Some of the signs were easier to read. One evening five months after the operation, Karen's father placed a ballpoint pen in her hand and she began to scribble on the bedsheet. Ecstatically the Emmotts handed her other familiar objects. They gave her a pair of sunglasses. She fumbled with them, then placed them over her eyes upside down.

"But then," Isabel wrote, "she took the glasses off and turned them right-side up and put them on. It's a miracle."

In January, the Emmotts brought Karen home. It was a momentous occasion. The five younger children joined with their parents in never doubting that someday Karen would be completely well. They joined them, too, in the long hours of teaching such simple tasks as putting on socks and tying shoes, tasks which now are well within Karen's ability.

Karen has much to learn from her family (which now includes a new baby brother), but they are beginning to wonder if it is not they who have the most to learn from her. I am sure it's true of me. Because little Karen Emmott has given me the answer to the question.

Yes—a doctor has a right to hold out hope to a patient. He has far more than a right: he has a duty.

When We Dare to Trust God
by Catherine Marshall

The Prayer of Relinquishment.

Like most people, when I first began active experimentation
with prayer, I was full of questions, such as: Why are some
agonizingly sincere prayers granted, while others are not?

Today I still have questions. Mysteries about prayer are
always ahead of present knowledge—luring, beckoning on to
further experimentation.

But one thing I do know; I learned it through hard experience. It's a way of prayer that has resulted consistently in
a glorious answer, glorious because each time power beyond
human reckoning has been released. This is the Prayer of Relinquishment.

I got my first glimpse of it in the fall of 1943. I had
then been ill for six months with a wide-spread lung infection, and a bevy of specialists seemed unable to help. Persistent prayer, using all the faith I could muster, had resulted
in—nothing. I was still in bed full time.

One afternoon a pamphlet was put in my hands. It was
the story of a missionary who had been an invalid for eight
years. Constantly she had prayed that God would make her
well, so that she might do His work. Finally, worn out with
futile petition, she prayed, "All right. I give up. If You want
me to be an invalid, that's Your business. Anyway, I want
You even more than I want health. You decide." In two
weeks the woman was out of bed, completely well.

This made no sense to me, yet I could not forget the
story. On the morning of September 14th—how can I ever
forget the date?—I came to the same point of abject acceptance. "I'm tired of asking," was the burden of my prayer.
"I'm beaten, through. God, You decide what You want for
me."

Tears flowed. I had no faith as I understood faith, ex-

196

pected nothing. The gift of my sick self was made with no trace of graciousness.

And the result? It was as if I had touched a button that opened windows in heaven; as if some dynamo of heavenly power began flowing, flowing. Within a few hours I had experienced the presence of the Living Christ in a way that wiped away all doubt and revolutionized my life. From that moment my recovery began.

Through this incident and others that followed, God was trying to teach me something important about prayer. Gradually, I saw that a demanding spirit, with self-will as its rudder, blocks prayer. I understood that the reason for this is that God absolutely refuses to violate our free will; that, therefore, unless self-will is voluntarily given up, even God cannot move to answer prayer.

In time, I gained more understanding about the Prayer of Relinquishment through the experiences of others in contemporary life and through books. Jesus' prayer in the Garden of Gethsemane is a pattern for us, I learned. Christ could have avoided the cross. He did not have to go up to Jerusalem that last time. He could have compromised with the priests, bargained with Caiaphas. He could have capitalized on His following and appeased Judas by setting up the beginning of an earthly kingdom. Pilate wanted to release Him, all but begged Him to say the right words—so that he might. Even in the Garden on the night of betrayal, He had plenty of time and opportunity to flee, but Christ used His free will to leave the decision up to His Father.

J. B. Phillips in his book on the Gospels brings Jesus' prayer into focus for us. "Dear Father, all things are possible to You. Please let me not have to drink this cup. Yet it is not what I want, but what You want."

The prayer was not answered as the human Jesus wished. Yet power has been flowing from His cross ever since.

Even at the moment when Christ was bowing to the possibility of an awful death by crucifixion, He never forgot either the presence or the power of God. The Prayer of Relinquishment must not be interpreted negatively. It does not let us lie down in the dust of a godless universe and steel ourselves just for the worse.

Rather it says: "This is my situation at the moment. I'll face the reality of it. But I'll also accept willingly whatever a loving Father sends." Acceptance therefore never slams the door on hope.

Yet even with hope our relinquishment must be the real thing, because this giving up of self-will is the hardest thing we human beings are ever called on to do.

I remember the agony of one attractive young girl, Sara B——, who shared with me her doubts about her engagement. "I love Jeb," she said, "and Jeb loves me. But the problem is, he drinks. Not that he's an alcoholic, you know. Yet the drinking is a sort of symbol of a lot of ideas he has. This has bothered me so much that I wonder if God is trying to tell me to give Jeb up."

As we talked, Sara came to her own conclusion. It was that she would lose something infinitely precious if she did not follow the highest and the best that she knew. Tears glistened in her eyes as she said, "I'm going to break the engagement. If God wants me to marry Jeb, He will see that things change—about the drinking and all."

Right then, simply and poignantly, she told God of her decision. She was putting her broken dreams into His hands.

Jeb's ideals didn't change, so Sara did not marry him. But a year later Sara wrote me an ecstatic letter. "It nearly killed me to give up Jeb. Yet God knew that he wasn't the one for me. Now I've met The Man and we're to be married. Now I *really* have something to say about trusting God! . . ."

It's good to remember that not even the Master Shepherd can lead if the sheep have not this trust and insist on running ahead of Him or taking side paths or just stubbornly refusing to follow Him. That's the why of Christ's insistence on the practical obedience: *And why call ye me, Lord, Lord, and do not the things which I say?** Our pliability must be complete, from our wills right on through to our actions.

When we come right down to it, how can we make obedience real, except as we give over our self-will in reference to each of life's episodes as it unfolds? That's why it shouldn't surprise us that at the heart of the secret of answered prayer lies the Law of Relinquishment.

So Mrs. Nathaniel Hawthorne, wife of the famous American author, found as she wrestled in prayer in the city of Rome one February day in 1860. Una, the Hawthorne's eldest daughter, was dying of a virulent form of malaria. The

---

* Luke 6:46

attending physician, Dr. Franco, had that afternoon warned that unless the young girl's fever abated before morning, she would die.

As Mrs. Hawthorne sat by Una's bed, her thoughts went to what her husband had said earlier that day. "I cannot endure the alternations of hope and fear; therefore I have settled with myself not to hope at all."

But the mother could not share Nathaniel's hopelessness. Una could not, must not die. This daughter strongly resembled her father, had the finest mind, the most complex character of all the Hawthorne children. Why should some capricious Providence demand that they give her up?

As the night deepened, the girl lay so still that she seemed to be in the anteroom of death. The mother went to the window and looked out on the piazza. There was no moonlight; a dark and silent sky was heavy with clouds.

"I cannot bear this loss—cannot—cannot . . ." Then suddenly, unaccountably, another thought took over. "Why should I doubt the goodness of God? Let Him take Una, if He sees best. I can *give* her to Him. No, I won't fight against Him anymore."

Then an even stranger thing happened. Having made the great sacrifice, Mrs. Hawthorne expected to feel sadder. Instead she felt lighter, happier than at any time since Una's long illness had begun.

Some minutes later she walked back to the girl's bedside, felt her daughter's forehead. It was moist and cool. Una was sleeping naturally. And the mother rushed into the next room to tell her husband that a miracle had happened.

Now the intriguing question is: what is the spiritual law implicit in this Prayer of Relinquishment?

Fear is like a screen erected between us and God, so that His power cannot get through to us. So, how does one get rid of fear?

This is not easy when the life of someone dear hangs in the balance, or when what we want most is involved. At such times, every emotion, every passion, is tied up in the dread that what we fear most is about to come upon us. Obviously only drastic measures can deal with such a gigantic fear and the demanding spirit that usually goes along with it. My experience has been that trying to deal with it by repeating faith affirmations is not drastic enough.

So then we are squarely up against the Law of Relinquishment. Was Jesus showing us how to use this law when

He said, *Resist not evil?** In God's eyes, fear is evil because it's an acting out of lack of trust in Him. So Jesus is advising: Resist not fear. (Note that He made only one exception to this: *Fear him*—(the Devil)—*which is able to destroy both soul and body in hell.***)

In other words, Jesus is saying, admit the possibility of what you fear most. And lo, as you stop fleeing, force yourself to walk up to the fear, look it full in the face—never forgetting that God and His power are still the supreme reality—the fear evaporates. Drastic? Yes. But it is one sure way of releasing prayer power into human affairs.

---

* Matthew 5:39
** Matthew 10:28

Why Me?
by William Gargan

The veteran actor tells how he found the answer to the question . . .

There's a question that, sooner or later, all of us seem to ask. When things go against us, when trouble comes or sickness or heartache, our hands go out in a gesture of bewilderment and we ask:

"Why me?"

Or perhaps you've heard it as "What have I done to deserve this?" Or "Why pick on me?"

Ten years ago it was my turn to complain to God in just those words—"Why me?"—and yet I could phrase them only in my mind. I lay in a Los Angeles hospital unable to talk. The only way I could communicate words was to write them. My larynx—or voice box—had been removed and I lay there deep, deep in depression. Here I was, an actor who could not speak. It was like being an athlete who could not run or a painter who could not see. For 35 years I'd been in the entertainment world, in movies, radio, stage, TV. Suddenly it was all over.

Yet, I was told I had reason to be cheerful.

"You're in good luck, Bill," the surgeon had said. "Cancer of the larynx is one of the most curable of all cancers. If discovered in time, we can save ninety percent of our patients." He smiled. "We got you in time."

It had been an odd quirk, finding that cancer in me. I had been playing in San Francisco in a drama about politics called *The Best Man*. Prophetically, I had the part of a president who was a cancer victim.

We were supposed to go on to Chicago, but the play was doing so well that the management decided to keep it in San Francisco for an additional two weeks. God works in wondrous ways. That decision saved my life. By waiting, we lost the theater in Chicago, and the show closed.

Back in Los Angeles, my wife, Mary, got after me. "You have the time now to get that throat of yours looked at," she said, forcing me to a doctor's office. For weeks I'd had a sore throat and couldn't shake it.

The doctor told Mary, not me, about the possibility of a malignancy, and for three days she carried that fear around in her heart. Then, just before I went to hear about the results of some medical tests, Mary tried to ease me into possible bad news. Even so, I was shocked when the verdict came. I had to make a choice, the doctor said. Operate and live; don't operate and die.

"When do you operate?" I asked angrily. I was so hurt by the news that I was mad.

"In a week or ten days," he replied. "You'll need time to put your affairs in order and . . ."

"I need twenty-four hours," I said forcefully. "If you can't take me then, I'm going down the street."

We settled on 36 hours.

It is true that when you know that death is near, life becomes intense and you live rapidly and deeply. And you learn things, too, which in all the years before you have not learned. I learned in the confusion of that day and a half that I was unafraid of death.

I didn't have far to go to talk to God in those 36 hours; He was no stranger. I talked to Him with the same prayer I have used each day for as long as I can remember:

Look down upon me, good and gentle Jesus, whilst before Thy face I humbly kneel, and with burning soul, pray and beseech Thee to fix deep in my heart, live sentiments of faith, hope and charity.

By the time I went into the operating room, I was calm and confident. I remember the last words I spoke. They were for Mary. I looked up at her. "I love you," I said.

And so the operation was a success, and there I lay in the hospital, totally depressed. I had not feared dying, but now I was afraid to live. Only a few days before my religion had been my strength but now, in self-pity, I began to weaken.

"Why me, God?" I asked with lips that brought forth no sound. "Is this some penance You're exacting for something I've done wrong?"

Every day, many times a day, I continued to say my

prayers, but in the gloom I suffered from the injustice I felt had been done me.

In a few weeks the doctor announced, "You're snapping back so fast, I'm going to make arrangements for your speech lessons."

I took out my pad and pencil. "Are you nuts?" I wrote.

"Esophageal speech," he said and went out.

"Never heard of it," I wrote on my pad, anyway.

So there I was propped up in bed looking like a chipmunk—my face was still puffed up from the operation—when a lady named Teckla Tibbs came in.

"I've come to let you hear what esophageal speech sounds like," she said in a hoarse, mechanical-sounding voice. I must have stared at her somewhat peculiarly. "You won't talk any better than I do, Bill, but at least," she said gruffly, "you'll talk like a member of your own sex!" Her eyes twinkled and for the first time in weeks I felt like laughing.

Teckla Tibbs went on to explain the basic facts of being a laryngectomee. She wore a large flat gold necklace around the lower part of her neck which covered the stoma or hole a surgeon had created in order to join the trachea to it. Since there was no longer any connection between the mouth or nose and the lungs, she breathed, coughed and sneezed through that opening. "To a large degree I've lost my sense of taste and smell, as you probably have," she told me, "but I can do almost anything I could do before—except swim."

It was the talking I wanted to learn about. She gave me some literature and after reading it, I began to feel the wonderful warmth of hope kindling inside me.

As soon as I was able to go home, the American Cancer Society telephoned, asking when I could come for my first speech lesson. I went immediately.

It was a grueling half hour in which I struggled in vain to make even the tiniest sound. Esophageal speech is a complicated process of developing false muscles, of forcing air into the esophagus so that its walls vibrate and cause a low-pitched sound. I'd take a sip of water and try to get the air down with it. I'd get the water down and eventually the air with it, but I couldn't produce the sound I was supposed to be able to make.

At home I practiced desperately. Day after day, Mary worked with me. "If you ask him a question and he doesn't try to speak, turn your back on him," the doctors told her.

Later, Mary said that was the hardest thing of all for her to do.

It got so that my friends would come in and work with me. Pat O'Brien, Jack Haley, Charlie Ruggles, Dennis Day, Ed Delaney—those guys spent hours trying to force a sound out of me. My old pal, Irving Pinsky of Queens, would call me long distance and demand that I talk to him.

In time, sounds came. First a gasp and a burp and then an "ah" and then an "ee," and then gradually I began to manipulate these "ahs" and "ees" and "ohs" into words.

Sixteen lessons later I graduated from speech class with a new voice. My teachers approved, but they urged me never to sing a song unless I wanted to empty a theater. Their joke suggested a problem which I had all but forgotten. I had a new voice, but it was not an actor's voice. How was I to spend my time?

Once again the American Cancer Society was on the phone. Would I make a speech on their behalf? This time it wasn't necessary to scribble out the question "Are you nuts?" I didn't ask it, either, but I wanted to. Still, I thought, nobody has misled me yet. They must know what they are doing.

"Sure," I agreed.

Once again I felt the excitement of stage fright. Some 20 people were there at a luncheon in Palm Springs when I was introduced. I was worried, not knowing if my voice would work or if I could be heard.

"Unaccustomed as I am to public speaking," I began. There was a laugh and I relaxed. I was home free.

After that the ACS asked if I would help in their fund-raising campaign. That year we managed to triple the quota in Palm Springs. Then I started speaking before "Lost Chord" clubs and other groups of laryngectomees the country over. There are approximately 20,000 of us in the United States today (about ten men to every one woman) and the clubs help new members over those first difficult months.

To sport my stuff again, to show off my special skill before newcomers and give them hope, was more thrilling to me than any play I'd ever been in.

Today I roam all over the country volunteering my services as a speaker. When I tell people that a checkup once a year and a close watch for the seven danger signals could cut cancer deaths by 50 percent, they're more inclined to follow my simple advice because of my raspy voice.

In this simple way, I am doing something to help others.

I believe that God forever is creating such opportunities for us, but often we are too involved in ourselves to grasp them. That's why the next time I'm inclined to complain with a petulant "Why me?"—I'll change that quickly to:

"Why not me, God?"

Desperate Enough
by Grace Perkins Oursler

A story that is now a part of American history.

The boy had fallen, running home after school, and skinned his knee in a briar patch. A simple scratch; there wasn't even a rent in his trousers. But by nightfall, the knee was swollen and was starting to ache. Nothing much, he still thought, being 13 and the son of a frontiersman. Besides, who on earth would lay down on chores because of a bothersome scratch? Ignoring the pain, he knelt in his nightgown and said his prayers, then climbed into bed in that upper room where he and his five brothers slept.

His ankle was swelling the next morning, but he still did not tell anyone. The farm kept the whole family relentlessly busy; always he had to be up at six with many assigned chores and jobs before school. And he must be thorough about them, with no sideswiping, or he would be sent back to do them all over again, no matter what else he had to miss, including meals. In their household, discipline was fair but stern.

Two mornings later the leg ached too badly for him to drag himself to the barn. That was a Sunday and he could remain behind, while the rest of the family drove into town. School homework finished, he sat in the parlor rocker, examining and comparing the three family Bibles; one in German that held the records of all their births and deaths; another in Greek that was his father's proud possession and finally the King James version shared by mother and all the sons.

One night this week it would be the boy's turn to lead the family devotions. He could select his own passages from the Old and New Testaments and read them aloud and try to get a discussion going; sometimes they became exciting. But now the pain blurred his attention; he put aside the Scriptures and dozed until his brothers returned from Sunday school.

Mom and Dad did not come home with them because Sunday was "parents' day off"; the boys cleared up the housework and cooked the big meal of the week, while Father and Mother stayed on in the village for the church service.

But by the time dinner was ready, the boy had given in and climbed back into bed. His left foot was turning black; shoe and stocking had to be cut off the swollen leg . . . Why on earth hadn't he told somebody? Go quick and fetch the doctor for your brother!

Mother bathed the knee, applied poultices and wiped the sweating forehead with a cloth that was moist and cool. She was an intense and vital creature, the only woman under this roof with her husband and six sons. Confronted with that angry wound, her manner remained serene. In a crisis there was never chatter, only quiet action. Mom had nursed her brood through accidents and ailments from toothaches to scarlet fever; one son she had lost, but that only made her calmer and more determined when she had to fight for the others. As the sick boy's eyes met hers, she gave him a smile and her small, tight hand gently shoved his cheek . . .

Old Dr. Conklin examined the leg and pursed his lips, as he pointed to a streak of red running from knee to heel:

"It's not likely we can save it!"

The invalid sat up stiffly.

"What's that mean?" he asked.

"It means," explained the doctor, as kindly as he knew how, "if things get any worse we'll most likely have to amputate."

"Not me!" stormed the boy. "I won't have it! You hear me? I'd rather die!"

His voice broke with an adolescent crack, but there was no adolescence in the eyes that defied the doctor's reproachful gaze. The eyes of mother and son met and held. She knew he meant what he said. He had all the plainsman's horror of being anything less than physically perfect and self-reliant.

Dr. Conklin snapped his false teeth, and stalked out, with a nod to the mother to follow him. And as he stood, explaining to both parents all that could and probably would happen, they heard the boy's voice calling for his brother:

"Ed! *Ed!* Come *to* me, won't you?"

And the elders could hear the older brother stamping in from the front yard; they watched him scoot past their whispering group into the sick room. And then, from behind the door came the sick lad's voice, high pitched with pain and eagerness: "If I go out of my head, Ed . . . don't let them cut off my leg, while I'm unconscious . . . Promise me, Ed— *promise . . ."*

"Imbecile fool boys!" breathed the doctor crossly, and would have gone on to argue, but the next moment Ed came out of the bedroom and strode down into the kitchen. Not a word was spoken until he returned.

"Ed—what's your brother asking for?" the mother inquired.

"Fork! To bite on, to keep from screaming."

After he went in, the boy's cries muffled down. Edgar came and stood outside the door, his arms folded. Father and mother looked at him with a sickening realization of a new problem to face. That was their son standing against the doorpost—but quite clearly he was on stoney guard.

Ed looked directly at old Dr. Conklin.

"Nobody's going to saw off that leg!" he announced.

"But Ed—it may mean death!" pleaded the doctor.

"Maybe so, doc. But I gave him my word."

And nothing changed that. If Ed had not stood his ground, father and mother might have yielded. Neither was yet convinced amputation was necessary, but they were doubtful. The adamant attitude first of the sick boy and then of his white faced, determined brother brought them up sharply with an almost incredible problem. Defiance of parental authority was unknown in this household. But there was Ed, leaning against the sickroom door—

"Guess we'll see how he looks by tonight, eh doc?" mother said softly.

Day and night Ed stood guard not even leaving to eat. He slept across the threshold, what little sleep he got, and only his mother was permitted in without every move being watched.

As the fever mounted, leaving the suffering boy babbling in a sweat of torment, the older brother grew gaunt. His eyes regarded the steadily mounting poisoning which climbed past the knee and reached, as the doctor foretold it would, the pelvis. But Ed was firm in his resolve, conscious of his promise to one who might be dying. The boy fully agreed with his kid brother; better to be dead than one-legged. His brother had made the choice—and he would have his will.

The parents could not make up their own minds. But they knew the younger one would hate them if they permitted the amputation. And so Edgar's attitude was decisive. The doctor, in helpless outrage, uttered the ugly word "murder" and slammed out with the verdict that "nothing but a miracle could save the boy now!"

Mother, father and son-on-guard shared the same thought as they looked at each other with dry-socketed glances. The dying boy's grandfather had been a vigorous and inspiring minister, farmer-leader of a religious community known as the River Brethren Colony in Pennsylvania. *He* had believed, and with good reason, in faith healings.

Without a word the three went on their knees. They were desperate enough—to turn to God.

They prayed, taking turns in leading one another in supplication. Father, mother,—and now even Edgar—would rise and go about the farm work and rejoin the continual prayer. One brought in a Bible and occasionally read a passage. During the night, outside the room, the other four brothers from time to time would kneel and join the prayers.

At early dawn the faithful doctor stopped by. His experienced eye saw a sign. He crept nearer the bed and leaned over. The knee swelling was going down. Dr. Conklin closed his eyes and made a rusty prayer of his own—a prayer of thanksgiving.

He went quietly off, leaving the family still at prayer. As the boy dropped into a normal sleep, one member after another kept the vigil.

It was nightfall again and the lamps were lighted when the boy opened his eyes. The swelling was way down, now; the discoloration almost faded away. By morning he could bend his knee.

And in three days, pale and weak, but with eyes clear and voice strong, the boy could stand up again.

And Ike Eisenhower was ready to face life.

PRAYER FOR A YOUNG SOLDIER

Lord, he is far away from home,
This is the first time on his own;
If he is torn and tempest-blown,
Comfort him, Lord, tonight.

May he feel for his country the same deep pride
As those before him who fought and died
To keep it free; but let him bide
In safety, Lord, tonight.

Whatever he sees of sadness and wrong,
May his trust in Thee stay sure and strong;
May he face the world with a smile and a song.
Bless him, O Lord, tonight.

Keep him from loneliness, fear, and despair;
Let him remember the joys that we share;
Wherever he is, as I make this prayer,
Lord, send him my love tonight!

BONNIE BIRD
Westfield, New Jersey

Thanks for the Miracle!
by Tony Conigliaro

He let go with a fast ball, high and tight, too tight. The ball slammed against my left temple, and I went down in a heap.

Things were going great. It was the middle of August, 1967, and my team, the Boston Red Sox, was on its way to the American League pennant, the club's first since 1946. To make it even sweeter, we had finished ninth the year before, so our comeback was to become the greatest in the history of baseball.

Personally, I was in my fourth season in the major leagues and having one of my best years. I had hit 20 home runs and was batting around .280 with six weeks to go. I felt I had an outside chance of reaching my 1965 homer output—32, tops in the league that year. Here I was, only 22 years old, playing right field for the team I had idolized as a kid and having a ball—on and off the field.

Then suddenly on the night of August 18, the roof fell in on me.

We were playing the California Angels in Boston, and Jack Hamilton, a hard-throwing right-hander, was pitching. When I came up to bat in the third inning, I checked the boxes behind our first-base dugout to make sure my family had made it to the game. Mom, Dad and my brothers, Billy and Ritchie, had come into town from Swampscott, Massachusetts, and when they saw me looking their way, they gave me a big wave. I smiled back.

Stepping into the batter's box, I took a couple of practice swings and then set myself, waiting for Hamilton's first pitch. He let go with a fast ball, high and tight, too tight. The ball slammed against my left temple, and I went down in a heap. Though I was wearing a plastic batting helmet for protection, it was not equipped with a side flap, so my skull absorbed the full shock.

Grabbing my head, I squeezed it hard, trying to stop the shriek that filled it, and at the same time I was gasping for breath. There wasn't any air; it was as if I were strangling. "Oh, God," I prayed, "let me breathe. Let me live." A few minutes later they carried me into the locker room where Dad and Billy and Ritchie had come from the stands.

I heard Dad's voice, but couldn't find him. Everything was dark. Then I realized that I was blind.

"I can't see, Dad," I said anxiously.

"Take it easy, son," he answered, taking my hand. "You'll be all right."

"Sure you will," echoed Buddy LeRoux, the trainer, but in muffled tones I heard them whispering and I knew that my face must be a swollen mess. At the hospital, X-rays showed that I had a broken cheekbone, but I was more concerned with my sight.

Doctors, however, assured me that the blindness I was experiencing was normal. "It and the internal bleeding will clear up in a few days."

"Thank God," said Mom in a response that was full of a gratefulness we all felt.

Mother has been the spiritual counselor for our family for as long as I can remember, reminding us of our obligation to God. Grace at meals, bedtime prayers, church every Sunday all came like clockwork at our house because of her. So prayer was no stranger to me that night, and I asked God to make me well, but I tried to suggest that He hurry. I had to get back to the ball team.

My prayers were reinforced many times, I was to learn later. From all over the country came letters from fans who said they were praying for me.

Though sight returned to my right eye in about 48 hours, it was seven days before my left eye opened. When it did, the doctors discovered a blister had formed on it and then broken. A perforated retina resulted, and there was a strong possibility it would be permanently damaged. With this news, I began to really worry.

"What about baseball?" I asked. "I can't hit a ball seeing like this." Everything was blurred, and the sight in my left eye measured 20–300.

"We'll just have to wait and see," the doctors advised, avoiding telling me what they really felt.

Now, I'd played sports all my life and I had been in some tight spots before. "When the going gets tough, the tough get going," I told myself. If I went into a batting slump, I would go out to the park early for several days and take extra practice. Hard work, willpower, concentration, determination—they all had worked before.

Slowly, however, I discovered I was up against a new kind of problem. The World Series rolled around, and I was still stumbling over blades of grass. What a tough pill to swallow that was, watching my team in the World Series and not being able to play. Some players wait a lifetime for the experience. Still, I thought I'd be back in the lineup by spring training.

After the Series I went with some athletes to Vietnam to visit our servicemen in hospitals there. I suspect Joe DiMaggio and Jerry Coleman, the ex-Yankee greats, invited me to go along for my own therapy as much as for the troops', but regardless, I went and was glad I did. There I saw something that really jolted me—thousands of young guys about my age maimed for life, but they seemed to accept their situations with a courage and faith that put mine to shame.

I shall never forget one encounter—walking up to one young soldier who was in traction with his head just a ball of white bandages. Doctors had told me that his face had been shot away and that he would never see again. I tried to carry on a conversation with him, but a watermelon lump kept coming into my throat that made it impossible. Finally I took his hand and mumbled, "Stay in there pitching, Bob."

As I turned to go, he called after me, "Tony, how's *your* eyesight?"

Imagine—this guy blinded for life being concerned about a blur in one of my eyes. Something happened at that instant that shook me in a way I won't ever forget. God was trying to tell me something through that wounded soldier— that whether I ever played ball again or not, life went on and I had to find my place in it.

Yet baseball was my occupation, and I continued to pray for a healing so I could play again.

I struggled through the long winter, trying not to be bitter at the thought I would never play again. I wasn't mad at Jack Hamilton who had hit me. It wasn't his fault. Getting hit is sometimes a part of baseball. Nor did I feel that God had brought this on me. All I knew was that I was angry with frustration.

When spring-training time arrived, I went South and tried to play ball again, but there was nothing I could do right. At the plate, I swung and missed balls by a foot. The other players and coaches tried to be encouraging, but they couldn't fool me. I was pathetic and knew it. So I went back to Boston, where I had another examination.

"If anything, your sight is getting worse," the doctors said. I walked out of the building in a daze.

Face it, Tony, you're through, a voice inside me said. *Don't give up, have faith,* argued another. It was about this time that I had a chat with Father Johnson, my athletic director at St. Mary's High School in Lynn, Massachusetts, where I had played football, baseball and basketball.

"Don't let your heart grow cold toward God, Tony. Don't blame anyone. Be patient. Have faith and continue to ask for His healing."

"But it would take a miracle," I protested.

"Then," he answered calmly, "we will pray expecting a miracle."

I tried, but it was not easy.

The summer dragged on. I went out to the ball park in the mornings and worked out with a pitching coach, thinking I might be able to make a comeback as a pitcher. I had done some pitching in high school and thought it might be easier than hitting. But when the doctors heard about it, they told me I might be endangering my eyesight, so I had to quit. After that I stayed away from the ball park. I couldn't bear to watch a game and not play myself.

Near the end of the season, however, my doctor advised me that my eye problem had stabilized and gave me permission to go to Florida and try pitching in an instructional league. My pitching was lousy, but amazingly I found I could hit the ball again. It was only against minor-league players, and there is a big difference, but it was enough encouragement that I went back to Boston and the Retina Foundation. There Dr. Charles Regan examined my left eye and exclaimed:

"I can't believe it. We've got a small miracle on our hands. Your vision is normal." Then, with a smile he added, "You must have been saying your prayers."

"Every day for a year," I answered.

That still didn't mean that I could win back my job on the Red Sox. Many players, after being hit, become gun-shy and aren't able to stand up to the plate without flinching. It has nothing to do with fear—it's psychological. I'd have to wait until spring training to find out.

In Florida the spring of 1969, I put on my spikes again and gave it a try. Everything felt all right, and I didn't have any trouble seeing the ball. But my timing was way off, and I had to begin a terribly slow relearning process.

Then came the day in Tampa when I hit my first home run since the accident. It was a big turning point. After that my confidence grew, and improvement came more rapidly.

On opening day I was in the starting lineup in Baltimore, and what a thrill it was to be back! Any other year it would have been sort of routine, starting another seven-month season, but this time I was full of excitement. It was my rookie year all over again.

In the tenth inning, with the score tied, I came to bat against Baltimore pitcher Pete Richert. He delivered one over the heart of the plate, letter high. It was just the pitch I'd been waiting for, and I could tell the way the ball left the bat it was on its way: a game-winning home run!

That was a tremendous thrill, but there was still a bigger one in store for me a week later when we had our home opener in Boston. Fenway Park was packed. Mom and Dad and Ritchie and Father Johnson were in the stands. And my brother Billy was playing alongside me in the outfield that afternoon.

When I came up to bat the first time (the first time in Fenway Park since I had been hurt), the crowd rose to its feet and let go with one of the most deafening roars I ever have heard. I tipped my helmet and stepped up to the plate, but the din grew louder. The fans stamped and shouted and applauded more.

"Step out, Tony," the umpire said, waving me out of the batter's box. "You might as well let them get it out of their systems."

It's a good thing he called time, because I had something wet in my eyes and I couldn't have hit a pumpkin right then, let alone a baseball.

"Thank you," I kept saying over and over. It seemed so inadequate, but it expressed everything I had in my heart. "Thank you. Thank you for your prayers. Thank you, God, for a miracle."

The Healing of Memories
by Agnes Sanford

---

*Even bad memories can be expunged, says this
authority on prayer and healing.*

Shortly after World War II, I used to go to an army hospital at visiting hours and walk through the wards listening
for what the Lord would have me do. So I once spoke to a
young German-born American soldier who had been bedfast
for two years.

His leg, riddled by shrapnel, was so full of osteomyelitis
and so easily broken that he'd been consigned to the incurable ward. "I know something that might help you get well," I
told him. "Would you like me to tell you about it?"

"I'm washed up this way," he said. "So you might as
well."

I explained to John the reality of God's healing power,
and then I prayed for the healing of his leg. At first it seemed
that God touched him in a most wonderful way. Within days
the doctors were speaking of a change that had begun to take
place. Soon he was on crutches. Within six weeks John—incurable John—was dismissed from the hospital.

Yet some months later, on one of my habitual visits, I
found him in another ward, back in traction. "It broke
again," he explained. "I was discouraged for a few days, but
then I figured there was something else God wanted me to
know."

And so there was. There were wounds in John's mind
deeper than the wounds in his body. I began to suspect that
unless we were able to reach these mind-wounds and heal
them, John would forever be breaking that leg. "I'll be doing
fine," he told me, "and then all of a sudden my feelings
change. I fly into a rage. Once, just before I broke my leg
again, I got so mad I picked up a typewriter and threw it on
the floor."

Well, this was quite a challenge to me. I gave John the New Testament, and the book greatly helped him; but still he suffered these fits of rage. I continued to pray for him in every way I knew. I prayed for an emotional healing—of the depression which made him break down and throw things. That did not work. I prayed for forgiveness—of the sin of a bad temper. That prayer did not help either. So I gave up trying to figure it out and said, "Lord, how *shall* I pray?"

It came to me that the trouble was not in the young man who lay in the hospital bed before me today, but in the little boy he had once been. That is, in the little boy who had grown up under the Nazi regime, the little boy whose father was in one concentration camp and whose mother was in another. He could not fight back, for the enemy was too strong. When Hitler Youth threw stones at him, he could not throw them back. So John held in his rage until, years later, it exploded and he threw typewriters.

"Yes, Lord," I said. "But how can I pray for that disturbed child? He is no longer here."

And deep within myself the Lord seemed to answer, "Yes he is. In John."

"But all that happened years ago."

Shatteringly, unbelievable, the Lord answered with a thought which set me on an entirely new prayer adventure: *There is no time.*

In Christ there is no time! "Yesterday, today and forever. . . ." Yes, I had read that in the Bible, but what did it mean? And then I saw. It meant that if in faith I opened the door to the past, Jesus Christ could go through that door and heal the wounds He found there.

Bit by bit, as I listened, I began to grasp this mystery. Christ came knowing that in the depths of men there are hidden wounds. He undertook to plumb these depths and to heal these wounds. Who can tell the anguish He underwent as He drew into Himself all the trouble of mankind: the sorrow and bitterness, the resentment and rage. Into these griefs He walked, taking them to Himself so that He might turn them into joy.

But why, if this is so, do we often walk heavily burdened, as John was doing? Why are all our old wounds not healed at once at confession?

Because He gave us free will. He will not come in uninvited, even to heal. We have to invite him into our wounds as they are recognized.

Moreover, as I struggled with these questions, Christ led me to see that it is often difficult for the one who needs healing to ask Him into the places where he is hurt, for his faith is too long weakened by suffering. But I could. In Christ's name I could open to John a door that he could not open himself.

I knew that it was impossible to do this in my own strength, so I undertook this work of prayer through the communion service. In faith one morning I went forward to receive the redeeming power of Christ not for myself but for a little boy who lived long ago. I was quite sure, as I walked back to my pew, that Christ was even then reaching little John. So I gave thanks for a child who was now healed.

In a few days I heard from John. "What has happened to me? All of a sudden I feel entirely different. And somehow I know that those old feelings of rage will never come back."

And John was right. In spite of the usual ups and downs of life, the rage has never come back, and neither has he broken his leg again.

This, then, is how I first ventured into prayer for the healing of memories. I soon discovered that there were two kinds of buried experiences that need to be dealt with: occasions when we have been sinned against, and occasions when we ourselves have sinned. Memories of our own sins are especially difficult to reach because of our ego. But the healing process is the same. When we allow the love of Christ to reach the depths of memory, a miracle takes place. Suddenly we recall an experience that used to make us ashamed or fearful and remember it with joy. For the memory is cleansed. "Thank the Lord," we can now say. "That experience no longer has the power to hurt."

Few people, however, reach this freedom without help from another human being. I've found that it's possible to act as this "other human being" through the written word. There is a prayer* below which people often find helpful as a guide to their own healing. If you are in need of healing remembered experiences, I should like you to join me in a simple and yet dynamic experiment with this prayer.

First, go through the following prayer to personalize it. Make it fit your own situation. For instance, when you speak of opening closed doors to "see if there be any dirty or bro-

---

* From *The Healing Gifts of the Spirit*, Lippincott, Philadelphia.

ken thing that is no longer needed," you will want to be specific.

Here is the prayer:

"Lord Jesus, I ask You to enter this person who has need of Your healing. I rejoice that as the light of Your love now fills this mansion of the soul, all darkness shall flee. Look and see, O Lord, whether there be any ugly pictures on the walls—pictures of old distressful and horrifying wounds of the past. And if there be such pictures, take them down and give to this memory-house pictures of beauty and joy.

"Go back, O Lord, through all the rooms of this memory-house. Open every closed door and see if there be any dirty and broken thing that is no longer needed. And if so, O Lord, take it away completely. Go back even to the years of childhood. Open windows long sealed and let in the gentle sunlight of Your love. Take a broom of mercy and sweep away the shame of ancient memories.

"Follow the soul of this Your child all the way back to the hour of birth and heal even the pain and fear of being born. I pray that You will restore this soul as You made it and will quicken it in all those creative impulses that You have placed therein, so that Your purpose may be fulfilled.

"I give thanks, O Lord, knowing that this healing of the soul is Your will and is the very purpose for giving of Your life for us . . . and that therefore it is even now being accomplished."

I suggest you might want to read the prayer through aloud, for this will have the effect of beginning to externalize your memories. Then, find a quiet time and slowly, confidently, allow the Lord to begin coming into your still-living past.

You can end with a word of praise, for when He heals our memories, they are really healed.

ANSWERED PRAYER

I asked God for strength, that I might achieve;
  I was made weak, that I might learn humbly to obey . . .
I asked for health, that I might do greater things;
  I was given infirmity, that I might do better things . . .
I asked for riches, that I might be happy;
  I was given poverty that I might be wise . . .
I asked for power, that I might have the praise of men;

I was given weakness, that I might feel the need of God . . .
I asked for all things, that I might enjoy life;
  I was given life, that I might enjoy all things . . .
I got nothing that I asked for—but everything I had hoped for.
  Almost despite myself, my unspoken prayers were answered.
I am, among all men, most richly blessed.

SOURCE UNKNOWN

"I'll Walk Home"
by Dr. Howard A. Rusk

---

*Juan Yepez from Bolivia is a courageous boy
whose faith, determination and good humor won
the hearts of people in two countries.*

They didn't speak much, the two men who stood waiting at
New York's Idlewild Airport that January morning in 1955.
They were too busy sorting out their anxious thoughts about
the passenger due to arrive from La Paz, Bolivia.

James Simon, the therapist into whose care the visitor
would come, was picturing the peculiar problems that lay
ahead. Big, strapping Ike Johnson, the driver who had met
dozens of planes before, was musing how he'd never met a
passenger like this one. Miles away, sitting in my office in
Manhattan, I was gazing at the clock; I, too, was trying to
look ahead. As Director of the Institute of Rehabilitation
Medicine, a unit of the New York University Medical Center, I was pondering whether my staff and I really could meet
the challenge we had so confidently accepted: to guide one
small, helpless human being to a life of usefulness and dignity.

The airliner taxied in and stopped. A ramp was rolled
up and a hatch door was opened. Ike Johnson hurried up the
stairs and into the plane's cabin. At last he reappeared with
Juan Irigoyen Yepez in his arms. The lad was being carried
because he had been born into this world with neither arms
nor legs.

Nine-year-old Juan was a *mestizo,* a boy of Spanish and
Incan heritage, and the face that peered over Ike Johnson's
shoulder that morning was a darkly handsome one. It was
also a face of bewilderment. In La Paz they had told Juan of
the impending trip to New York and that he might be gone
as long as eight months. But it was hard for a small boy to
understand where New York was—another part of La Paz,

Juan had thought at first, or perhaps a nearby village. He had cried and cried.

In the car driving into Manhattan, his firm body was still shivering, but his eyes were searchlights of curiosity. Juan's only words of English were "please" and "thank you" so communication was difficult, but by the time they reached the hospital, Juan had relaxed; the trip was over; he was ready for the next adventure.

That adventure, of course, was to belong to all of us. We had to create a set of what are technically called prostheses, mechanical arms and legs. The cost in effort and talent and money would be enormous, much of it to be paid for by such friends as Mary Boyle who only two weeks before had spied pictures of Juan on my desk. I had told this lovely lady, lifetime secretary to Bernard Baruch, about Juan and had added, sadly, that no funds were available to bring Juan to our Institute. "Oh, yes, there are!" she said. Then and there she had pledged her own personal financial aid.

There were to be other gifts, too, from the Simon Baruch Foundation and others, and from just plain people who wanted to help. And in negotiations with the Bolivian government I had told the Vice President, Dr. Hernán Siles Zuazo, "If we train this boy, it will cost a very large fee." Somewhat taken back, he asked what that fee would be. "If we demonstrate what we can do with the most severely disabled boy one can find," I said, "you, in turn, will see that a center is established in La Paz for other handicapped children."

The Vice President of Bolivia agreed.

Juan's faultless balance came from strong feet which from birth had been attached directly to his hips—and strong hands attached to his shoulders. His fingers were so nimble that he had taught himself to eat with them by leaning toward his plate—his only achievement in selfcare. All of us were astounded to find that Juan could roll himself wherever he wanted to go—as fast as the rest of us could walk. To accomplish this "spinning"—a feat not possible to other humans—nature had given him what doctors call a "secondary gain;" he could spin his body over the floor or ground without getting dizzy or sick.

Juan's childhood memories were checkered ones. He recalled primitive huts with dirt floors and of being locked in a grassy compound, alone and unattended. His mother would leave food where he could roll to get it while she was away for the day at work. But there were happy times, too. He knew what it was like to play with other children, and to be loved by his doting American friends, Dr. and Mrs. Beck, at the hospital where he had been a "boarder" after his mother died. Then there was Ann Wasson, a European living in Bolivia, who all but adopted him and arranged his trip to New York through the Save the Children Federation. And there was the surgeon from Kansas City, Dr. Terry E. Lilly, who wrote to me asking if something could be done to give this bright, unusual boy a chance at normal living.

When Juan arrived in New York, doctors formed a consultation committee including medical specialists, therapists, nurses and engineers. There were weeks of examination, of study, of discussions. Then came months of trial-and-error experiments. Juan was always helpful, always eager. Meanwhile he picked up English rapidly.

The Institute became Juan's busy home and playground. He was always the first to sense the terrible approach of homesickness in the children's ward. The head nurse there, Thelma Mihalov, came to realize that Juan's was the steadying hand of the older brother in her ward, even though he was often younger and littler than the youngster he comforted. Again and again I myself saw him display the compassion which is the hallmark of the afflicted, another of their secondary gains.

The first crude limbs we made for Juan were whittled out of wood. He rocked on them like a wooden soldier. "They won't work," Juan told us. And they didn't. We learned that Juan's judgment was always sound; we soon sought his opinions first.

A second set of prostheses were fashioned for him on entirely different engineering principles. And then others. And others.

A year passed.

Each set of prostheses meant hard and painful work on Juan's part, but each time we failed, Juan would be the first to shrug and smile his hopes for the next time.

One day two children in the ward were talking about "when we go home next week."

"When do *you* go home?" one of them asked Juan, who was sitting on the windowsill watching the cars on East River Drive.

"I only go home when I *walk* home," he replied with determination.

There were times, of course, when Juan's spirits would darken. Jim Simon, or Thelma Mihalov or social service worker Kay Perfect, who was especially close to Juan, were ready when the blues set in. However, his concern was always some normal kidlike disappointment or frustration because people refused to treat him as anything other than a handicapped child. "Some people try to make me feel handicapped," he confided to me, "but I know better than that." To Juan, the handicapped people of the world were handicapped in their spirits, not in their bodies.

Some 17 months after Juan came to us, and after four different sets of prostheses had failed, Juan was strapped into a sort of bucket seat which sat atop mechanical legs. With specially designed crutches, he grasped a small bar on the molded plastic hand sockets. He knew instinctively what to do. Summoning the power in his unusually strong shoulders he could swing his torso in a gait that lifted his body until, both legs swinging, he then caught his balance, repeated the swing through and away he went. Juan could walk!

He soon developed the skills that made it possible for him to walk as fast as a normal person. There were also special joint mechanisms developed so that he could unlock his knees without help. These made it possible for him to sit down.

Only years later were we to recognize that these prostheses were of far greater significance than any of us had realized. When over 5,000 babies were born deformed by the tranquilizer drug Thalidomide, Juan's prostheses were patterns waiting to help those very children.

"Many times," Juan said to Kay Perfect one day, "I have asked, 'What purpose have I in the world?' I believe God has a purpose for all men. But mine? And then come the times when He shows me that I can help others—maybe even more than if I had arms and legs."

As Juan gradually learned the difficult techniques of dressing and washing and caring for himself, and later how to telephone, type, and even drive a car, he walked each day to Sacred Heart School a few blocks away. He was a fair student, popular, mischievous and happy. But he was growing older.

"I think we coddle him too much," Kay Perfect said to me. "Juan must learn more about this independence we are giving him."

Juan's old friends, the Becks, were living now in California. It was arranged for him to go there to attend high school in Pomona, and later to take a two-year course at Pacific College. Whenever possible he returned to us for his vacation.

We knew that the time would come when Juan would have to leave us and return to Bolivia. We also knew that he had to have a job waiting for him. One day Ann Wasson in Bolivia arranged for us to meet the director of the United Nations' computer program for Bolivia's nationalized tin industry, Morton Kahl. When he learned that Juan was the champion chess player at the Institute he knew he had the basic aptitudes for computer programming. Soon Juan took the IBM aptitude tests, passed them, and began an intensive course in computer programming. Completing this, Juan was offered a well paid position in the Bolivian tin industry.

Twelve years had passed. It was the first day of December, 1967, and a group of us gathered at the airport. Jim Simon was there and Ike Johnson and many doctors, nurses, friends, photographers, TV men.

"How do you feel about going home again?" asked a reporter.

"I'm excited," Juan said. "And happy . . . and scared."

Juan was scared because, once again, he was heading into a new world. New York was his home, not La Paz. But he was ready. He would not fail us, or his countrymen or himself.

"Have a good trip and a happy landing," I said. Then I hugged him. "We all love you very much."

He looked up at me but he could not speak. I couldn't either. But I finally admonished, "If you don't write, I'll haunt you."

"I'll write."

Kay Perfect went aboard the plane with him. She had written ahead, specifying "a seat near the bulkhead with leg room." He was prepared to walk off that plane when it arrived in Bolivia.

And so Juan Yepez flew away, ready for the job awaiting him, equipped to live alone if he chose, eager to help out in the rehabilitation hospital established in La Paz while he was away. La Paz would be out to meet him—officials, doctors, Ann Wasson, Indians from the mountains, hundreds of eager new friends. Juan was no longer just a little boy without arms or legs in a far-away country. He had become a symbol of life's insistence, of people helping people, a passion built from compassion; the essence of goodness in the human spirit.

The Fire or the Scrap Heap?
by Arthur Godfrey

Millions were praying for the man behind the voice that everyone recognizes.

On the walls of my office in New York hang a number of wise sayings I have had lettered and framed. Most of them are well known, but one is not.

It reads:

The fire, Lord, not the scrap heap.

I hung it there to remind me of a story. There was once a blacksmith who had great faith in God in spite of a lot of sickness in his life. An unbeliever asked him one day how he could go on trusting in a God who let him suffer.

"When I make a tool," the blacksmith answered, "I take a piece of iron and put it into the fire. Then I strike it on the anvil to see if it will take temper. If it does, I can make a useful article out of it. If not, I toss it on the scrap heap and sell it two pounds to the penny. Maybe God tests us like this. When suffering has come my way, I know that I've come out the better for it, so much so that I can honestly say, 'Put me in the fire, Lord, if that's what it takes, just don't throw me on the scrap heap.'"

I like this story because it suggests a creative way of looking at things that seem to be pure disaster. It tells me something about this stubborn hunk of iron and the fires through which I personally have passed.

My first fire came when I was 28 years old. I had a radio announcing job in Washington, D. C., then, and I liked to take the night shift so that during the day I could drive out to the old Congressional Airport and fly a Franklin glider.

I was headed there one bright September morning in 1931, driving a 1926 Chrysler on narrow Riggs Road, when suddenly a truck coming the other way crossed the center line and hit me, head-on. It happened so quickly there wasn't time

227

to touch the brakes or turn the wheel. I remember the sound of crashing glass, the sight of a hot engine on the seat beside me and then nothing more for a full week.

The two guys in the truck came away with scratches, but when the police found me in the ditch beside the road they thought I was dead.

At the hospital a team of surgeons put back the pieces: four broken ribs, a hole in one lung, two smashed kneecaps, dislocated right hip, fractures of the right hip socket, left femur driven through its socket, 27 fractures in the pelvis, and other odds and ends of lesser consequence.

As I said, I was out about a week. When I came to one night I thought I was lying in my casket at my own funeral. There were flowers all over the place (sent in by radio listeners) and somewhere I could hear someone praying. Then I listened to the words and knew I was alive because the voice—a girl's—was asking God not to let me die. Later I wondered if the voice and the prayer weren't a dream, but the doctor told me that the same student nurse prayed over me every night during the time I was unconscious.

Anyway, when I became fully conscious, I discovered a cast from my collarbone to my feet. And there I stayed while the weeks stretched into months. Worse than the pain was the idleness: nothing to do all day and all night but listen to the radio beside my bed until 3 a.m. when the last West Coast stations signed off for the night.

And it was there, chained to the receiving end of the box that I'd only worked behind up till then, that I learned something which was to change my life. Something I might never have had an ear to hear if it hadn't been for that period of captive listening.

One day one of those "hello-out-there-you-in-radio-land" announcers read a commercial as if he were reciting Shakespeare through a megaphone to a full house at Yankee Stadium. "Heck, Buddy," I thought, "you don't have to shout. It's only me."

And suddenly I wondered if it weren't always "only me." Weren't radio announcers (me included) making a mistake in imagining we were addressing great numbers of people? In the aggregate, perhaps, but that was an abstraction that had no existence in reality. Wasn't the reality always one person listening to another one: the invalid in his bed, the salesman in his automobile, the housewife at her ironing board? I resolved that when I returned to radio I would in the future address myself to one person alone, as if I were actually standing right next to him.

The discovery I made in a Washington hospital bed transformed my career. I left the hospital four months after the accident, crippled, on crutches, but a tool sharpened a little better to do the work that lay ahead.

There have been other fires in my life, of course, and in every case it has seemed at the time that no conceivable good could come of it. This last time the name of the fire was cancer. In 1959 a pain sent me scurrying for an X-ray which revealed the presence of a tumor, not in the solar plexus where the pain was, but seven or eight inches above and a little to the left of center. Tests proved it malignant.

Fear has an antidote: hope—and this is what came to me now in cards and letters from every corner of the country. "I pray for you every day." "Keep it up, Arthur, we're all pulling for you."

A competent, courageous surgeon removed the cancerous lobe, and here I am as good as ever. Not exactly as good as ever: a little better. For in the fire, subtle changes took place.

During my first 58 years I think I took the gift of life a little lightly. Now I resolved to use my time better. I became a student again: art, music, literature, French. I've tried to do something about my hostilities and prejudices. I try to contribute something every day to the betterment of mankind.

That reads kinda tritely stupid, but that's the general idea. It could be, y'know, that the Man Upstairs had a little something in mind. What if He wanted me to tell the millions who follow TV and radio that cancer is not necessarily a sentence of death? What if, through me, He wanted to put this list of cancer danger signals in your hands?

Why then, I can look back at my bout with cancer and agree with the blacksmith: the fires we pass through are not to burn us up, but just to make us worth keeping on this good earth a little longer.

SEVEN DANGER SIGNS OF CANCER

1. Unusual bleeding or discharge.
2. A lump or thickening in the breast or elsewhere.
3. A sore that does not heal.
4. Change in bowel or bladder habits.
5. Hoarseness or cough.
6. Indigestion or difficulty in swallowing.
7. Change in a wart or mole.

Dark Night of the Soul
by Ray Cripps

---

*J.B. Phillips—whose translations of the Scriptures
have illumined them for people the world over—
tells of a time when his own faith wavered.*

Twenty minutes after I had driven up in front of J.B.
Phillips' Swanage, England, home, I was hearing a story from
him that I never expected to hear. My image of this great
Bible translator was comparable to the solid, gray stones
from which his house was built. He was in my mind a spiritual giant, invulnerable and unshakable. My interview revealed another side to this beloved man. But let me start at
the beginning.

When I rang the doorbell a woman answered and in
spite of the cotton housedress, I knew by the warmth of her
smile that this would be Mrs. Phillips.

"Come in, please," she said. "Jack is in his library. He'll
be right with you."

"Jack" is what J.B. Phillips is called by his friends.
When he came in, moments later, I had the feeling that I was
one of them, that I had known this kind-faced man all of my
life. He, too, was dressed casually, and his smile was as contagious as his wife's.

"Won't you come out to my hideaway?" said Dr. Phillips. He led the way outside again, and I saw, a little to my
surprise, that his library was in a separate building. The library itself was cozy and warm and in my mind's eye I saw
Dr. Phillips at work here, translating ancient Greek texts into
English as contemporary and gripping as tomorrow's news.

Almost from the first our interview took a direction I
could never have anticipated. I had heard about Dr. Phillips'
recent illness, of course, and he seemed to want to talk about
it. Yet not the physical illness, with its dizzy spells, but the
spiritual illness.

231

Was I hearing right?

"It's truly a devastating thing, you know," said Dr. Phillips, "to be ill in your innermost spirit. For the past four years I have been going through what many old-time writers on spiritual matters call 'the dark night of the soul.' That's perhaps too strong a term for it, but I've certainly come to know that the Devil—whom I believe to be real—can make all sorts of devious attacks upon us."

Dr. Phillips' time of testing really began years ago with the quite unexpected success of his writings. Phillips was a parish priest when he began "Letters to Young Churches," his translation of the Epistles. He started the work in 1941, largely for the sake of young people attending his church in London during the dreadful days of the blitz.

"I discovered," he said, "that to many of these young people the Authorized Version of the Bible, and particularly Paul's letters, were completely unintelligible. This was at a time, of course, when the message of them had never been more important."

C. S. Lewis saw a copy of the one to the Colossians, the first translation, and wrote Phillips a congratulatory letter. "It is like seeing an old picture which has been cleaned," Lewis wrote, and urged Phillips to translate the rest of the letters as soon as possible. It took six years to complete the task but the result was an immediate and dramatic success. The number of requests to preach, lecture, broadcast and write mounted alarmingly and the burden of correspondence alone became almost insurmountable to a man with a church to care for as well.

"This was the beginning of a difficult time for me which at first I tried to ignore and then to hide from myself," said Dr. Phillips. "But as pressures mounted I began to be aware as never before of the subtle and insidious dangers of success."

Dr. Phillips got up and walked to the window of his library. At first, he said, the new life had been exhilarating. His work took him on trips he could never have afforded as a parish priest. There were honors and V.I.P. treatment. There were interviews with the press. There were the ever-growing world sales of his books.

"And all the while something was going on which I did not see until it was too late," said Dr. Phillips, suddenly turning to face me. "Satan was mounting his most devastating attack on me. He was building an *image* of 'J. B. Phillips' that was not Jack Phillips at all. I was no longer an ordinary human being; I was in danger of becoming the super-Christian! Everything I wrote or said had to be better than the last. The image grew and grew until it was so unlike me that I could no longer live with it. And yet the thought of destroying it was terrifying too. It was on this dilemma that I hung."

The first result of Satan's attack was an end to the flow of creativity. "It was turned off like a tap," said Dr. Phillips. Not only in writing did he notice it, but in other areas as well. "One of my hobbies is painting," he said. "I found myself losing all sense of color. Shades which should have taken seconds to mix now took ages." Then nighttime battles began.

"Those were the worst of all," said Dr. Phillips. "I found that I could usually struggle on pretty well during the day. But at night it was as if I were the picked target of the Enemy. Irrational fears gripped my spirit, unreal guilt swept over me. Even my sense of God disappeared, though it never reached nihilism nor utter despair. Still, when I turned to God for help, He seemed remote and unapproachable."

I stared at this giant among present-day Christians in astonishment. Faceless fears? Haunting guilt? A God unreachable and far away? Why, he was describing *my* nighttime experience! But I had always imagined that such midnight torment was reserved for people of small faith and small learning like my own. Was it possible that it was the experience of mature Christians as well? And with the question came hope. For it was obvious that the man in front of me had emerged victorious from these lonely struggles.

Dr. Phillips' daughter, Jennifer, put her head in at the door to call us to lunch, and for the next half-hour the four of us spoke of lighter things.

But back again in his library after lunch, he gave me my answer. J. B. Phillips' return from darkness began with what might be called a vision—a vision which centered around a man who had followed much the same earthly path as Phillips himself: C. S. Lewis.

Lewis, too, had become a worldknown figure as the result of his Christian writings. He, too, knew what it was to live in people's imaginations as a kind of spiritual hero. His body, too, had succumbed to pressure: he was not well for several years before his death in 1963. Who was better qualified to speak to Phillips' condition?

Dr. Phillips described his experience to me. But he has also written about it in the preface to a new book, which was still in manuscript form on his desk at the time of my visit, and which is the first result of his fresh gift of creativity.* This is what he says about the extraordinary occurrence which made so deep an impression on him at a time when he most needed it.

"Many of us," he writes, "who believe in what is technically known as the Communion of Saints must have experienced the sense of nearness, for a fairly short time, of those whom we love soon after they have died. This has certainly happened to me many times. But the late C. S. Lewis, whom I did not know very well but with whom I had corresponded a fair amount, gave me an unusual experience.

"A few days after his death, while I was watching television, he 'appeared' sitting in the chair within a few feet of me. He was ruddier in complexion than ever, grinning all over his face and, as the old-fashioned saying has it, positively glowing with health. I was neither alarmed nor surprised. He was just there—'large as life and twice as natural.' "

And here are the words which C. S. Lewis spoke.

"It's not so hard as you think, you know."

At first, Phillips was baffled. What a disappointment to be visited by C. S. Lewis and to have nothing more important come out of it than an enigma. *What* wasn't so hard as you think? Could it be that Lewis was speaking about death, saying that death was not hard? But why this particular message to him? He was not aware of any special fear of death. And then suddenly he saw that the words could refer to that larger death of which physical death is but a part. And since the self with all its worldly ego and ambitious drives must be relinquished when we leave our physical bodies, how much better to get on with this beforehand.

This was the key that has helped J.B. Phillips emerge from his "dark night of the soul" and regain his creativity and vitality. For this glamorous image of an infallible mentor which had been built up around Phillips was in essence egofeeding. To destroy it was to destroy the false ego, in a real sense to kill it. C. S. Lewis's words made it easier for Phillips to begin. "It's not so hard as you think, you know," Lewis said.

I wondered suddenly if this very interview was not part of the process: Phillips seemed almost to be insisting that I

---

* *Ring of Truth* by J. B. Phillips, Macmillan, N.Y.C.

take him down from any pedestal where my humanness would like to place him.

"In this encounter," Dr. Phillips said before I left, "Dr. Lewis spoke to me as one who is no longer seeing through a glass darkly, but as one who has begun to see the glories of heaven face to face. He was kindly but firmly reminding me of something I knew but had almost forgotten—that the rewards of abandoning self are worth the suffering. Paul said it long ago, 'I reckon that the sufferings of this present time are not worthy to be compared with the glory which shall be revealed in us.' I'm beginning to see that the glories can start here on earth. It *is* a glorious thing to be yourself."

I had much to ponder on the way home. I felt that both Lewis and Phillips had spoken once again to our generation. For who of us does not carry around an image built both of our own pride and the expectations of others?—which is very different from the living man that God made. And who of us is not afraid to shatter that image so that the person God sees shines through? Should we not, with Dr. Phillips, take encouragement from these words:

"It's not so hard as you think."

A Place For You
by Dr. Paul Tournier

A famous Swiss psychiatrist, author and Christian layman tells about one of man's great conflicts.

One of my patients is a man who all his life had been dominated by other people. As a psychiatrist I see it as my duty to help such a person first discover and then assert himself. But this man is also a Christian. As his hidden resentments work their way to the surface in my consulting room, I see a conflict going on inside him, and I think I know what that conflict is.

He is reminding himself of the teachings of Jesus. Blessed are the meek. Turn the other cheek. Resist not. On the one hand his religion tells him that he must forget himself, seek not his own, live for others; and on the other I am urging him to self-realization, self-expression, self-fulfillment.

This problem tormented me, too, for many years. And then, because of a sentence spoken several years ago by one of my patients, I saw for the first time the possibility that these two approaches were not really opposites at all.

This particular young man came to me because he could not hold down a job. Although he was intelligent and hardworking he never seemed to fit in with the organization he worked for. As a psychiatrist I endeavored to find the root of this problem in his childhood, and I soon discovered that he had suffered—as have so many of my patients—from the marital conflict of his parents.

His father had been unfaithful to his mother, while she had felt a somewhat too-possessive love for her son. When the couple was divorced, the young man was utterly confused: full of hatred for his father and distrust of his mother.

Instinctively he started seeking a family or community to take the place of the one he had lost. First he went to the

Communists. But in the huge meetings and congresses he was always a lone figure.

When he became disillusioned with Communism, he started going about with the Existentialists. He would join them in their close, jampacked cellars, but no matter how thick the crowd he was still a solitary man.

Then he joined a gang that drove around on motorcycles in crash helmets and black leather jackets. But here again he could never feel a part of the group. What was emerging as the young man talked was a picture of a person seeking a milieu, a circle, a community, and yet, because of the wound which he carried in his heart, unable ever to become authentically incorporated in any community.

And it was at that point that he made the remark which struck me so strongly. "At bottom," he said, "I am always seeking a *place*."

I could not get those words out of my head. Man has a great need to have a place. In my work I am constantly hearing the dreams of patients in which they recall all the places of their lives—the places in which they were happy, the places in which they were unhappy. Each one of our feelings somehow remains attached to some place. A certain little corner in an attic, a certain turning in a road, a certain tree or rock. All our lives we are attached to places: Man is not pure spirit, he is an incarnate being and this attachment to place expresses his incarnateness.

He stands, in short, in need of a place in order to become a person.

And so I endeavor to give a patient like this young man a sense of place. My consulting room can become a real place for him. It becomes the place to which he can bring the despairs of his life in absolute trust. I light a fire, I pull two chairs up to it, and the room itself becomes for him an instrument of healing.

But what made me stop and think about my patient's remark was that I also remembered statements about place in the Bible. I remembered Abraham, the prototype of all believers. To Abraham God says, "Leave your country, leave your family." In short, leave your place.

I remembered Jesus, "The foxes have holes, and the birds of the air have nests, but the Son of Man has no place to lay his head."

I heard Him saying to St. Peter, "Leave your nets, leave your place, and follow Me."

So I was back again face to face with my old problem: the apparent conflict between the discoveries of psychiatry and the commands of the Bible. In order to heal my patient I endeavor to give him the place which he has lacked, while throughout the Bible rings out a call to leave one's land, to leave one's place and set forth on a spiritual pilgrimage.

I thought about it, as I say, very hard. And in the end I saw that there was a great difference between Abraham and my student.

Abraham *had* a place; my student had none.

It is to those who have a place that God sends the call to move on. We need to have a home before we can leave it. *We need to receive before we can give.* For no one can give that which he does not have.

There are then two movements which complete each other and are necessary one to the other. Receive, give. Grow up, and become as a child. Achieve selfhood, surrender that self to God. These two motions are not mutually exclusive, they are the rhythm of the Christian life. They are the breathing of the soul.

For a while I concluded that the first phase, then, must be the concern of psychiatry. It is the psychiatrist who endeavors to provide a place so that from there the soul may press on. But on examining the Bible I found that this was not so. God, long before psychiatrists, was concerned with giving His people a place. During the exile of the Jews, He honored their longing and nostalgia for Jerusalem. In the New Testament He is constantly supplying the needs of those who lack something. It is not to them that He speaks of renunciation. Renunciation He proposed to those who had already received. It was of the rich young man that He asked abandonment of riches, not of the poor. It was to Nicodemus the great scholar that He spoke of being reborn.

So there is the strongest link between the first movement and the second. The aim, the meaning and the sense of the first movement is to make the second possible. When a patient brings the misfortunes and tragedies of his childhood to my consulting room there will always be some worthy soul who says to him, "Why are you dragging out all these ancient histories? Forget the past. It's unhealthy to keep looking back."

But it is precisely in order to forget the past that these patients must look back. There is unfinished business back there that is halting their progress today. The past must be dealt with so that it can be abandoned. The first movement is aimed at making possible the second.

For a place can become a prison. Not all men have lacked a place. Some have had noted ancestors or remarkable parents, or a brilliant school record or an early success. They are well installed and settled in life, so much so that they risk falling asleep in their armchairs.

But we must all, sooner or later, leave our places if we are to arrive finally at the one which God has prepared for us. He does not give us our earthly place to settle down in, but to set out from.

We are a little like the trapeze artist. He swings for a while on one trapeze and then lets go to catch another. He must have good support from the first trapeze if he is to have the momentum to gain the second. But finally he must let go if he is ever to reach his goal. My patient with job troubles did not have a solid trapeze. It was my duty to give him this support so that he could, one day, make his jump.

For the goal is Christ, and His joy, and His life everlasting, and psychiatry can be a handhold to help some along the way.

Paul Tournier's Credo

In 1957, Paul Tournier's best-known book, *The Meaning of Persons,* was published in America. The response to it was immediate; over 60,000 copies have been sold. Since then eight additional books by the Swiss psychiatrist have come off the presses. Peoples the world over have found great help, and hope, in Dr. Tournier's insights into life. A devout Christian, Paul Tournier is a medical doctor as well as a practicing psychiatrist. His special gift is in communicating great truths in simple terms. One of his recent books, *The Seasons of Life,* contains this warm personal testimony:

In my childhood I had already come to know God, quite naively of course; nevertheless, I thank God for those who led me to Him. Yet, it took a revolutionary experience in order for this knowledge to go beyond the abstract nature of a few ideas about God, however right those ideas might have been. I had to meet Him in the full activity of adulthood, through dialogue with inspired men. They put my real life, my home and my medical work, under the light of God. Ever since, Jesus Christ has become my unseen companion of every day, the witness of all my successes and all my failures, the confidant of my rejoicings and my times of sadness. It is in this life shared with Him that the knowledge of God is continuously strengthened and sharpened. All that I can hope, when my time for action will be over, is that I may yet go further in the riches of this knowledge.

Section Six—

Great Dramas
of Faith

Section Six—
Introduction

A favorite story with Guideposts readers from the beginning has been the adventure-in-faith drama. The ten adventures in this section are some of the best examples of what can result when men put their trust in God—even when the odds are so staggering that faith seems folly. The very first article Guideposts published in 1945 was just such a story. War hero Eddie Rickenbacker wrote it, a stirring witness to the power of faith.

This set the pace for a continuous flow of action stories by and about people who didn't quit or give up their faith when faced with serious injury or death. These stories of spiritual courage have had a great effect on our readers' faith—we know because they have told us so.

Often these stories have appeared in Guideposts close on the heels of a news event such as Mrs. Stephen Armstrong's article about her moon-walking son, or Mrs. Lowell Thomas's terrifying experience in the 1964 Alaskan earthquake, or the 1960 Little Rock school confrontation written by James Gabrielle.

All of these stories testify that faith can indeed move mountains.

"I Believe in Prayer"
by Captain Eddie Rickenbacker

*In a day when heroes are scarce, this man's story
still qualifies him for the distinction.*

There are a lot of things about the human mind and soul
that we don't know much about. We get glimpses of them
when in times of danger or suffering we cross a little way
over the line of ordinary thought.

As I roared down the last stretch in an automobile race
years ago, I felt that I could control that machine with my
mind, that I could hold it together with my mind, and that if
it finally collapsed I could run it with my mind. It was a
feeling of mastery, of supreme confidence. But it was real.

If I had said such a thing then, the boys would have
called me crazy. Even now I can't explain it. But I believe
that if you *think* disaster you will get it. Brood about death,
and you hasten your demise. Think positively and master-
fully, with confidence and faith, and life becomes more secure, more fraught with action, richer in achievement and
experience.

Perhaps such things as the control of mind over matter
and the transmission of thought waves are tied up together,
part of something so big we haven't grasped it yet. It's part of
us and part of the Something that is looking after us. It's one
of the things that make me believe in personal protection and
in life after death. I don't know how to put it into words.

Another strange thing happened to me. A number of
years ago I was flying to Chicago. It was a Sunday afternoon
in the middle of December, and the weather was miserable.
There was a lot of ice. We suddenly lost the radio beam. For
a long time we cruised back and forth trying to pick it up.
Fog was all around us. We were lost, off the beam, and flying
blind. Our two-way radio went out, and we had lost all communication with the world. For seven hours we flew—where,

243

we didn't know. Nobody knew where we were; nobody even knew we were lost.

Darkness was coming on. Then, suddenly, we saw a break in the murk. The pilot brought the ship down to within one hundred feet, and we saw lights go flashing by on a four-lane highway.

"It must be going from some place to some place," I said, and we followed it for some distance.

Then we saw a red glow away off to the right, headed for it, and saw a river gleaming. We flew up that river, and out of the six-thirty dusk of winter sprang a town—Toledo! I saw the Toledo-Edison sign flashing as we swept over the bridge tops. Skimming the roots, we circled and landed at the airport a moment later. We had just enough gas left for eleven minutes of flight.

We had flown blind, without a beam, but we were on a beam, just the same. I like to think it was the "Big Radio" that kept us going—the Thing that keeps all of us flying safely through the fog and night, toward some mysterious and important goal. The "Big Radio" is a two-way job. You've got to keep tuned with It, and you have to talk back. I believe in prayer. I learned to pray as a kid at my mother's knee.

One day in France, with only one magneto on my Newport biplane functioning, I was attacked by three German Albatross planes. I came out of a dive so fast that the terrific pressure collapsed my righthand upper wing. No matter what I tried, I couldn't come out of that whirl of death. I often wish I could think as fast under normal conditions as I did during that drop. While I fought the controls and tried to get the engine going I saw all the good and bad things I had ever done, and most of them were bad. Then I began to pray.

"Oh, God," I said, "help me get out of this."

As a last desperate act, I threw my weight to the lefthand side over the cockpit and jammed the controls, then jammed the engine wide open. The thing suddenly sputtered and vibrated violently, and sailed away on her one good wing for France. I held it that way all the way home.

This escape and others I have had were not the result of any super-ability or super-knowledge on my part. I wouldn't be alive if I had to depend on that. I realized then, as I headed for France on one wing, that there had to be Something Else. I had seen others die—brighter and more able than I. I knew there was a Power. I believe in calling upon It for help.

I am not such an egoist as to believe that God has spared me because I am I. I believe there is work for me to do and I am spared to do it, just as you are. If I die tomorrow, I do not fear the prospect at all.

On a rainy night in February, 1941, I had the worst accident of my life. As I look back on those agonizing days in the hospital I realize there was a reason behind it all. It was a test and a preparation for what was to follow.

In the four months I lay in that hospital I did more thinking about life and death than I had ever done before. Twenty-one months later, I was adrift in an open lifeboat with seven other starving men, most of them so young they needed the strength and understanding of a man who had been down in the valley of the shadow, who had suffered and made sense out of his suffering. To those men I was able to bring the essence of the religion and philosophy I had distilled in the hospital.

Once I almost died from a throat hemorrhage.

"Here," I said "is death."

It dawned upon me in a flash that the easiest thing in the world is to die; the hardest is to live. Dying was a sensuous pleasure; living was a grim task. In that moment I chose to live. I knew from experience that abandonment to death was a sin. I was quitting. I had work to do, others to serve.

Many things came to me. I realized I wasn't *afraid* to die, because I have lived so much in good ways and bad that I no longer feel the youthful pang of not having lived at all. I knew only the sorrow of being unable any more to help other people. And when I finally came around, I saw life and death and the meaning of the Golden Rule more clearly than I had ever known.

I took that clarity with me to the rubber raft in the South Pacific after our plane crashed. I shall not recount that story again. I merely want to tell you the meaning of it. Of the eight men in those three rafts, I alone never lost faith that we would be picked up. Throughout those twenty-one days of blistering sun and nights of ghastly chill, we were adrift for a purpose. I saw life had no meaning except in terms of *helping* others.

I humbly think man distinctively does not interest himself in others. He does it by an act of will. He sees that "*I am my brother's keeper"* and *"Do unto others"* are the essence of all truth.

My experiences and the suffering through which I passed taught me that faith in God is the answer to life.

Recently, in a rehabilitation hospital, I addressed a group of airmen who had been badly wounded or nervously shaken. Many were discouraged, the future looked dark and unpromising. I knew how they felt . . . I too, had been through a lot, but had found a secret which brought me through and I urged them to find the same secret.

I said, "If you have not had an experience of God in your life, my advice is to get busy and get yourself one." For that is the sure way to win victories over inner defeat. It is the way a humble man meets life or death.

Neil Armstrong's Boyhood Crisis
by Mrs. Stephen Armstrong
(as told to Lorraine Wetzel)

An astronaut's mother tells the intimate story of
her son's boyhood crisis.

Most people think Neil Armstrong took the most important
step in his life when he set foot on the moon. But as his
mother, I remember an even greater step taken in our old
home on Pearl Street in Wapakoneta, Ohio, on another July
day—23 years earlier.

The story begins when Neil was two and his father and I
lived in Cleveland, not far from the airport. Like many
families during the depression days of the early 30s, one of
our inexpensive Sunday-afternoon pastimes was airplane
watching. Neil stood between us, his little face pressed so intently against the fence that it often left red marks. We were
always ready to leave long before he was, and his plea was
always the same: "Can't we see just *one* more airplane?"

I was often uneasy about Neil's obvious fascination with
planes. And I had to admit to myself that this child, our
firstborn, was very special to me. After Stephen and I married, I was haunted by the fear that maybe I couldn't
conceive. I had been an only child and often thought, *What
if I can't have even one baby?*

Then finally the day came when our doctor assured me I
was pregnant. The minute I got home I went down on my
knees and thanked God for His blessing to us and, in the
fullness of my heart, I dedicated this child-to-be to Him. In
the months that followed, I prayed steadily that this child
would be given a thirst for knowledge and the capacity for
learning which someday would accomplish noble deeds—
hopefully to serve the work of the Lord.

One Sunday morning, when Neil was five or six, he and

my husband left for Sunday school. When they returned, both had peculiar expressions on their faces. Stephen was a bit white-faced, but Neil was beaming from ear to ear.

"What is wrong with you two?" I asked. There was utter silence.

Suddenly a thought came to me. "Did you go up in that airplane I read about in the paper!"

Now they looked relieved. Yes, that is exactly what they had done. A pilot was barnstorming in town, and Stephen said rates were cheaper in the morning. He had not really enjoyed the flight, but little Neil had loved every minute of it.

One morning Neil and I were walking down the cluttered aisles of a dime store looking for cereal bowls. My husband and I now had a wonderful family of three active children who consumed vast quantities of cereal. Somehow the bowls were always getting chipped or broken. I was selecting five shiny new ones when I felt a tug at my arm. "Mom, will you buy this for me?" Neil held up a gaily colored box.

"What is it?" I asked cautiously.

"It's a model-airplane kit." The eagerness in his voice betrayed his excitement. "Mom, this way I could learn how to make airplanes. It's twenty cents."

Quickly I thought how 20 cents would buy two cereal bowls, but how could I resist the urgency and enthusiasm in my son's voice?

"Honey," I said gently, "could you find a kit for ten cents?"

"Sure, Mom!" His face radiant, he raced back to the toy counter.

Although Neil was then only eight years old, that was the beginning of two important occupations in his life. The first was his meticulous assembly line for many model airplanes. We put a table in one corner of the living room, and it was never moved—even when company came.

The second occupation made the first one possible. Beginning with his first model plane, Neil was never without a job, no matter how small. First he cut grass in a cemetery for 10 cents an hour. Later he cleaned out the bread mixer at Neumeister's Bakery every night. After we moved to Wapakoneta, Neil delivered orders for the neighborhood grocery, swept out the hardware store and opened cartons at Rhine and Brading's Pharmacy.

When Neil wasn't working or studying, he rode his bicycle three miles north on a gravel road to the Wapak Flying

Service Airport. Today this field isn't used, but in 1944 it bustled with activity. A young instructor, Charles Finkenbine, kept three light airplanes busy as trainers. Budding pilots came from surrounding counties to learn to fly, and Neil at 14 was a familiar figure sitting on the sidelines, his eyes glued to every takeoff and landing. One afternoon I was making grape jelly when the screen door banged as he rushed into the kitchen.

"Mom," he shouted, "Mr. Finkenbine let me *touch* one of the airplanes!"

"That's fine, son," I said.

"He says from now on I can be a grease monkey and one of these days he'll teach me to fly!"

"Are you sure you're old enough, Neil?" I tried to hide the anxiety in my voice.

He flashed his wide, confident grin. "Don't worry. I'll be careful."

The screen door banged again, and he was gone. I'm afraid his assurance did little to comfort me. By now I was beginning to wonder how the Lord could be served by a youngster so completely captivated by airplanes.

From then on every penny Neil earned went for flying lessons. At 40 cents an hour at the pharmacy it took him between 22 and 23 hours of work to pay for one nine-dollar lesson. But both Dick Brading and Charles Finkenbine were generous men: The first often let Neil off early to go to the airport, the latter managed free flying time for our son in exchange for odd jobs around the hangar. Neil's goal was to get his flying license as soon as he reached his 16th birthday in August.

In July our two boys, Neil and Dean, with their father as scoutmaster, attended Boy Scout camp in Defiance, Ohio. The evening they were due back I planned a special homecoming supper. They thought they'd be home at five o'clock, so I peeled potatoes and put them on to boil at 4:30, then started to set the table.

At 5:15 I picked up my darning basket and started to mend some of Dean's socks. An hour dragged by. I finished the socks and walked to the window. They were more than an hour overdue, and I knew something was wrong.

Then looking through the grape arbor, I saw our car drive into the garage. My husband appeared in the doorway, his face pale and drawn. Fear clutched my throat.

"What's wrong, Stephen? Has something happened to the boys?"

"No, they're all right. Dean is here with me, and Neil will be along soon. But there has been an accident."

"What do you mean?"

"Viola, come into the living room, and I'll tell you all about it." He put his arm around me, and together we walked to the sofa.

"We were on our way home this afternoon," he continued, "when we noticed an airplane flying parallel to us. Neil recognized it immediately as one of the trainers from the Wapak Flying Service. Some student was practicing takeoffs and landings in a field near the road. Then he must have dipped too low over the telephone wires, because suddenly the airplane was in trouble."

"Oh no!" I whispered.

"It nosedived into the field, and at the same time Neil yelled, 'Stop the car!' and before I knew it, he had climbed over the fence and was running toward the plane. Then we all got out and ran over to help too. Neil was lifting a young fellow out of the cockpit, and just as we got there he died in Neil's arms."

"Oh Stephen, how awful! That poor boy and his family." Then a terrifying new thought seared my brain. "It might have been Neil."

"Yes, Viola, it could have been." My husband's voice roughened with emotion. "Instead it was a young man from Lima whom Neil knew. Neil is staying with him until the ambulance comes."

A car door slammed, and I heard slow footsteps coming up the front-porch steps. Then suddenly Neil and I were in each other's arms, tears streaming down our faces.

"He was my friend, Mom. And he was *only* twenty!" I could hardly bear the anguish in his voice.

"I know, honey." I released him, with a mother's sudden awareness that her son was no longer a boy. I forced my voice to sound cheerful. "Do you want some supper?"

"No, thanks, I'm going up to my room." He stopped on the landing and tried to smile. "Don't worry, Mom. I'll be all right."

"I know you will, Neil." I watched him walk up the stairs and quietly close the door as dry sobs tore through me.

Stephen and I both thought it best to let him alone for a while. But we could not help wondering if Neil would want to keep flying. Both of us agreed he must fight this battle himself.

The next two days were the hardest of my life. As all mothers know, whatever hurts your children hurts you twice as much. And yet I knew he had to make this decision himself. Had our closeness with the Creator and the nightly prayers through the years prepared him to find the help he needed so desperately now? At this stage, it was out of my hands. All I could do was wait.

I tried to carry on a normal family life, but my heart and mind were always in that back bedroom with the iron bed, yellow wallpaper, the single overhead light fixture and the bureau covered with model airplanes. What was he thinking? What would he decide?

Finally, near dusk on the second day, I couldn't stand the silence and separation any longer. I baked oatmeal and raisin cookies and took a plate of them and a glass of cold milk upstairs.

"Neil, may I come in, please? Here are some cookies still warm from the oven."

He opened the door, and I walked into the stuffy little room and put the cookies on the bureau. What I saw made my heart leap. Next to a model airplane was an old Sunday-school notebook with a picture of Jesus on the cover. It was now turned to the page where years before Neil had written in his large childish hand, "The Character of Jesus," and had listed ten qualities of His. Among those that caught my eye were: He was sinless, He was humble, He championed the poor, He was unselfish. But the one which struck me the most was number eight—He was close to God.

Suddenly I felt like singing hosanna. "Honey, what have you decided about flying?" I asked him.

Neil's eyes held mine in a steady gaze, then he said firmly, "Mom, I hope you and Dad will understand, but with God's help, I *must* go on flying."

For a minute I was jolted as I thought of that other mother only a few miles away in Lima, brokenhearted and perhaps standing in her son's empty room at this very minute. I asked God for strength and the right words, and He gave them to me.

"All right, son. Dad and I will go along with your decision." My heart was pounding. "And, Neil," I said, "when you get your license in a few weeks, may I be your first passenger?"

There's a Girl Down There!
by Carol Balizet

The story of a woman who prayed, a God who heard and a man who acted.

A squall of rain blew across Florida's Route 60 that sultry August afternoon. Wearily, I rolled up the car window without taking my eyes off the road which was lined with an endless ribbon of scrub palmetto. I'd made the trip dozens of times from my parents' home in Vero Beach to the hospital in Tampa where I was a student nurse in 1953.

I passed a pick-up truck and felt sorry for the two men sitting in back getting wet.

Then suddenly, through the rain ahead of me, I saw a flashing red light. I stepped hard on the brakes. They must be repairing the road, I thought—and then I had no time to think. My car was skidding on the wet surface, moving sideways into the oncoming lane. I wrenched at the wheel but the car would not turn. Now the front wheels were off the road on the far side. The car was rolling down the bank. . . .

And then the sense went out of things. I was falling. My head struck something. The car seats fell out and tumbled around me. Suddenly everything was dark, I couldn't see! I groped for the door handle, but I couldn't find it. The steering wheel was gone too, the rear-view mirror, everything.

I put my hands to my head, trying to press some sense into it. Among the other impossible things my mind seemed to be telling me was that the car was still moving downward. It felt as though it were falling in uncanny slow motion, floating down toward the center of the earth.

And suddenly there was water in the car. Water was trickling down the walls, rising under my feet, dripping into my lap. It had a putrid, sour smell. The water seemed to come from everywhere, as though the car were surrounded by it. It was impossible, but it was happening.

252

The water kept rising. Not fast—the windows had been shut against the rain—but steadily, and at last I realized that somehow, somewhere, the car had fallen into deep water.

"Oh God," I cried. "Don't let me be trapped in here!"

Now the water was nearly at my waist, and the numbness of shock was wearing off. I began scrabbling frantically for the door, crawling first to one side, then the other of that car. At last my hand closed on a window crank. I pushed, but it would not budge. I hurled myself on that handle, straining like a madman. It didn't move. At last, panting and baffled, I leaned back and the handle gave in my hand. The crank worked backwards. I accepted the fact dumbly, as part of the whole world-gone-mad, and, backwards, rolled the window down.

Muddy, foul-smelling water spurted into the car, drenching my face and arms. I shut my eyes against the stream and cranked furiously. The window went down five inches and then stopped. No matter how I yanked and tugged I could not move it further.

Now I wound it hastily shut against the racing water and jerked off a shoe to batter the glass with. It was the soft black ballet slipper every teen-age girl wore that summer: it smacked soggily against the glass.

The water was at my shoulders. Mindlessly I flung myself at the solid metal above me, trying to tear myself loose by sheer strength. The water reached my chin. For the first time I understood that I was dying. Seventeen years old and dying.

Often I had been curious about God and had asked many questions but now that the moment to meet Him was here, I was terrified. What had I done to make life worth giving me? How would I account for myself to Him?

"God, pardon me!" I cried. "I should have been better but I wasn't and I'm sorry!"

It was a mental scream more than a prayer, but no sooner had I said it than a curious thing happened. Even as my body struggled for life and air, an indescribable peace surrounded me. Some part of me no longer struggled, some part of me did not belong to the agony, some part of me whispered, "I'm going to know! I'm going to have every question about God answered!"

The water climbed higher. I flattened my face against the metal ceiling above, sucking at the air. And then the water closed above me. I remember the roaring in my ears, my eyes straining from my head, and then nothing.

But all the while, above me, the drama on which my life hung continued. Here, as I pieced it together later, is what was happening. The flashing light I had seen belonged to a trailer truck pulled off on the side of the road. Three men were repairing a blowout on the truck when they heard the squeal of my tires on the road behind them. They peered through the rain but the highway was empty. Puzzled, they lay down their tools and started walking along the road. A hundred and fifty feet away, in the tall grass beside the highway, they came upon the underside of my car, sinking through the weeds, the rest of it already out of sight. Trapped inside, in the black night below those weeds, I had not known that the car had turned upside down. Even as the men watched unbelieving from the bank, the bottom, too, sank beneath the scummy surface, and only the waving swamp grass showed where a car had been.

The pick-up truck I had passed screeched to a halt behind them, and those three men ran to the ditch side. Six men now stared into the tangle of water plants.

The driver of the pick-up truck rubbed his jaw. "Nothing nobody can do now," he said helplessly. He nodded at the ditch. "There are cottonmouths down there."

Several men took a step backward. "I've got three kids," one of the trailer truckers said.

"Anyone in there's dead by now most likely," said another man.

"Killed when the car turned over," someone else agreed.

And then all at once one of the men leapt. His name was Theodore Henderson, a truck driver with a big hauling company. He landed in the center of the ditch. Six inches below the surface his feet touched the car, slowly settling through the muddy water.

"You'll drown!" the others shouted at him. "You can't do anything!"

But Henderson didn't answer. Perhaps he was thinking of his wife, expecting their fifth child in another month. Perhaps he was only bewildered because the car, instead of striking the bottom of the ditch as he had expected, still continued to sink away from him. At last in that incredibly deep canal, he was treading water, the car out of reach.

He took a long breath and dove after it. In the blackness under the surface he could see nothing. He swam straight down through weeds that grabbed at his arms and wrapped themselves around his waist. Ten feet down he touched metal. He found a door, braced his feet against the car's side and pulled. The door opened about an inch, then the weight of the water slammed it shut again, his middle finger inside.

His breath was gone. With his free arm he struggled to open the door again, but it held fast. At last he tore himself loose and shot to the surface leaving the end of his finger in the door.

A shout of relief went up from the other men as he reappeared. But Henderson, too winded to speak, climbed the bank and ran for the wrench he'd been using on the truck tire. Water streaming from him, finger dripping blood, he came back to the side of the ditch and jumped again.

Twice more he surfaced and then went down again through the foul water and strangling weeds, for someone he had never seen, who was probably dead. On the fourth trip he got the door open. He groped through the front seat: empty. He found me in the back where the somersaulting car had thrown me—in the back seat of a two-door car where I had found no door handle because there was none, where I had fought a window built to open only inches. . . .

The first thing I knew after my rescue was that it was light again. My eyes hurt and I closed them. There was pain in my chest. My head ached and I felt sick. I opened my eyes again. I was lying on some grass beside the road. A man kept saying: "You're going to be all right, Miss. We're going to get you to the hospital. You're going to be just fine."

But I was thinking only: I haven't seen heaven. I didn't find the answers. I was still too dazed to be glad I was alive.

And you see, I still didn't know the story of my rescue. I didn't yet know that a man had risked his life to save mine. I didn't yet know Theodore Henderson and his wife and their family.

But I do know them now. And I know, too, that I did catch a glimpse of heaven, and I did have an answer that August day. I had wondered about the meaning of life and God had showed me an act of love.

Editor's Note: Because Theodore Henderson's actions in his heroic rescue of Carol Balizet so epitomize the parable Jesus told of the Good Samaritan, Guideposts awarded him its Good Samaritan Medal.

Thank You for Daylight
by Maurice Ruddick

A coal miner with an extraordinary will to live.

We kept looking up at that tall blue sky, gulping that cool air. I guess coal miners always do that, just before they go down into the pits. It was Thursday, October 23, 1958. Around the pithead, 174 of us were waiting the rake* to take us down into Nova Scotia's Springhill Mine, the deepest mine in North America.

I thought about Norma, just home after the birth of our twelfth child. I was glad that Colleen, our oldest, had come from school as I left. She was 12, and a real help. And I'd be home by midnight, so I could give the baby her bottle.

The rake rose to the top and soon we were dropping into the eternal night of Number Two shaft. We stopped at 13,000 feet. Layton Reid and I switched on our helmet lamps and followed the circles of light down the wall to the coal face.

As we picked coal from the wall, we'd pack the empty space with timbers to support the roof. Once all the coal was removed from a level, we'd collapse that entire tunnel. There's a quirk of nature in deep-pit mining called a "bump." It happens when tunneling upsets pressures deep in the ground. Without warning, a section of the tunnel floor simply rises and smashes into the ceiling. The fewer tunnels open, the less danger of bumping. With our mine, safety came first.

At 6:00 we had a 20-minute break. At 7:45, Layton and I started packing in timbers. It was 8:05 when I started on my last timber.

"Okay," Layton said, starting down the wall. "I'm a movin' on."

---

* A vehicle used for mine transportation.

"I'm a movin' on," I sang softly. They were words to a song he and I harmonized on sometimes.

And then the world exploded.

I was lying on the floor with blackness all around me and a roaring in my ears. Somebody screamed. I tried to stand but I could not move my legs. In the dark, from far, far away, a tiny glow slowly turned into the luminescent dial on my watch.

I had moved one arm. I tried the other. Both arms all right. I reached up and found my helmet and lamp still intact. I switched on the lamp, and instantly wished I hadn't. Where Layton had started down the wall there was no tunnel at all, just a solid mass of rock and coal, splintered timbers and twisted track. Down the other way was worse, because I could see more. A narrow passage was still open. It was littered with the arms and legs of men I had worked with all my life.

I myself was buried to the waist. The scream came again. Frantically I dug at the rubble and freed my legs. Cautiously I arose and started toward the sound, stepping over dead men when I saw them, stumbling when I did not. Then out of the gray fog I saw head lamps. They were gathered around a man whose right arm was caught in a smashed timber pack.

"It's Percy Rector," I said.

"Get me out!" he screamed again. But his arm was crushed between great logs. For an hour we clawed away: it was hopeless.

"Maurice?" It was Garnet Clarke's voice. "There's no way out back there. How about up your way?"

I shook my head. "Closed up."

We were all silent for a moment, realizing we were shut in a space perhaps 80 feet long, almost two and a half miles under ground.

"Let's get the names of everyone here," I said briskly. Garnet wrote them on the wall with chalk. Garnet Clarke. Currie Smith. Herb Pepperdine. Doug Jewkes. Frank Hunter. Maurice Ruddick. Percy had fainted; Garnet added his name. "Seven of us."

"They'll come for us!" Currie's eyes begged us to agree.

But Herb spoke the words we were thinking. "How will they know anyone's alive down here?"

It was no sooner said than we set about to forget it. We found things to do. We searched every inch for food and water: two lunches boxes, two sandwiches in each box; seven water cans, very light.

A broken air pipe protruded from the debris and we set up shifts to keep up a rhythm of banging and listening. I crawled up the debris behind us until floor met ceiling. The picks were useless without compressed air. I clawed with my bare hands at the tons of earth and rock. One by one the other fellows did the same. Maybe we really hoped we could tear our way out; maybe we only wanted to get as far as possible from Percy's misery.

Gradually we found spots where we could stretch out. And suddenly I was praying. Without conscious thought on my part, the familiar words I had spoken at bedtime since childhood rose silently to my lips: "Thank You, dear Father, for this good day . . ." Sounds strange, I thought. But the words kept coming, of themselves. "Thank You for my wife. For my children. Thank You that they are digging, that they are looking for us."

No. Not strange. I had given thanks before when things looked bad to my short sight. I'd thanked Him for my children's health when one of them was so sick doctors had given up, and I'd seen the doctors fooled. I'd thanked Him for His plenty the time the mines closed, and my children ate that week and every week. "Thank You for Yourself, that we do not have to wait alone . . ."

Friday, Percy was worse. We were glad when his delirium began, when he no longer seemed aware of the heat and the smell of death and the weight of earth, but talked about a farm and horses and a well with endless water.

The thirst was hardest. Our tongues got thick, our lips cracked, our throats were lined with dust.

Sometimes we thought we heard them coming. Other times it sounded only like the gnawing of the great gray mine rats. "Thank You that they are coming . . ."

We were obsessed with time. My watch was our contact with the world of mornings and evenings. Saturday night I moved the hands back an hour. "Daylight Saving ends today," I said. It was so terribly important to keep touch with that world.

No matter how we hoarded our lamps, they dimmed and finally, one by one, faded out. Deep-earth dark is deeper than black, a dark without promise. "Thank You for daylight . . ."

Yet it was then that I really saw my buddies. Sunday I hefted the last water can. "We can't afford to drink today," I told them. "Each man just wet his lips." I held it for Percy. "We'll have to trust each other," I said. Five throats cried out for water, five pairs of hands clutched a life-saving supply of it, invisible, anonymous. The can came back to me as heavy as when it left.

Garnet's voice waked me from almost-sleep. "Is it Monday?"

I brought my watch to my eyes. "Yes."

"Then it's my birthday. My twenty-ninth birthday."

I sat up and groped for the lunch box. One bit of sandwich was left. 'We're going to have a party! Here's Garnie's birthday cake!" Seven pieces, each about the size of a lump of sugar—and about as soft. "Happy Birthday, dear Garnie!" Our voices were little more than whispers. Then we ate slowly, chewing a long time. "Thank You for food . . ."

Tuesday I crawled with the water can to Percy. I kneeled, feeling for his lips. My hand touched Percy's cheek. It was ice cold. I tried not to cry. Tears are water.

The hands of my watch hypnotized me: endlessly together and apart. It's Wednesday. Thursday. A week ago we were *out there*. Under the sky. The watch face was very pale: it needed light. All day we gnawed on the timbers. Doug Jewkes kept talking about Seven-Up. "Ice cold. Those little sweat drops, you know, down the side of the bottle." Friday. The word carried no meaning to starved brains.

Most of the fellows were too weak to take their turns at the pipe but Currie Smith and I kept at it. We lay by the broken pipe, too feeble to sit, spelling each other with the end of a coal pick. Bang. Bang. Bang. Stop. Listen. Bang again. Friday midnight. Who'd think we were alive after eight days?

On my watch, two pale, pale hands stood straight together. Then one hand moved on and it was Saturday. November. The watch and I were going out together. Norma, if they find me, put the watch in the sun. It needs light. "Thank You for light . . ."

Currie poked the pick at me. "I got to quit awhile," he croaked.

Bang. Bang. Bang. "Sure, Currie." I took the pick. Bang. Bang. Bang. I tried to lift it.

Currie's not pounding.

I'm not pounding.

"Currie!" I was screaming. "Currie, it's an answer! They're coming!" We were all screaming. Crying. Reaching in the dark for someone to hug.

We pounded that pipe nearly flat. The answering blows grew louder. We heard the rock wall in front of us giving way.

"Maurice!" a hoarse whisper. "We ought to give thanks. You're a praying man. You say thanks for us all."

I threw my hands over my eyes as a head lamp, incredibly bright, incredibly yellow, stabbed through a crack in the wall.

"Fellows," I said softly, "I've never stopped."

Hold My Hand, Look Straight Ahead
by James O. Gabrielle

An adventure in moral courage.

No one in New Orleans was especially concerned about the date November 14, 1960. It was, we all knew, the date set by the Federal Court for the integration of Negroes into the public school system. Some integration had already taken place—on the buses, in parks, at Louisiana State University—and all this had come about with very little ugliness.

There was one sign though, if we had known how to read it, that pointed to the trouble ahead. It was the petition that had gone around pledging those who signed to withdraw their children from any integrated school. My wife, Daisy, encountered the first hint of trouble one bright afternoon early in November.

She had built up a little business selling costume jewelry and was showing the new catalog to a neighbor when the subject of the petition came up.

"No," said Daisy, "I haven't signed. I don't think it's right."

The woman slammed the catalog shut. "I'm afraid," she said, "that you had better leave." The friendship of one neighbor, or maybe a two-dollar sale, Daisy thought, was all that her convictions were to cost her.

Monday morning, November 14, Daisy and little Lola stood in the doorway as our five older children set out for school. One of them Yolanda, our next-to-youngest, was on her way to William Frantz School, three blocks away. As Daisy watched her skip down the street she didn't know that another six-year-old, Ruby Bridges, was also on her way to Frantz. Ruby was a Negro.

I was out on my job as a meter helper when I heard the news. The trouble, it seemed, was mostly fear of trouble. As soon as they had heard about Ruby, mothers—hundreds of mothers—descended on Frantz School and took their children home.

The next morning my wife stood at our door as usual, inspecting Yolanda before school.

We didn't say much.

We had said everything there was to say the night before, over coffee in the kitchen. Daisy had become a serious student of religion in recent years. "If you don't put your beliefs into practice, what good are they?" she had asked. By the time the pot was drained she had my backing.

Daisy walked to school with Yondi, that day. But along the curb of the block opposite the school was a line of women. "Yondi," Daisy said, "those women may say things. If they do, you must not answer. Just hold my hand and look straight ahead."

Already the women were calling. "Hey, Daisy!" someone yelled. "Where you going?"

A few of the women crossed the street and came close. One of them let out a piercing catcall. "Yaaaa! Look at the nigger lover!"

Daisy and Yondi turned into the schoolyard and the women fell back. Inside, the empty halls echoed as they walked to Miss Kay's room. "Well!" said the teacher. "Hello, Yondi. I'm glad to see you. Come over here, dear, away from the window. . . ."

When Daisy left the building, the mob was waiting. All the way home they shouted vulgar words and threats and once Daisy was safe in the apartment, she collapsed into a chair. How was she going to keep up her courage?

Yet Daisy did, for three long weeks. She did it through a very powerful, very simple technique. She never looked around.

This is a most amazing thing about my wife. When Daisy becomes convinced that something is right, she fixes her eyes straight ahead as though they're fixed on Christ; she never looks around. She keeps her eye on the Light.

I used to believe this was just ivory-tower thinking. Not with Daisy. She brought it right down into the street, into the long three blocks between our home and William Frantz School!

"How can you stand it?" I asked her one night.

"I couldn't, Jimmy, if I looked at their faces. I'd freeze in my tracks the moment I saw anger and meanness. But those are surface things. I know some of these women. Deep down they are good people. If I look straight ahead I can remember the good things."

What a strange power there is to this idea. It kept Daisy walking the day the rotten egg broke on her dress. It kept her going when the rock crashed through our living room window and when a woman rushed up and struck her.

It worked so well that one day a neighbor called Daisy to say she wanted to join her. "Fine," said Daisy, and a few minutes later the two mothers and two children were walking down the street together between rows of hooting women.

They got to school with no trouble. But on the way home that afternoon, our neighbor forgot. She turned. She froze in her tracks. Like Lot's wife turning toward evil, she saw the hatred and the anger in the faces of 40 fist-clenched, stick-waving women. She didn't join Daisy again.

As the second week passed, the pressures continued to build. Daisy began to be afraid, not only for herself but for her family. So many rocks had come crashing into our home that we hung heavy blankets over the windows and lived in a perpetual twilight. Both Daisy and I had been threatened; all of us had lost friends. One of the older children spent her time in the kitchen listening to the radio. When you're a teen-ager, it is hard to lose every friend . . . "*Every friend,* Dad! No one will talk to me."

The pressure was telling on me too. When I came to work in the morning, everyone—except one man, God bless him—moved to the other side of the room. I was demoted. One day I was called into the head office. "Just had two phone calls, Gabrielle. Your little girl's been shot."

I ran out the door, tipped a taxi driver to speed, yet found Yondi playing in her room. It was a trick. I don't know how much longer I could have stuck it out, but the matter was taken out of my hands.

It was Wednesday of the third week. When Daisy and Yolanda left school, they faced another mob. Daisy's pulse beat faster. There was a new, deeper note in the voices around her. She warned Yondi again to look straight ahead.

And little Yondi forgot. Halfway home, she turned. Her mother felt her grip tighten. "Don't be afraid, honey," her mother said.

But Yolanda had seen the hate. At home she cried,

remembering the faces She hung on to her mother and she followed her everywhere. That night she could not sleep.

That settled it. We adults could stand for our principles in the face of hate, but couldn't force our children to do so. We were glad that there were 10 children in school now for we had to leave. We did, in the middle of the night, moving from the town where Daisy had lived 35 years. We left our furniture in the apartment.

Today, we live in the little town of Centerdale, Rhode Island. We're starting all over again, from new cups and saucers to new friends. Was it worth it, Daisy's stand?

There have been encouraging signs. We have heard that in a New Orleans school-board election the man who won was an outspoken foe of rule-by-the-mob. And then there are the letters from people who represent the real South, thanking Daisy for what she did.

But the most important event of all, perhaps, was the action of one single neighbor. This man taught us that an act done for God is never done alone. Where one act fails, another is begun.

This man lives in the same apartment building where we used to live. We didn't know him well. But on the day after we fled New Orleans, he changed his mind about integration. He walked through the same door as had Daisy and Yolanda. He took his son by the hand and started down the street between rows of hooting, jeering women. And as he walked, he looked straight ahead.

The Search for Little Wessie
by Ernest M. Snyder

The three-year-old boy had disappeared at 2 p.m. Now night was closing in. . . .

The news came over the car radio that April Sunday afternoon as my wife, Martha, our three-year-old daughter, Robin, and I were driving to my mother's house. A three-year-old boy was lost somewhere in Cunningham Falls State Park in western Maryland. He had wandered away from his family during a picnic.

"Just Robin's age!" I said to Martha. I thought of that rugged mountain terrain. "Hope they find him quick."

But hours later, driving home after dinner at Mother's, there was another bulletin. That little boy was still missing.

I looked at our own three-year-old sitting between us on the front seat. Then I wondered how many men of my National Guard unit I could locate on a Sunday evening. "Let's drive by the park," I said to Martha.

It was 6:15 when we reached the parking lot from which the search was being directed. The mountain slope seemed alive with searchers. I stopped a state trooper and asked if they could use some National Guardsmen.

"What can you give us?" he said.

"Mostly men and communications," I said, "and probably a Jeep or two."

From a radio car he phoned police headquarters and in a moment had the necessary official request. I drove Martha and Robin home, called three local radio stations and asked them to broadcast an appeal for Guard volunteers. I also contacted Staff Sgt. Charles Lockard, the unit's full-time employee, and asked him to open the armory.

By the time I had changed into my uniform and driven the ten miles to the armory in Frederick, men were already gathering. I went through a mental list of items needed—radios, compasses, flashlights, a radio vehicle, batteries, maps. Twenty minutes later I was enroute to the park in the radio Jeep with the first contingent.

As we reached the park our eyes fell on the sight everyone dreads in a search operation. Firemen with grappling hooks were dragging a small pond just south of the picnic area where the young boy had been playing. After setting up a command post for the Guard activity, I questioned the police about the details of the disappearance.

The boy, Wesley Eans, three-year-old son of Mr. and Mrs. Claude Eans of Laurel, Maryland, had been playing with his six-year-old brother and four older children a short distance from where his mother was setting out their picnic lunch. At 2 p.m. when she called them to eat, little Wesley— or "Wessie" as he was called—failed to appear. His parents started hunting at once, joined by other picnicking families, and then, as anxiety mounted, by park rangers and the state police.

I went to talk to Wessie's parents now, where they waited in their white station wagon, assuring them that the Guard would stay until Wessie was found. Night was closing in fast; I could see in the couple's eyes that hope would be hard to maintain in the dark. The only consolation was that the dragging operation in the pool so far had turned up nothing.

Returning to the Jeep, I reviewed the patrols that would go out as soon as enough men arrived. We planned a fan operation based on compass azimuths, continuing until all of the park within one and a half miles in all directions from the base point had been covered. Soon the first patrol of six men started up the mountain. Throughout the night and into the early morning, as more of my company arrived, they were dispatched into the surrounding areas.

It grew cold. The temperature fell to near freezing, and as I shivered in the open Jeep I thought of a small child in a thin cotton jacket somewhere on that mountain. At approximately 2:15 our last group went out on a three-quarter-ton truck with a generator and flood lights. They were to travel the small trails west of the park, an area dotted with open cisterns.

And meanwhile the earlier patrols were returning. We began sending men home as they came in, because there seemed no place left to search. A bloodhound pack had just come back with no results either. The dogs had picked up a trail that led up into the rugged, rocky area to the northwest. After struggling after the hounds for more than a mile over terrain difficult even for adults, the search party decided the dogs had crossed scents. Doubtless the men were right: One of our Guardsmen, Staff Sgt. John Wilcox, had injured an ankle trying to get into that same area earlier. It was generally agreed that a three-year-old could not make such a climb.

About 2:30 a.m. I walked through the floodlights illuminating the parking lot to the white station wagon. I leaned down to the window and was murmuring the conventional reassurances to Mr. and Mrs. Eans when all at once my voice just stopped functioning. My throat choked up, my eyes burned. Astonished at myself, I whirled away and walked back toward my command post.

I kept walking, into the cover of the woods, and there they began, great racking sobs that I thought would tear me apart. And along with them, a sense of helplessness that I had never known before. Then, perhaps because the whole experience was so strange, I did something else completely out of character for me. I looked up through the branches to the stars shining cold and brilliant, and I said a prayer.

"Dear God," I said, "please help these people! Don't let this suffering continue. You know where Wessie is. You see him right now. Show us, dear God. Show us." It must have been ten minutes before I went back to the Jeep.

About 3:30 our last group came in, and with them the expected bad news: no sign of Wessie. The police had checked into the family's history and financial status and found no motive for kidnapping. But there is always the deranged individual, and opinion was growing that Wessie was not in the park at all. Nevertheless it was announced that the search would resume as soon as it was light.

I went home to catch a little sleep. Before turning in, I stepped into Robin's room and stood there for a minute looking down at this three-year-old snug in her own bed. Martha was awake. "I've looked at her a dozen times tonight," she said.

By 6:30 Martha was fixing eggs and coffee. I looked out the kitchen window to the mountains west of the park and realized what I had somehow known ever since that prayer was wrenched from me under the stars—that I was committed to this search until the child was found.

When I reached the park, between 600 and 700 people were gathering in the pale dawn light. Sergeant Wilcox was there, hurt ankle and all. He said he could still work the radio in the Jeep. With me at the wheel and two state troopers in the back seat, we started the Jeep up a trail northwest into the mountains.

The going was rough, and soon I had to shift into the lowest gear in four-wheel drive. Occasionally the two troopers would call out the boy's name. Then I'd have to stop and shut off the engine so we could listen. We passed the place where Wilcox had twisted his ankle in the dark. Now we were approaching the ruggedest part of the park, an area known as Cat Rock. Two miles from the base, the four of us reached the same conclusion earlier search parties had—a three-year-old could not have made it up here.

We had made about half a mile on the return leg and were descending a downgrade with the engine roaring and the squelch on the radio going, when somewhere off to my left I heard the sound I can still hear today. It was a voice, a deep male voice, saying the word, "Here."

I slammed on the brakes. The others turned to stare at me. Not a sound came from the woods around us.

"What's the matter?" Trooper Mills said.

"Nothing," I said.

And yet there had been something. I was so sure of it that I climbed out of the Jeep and walked 150 feet back up the trail. The three others were getting restless. "What are we waiting for?" one of them called.

I knew it sounded ridiculous, but I said it anyway: "I heard something."

At that Trooper Mills stood up and shouted Wessie's name. Immediately I heard another voice, but this time it was a child's voice. The others still had heard nothing. When it came the second time, I determined the direction and plunged into the woods toward it, the two troopers right behind me. Over rocks and fallen logs we scrambled, branches lashing our faces.

I reached him first, sitting behind a log, not at all surprised at seeing us. I scooped him up and crushed him to me. "Where's Mommy and Daddy?" he asked me. "I couldn't find them. I bet they went home."

We assured him that they had not. And then we looked around for the direction we'd come in. We were 250 to 300 yards from the Jeep and had got turned around. I remember that we yelled for Wilcox several times before he heard us, and when he shouted back, we could barely hear him.

As he caught sight of us, Wilcox radioed back that we were bringing Wessie in safe and sound. We found a cheese sandwich which the little fellow finished in no time. As we started the return trip down the mountain, Trooper Mills looked at me. "You could not possibly have heard that boy," he said.

"I know," I said.

Before the Jeep had completely stopped, Wessie was in the arms of his parents. Then all three were whisked away in a police car to the hospital in Frederick. The doctors' examination there confirmed what our eyes had shown us: Wessie was fine.

Wessie now is probably well on the way to forgetting what many will remember for years to come. I know that I for one have returned to that spot in the mountains where we found him. I have sought an explanation from all points of view, and I know that the only answer is the one that came to me on that day.

Wessie was miles from anyone in a cold, lonely, dark mountain. Yet he was not alone. And, for that matter, from the moment I cried out to God for help, neither was I.

God, Send Someone!
by Dick Sullivan

Suddenly the bank caved in, and tons of dirt came crashing down on Jack.

At 4:00 P.M., June 14, my brother, Jack Sullivan, was just crawling down into a ten-foot-deep trench, which ran down the center of Washington Street, a main thoroughfare in West Roxbury, Massachusetts.

It was near quitting time. Jack is a welder, and he wanted to finish one particular part of his job before he left. Jack said goodbye to the other men as they quit, took his welding lead in his right hand, lowered himself and his electric power cable into the trench. His head was well below the street surface.

Traffic up above was heavy. Jack could not see the cars and trucks, but he could feel their vibration as the earth shook slightly. Occasionally a pebble would break loose from the side of the trench and fall. Jack paid no attention to it.

It was Jack's job to weld the joints of a new water main both inside and out. First Jack crawled into the 36-inch diameter pipe, lowered his mask to protect his eyes against the bright welding arc, then went to work. After completing the inside of the joint he crawled out of the pipe. It was 4:30 P.M. He began to weld the outside. Half way through he stood up to get the kinks out of his legs. Jack stretched, turned towards the pipe, pulled down the shield again. And then it happened.

The bank caved in. Tons of dirt came crushing down on him from above and behind.

Jack was rammed against the pipe with the force of a sledge hammer. He went down, buried in a kneeling position; his shield slammed against the pipe; his nose flattened out against the inside of the shield.

The pain started. He felt his shoulder burning against

270

the red hot section of pipe he had been welding. He tried to move his shoulder back from the pipe. He couldn't.

His nose began to pain him. It was bleeding. He couldn't move his head.

Jack tried calling. Three times he shouted. The sound of his voice died in his shield. He tried to breathe slowly to preserve the supply of oxygen.

It crossed Jack's mind that he might die.

Slowly he began to pray. Going to Mass at St. Patrick's once a week suddenly seemed quite inadequate. My brother continued to pray. He had his eyes open. It was black.

Something cool crossed his right hand. He wiggled his fingers. They moved freely. His right hand had not been buried. He moved the hand again. He tried to scratch around with his hand to open up an air passage down his arm. But the weight of the earth was too great. It didn't do any good.

Then it occurred to him that he'd been holding the welding lead in that hand. So he fished around with his fingers. He found the rod, still in the holder. He grasped it tightly and moved it, hoping it would strike the pipe. Suddenly his wrist jerked and he knew he had struck an arc—the electric current would be making its bright orange flash. So he kept on tapping the pipe, making an arc, hoping it would draw attention.

"That must look like something," Jack thought to himself. "A hand reaching out of the ground striking an arc against the pipe. That must really look like something."

He began to figure how long he'd been buried. Of course there was no way of telling time. He wondered how much gasoline was left in the engine-driven welder up on top of the trench—whether it would last until dark when the orange arc might draw attention. Then he remembered that it was almost the longest day in the year; darkness wouldn't fall until nearly nine o'clock. Still, if he had enough oxygen in his little tomb and if the gasoline held out, maybe . . .

He thought of all the hundreds of people passing within feet of him up above . . .

He thought of his family and wondered if he'd ever see his little grandson again . . .

He thought of Tommy Whittaker, his assistant, out on another job on Route 128 . . .

He figured there wasn't anything to do but lie there and wait and keep tapping flashes, and hope enough air filtered into the mask to keep him alive . . . there wasn't anything to do but lie there and pray . . . God, send someone . . . someone . . .

In another part of Boston, out on Route 128, Jack's assistant, Tommy Whittaker, quit his work for the day. Whittaker was 47 years old. Jack was 41. They had known each other for over 15 years and were close friends. So close that within the next few moments one of the strangest prayer phenomena in modern times took place.

Tommy Whittaker did not know that Jack was on the Washington Street job. Whittaker got in his truck and started off down Route 128 with the full intention of driving directly home. Route 128 is a main artery, a super highway that could take him home within minutes.

But as Whittaker drove, he began to have the feeling that something wasn't right.

He tried to shake the feeling off. He kept driving. The strange and inexplainable sensation grew. He thought that he ought to drive up to the Washington Street job and check it. He dismissed the idea. It meant driving six miles out of his way at the peak of the rush hour. Whittaker approached the intersection of Washington and Route 128.

Suddenly he turned.

He did not try to explain it to himself. He just turned.

Meanwhile, Jack continued to pray. It was the same simple prayer: "God, send someone." The bleeding in his nose hadn't stopped, and the blood ran down his throat and began to clot. "God, send someone." He spat the blood out, but it was getting more difficult. All the while he listened to the muffled sound of his welding motor outside. He wondered if it was dark yet. It seemed an eternity.

Tommy Whittaker drove along Washington Street. The job was divided into two sections. He stopped his truck at a spot several blocks away from the cave-in, got out. He chatted with an engineer for the Metropolitan District Commission for 15 minutes. Whittaker did not mention the gnawing sensation that still would not leave him alone. The time was 5:45 P.M. It was still broad daylight . . .

Back in the trench, Jack struck some more arcs. He thought it might be dark by now. He listened to the welder popping. He hoped someone would come, soon. The clot of blood in his throat was getting harder to bring up. He was a little surprised that he wasn't in panic. My brother just continued to pray, "God, send . . ."

Up above, a little way down Washington Street, Tommy

Whittaker got into his truck, said goodbye to his friend, and started up again. The gnawing sensation, if anything, grew stronger. He reached a stop light. It was his turn-off to get back to 128 by a short cut. If he stayed on Washington Street, he's have to go still farther out of his way. Tommy Whittaker braked his truck for a brief instant, then continued on up Washington.

Underground, Jack finally gave up striking the arc. It was making him breathe too hard. He didn't think he could last much longer. He couldn't get the blood clot out of his throat. He was gagging . . .

At that moment up above on Washington Street, Tommy Whittaker arrived at the spot where his friend was dying. Nothing seemed unusual. He noticed the stake-body truck. But it was a truck that Sullivan never used. Whittaker thought another man from the shop was down in the trench. Whittaker pulled up. He got out of his truck, noticed the welder was running. He thought someone was inside the pipe, welding the inner circle. Nothing, still, struck him as unusual.

Then Tommy Whittaker saw the hand . . . the hand moved.

"Oh, God!" he whispered.

Whittaker jumped down into the trench and dug like a chipmunk with his hands. The earth was too packed. He scrambled out of the trench, looked back at the hand, shuddered. He shut off the welder and raced through traffic across the street to a garage.

Underground, Jack heard the pop-pop of the welder stop. It was then that he began to prepare to die. He knew it was all over. He was gagging and trying to throw off the mist that come over him.

Tommy Whittaker, feet away, shouted to the men in the garage. "There's a man buried alive over there! Get a shovel."

Back across the street Whittaker raced, carrying a snow shovel. He ran to the place where the hand stuck up, still now knowing it was his friend; he jumped down . . .

My brother, below, felt an extra pressure on top of his head. He knew someone was above him. He fought to keep from fainting.

The garage men hurried over.

"Send for the police. There's a fire box down the street. Pull the box," Whittaker called.

Tommy Whittaker began to dig. He uncovered a wrist

watch. He thought he recognized the watch band. He kept digging, until he uncovered the man's side. He saw the man was still breathing; the respiration was very weak.

Then Tommy Whittaker recognized my brother. Jack had fainted. Whittaker dug more frantically.

The rescue squad arrived. They applied an oxygen mask to Jack while they were still digging him out. From busy Washington Street, a crowd gathered now.

Jack revived slightly when they put him on a stretcher. It was 6:30 P.M. He spied Tommy Whittaker. "Who found me?" he asked.

"I did," said Whittaker.

With his lips, Jack formed one word.

"Thanks."

There was no more powerful word than that.

The gnawing sensation that had been bothering Thomas Whittaker went away.

That Bad Good Friday
by Mrs. Lowell Thomas, Jr.

By the time we reached the front hall, the whole house was beginning to shake.

It began as such a happy day, Good Friday, 1964. The snow which had been coming down for two days let up suddenly which meant that my husband Lowell could fly to Fairbanks, and get back in time for us to have all of Easter weekend together.

The children and I waved goodbye as he drove off to the airport, then shut the door quickly because it was still below freezing outside. About five o'clock, feeling lonesome for him, Anne, eight, David, six, and I went upstairs to watch TV. Anne and David wore blue jeans and cotton T-shirts; I had on a wool dress and nylon stockings. We took off our shoes so we could sit on the bed.

It was half an hour later that I heard a rumbling sound. Although we frequently hear a similar roaring—the firing of guns at a nearby Army base—I knew instantly that this was the sound of an impending earthquake.

I leaped up, called to the children to follow, and raced for the stairs. By the time we reached the front hall the whole house was beginning to shake. We ran outside into the snow, David crying, "Mommy, I'm in bare feet!"

We were about 10 feet beyond the door when the world around us fell apart. We were flung violently to the ground which was jolting back and forth with unbelievable force.

The hallway through which we had just run split in two. We heard the crashing of glass, the ear-rending sound of splintering wood. In front of us a great tree crashed full length onto the ground. Our garage collapsed with a sharp report.

Now the earth began breaking up and buckling all about us. Suddenly between Anne and me a great crack opened in

275

the snow. I stared in disbelief as the trench widened, apparently bottomless, separating me from my child. I seized the hand she stretched out to me in time to pull her across the chasm to my side.

By now the whole lawn was breaking up into chunks of dirt, rock, snow and ice. We were left on a wildly bucking slab; suddenly it tilted sharply, and we had to hang on to keep from slipping into a yawning crevasse. Though sobbing, Anne had the presence of mind to hang on by herself—thank God, for I was holding David with one hand, our bit of ground with the other.

Now the earth seemed to be rising just ahead of us. I had the weird feeling that we were riding backward on a monstrous Ferris wheel, going down, down toward the water (our house had stood on a high bluff overlooking Cook Inlet). When the worst of the rocking stopped, I looked around and saw that the entire face of the bluff had fallen to sea level. A few feet away, at the water's edge, lay the roof of our house.

All I could think of was that the water would rise as earth tumbled into it and we would be trapped. The cliffs above us were sheer, with great sections of sand and clay still falling.

The children both were hysterical, crying and saying over and over, "We'll die! We'll die!" I realized we'd have to find a way up that cliff but the children were too frightened to walk.

I suggested that we say a prayer asking Jesus to take care of us and guide us. Both children stopped crying, closed their eyes and fervently pleaded with Him to come and help us. This had an extraordinary effect on them and on me, and we set out with the first real stirrings of hope.

The next 20 minutes were one great nightmare as we clambered up and down the great slabs of earth and snow, our bare feet aching and raw in the cold. I found a large tree leaning against the cliff and thought for a few moments that we might be able to shinny up it, but we gained only a few feet. We kept moving to the right, trying to avoid holes which opened at our feet and rubble still falling from the cliff.

Suddenly a man appeared above us. "Help!" we called to him. He shouted down that he would hunt for a rope, then disappeared. As we waited we were aware for the first time that we were soaked to the skin from lying in the snow; the children were shaking and their lips were blue.

At last six or eight men appeared at the top of the cliff. One of them, a stranger to us, started down toward us, finding one less steep spot. The children threw their arms around him as he reached us. He took off his black wool jacket, put it around Anne, then boosted David into his arms and led us all back up along the rope.

At the top there was a steep, sheer rim which I doubt I could have scaled by myself. But willing hands hauled us up and tucked us into a waiting car. When I turned to thank our rescuer, he had gone. But nearby I saw the strained, white face of our neighbor Wanda Mead. Someone told me that two of her five children were missing.

We were driven to the home of friends who lived well away from the devastated area. They wrapped us in blankets, but there was no heat in the house nor any way to make a hot drink.

The children were offered beds but refused to leave my side where I huddled with the others over the portable radio; they finally curled up in sleeping bags on the floor. Sleep for me was impossible until two questions were answered; had Fairbanks, where Lowell was, felt the quake, and how could we get word to him that we were all right?

The radio reported all the homes along our street destroyed, and that the two Mead children were still missing. I winced at the frequent pleas, "Urgent to Dr. Mead . . . needed immediately at Providence Hospital."

Perry Mead, Alaska's only neurosurgeon, spent the next 24 hours going from bed to bed at the hospital, tending to the needs of others while tears for his children streamed down his face.

The radio listed tremendous damage in the downtown area. We, living in Anchorage, watching it grow day by day, had felt personal pride in each new building that rose. Now the tally of damaged schools, stores and office buildings mounted by the hour.

There was a continuous stream of "Tell John his father and mother are at the Stewarts," or "The Johnson family wants to know the whereabouts of daughter Ann." It seemed an eternity to me before radio contact was reestablished with Fairbanks and we learned that it had felt merely a strong jolt. Planes were arriving from there with doctors and supplies, and I knew Lowell would be aboard one of them.

Then suddenly the announcer's voice said, "If anyone knows the whereabouts of Mrs. Lowell Thomas and family, please contact us immediately." I ran to the telephone and was so overwhelmed to find it working that I could hardly talk to the person who answered. But I got the essentials through, and just half an hour later Lowell walked through the door.

Words cannot describe our reunion. The kids and I were tremendously relieved, but Lowell's emotions were those of a man who had not known for many hours whether his family was dead or alive.

Next morning, Easter Sunday, Lowell, Anne, David and I rose early. We put on the same clothes we had been wearing for two days: Anne the coat provided by our unknown rescuer, far more meaningful to her than any Easter bonnet; David a pair of pants too small to button, me some men's corduroy trousers.

Many in the Easter congregation wore similar misfits, and the air in the heatless church was so cold that our breaths hung white above us as we sang "Hallelujah!" But it was an Easter service to remember.

At the rear of the church the minister had pinned two sheets of paper, one to be signed by the "haves"—those who had clothing and household goods to contribute—and one where the homeless could write down what they needed. At least 20 families there that morning had lost everything, yet as we left the church I saw that not one person had signed the "have not" list.

For what was there that we did not have? We had new gratitude for the gift of life and for the fact that, in one of history's worst earthquakes, loss of life had been as small as it had. We had a state to rebuild with a new love for the word "Alaska" born the night we watched our neighbors rise to heroism. Above all we had the Easter message ringing in our hearts.

For the first Christians, too, lived through a sorrowful Friday, a Friday when their dreams collapsed, their hopes lay in ruins, when by every earthly standard they had lost everything. And then on Sunday morning they were the first to whisper the news that has transformed every loss from that day on, the news that love had won, that God had the final word, that death was overcome, that He had risen.

S.O.S. Anyone, Anywhere!
by Beth Black

> Her husband had collapsed at the controls of the
> plane, and she didn't know how to fly.

It was a perfect night for flying. Two thousand feet below us
the friendly lights of the Dallas suburbs made an endless
necklace against the dark earth. Above us, the soft spring sky
was spangled with stars. The engine of our little airplane, the
Blue Bird, droned steadily. My pilot-husband said happily, "I
love flying at night, don't you? Just the two of us."

I nodded, too contented to speak. It seemed to me that I
had everything in life that a woman could ask for: an adored
husband, a houseful of children waiting at home, security,
happiness. . . . And then without warning, like a hammer
smashing down on a crystal vase, came panic and terror. I
heard Spence gasp, felt the plane lurch. I saw him clutch at
his chest with one hand. "Darling!" I cried. "What's wrong?"
There was no answer. The look of pain faded from his face,
his head fell back, his shoulder sagged against mine. His
other hand slipped from the wheel.

"Spence!" I screamed. I leaned across him and grabbed
the wheel with both hands, trying to steady the plane. Even
as a passenger, I knew that if you pushed the wheel forward,
the plane would nose down. If you pulled it back, the *Blue
Bird* would rise. If you turned it like the steering wheel of a
car, the plane would bank to the right or left. But that was
all I did know. I was two thousand feet above the darkened
earth in a plane that I didn't know how to fly.

The gauges on the instrument panel were a menacing
jumble of needles and figures. But in those first dreadful seconds all I could think of was Spence. His eyes were half
open; he seemed to be breathing faintly. I took one hand
from the wheel and groped for his pulse. Spence was still
alive, but some deep instinct told me that this was a fatal
heart attack.

Suddenly something in me seemed to cry out, if Spence is dying, then let me die too. Let me go with him, and not hurt anyone else by crashing into a house, or—worse, perhaps—colliding with another plane. I twisted the wheel, turning the plane, heading for the dark areas away from the lighted suburbs, away from the crowded airlanes between Fort Worth and Dallas. Above some open field I could shove the wheel forward, or just let go. . . .

This was my first reaction, but then, right on its heels, came a more rational thought: what about the five trusting children waiting at home? Did I have the right to rob them of *both* parents? Of course I didn't! I had to get back to them.

I knew that if I was to have any chance at all, I would have to get through to the control tower at the Dallas airport. I picked up the radio microphone and pressed the sending button as I had seen Spence do. "S.O.S." My voice was shrill with grief and terror. "S.O.S. Love Field! This is Nine Seven Charlie calling Love Field. I'm in trouble, terrible trouble. Please help me."

Static crackled from the loudspeaker-receiver above my head, but only static. Perhaps I was sending on the wrong channel. Frantically I twisted the selector switch and tried another frequency. "S.O.S. Love Field. S.O.S. anyone, anywhere! I need help! Oh, God, won't someone help me?" It was more than just a question. It was a prayer, the most desperate and urgent prayer I had uttered in my life.

And although I didn't know it, the prayer was being answered. In the tower at Love Feld, the traffic controller, Donald C. Potter, did hear me faintly. Instantly emergency measures were taken. Potter's supervisor, Lester Reece, ordered his radar room to try to get a fix on the *Blue Bird*. Two airliners and a private plane waiting to land were sent into a holding pattern away from the field. Crash trucks and firemen were alerted. Don Potter kept calling to me, asking me to identify myself, but I could not hear him. In my panic I was switching frequencies so rapidly that he could not get through to me. Eventually Lester Reece realized this, and gave orders to start calling on all 16 channels.

Now a bumpy wind sprang up, buffeting the little plane, making it swoop and lurch more wildly than ever. Once the lights below came rushing up at me. In terror I tugged back on the wheel and saw the stars glitter as the *Blue Bird* climbed. Reaching across Spence to hold the wheel was awkward and difficult. I knew the controls could be swung over to the passenger's seat, but I was afraid to attempt this, afraid I might lose control altogether. "Help me, help me?" I sobbed into the microphone, but my only answer was static and a jumble of faraway voices.

Below me I saw a brighter light and, looking down, I recognized the 22-story Southland Life building. I was over downtown Dallas. Now, at least, I knew where Love Field was. I headed for it, pushing the wheel forward.

Now the altimeter read 1,000 feet. Now it was 800. Ahead of me I saw two parallel rows of blue lights. A runway, I thought: this would have to be it. Down, down. . . .

"Pull up! Pull up!" A frantic voice from the loudspeaker suddenly ripped into my ears. "Aircraft south of Love Field, pull up! You're going into the downtown area!"

For one heart-stopping second, I was paralyzed. Then I knew. Those blue lights below me didn't mark a landing strip. They were the parkway lights of an expressway! In a frenzy of fear, I yanked the wheel back. The *Blue Bird* climbed steeply. Below me I saw cars and the massive shadow of an overpass. I don't know how close I came. It seemed like inches.

"Turn around!" cried the loudspeaker. "Turn around!"

Somehow I turned the plane back toward Love Field. This time I picked an actual landing strip, Runway 31. I was coming in cross-wind, and I still was frightened, but a strange thing had happened in the darkened cabin. I could feel Spence's shoulder solid against mine, and suddenly some of the panic left me. A surge of strength and determination seemed to come from outside me, as if God had heard my prayers, as if Spence were somehow helping me too. It was an extraordinary sensation, this feeling that God and my husband were with me, two separate, strengthening spirits trying to calm and reassure me, give me courage. . . .

I reached out and punched the button marked "flaps," as I had seen Spence do. I punched the one marked "landing gear." The plane was weaving badly; I couldn't control it. I knew I was going too fast, but I was still afraid to touch the throttle. I decided the only way to slow down was to cut off the engine. I reached out and turned the ignition key. In the sudden silence, the wind shrieked and the voice on the loudspeaker kept calling instructions, but I could do nothing except cling desperately to the wheel. I saw the ground rushing up, but I didn't feel the plane touch the concrete. I didn't feel or remember anything. I don't to this day.

They tell me that the *Blue Bird* slammed into the ground at an angle of 25 degrees, bounded 40 feet in the air, then slid another 300 feet in a screeching mass of tangled wreckage. The horrified watchers were sure that no one could have survived. But when the crash trucks pulled alongside, I was sitting on the edge of a crumpled wing, jaw cracked in three places, left arm smashed above the elbow, dazed and bleeding, but alive—and asking for help for my husband. But Spence was beyond all help. The doctors believe he died before the crash. I think so too.

Has this experience changed me inwardly? Of course it has. Until that night of May 14, 1960, I never stopped to wonder whether the Power that rules the universe cared about me. By rights, I should have been killed in the crash at Love Field. But I wasn't. And years later, I still remember that extraordinary sense of being sustained and protected by a Power beyond all human comprehension. That was the contact that brought me through the worst crisis of my life.

Section Seven—

A Quiet Faith

Section Seven—
Introduction

All magazines look for "big" stories about important, world-moving themes and about prominent people with money, fame and influence. Yet Guideposts discovered early in its history that there are many heart-warming stories which never make headlines. Often they are about little-known people doing small tasks and kindnesses which together have a great cumulative effect on society. We named these folks "Quiet People," and over the years hundreds of stories have been printed about them.

They may work in train stations (like Ralston Young, Redcap 42) or drive a bus (like Singin' Sam) or work with a jackhammer (like Joe Sceppa), but each in his own way contributes more than muscle. The Quiet Person brings faith to bear on his and other people's problems, using gentleness, tolerance, selflessness, reasoned action and understanding.

We think you will like these stories, because they are about people easy to like. Just Quiet People.

Track Thirteen
by Chase Walker

A man who took his faith to work.

As Station Porter No. 42 pushed his empty baggage carrier up the ramp in Grand Central Station, another Redcap hailed him.

"Hello, Preacher."

Redcap No. 42 turned and smiled easily into the irreverent face of his co-worker.

"I don't mind your calling me that," he said, "but take off the 'P' and make it 'Reacher,' will you? All I'm trying to do is reach out a bit and help other people find themselves."

The other porter grinned back. It was hard to get irritated with this good-natured Negro.

Ralston Crosbie Young, the porter No. 42 in question, was, until his retirement, known to millions as Grand Central Station's "Most Unforgettable Redcap." A medium-sized man, Ralston made a career of carrying luggage and offering comfort to the discouraged and the bewildered. This eager disciple of God discovered that a busy railroad terminal is an ideal place to practice religion every day of the week.

Each Monday, Wednesday and Friday noon Ralston conducted the now famous "Track Thirteen" worship service. Executives and clerks, railroad employees and officials, travelers, men and women of all walks of life would gather on these days at the stroke of twelve in front of Track 13 in New York's Grand Central Station. Ralston then would unlock the gate and all would file down to a vacant coach for a fellowship prayer meeting.

"We're just a group of people who like to talk and pray together and find a solution to our problems through Christ," Ralston would explain simply.

The meetings began back in 1944 when Ralston, having heard about other small prayer groups which were meeting regularly in shops, factories and offices, gathered together several interested persons.

When the Reader's Digest featured Ralston and his unique prayer service, men and women of faith throughout the world made a mental note to attend should they ever get to New York. But along with the cheers came the inevitable jeers. Jibes from some of his fellow workers cut deeply at first. Dislike for several of the men welled up so strongly in Ralston at times that he got down on his knees and prayed about it.

"I had to learn to love the hate right out of my system," he declared.

Passing through the employee's locker room one day, he noticed a small group in the middle of a discussion. One called over to him.

"Say, Ralston, I suppose you know that the Bible has more filth in it than any book ever written?"

Ralston was on guard. "Which part of the Bible?"

"I don't remember which part . . . most all the way through it, I guess."

Another chimed in. "He's right. The Bible is full of dirt."

Ralston steadied himself to meet this new attack. "One at a time, boys." Then to the first, "Did someone tell you this, or have you read the Bible yourself?"

"I read it, but I don't remember which sections."

Ralston dismissed him with a wave of his hand. "You can't tell me where you read this filth, so that lets you out." To the others. "Can anyone name a part of the Bible which is filthy?"

One thought he knew and named a chapter.

Ralston had himself well under control now. "Here's my answer to that. The Bible is history. History, both the good and the bad, has to be recorded as it happened. You can't call the Bible filthy for stating true historical facts. Besides the Bible deals not only with God Almighty, but with man and his transgressions."

These answers had enough logic to satisfy most of the group. Several wanted to argue further, but Ralston had made his point. Besides it was getting close to noon and time for his regular "Track Thirteen" meeting.

On this particular Wednesday Ralston arrived at the track gate to greet several old friends including a retired railroad official, a pastor from New Jersey and a Mr. Johnson from Pennsylvania. Then he introduced himself to three new-comers: a young blond giant who looked like he could play football for anybody's team, a slim merchant seaman, and a Guideposts reporter.

This group—an interesting cross section of American life—filed down to an unlighted coach, which was illuminated solely by rays from the platform lights. Coach seats on both sides of the aisle were adjusted to seat seven. The atmosphere was informal, relaxed.

Ralston opened with a short prayer, calling for peace and understanding in a troubled world. Then he began the discussion by telling of the incident where he was called on to defend the Bible.

"I knew they were trying to put me on a spot," he said, "but I controlled myself and waited for the Lord to give me the right answer."

Others then joined in the discussion, eager to tell of their own special problems. As they talked each one found himself being drawn more closely to the others. Barriers slip away easily somehow when people *know* they are in the presence of *Him*.

The merchant sailor was the last to join in the conversation. Shy at first, the lad soon talked freely. He had read about Track Thirteen while on shipboard thousands of miles away from home. Inspired by the story, he had resolved that some day he would get to New York and attend a meeting.

"Now that I've had a chance to meet with you people, I can see that Track Thirteen can go on forever. On my next voyage I'm going to try and organize a meeting like this on shipboard." The young man's enthusiasm left an atmosphere of quiet elation in the coach.

The meeting then broke up. Spiritually refreshed, all started back to their normal routines, each one feeling a new strength and vigor to meet the problems of the day.

Ralston, however, was still willing to talk further about Track Thirteen.

"Years ago," he stated to the Guideposts reporter, "I tried everything to find happiness. Nothing lasted. Then I began to live my life for Christ. It was as simple as that. I then found the happiness I had looked for so long."

"It hasn't all been easy though," he continued. "I've made mistakes and gotten off the course many times. But just when I feel lowest, something always happens to give me a new zest for life and even more faith in God.

"Take Mr. Johnson who was here today," Ralston said. "He had a brother who was very sick. Hearing of our Track Thirteen prayer fellowship, he came one day simply to pray for his brother.

"When he told us about his brother, we all prayed for him too. Then he returned for a second time, and a third. Finally, he told us that he believed our prayers were doing more good than anything else to help his brother pull through. We felt wonderful about it.

"Mr. Johnson's faith in his brother's eventual recovery grew with each visit. For a time it did seem that his brother would recover. Then suddenly he died.

"As far as Mr. Johnson was concerned," Ralston went on, "that did it. He was through with us—and worse—with God. He figured that God had let him down. I felt very bad. It was just one of those things hard to understand and explain. Mr. Johnson was a fine man, but his hurt was more than he could take at that time.

"This all happened over a year ago. We didn't see Mr. Johnson again as the months went by, but we never forgot him in our prayers. One week I was in a particularly low mood. Troubles seemed to be ganging up on me from all sides. I guess the Lord decided one Friday that I needed a special lift. That noon when I came to Track Thirteen. . . .

"*There was Mr. Johnson.*

"He didn't have to tell me why he had finally come back. I knew he would some day. He had found out that living a life without God is living without hope or happiness."

"Ralston," Mr. Johnson said to me later on, "I suddenly realized that all along I had been asking God to give *me* something. I had never once tried to give something to *Him* in return. You just can't deal with God that way."

It was time for Ralston to go back on duty. As he locked the gate and turned toward the congested station floor, a gleam of excitement and—something else—came into his eyes. "You know, Grand Central Station is a parish—a big one and a mighty good one. I wouldn't trade my job here for any in the world."

Don't Bring Lulu
by Charlotte L. Dulcie
(as told to Leona N. Hands)

A broken relationship healed.

The first time I walked into the factory, I had a feeling I didn't belong there. When I asked for Mr. Funt, the plant superintendent, I was directed to a plump, red-faced man with a big cigar between his teeth.

He was standing with several girls, listening to one tell a story. She finished and everyone doubled up with laughter.

"You take the cake, Belle," he said. "I don't know where you find them stories, but they're all dillies."

Then he noticed me in the background of the group and walked toward me. "You the new girl?" he asked.

When I nodded, he introduced me to the other girls. "Meet Charlotte," he said. "I'm putting you in Belle's group. She's the fastest worker we got. Don't try to compete with her. Just let her show you how to do the work."

I could tell Belle was looking me over as I followed her to the assembly-line. Being so small in size and uncertain, I must have seemed unfriendly, but Belle gave it a try. She repeated the story she had told the boss. I looked blank. Belle thumped me on the back. "You didn't get it, did you, Kid?"

When I still didn't respond, Belle looked at me suspiciously.

The plant produced leather goods and our unit put together handmade billfolds—one of the company's most expensive items. Belle patiently showed me how to shape the pieces of leather. Although my hands are small, I have nimble fingers and catch on quickly. In a matter of a few days I was one of the fastest workers. I was anxious to make good because it had taken me weeks to find this job and I needed extra money for my mother who was seriously ill.

289

I liked the work, but soon realized that the other girls were different from those I knew in the small farming community where I had been raised. The conversation was full of dirty words which made me blush. My embarrassment and lack of response annoyed Belle. She began to ride me; when I tried to ignore her this made it worse.

Then came the episode at lunch about a week or so after I had been on the job. For the first few days I had eaten my lunch by myself in a corner. One of the girls tried to be helpful. "They feel you're high-hat and too good for them," she said. "I didn't like their language or stories either when I first came here, but I soon learned that you either joined in, or you get the business. If you need this job, you'd better be friendly."

I wanted to be friendly. The problem was I didn't know how. So this day at lunch I picked a seat in the middle of the other girls close to Belle. No one really knew my full name or my nickname, so somewhat hesitantly I told them:

"You know, my full name is Charlotte Lucinda Dulcie, but for some reason I've always been called Lulu."

At first no one seemed the least bit interested. Then someone giggled.

"Well, I'll be d. . . .," said Belle. She seemed struck by something, began humming. Then out came the words:

"You can always bring Kate
For she's a good skate
But don't bring Lulu."

Other voices joined in, and they repeated the "Don't bring Lulu" verse over and over again with great hilarity. My face got redder and redder.

Then the singing stopped while Belle launched into a long story, spliced with epithets and vulgarity. I couldn't take it any more and slipped away to the washroom where I stayed until the lunch period was over.

This episode made the break between Belle and me complete. I was stung by the way she made fun of me. Belle was furious when I walked out in the middle of her story.

I am small and shy and awkward socially, but I am no quitter. The job was important to me and I was determined to do so well that they couldn't fire me. The harder I worked, the worse the abuse from Belle and the others. I kept silent, but I couldn't stand them and they had nothing but contempt for me.

One night several weeks later, however, I was ready to

give in. There seemed to be no one who cared. My mother was so sick I couldn't confide in her. It seemed so utterly hopeless. Yet there was One to turn to. . . .

On my knees I poured out my heart to Him, "I can't stand it another day. It's impossible. I just can't work there any longer."

The tears came and I don't know how long I sat there just feeling sorry for myself. But after a while there came a feeling of peace. And then the words, "But you haven't really tried to tell them of Me."

Was I hearing things? What an impossible request! God couldn't really expect me to try and inject religion into that sordid situation.

Not religion—but Me!

I couldn't get to sleep thinking about it. It was fantastic: how could a mousy person like me even get their attention; much less be a witness to a Higher Power?

The next morning was a blur as my thoughts raced and my head pounded. Lunch came. I let the other girls go in first, then I walked into the midst of them.

"Here's Lulu," cried one girl. "Belle, how about a good story for Lulu."

"What for?" mocked Belle. "She'd never get it. She's a virgin."

I didn't say a word, but took my sandwich and thermos and placed it at the seat directly beside Belle. She looked surprised. I sat down and began to unwrap the paper from my sandwich. *Oh, Lord. How do I say it?*

The room had grown quiet, much too quiet. I cleared my voice and turned to Belle. "I would like to say something to you," I began.

Belle's face was cold. "Speak up, Kiddo. It's a free country."

"I'm not very good at saying things," I began. "And I don't know how to get along with most people. It isn't because I don't want to be friends. I don't know how."

My eyes began to fill with tears. Angrily I tried to hold them back, to brush them away, but they streamed down my face. I couldn't stop now.

"I came here to work because I needed this job. I never worked in a factory before. What you girls say and do is all strange to me. Most of all I don't like dirty jokes. Someone told me to pretend I do and laugh with everyone else. I suppose I could learn to do this after a while, but there is something else that will always keep me from doing it."

The room was completely still now. I gulped, swiped at my tears and went on.

"There are certain words you use all the time: God and Jesus. You say them with scorn and as swear words. To me, these words are very precious. Years ago I made certain vows to Jesus Christ. When I hear His name used the way you do it makes me feel all sick inside. I tell myself that you really do not mean to take His name in vain, that in your way, you may be as good as or a better Christian than I am. But every time I try to reach out to be friendly, something you say makes me freeze inside. Do you have to use this kind of language?"

Someone laughed scornfully. Belle turned on the girl. "Be quiet. Let her finish."

But I had said it all except one thing. "I would like to be your friend, Belle, if there is any way I can."

The hardness was gone from Belle's face. "Eat your lunch, Lulu," she said to me gently. Then she turned to the other girls:

"If there is one thing I like in a person it's courage. Lulu has it. What she just said took guts. What's more I think she's right. Our talk has been pretty bad, and mine has been the worst. It's time we changed."

I seemed to float through the rest of the day. There were smiles and nods now from nearly everyone. And the atmosphere in the factory did change in the weeks that followed. Not that all the profanity stopped, but it did around me.

To my surprise, Belle and several other girls whom I considered so crude at first, became my close friends. A couple began attending church with me.

Months later, however, I had to quit my job and give fulltime care to my mother. To my amazement, the girls gave me a farewell dinner. It was Belle who presented me with a gift of some money, and then gave a little speech:

"Lulu, you put me in my place once. But you did it like a lady. I thank you for that and for the way you stand up for what you believe. And, Lulu, I always want to be your friend."

Why, Lord, are we so fearful of stepping out in Your name when the results can be so amazing?

Singin' Sam
by Sidney Fields

They call him New York City's "happiest bus driver."

Sam Cascavilla closed the door behind the last passenger boarding his bus at a midtown corner in New York and was about to drive off when he saw two middle-aged women running to make it. He opened the door again, got out of his seat and called out to them:

"Don't rush, young ladies. There's time. There's always more time than money."

They climbed aboard panting and grinning. The other passengers smiled too. They always do with Sam. Sam's bus is a sort of special world, and anyone stepping into it immediately feels free of the city's frenzy and indifference.

"Time now is 10:03 and 45 seconds," Sam announced. "Temperature 61 degrees. No rain due. This is 50th Street. Change for Radio City Music Hall. The Waldorf Astoria. Stay healthy and say a prayer for me. Thank you."

Sam drives along Eighth Avenue through factory and business districts, through slum, middle-class and elegant areas. His passengers include the rich and poor. He is known as Singin' Sam not only in New York but in far corners of America where visitors have carried the story of the bus driver with the friendly patter.

Between announcements and greetings this particular day, Sam broke into song with lyrics of his own . . . "Trala lala lalala I love you. I love you. Oh I love you."

When a taxi cut across his path, he waved it through. "Go on, go on and God bless you!" he called.

Spotting an elderly man across the street, apparently uncertain of where he was, Sam opened the window, gave him the directions he needed and then apologized, "Sorry I can't turn around and take you there, young man." Laughter filled the bus.

No matter what the age of his passengers they're always "young lady" or "young man" to Sam. And "They're all wonderful," he says. "Wonderful." And when he says it it sounds truly joyous.

A very young lady boarded the bus with her mother. "I'm seven years old today," she confided to the bus driver. Sam congratulated her, then burst into a birthday song. Off came his hat which was passed through the bus. Six dollars was collected for a birthday gift—much to the delight of the girl and over the embarrassed protests of Mother.

Driving by the park Sam called out, "Look at the magnolia tree. Beautiful, isn't it?" Then in almost a sing song he told the whole world, "Oh, it's nice to be here. God puts a touch of heaven here too, you know."

Near the end of his run Sam stopped to yell out to a fruit dealer, "How's your sister-in-law?"

"She came home from the hospital yesterday."

"Tell her I'm praying for her."

The fruit dealer leaned inside the bus and handed him a pear. At the corner Sam gave it to a policeman.

For over 30 years Sam has driven a bus. People wait for him. His chatter is a bonus that seldom comes with the fare. When he isn't driving a bus, Sam and his wife love to visit their daughter, son-in-law and two grandchildren.

"Playing with the *grandkids* and working in the garden and driving a bus. That's my life," says Sam with a contented smile that belies the fact that he has had some dark days few people knew about.

Sam met his wife, Josephine, when she and her parents were steady passengers on the open trolly car he drove back in the late '20s before he switched to buses. Some years after their marriage Josephine developed a bad cough. The x-rays showed spots on both lungs.

One doctor suggested an upstate sanitarium where Josephine might have a chance—or pass her final days in clean, fresh air. Sam had little money, so he worked double shifts to pay the heavy bills.

"I never stopped praying and believing she would get well. Never," Sam declared.

He carried his burden for eight years, alone. But one bright day, Sam's prayer was answered: Josephine came back to him, smiling, healthy.

"You should see her now," he said, "like a girl of 25."

Then Sam confided, "I learned a lot during the years Josephine was sick. When people have trouble—and we all do—it's easy to be grouchy; hard to smile. I didn't want to burden my daughter, my wife, my in-laws, my passengers with my troubles. So while I drove I talked, whistled, sang and laughed. The result was others around me smiled and talked and felt better. And seeing them feel better made me happier.

"I'll drive as long as they let me. If I were rich I'd pay the company to let me drive, and pay the passengers to let me ride with them."

Could You Have Loved This Much?

by Bob Considine

An award-winning newspaper columnist and author tells an unforgettable story.

This is the story of a woman's love for her husband. Whether he deserved that love—and why he acted the way he did—are questions I can't answer. I'm not going to write about Karl Taylor, this story is about his wife.

The story begins early in 1950 in the Taylors' small apartment in Waltham, Massachusetts. Edith Taylor was sure that she was "the luckiest woman on the block." She and Karl had been married 23 years, and her heart still skipped a beat when he walked into the room.

Oh—there'd been tough times during those years, times when Karl had been depressed, unable to keep a job; but she had helped him through the low times and she only loved him more because he needed her.

As for Karl, he gave every appearance of a man in love with his wife. Indeed, he seemed almost dependent on her, as if he didn't want to be too long away from her. If his job as government warehouse worker took him out of town, he'd write Edith a long letter every night and drop her postcards several times during the day. He sent small gifts from every place he visited.

Often at night they'd sit up late in their apartment and talk about the house they'd own . . . someday . . . "when we can make the down-payment" . . .

In February, 1950, the government sent Karl to Okinawa for a few months to work in a new warehouse there. It was a long time to be away, and so far!

This time, no little gifts came. Edith understood. He was putting every cent he saved into the bank for their home.

Hadn't she begged him for years not to spend so much on her, to save it for the house?

The lonesome months dragged on, and it seemed to Edith that the job over there was taking longer and longer. Each time she expected him home he'd write that he must stay "another three weeks." "Another month." "Just a couple of months longer."

He'd been gone a year now—and suddenly Edith had an inspiration. Why not buy their home now, before Karl got back, as a surprise for him! She was working now, in a factory in Waltham, and putting all her earnings in the bank. So she made a down payment on a cozy, unfinished cottage with lots of trees and a view.

Now the days sped past because she was busy with her wonderful surprise. In two months more, she earned enough to get the floor laid in one of the bedrooms. The next month, she ordered the insulation. She was getting into debt, she knew, but with what Karl must have saved . . .

She worked feverishly, almost desperately, for now there was something she didn't want to think about.

Karl's letters were coming less and less often. No gifts she understood. But a few pennies for a postage stamp?

Then, after weeks of silence, came a letter:

"Dear Edith. I wish there were a kinder way to tell you that we are no longer married . . ."

Edith walked to the sofa and sat down. He'd written to Mexico for a divorce. It had come in the mail. The woman lived on Okinawa. She was Japanese, Aiko, maid-of-all-work assigned to his quarters.

She was 19. Edith was 48.

Now, if I were making up this story, the rejected wife would feel first shock, then fury. She would fight that quick paper-divorce, she would hate her husband and the woman. She would want vengeance for her own shattered life.

But I am describing here simply what did happen. Edith Taylor did not hate Karl. Perhaps she had loved him so long she was unable to stop loving him.

She could picture the situation so well. A penniless girl. A lonely man who—Edith knew it—sometimes drank more than he should. Constant closeness. But even so (here Edith made an heroic effort to be proud of her husband)—even so, Karl had not done the easy, shameful thing. He had chosen the hard way of divorce, rather than take advantage of a young servant-girl.

The only thing Edith could not believe was that he had stopped loving her. That he loved Aiko, too, she made herself accept.

But the difference in their ages, in their backgrounds—this couldn't be the kind of love she and Karl had known! Someday they would both discover this, someday, somehow, Karl would come home.

Edith now built her life around this thought. She wrote Karl, asking him to keep her in touch with the small, day-to-day things in his life. She sold the little cottage with its view and its snug insulation. Karl never knew about it.

He wrote one day that he and Aiko were expecting a baby. Marie was born in 1951, then in 1953, Helen. Edith sent gifts to the little girls. She still wrote to Karl and he wrote back: the comfortable, detailed letters of two people who knew each other very well. Helen had a tooth. Aiko's English was improving, Karl had lost weight.

Edith's life was lived now on Okinawa. She merely went through the motions of existence in Waltham. Back and forth between factory and apartment, her mind was always on Karl. Someday he'll come back . . .

And then the terrible letter: Karl was dying of lung cancer.

Karl's last letters were filled with fear. Not for himself, but for Aiko, and especially for his two little girls. He had been saving to send them to school in America, but his hospital bills were taking everything. What would become of them?

Then Edith knew that her last gift to Karl could be peace of mind for these final weeks. She wrote him that, if Aiko were willing, she would take Marie and Helen and bring them up in Waltham.

For many months after Karl's death, Aiko would not let the children go. They were all she had ever known. Yet what could she offer them except a life like hers had been? A life of poverty, servitude, and despair. In November, 1956, she sent them to her "Dear Aunt Edith."

Edith had known it would be hard to be mother at 54 to a three-year-old and a five-year-old. She hadn't known that in the time since Karl's death they would forget the little English they knew.

But Marie and Helen learned fast. The fear left their eyes, their faces grew plump. And Edith—for the first time in six years, Edith was hurrying home from work. Even getting meals was fun again!

Sadder were the times when letters came from Aiko. "Aunt. Tell me now what they do. If Marie or Helen cry or not." In the broken English Edith read the loneliness, and she knew what it was to be lonely.

Money was another problem. Edith hired a woman to care for the girls while she worked. Being both mother and wage-earner left her thin and tired. In February she became ill, but she kept working because she was afraid to lose a day's pay; at the factory one day she fainted. She was in the hospital two weeks with pneumonia.

There in the hospital bed, she faced the fact that she would be old before the girls were grown. She thought she had done everything that love for Karl asked of her, but now she knew there was one thing more. She must bring the girls' real mother here too.

She had made the decision, but doing it was something else. Aiko was still a Japanese citizen, and that immigration quota had a waiting list many years long.

It was then that Edith Taylor wrote to me, telling me her story and asking if I could help her. I described the situation in my newspaper column. Others did more. Petitions were started, a special bill speeded through Congress, and in August, 1957, Aiko Taylor was permitted to enter the country.

As the plane came in at New York's International Airport, Edith had a moment of fear. What if she should hate this woman who had taken Karl away from her?

The last person off the plane was a girl so thin and small Edith thought at first it was a child. She did not come down the stairs, she only stood there, clutching the railing, and Edith knew that if she had been afraid, Aiko was near panic.

She called Aiko's name and the girl rushed down the steps and into Edith's arms. In that brief moment, as they held each other (cover photo), Edith had an extraordinary thought. "Help me," she said, her eyes tight shut. "Help me to love this girl, as if she were part of Karl, come home. I prayed for him to come back. Now he has—in his two little daughters and in this gentle girl that he loved. Help me, God, to know that."

Edith and Aiko Taylor and the two little girls began to live together in the apartment in Waltham. Marie became the best student in her second grade class; Helen's kindergarten teacher adored her. And Aiko—she began studying nursing. Someday, she and Edith would like a house of their own. At night they sit up late and make plans. Today Edith Taylor knows she is "the luckiest woman on the block."

The Old Fisherman
by Mary Bartels

"I was tempted to turn him away. He was so ugly."

Our house was directly across the street from the clinic entrance of Johns Hopkins Hospital in Baltimore. We lived in the downstairs and rented the upstairs rooms to outpatients at the clinic.

One summer evening as I was fixing supper, there was a knock at the door. I opened it to see a truly awful looking old man.

"Why he's hardly taller than my eight-year-old," I thought as I stared at the stooped, shriveled body.

But the appalling thing was his face—lopsided from swelling, red and raw.

Yet his voice was pleasant as he said, "Good evening, I've come to see if you've a room for just one night. I came for a treatment this morning from the Eastern Shore and there's no bus till morning."

He told me he'd been hunting for a room since noon but with no success. "I guess it's my face. I know it looks terrible but my doctor says with a few more treatments . . ."

For a moment I hesitated but his next words convinced me, "I could sleep in this rocking chair on the porch. My bus leaves early in the morning."

I told him we would find him a bed, but to rest on the porch meanwhile. Then I went inside and finished getting supper. When we were ready I asked the old man if he would join us.

"No, thank you. I have plenty," and he held up a brown paper bag.

When I had finished the dishes I went out on the porch to talk with him a few minutes. It didn't take long to see that this old man had an oversized heart in that tiny body.

301

He told me that he fished for a living to support his daughter, her five children and her husband who was hopelessly crippled from a back injury. He didn't tell it by way of complaint; every other sentence was prefaced with a thanks to God for a blessing. He was grateful that no pain accompanied his disease, which was apparently a form of skin cancer. He thanked God for giving him the strength to keep going.

At bedtime, we put a camp cot in the children's room for him. When I got up in the morning, the bed linens were neatly folded and the little old man was out on the porch. He refused breakfast but just before he left for his bus, haltingly as if asking a great favor, he said, "Could I please come back and stay the next time I have to have a treatment? I won't put you out a bit—I can sleep fine in a chair." He paused a moment and then added, "Your children made me feel at home. Grownups are bothered by my face but children don't seem to mind."

I told him he was welcome to come again. And on his next trip he arrived a little after seven in the morning. As a gift, he brought us a big fish and a quart of the largest oysters I had ever seen. He said that he had shucked them that morning before he left so they would be nice and fresh. I knew his bus left at four a.m. and wondered what time he had to get up in order to do this.

In the years he came to stay overnight with us there was never a time that he did not bring us fish or oysters or vegetables from his garden.

Other times we received packages in the mail, always by special delivery: fish and oysters packed in a box of fresh young spinach or kale, every leaf carefully washed. Knowing that he must walk three miles to mail these and how little money he had, made the gifts doubly precious.

When I received these little remembrances, I often thought of a comment our next-door neighbor made after he left that first morning, "Did you keep that awful looking old man last night? I turned him away. You can lose roomers by putting up such people."

And maybe we did, once or twice. But oh! if only they could have known him, perhaps their illnesses would have been easier to bear. I know our family always will be grateful to have known him; from him we learned what it was to accept the bad without complaint and the good with gratitude to God.

Recently I was visiting a friend who has a greenhouse. As she showed me her flowers we came to the most beautiful one of all: a golden chrysanthemum bursting with blooms. But to my great surprise it was growing in an old, dented, rusty bucket. I thought to myself, if this were my plant I'd put it in the loveliest container I had. My friend changed my mind.

"I ran short of pots," she explained, "and knowing how beautiful this one would be, I thought it wouldn't mind starting in this old pail. It's just for a little while, till I can put it out in the garden."

She must have wondered why I laughed so delightedly, but I was imagining just such a scene in heaven. "Here's an especially beautiful one," God might have said when He came to the soul of the fisherman. "He won't mind starting in this small body."

But that's behind now, long ago, and in God's garden how tall this lovely soul must stand!

No Tips Today, Please
by Milton Bronstein

A simple example of what one person can do.

One November, just before election time, I heard a guy say to his buddy, "Who you gonna vote for, Jim?"

"Don't know," said his friend. "Probably no one. I got a rough day Tuesday."

"Me too," said the other. "What's one vote anyway?"

I thought to myself, "Who do these guys think they are? They live in a free country; they get a chance to vote for anyone they like and they haven't got time."

I guess they're free *not* to vote, just as they're free to vote, but I still don't like it. I'm not trying to wave the flag about, but I'm certainly not too proud to say that I love my country. I drive my own cab, have a wonderful wife and two great kids. Our cab association is made up of guys who fought in World War II. In a way we're still fighting for the things we believe in.

Anyway, all this gives me an idea. The day before election I get out paint and brush and go to work on the side of my cab. The next day I pull up by our administration office—the American-United Cab Association—proud of my art. On the side of the cab is this sign:

"Be American. Ride American. No matter how you vote. . . . Vote today. Your ride free to the polls."

I showed the sign to the other cabbies. "What do you guys say? Want to join me?"

Fifteen did.

See what I mean about our company!

Now I've no axe to grind about politics. I just believe in taking advantage of the rights we got in this country. We handled a lot of business free, that day. As for the lost fares, so what!

We got our cab association going the hard way after the

304

war. There's nothing tougher than breaking into a big city like Chicago with a new cab outfit. We stuck together, pooled our money and ideas and made a go of it. Some of our veterans were full colonels, one an air-base commander in the war. We own our cabs, come an emergency and we're mobilized, ready to go as members of the Civil Defense Corps.

I got a formula that I've followed ever since I started driving: For every dollar in my pocket, fifty cents belongs to anyone in need. I'm no fall guy; I just like helping people. A lot of my buddies feel the same way.

Don't put us down for no halos. The guys are rough-and-ready; several have trapped thugs and brought 'em in. Sometimes we scrap a little among ourselves, but let anyone else try to muscle in and see what happens.

On certain days we give free rides to anyone who will give blood to the Red Cross. Some of the guys have given so much blood, their arms are full of needle holes. I don't see how they walk around.

One day about 15 of our cabs jammed up the traffic in front of the blood center. A cop came running up, waving his arms and shouting, "Get these cabs outa here." But he quieted down quickly, and later went in and gave some blood himself.

Some days we put a sign inside our cabs, asking riders who intend to tip, to put it in the can for March of Dimes. We do the same thing, too, for the Cancer Fund, Crippled Children and so forth. We raised $48,000 for the Cancer Fund alone. One of my favorite jobs is to drive up to the Navy Base and pick up vets and give 'em a free ride to town and back.

But the rides I like best are with my own family. A number of years ago my wife and I started giving kids a special geography lesson every year during our vacation. I asked the family what state they'd like to visit. They said Wisconsin. We studied every inch of the map; we knew every important spot, and then the four of us—Margaret, my wife, Sandy, Sharon and I—all hopped into my cab and we started off.

We really covered that state. In three weeks we stopped at tourist cabins, visited historical spots, the capital, the parks, traveling up and down and crosswise. Did we love it!

The next year it was Michigan—then Colorado, Illinois, Indiana, Minnesota, and Pennsylvania. Lots more to go and plenty of time to do them.

There's too much living to do to waste any of it being unhappy because we haven't the money we'd like or don't belong to the best clubs.

Sometimes I've been hurt by cracks made about my religion. Happened several times in the Army. One answer always stopped 'em.

"That's okay with me if you feel that way, fellas," I'd say after some dig. "But if any of you men get hit by a bullet, I'll be glad to give you my blood. Then you'll have Jewish blood in you too."

After all, does it make any difference what your race or religion is if you try to keep God in your heart?

"People Is Like Onions"
by S. D. Matthews

Our cleaning woman's philosophy was hard to argue with.

The first time I saw her was just before the last world war, when Mother had advertised for a cleaning woman.

Mrs. Tindle came in without knocking, just breezed in and took over. A big, red Irish woman with wrinkled brown cotton stockings, a purple apron flapping underneath a patched gray coat, and her hair leering saucily from under a man's crushed hat.

"Mighty purty house y' got here . . . my! Aren't those chandeliers grand! An' vernition blinds! They're a real caution t' dust, but I kin handle 'em."

We showed her through the house, the tour punctuated by her ohs and ahs. But, when we reached the bathroom, she was struck speechless. She looked at it in the same way she might have looked at the pearly gates. "Now thet there's lovely!"

"It's only a bathroom."

"Only a bathroom! An' me willin' to die fer one half as good! All m' life I've dreamed of havin' one. Jest think—a *moderate* house!"

Deep in the heart of every person, there is a secret dream, stronger than just desire. Mrs. Tindle had such a dream—a "moderate" house.

"Oh," I laughed, "you'll have a bathroom, too, some day."

She shook her head sadly. "Well, as Barney was sayin',—there's more pleasure to wantin' than gittin'."

Barney Tindle, it developed, was wisdom itself. Seldom did Mrs. Tindle, who could neither read nor write, ever start a sentence with other than "Barney says. . . ." That Barney had often been anticipated by Lincoln, Shakespeare, and the

Bible, did not lessen the importance of his pronouncements. Indeed it was something of a shock when anyone met Barney Tindle, for he was a shabby, wizened little man, a good foot shorter than his wife.

The early years of their married life had been spent in a tent, where Mrs. Tindle reared six children. They had followed Barney on road construction jobs until his health gave out, and then he got a job with the city as a street sweeper. They lived in a tipsy structure which sagged despondently on the outskirts of the city. It had no plumbing.

Over the years, first one child died, and then another, until there were four. One daughter left a grandchild for Mrs Tindle to rear.

Mrs. Tindle "helped out" my mother on Fridays, and she performed the cleaning with a robust will. But it was when she reached the bathrooms that she excelled. That our house boasted not one, but two bathrooms, was a never-ending source of wonder to her.

In her spare time, Mrs. Tindle made quilts.

"Kin I have it fer quilts?" was a constant request. One day I grinned at Mother after Tindle left. "She must have quilts piled to the ceiling by now," I said. "Surely she doesn't expect to sell enough for that bathroom of hers—not those funny-looking things."

"She doesn't try to sell them," Mother said. "And it's true they are funny-looking. The stitches are big and often the quilt is lop-sided, the stuffing lumpy, but they have kept a good many children warm."

Tindle became a fixture around our house, speaking her mind as freely as a member of the family.

I was sitting in the kitchen one afternoon watching her eat Bermuda onions. She'd slice them neatly, admiring the pearly juice that dripped from each slice before popping it into her mouth.

"There's nothing as good as onions," she observed, propping her feet on a kitchen chair. "Onion's got real substance. Most people don't appreciate th' solid things in life."

"Like onions?"

"Yep," she nodded sagely. "Onions plumb takes the meanness outten a person. You take Sample Jones, now—he oughta eat onions—boughten ones, not stole ones."

Sample Jones was one of Tindle's neighbors, with a habit of "sampling" anything not nailed down.

"He in jail again?"

Mrs. Tindle wagged her head sadly. "Them poor little children o' his an' thet wore-out wife—I jest couldn't stand nohow to see 'em grieve so."

I sat up straight. "You didn't bail him out again?" Her face told me the answer. "Tindle, you know Sample's rotten all through—he'll just get caught again! Anyway, how do you expect to get a bathroom if you keep throwing your money away?"

She shrugged her shoulders. "Bought a awful lot of happiness for Sample's fam'ly—thet ain't throwin' money away. Tain't often y'kin buy happiness." She smacked her lips and wiped the paring knife on her purple apron. " 'Sides, people is something like onions—look rotten from th' outsides, but peel off enough layers an'y'kin find some good."

No one asked of Tindle and went away empty-handed. And each time she gave, her dream was postponed a little.

Finally Tindle announced that she was retiring. Barney was working, the children were on their own, and at last she had saved enough to pay for the addition to her home!

But sometimes dreams have a way of fading before your eyes. I went down to her shack when the tragedy struck. The doctors could not put off telling her about the cancer operation.

"Ah, well . . ." she sighed to me as we discussed the medical bills, "this old house is kind o' antiquidated an' I reckon a bathroom would be out o' place anyways."

On the day she entered the hospital, her son, Billy, and all the men on his construction gang, took the day off. They gathered at her shack to build a bathroom. Somehow the word got around and others began to come—everyone who had known Tindle—those who had needed money, the children, grown now, who had slept under her quilts. A plumber offered his services free, and a local builder hauled over some scrap lumber. A wealthy lady donated the fixtures and Mother went over with a hot meal for the workmen. And, in one day, they really built it.

When the room was finished, it looked more like an afterthought—but it *was* a bathroom. The only bathroom in the world with a stained glass window!

During the building they found that a window was lacking. The neighbors supplied the need by installing a small, stained glass window salvaged when a nearby church had burned.

Now to some that may seem funny—a stained glass window in a bathroom. But I saw it, and I'm telling you that there was something wonderful about that bathroom. It was built out of love—and the window seemed just right.

And, since I believe in a life after this one, I like to think that Mrs. Tindle knows all about that room, too. Because Mrs. Tindle never saw her dream come true—she died on the operating table.

I had often wondered what it was that Mrs. Tindle, of all people, found in life to make it so wonderful, so full of joy. But I think I know the answer now. It must be that happiness in life is not so much a matter of achieving a goal, as it is of reaching for one—with a great deal of love.

Trouble At the Inn

by Dina Donohue

It was unlike any Christmas play the audience had ever seen.

For years now whenever Christmas pageants are talked about in a certain little town in the Midwest, someone is sure to mention the name of Wallace Purling. Wally's performance in one annual production of the Nativity play has slipped into the realm of legend. But the old-timers who were in the audience that night never tire of recalling exactly what happened.

Wally was nine that year and in the second grade, though he should have been in the fourth. Most people in town knew that he had difficulty in keeping up. He was big and clumsy, slow in movement and mind. Still, Wally was well liked by the other children in his class, all of whom were smaller than he, though the boys had trouble hiding their irritation when Wally would ask to play ball with them or any game, for that matter, in which winning was important.

Most often they'd find a way to keep him out but Wally would hang around anyway—not sulking, just hoping. He was always a helpful boy, a willing and smiling one, and the natural protector, paradoxically, of the underdog. Sometimes if the older boys chased the younger ones away, it would always be Wally who'd say, "Can't they stay? They're no bother."

Wally fancied the idea of being a shepherd with a flute in the Christmas pageant that year, but the play's director, Miss Lumbard, assigned him to a more important role. After all, she reasoned, the innkeeper did not have too many lines, and Wally's size would make his refusal of lodging to Joseph more forceful.

And so it happened that the usual large, partisan audience gathered for the town's yearly extravaganza of crooks

311

and crèches, of beards, crowns, halos and a whole stageful of squeaky voices. No one on stage or off was more caught up in the magic of the night than Wallace Purling. They said later that he stood in the wings and watched the performance with such fascination that from time to time Miss Lumbard had to make sure he didn't wander onstage before his cue.

Then the time came when Joseph appeared, slowly, tenderly guiding Mary to the door of the inn. Joseph knocked hard on the wooden door set into the painted backdrop. Wally the innkeeper was there, waiting.

"What do you want?" Wally said, swinging the door open with a brusque gesture.

"We seek lodging."

"Seek it elsewhere." Wally looked straight ahead but spoke vigorously. "The inn is filled."

"Sir, we have asked everywhere in vain. We have traveled far and are very weary."

"There is no room in this inn for you." Wally looked properly stern.

"Please, good innkeeper, this is my wife, Mary. She is heavy with child and needs a place to rest. Surely you must have some small corner for her. She is so tired."

Now, for the first time, the innkeeper relaxed his stiff stance and looked down at Mary. With that, there was a long pause, long enough to make the audience a bit tense with embarrassment.

"No! Begone!" the prompter whispered from the wings.

"No!" Wally repeated automatically. "Begone!"

Joseph sadly placed his arm around Mary and Mary laid her head upon her husband's shoulder and the two of them started to move away. The innkeeper did not return inside his inn, however. Wally stood there in the doorway, watching the forlorn couple. His mouth was open, his brow creased with concern, his eyes filling unmistakably with tears.

And suddenly this Christmas pageant became different from all others.

"Don't go, Joseph," Wally called out. "Bring Mary back." And Wallace Purling's face grew into a bright smile. "You can have *my* room."

Some people in town thought that the pageant had been ruined. Yet there were others—many, many others—who considered it the most Christmas of all Christmas pageants they had ever seen.

Faith in Action

In the closing days of World War II a group of American prisoners in Europe showed their Nazi captors a sample of faith in action.

The rumor spread within the camp that the Jewish soldiers among them were to be separated from the others for "special treatment." All the men in the camp were talking about it. The Jewish boys urged their buddies not to stick their necks out for them.

The following day when the command was given, "All prisoners of Jewish blood step forward," every single soldier stepped out.

Submitted by D. LUBEN
Sierra Vista, Arizona

I Speak for the Bums
by Leonard E. LeSourd

---

*"Churches don't care," he was told, so he decided
to find out himself by posing as a drifter.*

"Why waste your time working for a religious publication?"
the man asked me. "Take it from me, churches are too selfish
ever to do anything really constructive."

He then offered me an excellent job. Back in 1945 I
had, after careful deliberation, chosen work in a field which I
deeply felt lay the main hope of civilization—religion. Nothing the man said caused me to doubt my choice, so I didn't
take the job offered.

But I did take his words to heart. Churches are the
backbone of society, yet how account for people who held
this opinion of them? I decided to go and see for myself—
how, for example, would churches receive a man, broke,
friendless, down-and-out? I'd be a bum and find out.

I let my hair grow, dug up old clothes and took the
name Al Barrow. In this role I'd simply be a drifter in from
Ohio who had gotten in bad company and had been robbed
of money and belongings.

It was midnight on a warm summer evening when I
strolled out of my apartment. My possessions (besides
clothes) included a comb, handkerchief, pencil, note paper
(to record incidents)—*no money or identification of any
kind*. I headed for the Bowery in New York, a typical subject
for rehabilitation.

At Lincoln Square Park I stretched out on a bench.
There was little sleep for me that hot night, and in the morning I was stiff, tired, hungry, dirty. A short stroll took me
into the environment of drunks sprawled in doorways, of
dull, beaten faces, of debris littered sidewalks.

For eight days I lived my role completely. I ate in bread

lines and soup kitchens, slept in flophouses and missions, panhandled, and tramped along the avenues seeking odd jobs.

My first day was joltingly rough. After the dreary night on a park bench, I joined up with two bums who were panhandling. I was a miserable failure despite coaching from my hobo pals. Most people brushed by as though I were something unclean.

Not until 2 P.M. did I have my first food—a bowl of watery soup from a soup kitchen. At nine o'clock that night came my second handout—bread, coffee and more soup, served in a mission after a two-hour service. I also lined up to spend the night on the cement basement floor, but the attendant soon discovered that I had no social security card and asked me to leave. Was a man without identification (granted that he might be a questionable character) too low to shelter?

The missions are helpful to many bums, and while the food is understandably poor, they do feed a man—yet a saloon in the Bowery is noted for free food, good and no questions asked. Why, I asked myself, don't restaurants, bakeries and families supply missions with the days remains? Couldn't a system be worked out so that all contribute and nothing go to waste?

By 10 P.M. I was thoroughly "down." Another night on a park bench loomed up, my stomach cried for food, and there wasn't money even to call and reassure friends.

On the park bench beside me was a perspiring fat man reading a newspaper. Struck by a sudden hunch I turned to him. "Pardon me, Mister, but do you have faith in people?"

"Yes, I think so," he answered.

"I'm not a bum, just down on my luck. If you have faith enough in me to give me a dollar, I'll send it back when I'm on my feet. But I won't take it unless you give me your name and address too."

He reached into his pocket, drew out a wallet and handed me a bill together with his card. "I'll believe in you, Johnny. Send it back when you can."

Aglow with thanks, I took the dollar. Never did a hamburger and an orange drink taste so good.

As I wandered back to the Bowery, the pattern of days ahead shaped up. I'd be humble, sincere, though very ragged, asking for a job, or for help only on the basis that I would pay back any money when on my feet. The idea of fulfilling the faith people might have in me was exciting. They'd receive a note along with the money, thanking them for their trust.

My travels (by blistered feet) took me into some 60 churches, as many or more businesses; I approached all kinds of people—cabbies, ministers and businessmen.

The clergymen were for the most part away on summer vacation, but those I did see showed warmth and kindness. Several gave me money on faith. In one church I was offered a job as janitor, the first constructive help toward getting me on my feet. One church ran a famous breadline.

But I sensed an over-all attitude of resignation, even defeat. And while most clergymen were kind, others in the church were not.

A big Fifth Avenue church looked inviting. "I'm down on my luck and need help," I informed the receptionist inside. She pointed toward the superintendent who shook his head. "Nothing."

"I figured the church was one place where someone down on his luck could get help," I persisted.

"Don't come in here with a chip on your shoulder," he said sourly. "Go down to the police station—they'll take care of you."

My face felt hot. "And I thought people in a church applied the teachings of Christ."

He swelled so with hostility that I turned and walked out.

"We have twenty like you in here every day," the sexton of another church told me. "If we gave you something, we'd have hundreds."

"We have to run the church like a business," still another sexton informed me. "You've gotta put something in the church to get anything out of it."

I felt greatly let-down by these experiences. What if helping one does bring a horde of derelicts—*is that bad?* And if 200 take advantage of charity and only two are rehabilitated, would the cost be too great?

As I tossed and turned one night on a hard mission bench, these thoughts tumbled about in my head. About 50 men crowded together, sleeping on benches and floors, were coughing, groaning, snoring in their sleep. The stench of hot bodies was overpowering—I could almost hear souls writhing in torment.

Even the poorest of churches could avail themselves of information that could help the down-and-outer, I thought.

Personnel could be instructed as to where and when a bum could obtain food, clothing, medical care, shelter. It cost nothing to show kindness and a smile.

Perhaps the Communists might give me a warmer reception. But how to get to them?

Several phone calls soon uncovered information about a Communist Waterfront District meeting that night. I'd go there.

Outside of the assembly room (on second floor of plain walk-up rooming-house type of building) sat a woman at a table collecting dues. I told her I was interested in the party and wanted to sit in on the meeting. I suddenly realized how shabby I looked in contrast to everyone else. The members of this Communistic group had the appearance of comfortable prosperity—at least in their attire.

"Frankly, brother, we've nothing here for you," said a man who had been standing near by. "You gotta pull yourself together. Get a job, join a union, then come back and we'll have something for you to do."

I was no use to them as a bum.

Inside me was a feeling of deep relief. If they had done something to help me—toward putting me on my feet, it would have been hard to take, coming from the most anti-religious of groups. Where was the brotherhood they spouted? Only for the solvent!

My wanderings carried me into a mission in a poor section of town. Soon a man with frayed collar and poorly fitting suit approached—the minister. He looked shabby from the neck down—but his face was immaculately dressed with warmth and kindness.

When I had related my story, he smiled. "You're a young fellow. No need for you to stay down long. Are you hungry?" He pulled out a handful of change and counted out four quarters. Then he wrote down the addresses of several places where food and lodging could be obtained.

I watched him fascinated. Humble kindness and love shone from his eyes. His was the true spirit I had been seeking. Before leaving he asked me to join him in a word of prayer. Here was sincere spiritual help too.

At the end of eight days I had myself shaved, sheared and fumigated (from bedbugs and lice), and went back uptown. But as days passed, my Bowery experiences haunted me. I could never turn down a bum again without offering some kind of help, whether to treat him to a meal or give him money. Passing one by would also cheat me of the spiritual benefit that goes with giving—and if but one out of 20 or 100 were helped, it would be double return.

I decided to visit some of the ministers, tell them of my experiences and find out the reasons for the generally cold treatment given to bums.

"Don't judge all churches by this city, with its congestion and overflow of humanity," said one. "We each have more to do in our own parish than strength can accomplish."

Another explained: "There's no excuse for church personnel treating any human being with contempt, and if my workers do it, I want to know."

"Most bums know of the agencies he can go to if he really needs help," said still another. "We should all aid these agencies far more than we do. The church isn't a social service, but certainly the people of the church should learn to 'love thy neighbor as thyself.' "

In the final analysis, the problem comes right down to *you* and *you* and *me*. We make up the church congregations and decide church policy; we are to blame if charities and missions are staffed with people "who do not care"; and we are the ones who feel too often that failure and poverty are a disgrace, a mark of weakness and sin.

Misfortune can hit anyone, since many of the bums were intelligent and obviously at one time respected members of their community. Many now are too defeated to try to come back even though jobs are open to them. But they might be inspired to give it a try if people with real love in their hearts took a personal interest in them as individuals.

Begging is a harsh lesson in humility, and as a beggar I saw deep behind the eyes of many people. It wasn't a pretty sight. Perhaps they would have reacted differently if they knew me as a reporter.

There is a phrase in the Bible which says: *"Inasmuch as ye have done it unto one of the least of these, my brethren, ye have done it unto Me."*

For that matter, how can you be sure that the next person who stops you on the street for help won't be the Master, Christ Himself?

Jackhammer Diplomats
by Joe Sceppa

The United Nations isn't the only place where peaceful negotiations take place.

One spring day in the early '50s, one of our timber cutters was down in the hole shoring up a span of pipe that would run into the United Nations. A big diesel shovel was working near him, and this cutter didn't like the way the bucket swung out over his head. Once in a while the shovel operator had to balance a ton rock on the teeth of the bucket. If that rock slipped and fell, it would have crushed the cutter on the spot.

"Swing that load out the other way!" the cutter yelled above the noise of the drills. When nothing happened he got mad.

I don't blame him for getting mad, but I do blame the way he settled the thing. He just ups himself into the cab, pulls the operator out by his lapel and starts in on him. We had to pull them apart and bring them both in for coffee, till they settled the thing on some other grounds than who was the strongest.

Later we got to talking about how this was like the United Nations. We did a lot of talking about the UN down in the hole. The big guys up there in those plush conference rooms sometimes have the same problem as the shovel operator and the cutter: They can't get their work done for arguing about *how* it should be done.

People from those offices would come around, ask us what it's like building the UN.

"Do you know how big this job is?" they'd say. And mostly we didn't answer. But when we'd grab ten minutes for coffee . . . there's nothing better than coffee around an oil drum fire . . . we'd talk about whether this job *is* different.

In many ways all heavy construction's the same. You

know you'll work with mud and rock. You work with drills
and your hands throw a plunger that dynamites tons of rock
at a time.

I'd been a heavy construction man for over 15 years
around New York. Whenever visitors would come from out-
of-town, I could take them almost anywhere and say, "I built
that." The 6th Avenue Subway, the Midtown Tunnel, Natural
Gas Lines—I'd laid miles of conduits and knew the secrets of
New York's underground life.

New York is my city, was my father's before me. He
came from Italy to work on construction crews, building, like
I do. He's an American now, and he gave me New York; his
city belongs to me, because I helped build her.

When I started working on the UN it was the same mud
and rock, the same noise of dynamite and drills, but somehow the job promised to be different. Of course, some of the
men up there in those conference rooms might be putting on
a big act. Maybe they were shouting for peace and dressing
for war. If that's true, then I was wasting my time; I'd rather
work on sewers. Because nothing's as honest as a sewer.

They could come down here in the mud, those men in
the conference rooms and, by watching us and by knowing a
little about the land the UN is built on, they might get a few
ideas.

They tell me that the ground between 42nd and 48th
Streets is blood ground, and during the Revolution, British
soldiers had a warehouse at the foot of 45th Street, and the
Liberty Boys fought for it on a midnight in 1773. Three
years later Nathan Hale was hung on the same spot where
the UN building stands.

But it was blood ground more recent than that. I
remember the slaughter houses that stood on the UN ground.
Cattle boats sailed up the East River and in a good week one
house could kill 3,000 head.

The stink was pretty bad, and nobody wanted to live
there, so the ground that wasn't bloodened by sudden death
was covered by tenements where death was slower. The whole
area was slums—tough, saloon, leadpipe slums, and the old
timers tell how sometimes a steer would break loose and run
wild in the streets, getting even with men.

We brought in wrecking crews to tear down the slaughter houses and gashouse slums. Underneath them, hidden by
layers of pavement, were the secret arteries that keep New
York alive—steam pipes, sewer lines, water mains, gas pipes,

signal conduits, electric and telephone lines and wire cable so complicated that New York had to draw up a special map to keep us construction men from cutting them. We had to tear up these arteries; and stick 'em back just right, so you couldn't tell there'd been an operation.

But digging up old lines was only the beginning. Under this part of Manhattan is about 80 feet of solid bedrock called Manhattan Schist. Just a few generations ago it would have been impossible to work in this tough rock. But with to-day's drills that bear down and explosives that shatter from the inside we were able to go down through bedrock to build foundations for the United Nations. Then came the shovels that scoop up nine cubic feet of broken rock, and the heavy trucks with vertical exhausts which haul the rock away.

Like I say, I wasn't sure my job was important when I first went there. But I noticed something: The more I put my own back into the UN, the more important it became to me.

I think the delegates must have felt the same way. Every morning they would come from all over the world, many of them wearing long robes or turbans or different shoes from ours, to watch the shovels and trucks. I liked to think about them maybe sitting down over a cup of coffee, trying to solve their differences, like we did. And we'd plenty of them.

In the first place, there was every kind of person working in the hole: college men and immigrants, Jews and Christians, black and yellow men. They all put their sweat into this job. If we couldn't keep harmony on this job of building the very foundations of the United Nations, we certainly couldn't expect these people in different dress to do any better. Every man has a right to gripe, that's only human. But we solved our gripes over coffee; we let people spout off, but we didn't settle our problems on the basis of who was strongest.

The delegates seemed fascinated with the idea of building the UN on solid rock. I hope they realized that just as it takes drills and dynamite to build in rock, it would take hard-cutting tools to blast away at some of their old ideas and policies that have led to war after war.

As the verse in the Bible says:

*"He is like a man who was building a house, who dug deep and laid his foundation upon the rock, and when there was a flood, the torrent burst upon that house and could not shake it, because it was well built."**

---

* *Goodspeed version of Luke 6:46-49*

The Span

Life is but a bridge we build
To link Before and After,
And wise the man who builds his span
Of faith and love and laughter.

JILL TAYLOR

Section Eight—

Faith Through the Master

Section Eight—
Introduction

Guideposts over the 25 years of its history has regularly presented articles by and about people who have experienced a close walk with Jesus Christ. The insights by Christians who have seen great examples of His love and compassion in their own lives have strengthened and nurtured the lives of others new in the faith.

Special features have included depictions of the Lord by leading artists. They include a wide range of interpretations from the works of such men as Howard Chandler Christy and Warner Sallman, whose head of Christ has been reproduced millions of times, to such contemporary talents as Austin Briggs, Ben Stahl and William Hofmann. In many cases, Guideposts discovered upon investigation by our writers and editors a fascinating story was "behind the painting." We include here some of the most inspiring.

But not all visualization of the Lord has been left to the artists. Guideposts has also published many word-pictures of the Man from Nazareth. These portraits are as diverse as the ones attempted by painters. One thing, however, seems to come clear: The gentle-Jesus-meek-and-mild image, too long perpetuated, has given way to one of a Man whose physical strength was as commanding as the inner strength He carried all the way to the Cross.

... At the Ninth Hour
by William Hofmann

Faced with a deadline, this painter was suddenly filled with inspiration.

There was darkness over all the land. And at the ninth hour Jesus cried with a loud voice, saying, "My God, my God, why hast Thou forsaken Me?"

These words from John Stainer's cantata, "The Crucifixion," were the inspiration for one drawing of mine. In fact, his powerful composition is the reason for it. Let me tell you why.

In January, 1953, the First Lutheran Church choir, Bronx, New York, began rehearsing "The Crucifixion" for presentation at Easter. I was given two bass solo parts.

Nineteen years old and just starting out as an artist, I was long on time and short on work. Anyway, I loved to sing. One night after rehearsal I talked with the minister and choir director about doing a poster to publicize the upcoming performance.

"Maybe I could do a drawing of Christ which could be placed in the vestibule," I remember saying. They liked the idea and I had myself a job.

Before I sit down to paint I like to carry an idea with me for a week or two. By waiting, not forcing an assignment, I find that I give the project time to sink deeply into my subconscious. I try to immerse myself in the subject using odd moments to meditate upon it. I feel this process is building an empathy or oneness between myself and the Spirit within me, and by joining the two I reach a Source which is not subject to human limitations.

The day I drew the picture in a shabby, cupboard studio on 41st Street in Manhattan, was not unlike other days. In the morning, I remember doing an illustration of a plumber repairing some pipes: it was for a newspaper ad. Around noon I unwrapped the sandwich Mother sent along with me, and as I munched on it I thought about the choir poster. It was due, overdue.

Opening a pad of tracing paper, I ripped the corner of the sheets, 40 to 50 of them, I suppose. When an artist is probing for an idea, he often runs through a whole pad, and more, without satisfaction. I fully expected to use all of the sheets when I started.

As I stared at the snow-white sheet in front of me, John Stainer's words came to my mind and were joined by a melody from somewhere within . . . *There was darkness over all the land. And at the ninth hour Jesus cried with a loud voice, saying, "My God, my God, why hast Thou forsaken Me?"*

Darkness. I reached for a piece of black charcoal and began to sketch the face of Christ as He seemed to me when the God-man conflict reached its pinnacle. I saw the *humanness* of Christ for the first time as He experienced an ordeal which He could have avoided. I saw anguish, mercy, strength, suffering.

All the while I was drawing—not a head, eyes, nose, crown of thorns, but *Christ*. The charcoal seemed light on the toothless paper; it practically flew in my hand. Within a few minutes, it was completed—on the first try! As I studied the finished product, I felt as if I had watched it being drawn; as if someone else had taken my hand.

Now as I stood and looked down upon it, I saw something more than anguish, mercy, strength, suffering. In His face, I saw victory—the victory that overcomes the world.

Now I See

by Howard Chandler Christy*

Doctors said this famous painter would soon be blind, but their predictions were wrong.

To have spent one's boyhood on an Ohio River Farm—during the Steamboat Days—would breed romance in any youngster's life—never to be forgotten.

Our farm was on the crest of a hill overlooking the lock and Canal—through which the big Ohio River steamboats had to pass—and no matter what time of day or night I never missed the thrilling sight of seeing them lock through. I knew all the Captains and Pilots and they would never forget to look up, and give the wave of the hand to the small boy looking on.

Sometimes the morning boats would steam up the river carrying picnickers, and on the hurricane deck would be a beautifully uniformed band—one in particular with horns all in silver—and how those bands could play. They sent joy and enthusiasm out on the clear sparkling morning air, bringing with it the thought, "God is on His throne—all is well with the world."

Often in the nighttime could be heard—miles down the river and echoing from hill to hill—the beautiful chime whistles, and the deep sound of the bell drawing closer and clearer. It was just impossible to lie in bed, so out of the window I would go (so as not to awaken anyone), and out to the crest of the hill overlooking the lock. Then would appear the brilliantly lighted steamboat—activity everywhere. Sometimes the furnace fire leaping out of the tall smoke stacks—especially when two of these big boats would happen to be coming on together and racing for the lock, taking chances in order to win meant nothing to either the Captains or crews.

---

* (See p. 363)

Everything went into the furnaces which fairly roared as they came plowing up the river.

I could well understand Mark Twain's saying that he was jealous of the cabin boy, who shook the tablecloth out over the railing—for this boy had been places—and was going somewhere—while my big brother and I worked hard on the farm.

There were times off when we could go fishing. Even now I can see clearly and feel the thrill of my brother going ahead (with his dog following)—carrying a bamboo fishing pole—a tin can full of worms—and what could possibly be better than this in a boy's life?

He knew how and when to fish—and caught them, too! I was not so good, because in spite of all the excitement I could not help but admire the beauty of the river—and trees overhanging its banks—and when the early morning steamboat would loom big and overpowering out of the fog—and go roaring by—fishing to me was forgotten.

At the age of 16, I had earned one hundred dollars and my mother matched it with one hundred more (this is the only money I ever had given me), and I came to New York to study and look at great paintings.

The next time I came—I came to stay—at the age of 19.

Two years with William M. Chase at Shinnecock, and in his New York Studio at 51 W. 10th Street, completed my art studies and then—money all gone, I began to work for an existence.

In my first little studio I slept on the floor for the first weeks—then sold a few drawings, and bought two empty boxes from the grocer—nailed them together and slept on them for several months. It's all the same old story of a young fellow cooking his own meals—and trying to get started selling his work for almost nothing. And glad of the opportunity of doing so.

I gave up painting for the time being. Soon came the Spanish American War—and of course—I followed the tradition of my forefathers and had to go, and in the very first expedition on board the S. S. Yucatan were five hundred Rough Riders—Teddy Roosevelt, and Colonel Wood, where also was Colonel Wherry in command of two hundred Regulars 2nd Infantry U. S. Army.

Leslie's Weekly and Scribner's gave me commissions to illustrate the War as I saw it. And this was my real beginning which kept me busy for many years thereafter with illustrations for most of the big publishers and well known authors.

Finally one day, I discovered my eyesight was becoming dimmed—so much so that I was unable to do my work. Experts said I would be blind in a short time, but I felt that something would come to me—which would restore my perfect sight—that it would be nothing short of a miracle. So much ahead I wanted to do—so much to accomplish—and on one day which seemed the darkest came this miracle.

A relative of mine who was a Practitioner, came to see me, and asked if I would like a treatment. My reply was: "Yes." Instantly I knew that *this* was the Truth—that God was the only power—and that at last—I was being set free.

The room suddenly became full of light, and I interrupted the Practitioner with the remark, "It will be a good day after all, for the sun is coming out from behind the cloud."

She replied, "The sun has been out all the time, what is really happening—you are being healed."

From that day to this, I've never needed eye glasses to do my work, in fact they would be in my way.

This was 41 years ago, and now I find that gratitude is one of man's greatest blessings.

---

* *Howard Chandler Christy was born in Duncan Falls, Ohio, on Jan. 10, 1873. A famous illustrator and portrait painter, he has received medals, honors and recognition too numerous to list. Perhaps his best known work, "Signing of the Constitution," hangs in the Capitol Building, Washington, D. C.*

The Forgotten Side of Christ
by Catherine Marshall

A fresh insight into the personality of Jesus, revealing Him to be a Man not only of sorrows and
grief but of gentle wit and warm humor.

It was a typical after-dinner family scene—father, mother
and children gathered in the living room. The father, with his
four-year-old boy on his lap, read these words of Jesus
from the book of Matthew:

Why do you look at the speck of sawdust in your
brother's eye, with never a thought for the great plank in
your own?*

The boy chuckled loudly. Surprised, the father looked up
to see if his son had been diverted by the cat or his brother.
No, the boy was laughing over what had just been read. He
thought it was funny.

The father was Dr. Elton Trueblood—Quaker, professor
and author—and this simple experience opened his eyes to a
new facet of Jesus Christ: the Master's words had a quality
of humor in them. The result of that discovery was a book
published some years later by Doctor Trueblood called *The
Humor of Christ*.**

This book fascinated me because it verified something I
had been discovering firsthand. Writers and speakers have
emphasized Christ as the Man of Sorrows carrying the burdens of the world, or as the forceful Christ Who could show
righteous indignation, or as the compassionate Jesus. But one
dimension of the Man has been ignored almost completely:
This carpenter loved people, loved to mingle with them, loved
to laugh and engage in light banter with them. In short, He
had among other great qualities a rare sense of humor.

* Matthew 7:3 NEB
** Published by Harper & Row, New York City.

My first brush with the wit of Jesus came in a personal way back in 1944. It's a story I've told before. Bedridden for several years with a lung ailment, I was discouraged, full of self-pity. One night I awakened in total blackness. Suddenly I was aware of a Presence, a Power in my room.

My physical eyes saw nothing, yet somehow I was given a new way of seeing the Kingly Presence beside me. Through His tenderness shone the fact that He looked upon me as a child, a quite foolish child at times.

"Why do you take yourself so seriously?" He asked me. "Relax! There's nothing here I can't take care of."

His reassurance and love that night helped me to throw off self-pity. It was the turning point of my illness. From then on, I was on my way to health and a normal life.

Yet surprisingly, it was the light joshing quality of Christ's voice that has lingered so clearly through the years. I had been so solemn and serious—He seemed almost gay, with a teasing light banter.

That experience sent me back to the Gospels to check out my new understanding of Christ. I was genuinely puzzled because the One I had met was, oh, so different from the Jesus pictured in most Sunday-school books or painted by most artists—solemn, sad-eyed, meek to those who abused Him, plodding on His sorrowful way to Calvary.

In my search I read of Christ's blast against the hypocrisy of the Pharisees in the 23rd chapter of Matthew and blinked when I came to the words: *You strain off a midge, yet gulp down a camel!** How could we miss the humor in this word-picture of a Pharisee elaborately straining a gnat out of his drink, then swallowing an unwieldy camel?

Here is the humor of gross exaggeration, beloved in folk tales. Jesus, remember, was from simple folk, and *the common people heard Him gladly.*** We Americans are familiar with the humor of the deliberately preposterous through the tall tales of Texas or the Appalachian frontier, especially the Kentucky and Great Smoky Mountain areas. But the humor that I had met firsthand in Christ was more akin to banter.

For instance, Jesus' talk with the woman at the well in Samaria. She was a woman of unsavory character. Jesus knew that, yet at one point in His conversation with her, He suggested, *Go home, call your husband and come back.*

---

* Matthew 23:24 NEB
** Mark 12:37

She answered, "I have no husband."

"You are right," said Jesus, *"in saying that you have no husband, for although you have had five husbands, the man with whom you are now living is not your husband; you told me the truth there. . . ."*

Instinct tells us that the words "You told the truth there" were accompanied by a quizzical smile. Then we realize one obvious reason why we have not recognized so much of Jesus' humor: We are missing the tone of voice and the facial expressions. This is a great loss, for much of a person's wit and banter are revealed by his gay expression and personality.

Yet Jesus' wit differs from ours in that we have no record of His having made use of the funny story for its own sake. When we try to get a laugh for a laugh's sake, usually we are trying to get the center of the stage and boost our ego. I believe Christ used humor for a purpose. Sometimes a witticism became His bridge to an individual whom He would otherwise have had trouble reaching. Most often it was used to illuminate truth.

There was the occasion when Christ joshed His disciples about spiritual timidity: *Do you bring in the lamp to put it under the mealtub, or under the bed?** (Hardly the latter, for the mattress was usually made of straw.) He said in effect, "I need disciples who don't hide their light." When the apostles became so impressed with the size of the crowds Jesus was drawing that they began taking head counts, He, knowing full well that crowds gather for many reasons, commented dryly, *Wherever the corpse is, there the vultures will gather.***

How can we miss the twinkle in His eyes when Jesus spoke about the hypocrisy of the priests and Pharisees: *Do what they tell you . . . but do not follow their practice.****

Not that His apostles always saw or understood any more than we do. There were times when Christ's unlettered apostles failed to get His point, occasions when He chided them for taking His humorous images and analogies with stodgy literalness. *Are you still as dull as the rest?***** He once asked them.

---

* *John 4:16-19 NEB*
** *Mark 4:21 NEB*
*** *Matthew 24:28 NEB*
**** *Matthew 23:3 NEB*
***** *Matthew 15:17*

The Master undoubtedly knew that the only way His teaching would be remembered (and eventually recorded) was to put truth into the form of the ironic, often exaggerated, metaphor. And He was right: the simple Galileans recorded not only the metaphors, but even their own goofs at not understanding.

Once we reread the Gospels, watching for Christ's wit, we find it everywhere. *Can one blind man be guide to another blind man? Surely they will both fall into the ditch together.** Or the comment made about the rich man who valued his possessions too much. *It is easier for the camel to go through the eye of a needle than for a rich man to enter the kingdom of God.***

Thus if we will read them carefully, the Gospels give us a picture of a Christ Who would not let people be unobservant about life, about the actions of others, or most of all, about themselves. He wanted them awakened at every level of their being. And so He used every weapon of language and thought and communication to achieve his goals; most effective were banter, the humorous thrust and sardonic comments about those who put on airs and think more highly of themselves than they should. As one of sound and balanced mind, He could not observe humankind and fail to see our incongruities and absurdities. He did see, and He laughs along with us.

We should be relieved to rediscover Him so truly human as well as divine. For when our concept of Him is limited to that of a nebulous God, an odd thing results: much of *His* greatness disappears for us and, along with it, much of *our* spontaneity and fervor in worshiping Him. And how we need this "new-old" understanding of Him in our society today! He would not tolerate strutting pompousness or inconsistent hypocrisy any more than He would tolerate dishonesty or hatreds or greedy materialism.

At a time when our nation aches for a true hero, all that we long for in a hero is there—in Christ. Is it not possible that many Americans, hungry for something beyond materialism, eagerly pursuing the occult, fascinated with spiritualism—are really hunting for Christ—but don't know it because we have not presented to them the complete Man? I believe, too, that American youth, idealists that they really

---

* Luke 6:39 (Phillips)
** Luke 18:25 NEB

are, and fed up with so much talk about "the establishment," would discover in this incredible Man that rare blend they can find nowhere else—purity, strength, compassion and rare and sparkling humor.

The Picture of Christ In Our Home

by Doris D. Forman

It was not what the interior decorator had in mind, but. . . .

Several years ago, after a series of material blessings, we were able to buy a fine new home. "Since God gave us the increase," my husband said, "what about having a picture of Christ in our living room?"

Outwardly, I agreed with him, but inwardly I wasn't so sure.

Busy days followed with the many details of moving into a new home. When the decorator came out to check on lamps and pictures one day, he found the 16x20 print of "The Saviour," by Coleman, which my husband had hung over the piano in the most prominent place in our living room.

"We must select a picture to go in that spot," the decorator observed.

"We have, and that is it," my husband answered.

"Hmmm, a picture of Christ? Well, of course if you could have an original it might be all right, but a print . . ."

"We like it, and that's where it stays," my husband replied firmly.

Since the matter of the picture first came up, I had been struggling with conflicting emotions. Of course, we were Christians and, of course we loved God—but a large picture of Christ hanging in the living room . . . and in a spot where everyone who stepped into the room would see it . . . wasn't that being a bit fanatical?

Most of our friends were professed Christians, but they lived largely in a world of club affairs, cocktail parties and bridge luncheons. What would *they* think? . . .

But even as I began thinking that the picture might look better on the bedroom wall (where few would ever see it), a Bible verse kept nagging at my mind: *Whosoever therefore shall confess me before men, him will I confess also before my Father which is in heaven. But whosoever shall deny me before men, him will I deny before my Father which is in heaven.**

Was I being ashamed of Christ? Did I have a nice compartmentalized religion that allowed me to go to a fine church in my good clothes on Sunday, but didn't permit me to confess Christ any other way, at any other time? By my reluctance to hang His picture in my living room, was I—as did Peter—denying my Lord . . . *I do not know the man.***

I did much soul searching and what I found did not make me happy—so I just kept quiet. The picture remained on our living room wall.

During the next two years, many things happened to us because of this picture. A salesman once looked at it and then almost in awe whispered, "He not only looks at you, He speaks to you."

Recently, after coming to my house for monthly Cub Scout meetings, a friend commented, "It's such a joy to come here each month, and relax in the peace and warmth of your home."

But wasn't it His peace and His presence that she really felt?

And then a few months ago I became conscious of a strange happening. Total strangers—such as the man who delivers our papers—began telling us their troubles. As more and more people began unburdening themselves, I suddenly realized the reason—it was that picture of Christ. Consciously, or maybe unconsciously, they felt that we must know Christ, and if we knew Him, maybe we could mention them in our prayers (which we do) and He could help.

Our club friends? We see them, but now our relationships are much less superficial. There is not very much time for bridge. And since we work so much with our church teenagers, cocktails just don't seem to fit into our world anymore.

To sum it up, our life today has more purpose, more meaning and more beauty.

But I often wonder what would have happened if we

---

* *Matthew 10:32-33*
** *Matthew 26:72*

had hung a landscape instead of His blessed picture. The skeptic may say the picture had nothing to do with it—and, of course, there were other factors. But this much I know—you can't live in a house with Him, and ever be the same again.

A Prayer for Older People

Father, Thou knowest I am growing older. Keep me from becoming talkative and possessed with the idea that I must express myself on every subject. Release me from the craving to straighten out everyone's affairs. Keep my mind free from the recital of endless detail. Seal my lips when I am inclined to tell of my aches and pains. Teach me the glorious lesson that occasionally I may be wrong. Make me thoughtful but not moody, helpful but not bossy. With my vast store of wisdom and experience, it seems a pity not to use it all, but Thou knowest, Lord, that I want to keep my friends until the end. Amen.

—ANONYMOUS

The Way of the Cross
by Ben Stahl

An assignment that brought painter and subject closer than ever before.

There are countless spiritually attuned people who, asking God to give direction to their lives, receive this help. I contend that there are countless other people, people like me, people with only a nodding sort of acquaintance with God, who do not consciously seek guidance but receive it just the same.

They are the people puzzled by some strangely recurring experience, the inexplicable twist of events, an insistent idea in their minds. They are the ones unequipped or unwilling to come to grips with the feelings tugging at them. This is much the way I was back in 1952, the year an odd drama began to unfold in my life.

For over 35 years I have made my living by illustrating books, magazines, advertisements. Simultaneously I have painted. I don't paint objectively, in fine precision. I draw romantically, with surging lines and full figures. I love shadows; I love action; I love mood and emotion and I want my pictures to exude a kind of excitement of the senses.

I mention these things because my style in art is also my style in living. In many respects I am the cliché artist. I gobble up sights and sounds and take joy in the texture of things. I've always loved to eat, drink, work hard and look at beautiful women.

In 1952, a publisher came to my home in Connecticut with a lavish commission to paint some pictures for a new edition of the Bible. "I've searched everywhere for the right artist," Leonard Davidow said to me.

I was dumbfounded. I was the most unlikely prospect for an assignment so deeply reverent. Growing up in Chicago, I had gone routinely to Sunday school, but in my ma-

338

ture years there had been no room for religion. I asked, "But why have you picked me?"

"I saw your show," he replied.

This only confused me more. Davidow had seen my one-man exhibition of oils at a Chicago gallery. About 75 per cent of the paintings were nudes. There wasn't anything remotely religious about any of it. "What sort of pictures do you want?" I asked, probing.

"The fourteen stations of the Cross," Davidow said, and laughed as my expression revealed only the faintest knowledge of what he was talking about. I knew only that these "stations" were religious subjects and great painters of the past like Tiepolo had painted them. Now I learned that they were 14 representations of specific acts in the final drama of Christ's life, beginning with Pilate's judgment and ending with His burial. The stations of the Cross are found in Roman Catholic churches, and meditation before each of the 14 is a familiar devotion.

I told Davidow I would have to do a great deal of research and study. "I'll pay for your study," he said quickly, "at the source. I'll send you to Palestine."

So it was that my wife, Ella, and I went to Jerusalem. I went as a reporter would go, in search of cold fact. But it was as an artist, sketch pad and camera in hand, that I began to warm to the task. Palestine stimulated me. The land was rock, scarred as though clawed by a tiger. The sky had its own distinctive sun-color. Jerusalem itself—said to look much as it did 2,000 years ago, even though it has been rebuilt many times—immediately started me picturing the crowded streets through which this Man struggled and stumbled.

Fact piled upon fact, sketch upon sketch, but after a month, I had to leave. As soon as we got home, my schedule was cleared for the job and I was ready to start painting, but I soon found myself stalled. I would go into my studio and just sit. Here I was, an illustrator with a story full of court trials, mobs, hatred, love, death, suffering—the greatest, most dramatic story in the world—and I couldn't even start on it. The truth was, I was afraid. In some unexpected way, Jesus had humbled me. The simple fact is, you can't come close to Him or to His story without feeling humility.

At last, however, I forced myself to take brush in hand. I worked slowly, more painstakingly than I ever had before, blocking in backgrounds, filling in a few people, hesitating to approach the central figure of Christ. Then there came the time when I knew I had to draw Him. And a strange thing occurred.

As soon as I put brush to canvas my hands moved with a speed and a facility I had not known in months. No hesitation at all. No standing back, pondering. Just work. And especially when I painted Christ's head—ten strokes of the brush, there, it's done!

On all 14 canvases, it was the same story. Whenever I painted the figure of Jesus, it was almost effortless.

At long last, the work completed, I packed up the paintings and sent them off. It had been a memorable and deepening and somewhat bewildering experience for me, but that seemed to be that. I turned to other jobs.

Yet I couldn't get away from those pictures. Davidow seemed pleased, but I couldn't get over the feeling that I could have done them better. But this is usual with me.

Time passed. My family and I moved to Sarasota, Florida. Intermittently, that feeling about something I had not done with the stations would come back and gnaw at me. Then, one day in my studio, apropos of nothing, it came to me. Indeed I hadn't done the job I had wanted on those pictures of Christ. I would redo them. This time I'd paint them on an enormous scale, on vast canvases, and I'd fill those canvases with as much power and pity and love as I could summon.

Out again came the notes and sketches. I stretched the first canvas six feet by nine and flew to work. This time I wanted to give people the impression of being there at that very moment. I wanted to shatter them with the viciousness of the mobs, Mary's anguish, the physical suffering of Jesus. Yet somehow I would paint Jesus in such a way that one would want to follow Him in spite of the obvious peril. And this time I wanted to add a 15th painting—the Resurrection.

Once more it happened. I would labor hard over a face in the crowd, but when I went to paint Jesus, my brush moved smoothly. Sometimes, looking over a day's work, I would find things I had not planned. I recall being surprised by the manner in which I had painted Christ's hand grasping the heavy cross, I had given the hand more the quality of a caress than a grasp. At first that seemed wrong to me, but as I looked longer, it came to me that the subtlety of a caress was right—before my eyes Christ was turning the cross, a thing as ugly as today's electric chair, into a symbol of love.

Canvas after canvas came off my easel and began to

jam my studio. I could not explain to anyone why I was painting them or, for that matter, what I was going to do with them. I simply didn't know.

Gradually people began to ask to see them. Some actually arrived on my doorstep. Then I began to get offers from people who wanted to exhibit the paintings, *all* of them.

Actually, by this time, I was surprised at nothing about those paintings. At last I was beginning to have some personal concept of this thing which I later found to be called guidance. I went on working, at peace with myself, enjoying the fervor of creation, always at ease when someone came up with some new plan for showing my work. Pictures are painted to be seen, and if these were to be seen, God would help me find a way.

After several offers that proved impractical, one in particular that would have made the paintings into a circus exhibit, I got the idea to show the paintings myself in a building constructed for that purpose. It would have to be a building with dignity and beauty. I spent weeks creating a model of the type of building I wanted. Then one afternoon a friend of mine in Sarasota, John Hamel, telephoned me.

"I found your building. I just drove by. It's on the South Tamiami Trail. It's vacant and waiting. It's round and glass. It's beautiful. It's your building. I know it is!"

And it is. From that moment on, the paintings have had a home. I leased the building, getting help from every side—from friends, from banks, from the city of Sarasota. My paintings are on permanent exhibition in the Sarasota Museum of the Cross.

I cannot tell you what effect the exhibition of these paintings will have on those who see them. I do know that the paintings have brought me closer to the most perfect of all men, and that is a stirring and humbling experience. I now believe that God, at times, will quietly reach into the minds of people like me. We don't always know what to do with this guidance, but I'm convinced God can be more persistent than we can. He can wait for us.

The Carpenter
by Peter Marshall

Unlike any man who walked the earth before or since.

There are many of you who think of Christ as someone who belongs to history—like Caesar, or Washington, or Napoleon.

You think of Him as one who lived on earth and passed away. A great Man, to be sure, but nothing more.

Perhaps you even have an inner contempt for the mild, suffering Jesus so often pictured. It is a curious thing that so many artists have portrayed His gentleness, meekness, compassion, rather than the other equally true sides of His personality ... strength, tireless energy, uncompromising will.

Perhaps it is this one-sided picture of the long-suffering Christ that you and I *want* to see. Perhaps it is the picture which more nearly suits our generation with its broadmindedness and its easygoing compromises.

But when we throw away our preconceived ideas and turn to the New Testament, we come away with an altogether different conception. In the Gospel of John, for example, there is this dramatic scene in the Temple of Jerusalem at the start of Christ's ministry ...

It is early morning, but already the temple court is a bedlam of activity and noise. Among the tables of the money changers, the cages of doves and the stalls of cattle, shrill voices are bargaining and bickering.

All the signs of greed can be heard just outside the Holy Place. Then, suddenly, there is a lull in the confusion.

Startled at the sudden quiet, they look up to find a strange figure standing between two of the gigantic stone columns.

In a few long strides He is across the court. Picking up the boxes filled with money—scornfully and deliberately—He empties them on the stone floor. The coins spill with a clatter and go rolling in a hundred directions. The tables too go crashing to the floor. And then He drives the terror-stricken cattle from the temple. There is no mildness or meekness here. In fact, the muscles of His arms stand out like cords; lights dart from His eyes. His magnificent figure dominates the scene.

Meanwhile, not a voice is heard in protest . . . not a hand is raised against Him.

Finally, His voice rings out like the voice of God Himself:

"It is written, My house shall be called the house of prayer, but ye have made it a den of thieves."

Who is this Christ?

Whence did He come?

His home was in an obscure village of an occupied Roman province. He was born in a stable; His parents were poor working people.

The only records we have of Him are silent about the greater part of His life. This remains one of the most intriguing historical mysteries of all time.

It is reported that after Joseph's death He took over the family carpentry shop—first in Nazareth, then in Capernaum.

His formal education was in the local synagogue school, it stopped when He was 12.

He left no writings.

Never did He travel more than a hundred miles from home.

When He began preaching, His family tried to talk Him out of it, saying that He was mad.

His friends were mostly as poor as He was—fisherman and peasants. He loved to mingle with forgotten men, talking to outcasts, knowing no social barriers, caring nothing for money, concerned mostly with sinners.

He attracted great crowds, for He walked among the sick, touching here a blind eye, there a palsied limb, here a running sore.

Even His enemies were later to admit these miracles.

But finally the crowds drifted away, for His counsels were too difficult. Men were not ready to accept this hard way of love.

In the end, most of His own followers fled in fear, caring more for their own safety than for Him.

He died a criminal's death, reviled and mocked, tormented and laughed at, hanging between two thieves.

They buried Him in a borrowed grave.

But the story was not finished.

For suddenly His disciples, the same men who had run away, came back boldly into the streets of the city which had crucified Christ, proclaiming that He was not dead at all—that He was alive.

The body with the marks of the nails had disappeared. On this everyone was agreed.

There were many attempted explanations, but somehow none was adequate. All that His enemies had to do to silence forever the rumor of this resurrection was to produce the body—but they could not.

Whatever anyone else in Jerusalem thought, Christ's Disciples were convinced beyond any doubt that their Master was alive.

For they were different—not the same men at all.

They spoke boldly.

Threats did not intimidate them.

Their ringing assertions echoed and reverberated:

"This Jesus whom ye crucified is risen from the dead and now demands that every man repent."

The wild story traveled fast . . . to Asia Minor . . . to Rome.

There was derisive laughter. But when this Jesus began to be talked about too much, the Roman Empire tried to stop the talk by threatening. "Don't tell these tales again," the Disciples were told, "if you value your lives."

The threats only made these Apostles more eloquent and bold.

Thrown into prison, they made the cell a pulpit and the dungeon a choir. Stoned, they rose from the dust bleeding and bruised, but with a more convincing testimony.

Lashed with whips, they praised God the more. Hunted and persecuted, thrown to the lions, tortured and killed, still the number of those who made the sign of the Cross grew.

Rome could not stop Jesus.

Her grandeur toppled and fell; Jesus lived on.

Incredibly, in A.D. 325 under the Emperor Constantine, Christianity won recognition from the empire which had once avowed to crush every follower of the Nazarene.

In all of history, there has never been such an extraordinary sequence of events—never been such a Man as the Carpenter of Nazareth.

The other day while trying my luck at ice skating I fell— many times. Each time it seemed more difficult to get up until someone yelled, "Get up on your knees first." I tried it and it worked.

Later I thought—there are so many ways in which we fall and fail; what better advice than to "Get on your knees first," *then* pull yourself up. This works too.

ROBERTA RENNIE LASH
Finleyville, Pennsylvania

The Five Christs I Have Known

by Leonard E. LeSourd

A person's understanding of Christ's nature changes as his faith matures. Here, the executive editor of Guideposts tells about . . .

Ten people at a dinner party began to discuss a movie about Jesus Christ. A gay young woman, bored by the subject, said blandly, "Why would anyone ever want to be like Jesus?"

There was silence for a moment, then the conversation veered into another direction. Yet I found myself fascinated by that silence. What thoughts, unexpressed, went on in the minds of the other nine people? How many wanted to state their feelings for Christ but did not because of embarrassment? How many shared the girl's boredom? How many simply had no thoughts about Him at all?

I can think of at least five different reactions I would have had in the past 45 years. In my youth, I couldn't have cared less about Him. Today I think that what an individual does about Jesus Christ is the most important decision he can make.

At ten the *first Christ* I knew was the pale, anemic face on the Sunday-school wall. "Gentle, mild Jesus" did not inspire this boy whose obsession was athletics. As a youth, I believed in God, went to church, became a perfunctory Christian but outside of church never gave Him a thought.

In college I encountered the *historical Christ*. Now here, I found, was a comfortable position to take toward Him. The historical Jesus is usually set far back in the stream of life.

With this approach, one is not likely to be shunned or considered a fanatic for his beliefs. He can join the intellectual chorus and recite the words, "Jesus was a good man. He had some good advice for us, but let's be realistic about those myths and fairy tales in the Bible."

In my case, putting Christ in this setting was a simple solution during college and four years as an Army Air Corps pilot. The historical Jesus did not interfere with anything I wanted to do.

True, faced with the cold, clammy fear of death during World War II, I desperately needed a philosophy. The historical Christ was too remote to be of any help. And so I settled on an attitude of nonchalance which meant that nothing was really important, not even life itself.

My drift from this "historical" relationship with Christ to a third stage—*Christ the Teacher*—began in 1946. I had been out of the Air Corps for a year, wandering around the country collecting material to write a novel. But the novel did not materialize; my philosophy of nonchalance left me unadjusted to face the competition and realities of the post-war world.

Through the guidance of my parents and an unusual chain of circumstances, several months later I found myself applying for and accepting a job I did not think I wanted. It was to write articles for a small new religious magazine named Guideposts.

Soon a spiritual change began to take place inside me as I interviewed for the magazine people of achievement who had at the core of their lives a strong faith. I began to want what they had.

"Christ is the greatest Teacher," a sales manager for a paint company told me one day, "and there is practical value in the Gospels for us today." I began to see that what the Master said nearly 2,000 years ago could be applied to me, now. For example, His words, *Ask, and it shall be given you; seek, and ye shall find; knock, and it shall be opened unto you.** Here was helpful advice for an ambitious young man. I was also intrigued by the passage, *I can do all things through Christ which strengtheneth me.*** Christ the Teacher was a good psychologist. He understood people. The phrase "spiritual technique" entered my vocabulary. All this was fine as far as it went. The unfortunate part was that I became interested in Christ not for what He was and is, but for what He could do for me.

---

* *Matthew 7:7*
** *Philippians 4:13*

It took a fellowship group to nudge me into the fourth stage—where I encountered *Christ the Person*. I walked into the Young Adult Group of Marble Collegiate Church one night in 1947, 28 years old, cynical and lonely.

As I entered the door, I told myself that these church meetings were a waste of time—stuffy people talking about a stuffy religion. To my surprise, instead of pious types, I found attractive, intelligent people who were genuinely friendly.

Before I knew what had happened, I was pulled into some of their activities. They obviously found Christ to be more than a teacher. Through them and through books, particularly *The Man Nobody Knows* by Bruce Barton, my concept of a pale, meek and mild Jesus changed to one of a virile Man with great stamina. I also began to picture the sense of adventure which the Disciples must have felt following such a Man.

Then I attended a weekend retreat in June, 1948, with some of these young adults. This particular affair combined a series of discussions, quiet meditation, and some recreation. The central theme was on the importance of making a personal commitment to Jesus Christ.

At first I decided that I already had done this. After all, I was a member of a church. Soon I began to realize, however, that they were not talking about church membership, but a specific personal step that for most people went beyond this.

When one of the group described how he had gone into a small chapel nearby, knelt at the altar and made this commitment, I became uneasy. This was an emotional religion which I always had avoided. It was the threat to my self-control—to the veneer of sophistication carefully built up over the years.

Yet, I felt myself drawn to a quality of life I was seeing in these "committed" young people.

Before the weekend was over I found myself in this chapel, on my knees before the altar, saying a simple prayer, "Lord, I don't know how I happen to be here, but I want to give my life to You. I do so now. Show me how to be a good disciple."

Immediately there was a great sense of release and exhilaration; also a kind of cleansing. This experience climaxed my growing relationship to Christ the Person.

The years which followed this "surrender" experience were full of exciting creativity. I felt close to Christ. I had an enthusiastic witness for Him which I gave regularly. What more was necessary?

Yet somehow I was not spiritually undergirded at all for a calamity in my personal life which unexpectedly came when I was 39. The breakup of a marriage is devastating. The question I asked was, "Why?"

I had turned over my life to Christ; had worked hard at being a good Christian. Behind my self-pity was the feeling that all this Christian effort somehow should have made me immune from a personal disaster.

In the period of discouragement that followed, I came face to face with the spirit of evil. Never again will I think of the Devil as a comical red-robed figure with a pitchfork. He is subtle, suave and persuasive. I discovered one of Satan's best tools for the conquest of a human being is self-pity.

When one is falling, the instinct is to reach out for something to hold onto. I did this and found one handle to clutch—my commitment experience kneeling at an altar ten years before. This was still very real to me. And so I knelt once more and sought Him again as I had before.

With this act of submission came a new recognition and acceptance of my frailty. Before I had, in effect, congratulated Christ for having found me. Now I realized that it was not enough to have Him just as a Leader, or a Guide or Presence. I needed His Spirit within me.

Thus began my fifth and most meaningful relationship with Jesus—my contact with the Holy Spirit or the *Indwelling Christ*.

I see now that the first disciples likewise had their moments of great defeat. Humble, dedicated, they had all committed their lives to their Master, yet their commitment was not enough. When trouble came, Judas betrayed Christ, Peter denied Him; the rest fled in panic when Jesus was arrested and crucified.

Yet the great miracle of Christianity is what happened to these confused and inadequate men at Pentecost. Christ appeared and said, "You shall receive power when the Holy Spirit has come upon you."*

The Disciples gathered in the Upper Room and prayed deeply for many hours. The Bible describes the "rush of mighty wind" that came, and how "they were all filled with the Holy Spirit." What a sight this must have been! How in-

---

* *Acts 1:8*

describable the joy, the elation, the resurgence of power as these men were reborn! The Holy Spirit filled them all with such power that they were able to go forth and bring Christianity to the world in spite of ridicule, beatings, imprisonment and execution.

Is the same power available to us today?

I believe so with all my heart. Though only a beginner in my experience with the Holy Spirit, during the past years my life has been blessed in ways I could never have believed possible during my deep despair back in the mid-50s. My feeling now is one of overwhelming gratitude and joy—the kind of deep joy that can even bring tears unexpectedly. And also love—love for my family, for friends, for work, and most of all for Him.

The Story Behind My Painting
by Warner Sallman

The most famous portrait of Christ.

Many times I have been asked how I happened to paint the *Head of Christ* that has received such wide circulation since it appeared as a painting in 1940.

"Did you have a vision beforehand?" they ask.

"Did you feel Christ's presence?"

"Did you have some kind of religious experience?"

The answer is *yes* to all these questions, but the real story behind the picture begins with a change that took place in my life shortly after my wedding.

When I married Ruth Anderson, an attractive and dedicated choir member and organist, back in May, 1916, I was 24 years old, was employed as an artist in the field of men's fashions and was prospering financially. In all, it seemed like a cloudless sky, but storm clouds already were forming below the horizon.

Years before, I had had a tumor in my shoulder but a surgeon had removed it and it apparently was healed. Then came a major complication in the same area. By the following spring—1917—the pain was acute. I went to several doctors and took various treatments, but the affliction grew worse. Finally, I consulted a specialist who made extensive tests.

"You're pretty sick, my boy," he said kindly.

"Tell me the whole truth, doctor," I replied. "I ought to know what's wrong with me."

"You have tuberculosis of the lymph glands," he continued. "I recommend surgery." He hesitated a moment, took my arm, then continued. "Otherwise I cannot give you much hope beyond three months."

351

The physician's words jolted me severely. I left his office in a daze, and with uncertain step made my way to a streetcar. On the car I moved up until I was close to the motorman, feeling some protection in his presence. It gave me an opportunity to do a little thinking.

"What shall I do?" I asked myself. "Shall I tell Ruth the whole truth, or conceal what the doctor said until after the baby is born?" It was July, and our first little one was due in September. I feared the revelation would so upset her that serious complications might develop.

I prayed for guidance, and I believed God was directly speaking to me when the conviction suddenly came over me that "Ruth is brave, has a deep faith, and can take it. I'll tell her all."

This I did, not minimizing the "three months to live." Ruth received my words with utmost calm . . . A feeling came over me that she was like a rock—and that through her the Lord would guide us aright.

"Let God's peace come into your heart, Warner," she told me, putting her arms around my neck and looking squarely into my face, her eyes aglow with love. "We'll pray and whatever is God's will for us, we gladly will do it. In three months we can do a lot for Him: and if it be His will to spare our life together for a longer period, we will thank Him for it and go ahead serving Him."

I do not remember the words we used in our prayer together, but I do know we did *not* ask for a longer life span. We only asked God to guide and bless us and use us. The heart of our prayer was a plea reminiscent of our Savior's in Gethsemane: "Dear Lord, we pray that Thy will be our will, and that in all ways Thy will be done."

In no manner did we forego medical or surgical help, but we felt that if the latter was to be for me, God would make it known. We continued the medical treatments as before, but no revelation came regarding the proposed surgery.

However, something else did happen: by the alchemy of nature or in the Providence of God, the pain gradually grew less, and there were signs of amelioration of the disease. It took months, but complete healing finally took place. We do not minimize the powerful influence of mind over matter— we implicitly believe the Lord can and does heal.

What better proof can there be than that the predicted three months have stretched into 44 busy, fruitful and happy years—with the added blessing of three sons born to our union—and that now, as I near the 70-year mark in this year 1962, I feel almost as vigorous as ever, am well occupied with my work and have the joy of Ruth's unfailing companionship?

Yet the important part of this experience is not that I was healed, but that I learned an exciting and dynamic principle: When we turn our lives over to God, without reservation, He can and will do remarkable things through us.

It was this personal philosophy that made it possible for me to do the *Head of Christ*. It began as an assignment from a small Christian youth publication in January, 1924, for a cover design. I thought to do the face of Christ. My first attempts were all wrong. Finally there were only 24 hours until delivery date. I tried again and again the preceding evening, but the impressions that came to my mind were futile. I felt disturbed and frustrated.

I went to bed at midnight, restless in spirit but did ask God once more to give me the vision I needed. Suddenly about two o'clock I came out of my fitful attempts at sleep with a clear, beautiful image of the *Head of Christ* startlingly vivid in my mind. I hastened to my attic studio to record it. I made a thumb-nail sketch, working as fast as I could in order that the details of the dream might be captured before fading out of my mind. Next morning I made a charcoal drawing from it.

This *Head of Christ* hardly caused a ripple of comment when it first appeared. But years later I made an oil painting of the "Head" and since that time its distribution has attained phenomenal proportions.* Yet I always think of the portrayal as something God did—through me.

For Ruth and I believe that as disciples of Christ our task is primarily seed-sowing of good deeds, good thoughts and good purposes.

Yet we are human enough to enjoy hearing or knowing of results—often strange and unpredictable—accompanying our labors. For instance, there was a recent incident in Los Angeles. A robber rang the doorbell to an apartment. When the lady opened the door he thrust a revolver in her face and snapped, "This is a holdup. Give me your money and jewelry!"

---

* *More than 100,000,000 copies have been published and distributed throughout the world.*

Just then he looked up and saw behind the woman a large picture on the wall. It was the *Head of Christ*. For a moment he seemed to freeze. Slowly he lowered his gun.

"I can't do it, lady," he gasped, "not in front of that picture." And he turned and ran down the stairs.

Three Months In His Presence
by Virginia Lively

---

*This Florida housewife cannot explain her strange
spiritual revelation. All she knows is that it
changed her life.*

When friends ask how I first discovered that my hands have
been given a ministry of healing, I'm sure they don't expect
to hear the kind of story which I am about to set down. Apparently the fact that I am a suburban housewife who saves
grocery stamps and has to watch her weight seems a poor beginning to a story of divine intervention.

It started the year my father entered the tuberculosis
sanitarium in Tampa. We had long since given up hope. He
was too old for an operation and we had seen the x-rays. The
last thing on earth that would have occurred to any of us—
Mother or my sister or me—was to ask God to step in and
change medical facts.

And yet my husband, Ed, and I were active church
members. As a banker, Ed was head of fund-raising, our two
children went to Sunday school and I belonged to all the
groups. We were, in short, typical, civic-minded churchgoers.
Which is why the tears, when they began, caused Ed and me
so much embarrassment.

It was in October, driving home from a PTA meeting,
that I suddenly began to cry. I was in charge of the Hal-
loween Carnival that year, and at the meeting there'd been
some criticism of the plans. When I was still crying at bedtime, Ed put his arms around me and said:

"Honey, no carnival is that important."

But it wasn't the carnival. Even as I cried I knew that
these tears were for something far bigger. I cried myself to
sleep and in the morning as soon as I opened my eyes the
tears started again. I choked them back, but as soon as Ed
and the children left, the tears burst out again.

355

This incredible state of affairs lasted four days. I took to wearing dark glasses even in the house so that the family would not guess how constantly I was crying. I was sure I was having a nervous breakdown.

It was on the morning of the fourth day, after Ed and the children had left, that a curious change took place. I saw nothing. I heard nothing. Yet, all at once there was power in the air around me. The atmosphere itself seemed to hum and crackle as though I stood in the center of a vast electric storm. As I try to put it into words it sounds fantastic, but at the time there was no sense that something beyond the possible was taking place.

I had sunk into the high-backed chair in the living room when suddenly through the window I saw the eastern horizon. Trees and houses stood between me and it, but I seemed to see right beyond to the place where earth and sky came together. And there, where they met, was a ball of light.

This light was moving, traveling toward me with incredible speed. It appeared white, yet from it poured all the colors I had ever seen.

And then it was beside me. Although it seemed impossible that anything with such energy could hold still, it took a position at my right shoulder and there it stayed. And as I stared, I started to smile. I smiled because He was smiling at me. For I now saw that it was not light, but a face.

How can I put into words the most beautiful countenance I have ever seen? "He is perfect" was the first thought that came. His forehead was high, His eyes exceptionally large. But I could never fix the color of His eyes any more than I could the color of the sea.

More, much more, than individual features was the overwhelming impression of life—unhampered life, life so brimming over with power and freedom that all living things I had seen till that moment seemed lumps of clay.

Not for a moment did I hesitate to call this Life at my side Jesus. And two things about Him struck me most. The first was His humor. I was astonished to see Him often break into outright laughter. And the second was His utter lack of condemnation. That He knew me down to my very marrow—knew all the stupid, cruel, silly things I had ever done—I realized at once. But I also saw that none of these things, or anything I would ever do, could alter the absolute caring, the unconditional love, that I saw in those eyes.

I could not grasp it. It was too immense a fact. I felt

that if I gazed at Him for a thousand years I could not realize it all.

I did not have a thousand years; I had three months. For as long as that, the face of Jesus stayed before me, never fading, never withdrawing. Many times I tried to tell someone else what I saw but the words would never come. And meanwhile I carried on with my tasks—meals and shopping and the PTA carnival—but effortlessly, scarcely knowing I was doing them, so fixed were my thoughts on Him.

At the same time, I had never seemed so aware of other people. How this was possible when my mind was full of Him alone I don't know, but it was true. My husband, especially. Far from feeling that a third person had entered our marriage, I felt that Christ *was* the marriage, as though all along He had been the force drawing us together.

And the Bible! All at once I couldn't read enough of it. It was like tearing open a letter from someone who had known this Presence as a flesh and blood person, full of just the kind of specific details I longed to hear. Certain passages in particular had a strange effect on me: when the Bible described Jesus healing someone, the actual print on the page seemed to burn. The hand that touched it would tingle as if I had touched an electric current.

And then one afternoon before the children got home, I was sitting, just looking at Him, when all of a sudden in a patch of sunlight on the wall appeared the x-ray of my father's chest. It was all scar tissue and cavities. Then as I watched, a white mist moved slowly up the wall. When it passed the diseased tissue, there appeared on my wall a picture of a healthy lung.

"Then Dad's well!" I said aloud, and at that the Person at my side burst into peal after peal of joyous laughter which said that wholeness was always God's way.

I thought my heart would burst as I waited for next Wednesday's x-ray. I enjoyed the scene in my mind again and again, imagining the ring of the telephone and Mother's voice stammering with excitement, "Darling—the most amazing—the most glorious—"

But when Mother called, her voice was flat. "The most annoying thing, Virginia. They got the slides mixed up! Poor Dad's got to go back for x-rays tomorrow. Why, they sent down pictures of someone who never even had TB . . . !"

But, of course, the x-rays next day showed no sign of

disease either; Dad was healed and lived out his long life in thanksgiving to God.

And it was Dad's healing that convinced me I must try to describe the indescribable that had happened to me. I went to an elderly pastor whom I had known a long time. To my astonishment he understood me at once. He gave me some books which described fairly similar things.

Then he said the words I have wished unsaid so often.

"Don't be surprised, Virginia, if the vision fades after a time. They usually do, you know."

"Fade!" I thought, as I drove home with that joyous Presence beside me. Oh, it can't, it mustn't! For the first time in the whole incredible experience my attention veered from Him to myself. And in that instant the vision was diminished, actually disappeared for a second or two, though right away the radiant face was beside me again.

But the damage was done. The seed of self-concern was sown. The bright Presence would sometimes be missing for an hour or more. The more worried I got, the more self-centered I grew. What have I done? What will I do without Him? When He did return there would be no accusation in His eyes, just a tremendous compassion as though He realized how difficult it had become for me to see Him at all.

At last all that was left of this experience was the strange tingling in my hands as I read the Bible stories of healing. One day I was visiting a friend in the hospital. She was hemorrhaging and in pain. On an impulse I reached out and touched her. My hand began to burn just as it did during the Bible reading. My friend gave a little sigh of comfort and fell asleep. When the doctor examined her, he found that the hemorrhaging had stopped.

Over the next eight years there were dozens, scores of experiences of this kind, all as inexplicable as the first. And yet for me they were still years of emptiness and waiting. "I will always be with you," He had told me when I last saw Him.

"But how will I know if I can't see you?" I called to Him, for He had seemed so far away.

"You will see Me," He said, and then He was gone.

But the years went by and the vision had not come back. And then one day, while speaking to a church group, I saw those love-lit eyes smiling once again into mine. I looked again. The eyes belonged to a lady in the second row. Suddenly the room was full of Him; He was in the eyes of everyone in the room. "You will see Me. . . ."

I used to wonder what would have happened if the old pastor had never spoken of the vision fading. Might I have had it forever? I think not. I think that the days when Jesus was real to my eyes were the days of the "childhood" of my faith, the joyous, effortless time of discovery. But I do not think He lets it stay that way for long.

He didn't for His first disciples, He doesn't for us today. He gives us a glimpse only. Perhaps He let me look so long because I am slow to learn. But, finally, He takes away all sensory clues. He is bigger than our eyes and ears can make Him, so He gives us instead the eyes of faith, and all mankind in which to discover His face.

Section Nine—

Faith Can Change the World

Section Nine— Introduction

Few will disagree that the world about us is sick and suffering from a spiritual malnutrition which needs immediate attention. In fact, changes must take place if the earth is to survive. The problem comes when one tries to get specific: Who needs changing? When? How?

The first answer is, of course, that change begins with me—and you. When? Now. How? That answer can come to each individual when he really gets honest with himself—and the Lord.

In this section, we present articles by people who have found their own "how" and have passed it on to others. Read these stories closely. Maybe one of them will prompt you to act on some simmering action you have wanted to take but haven't.

With many persons, unfortunately, there is a lack of faith that their individual change can influence the whole picture. Since the inception of Guideposts, over and over again we have illustrated the principle that one person is an army with God. Faith—the kind which brings inner spiritual change resulting in creative outward actions—is, in our opinion, the best way peace and cooperation among the people of the world can be accomplished. It is the kind of peace promised by Christ, a peace that passes understanding.

Somebody Needs You
by E. Stanley Jones

A great missionary calls for a new antidote for old problems: An outpouring of love.

I believe the most dramatic moment in history occurred 2,000 years ago, as a little group of listeners leaned forward to hear Jesus' answer to a certain question. There were 3,600 commandments at that time in the Jewish law: the question they had put to Jesus was, "Which one is the greatest?"

It was not only a matter of great import to the Jews of those days; on His answer would depend the place He would hold in our lives today. Would it be the answer of a man speaking to his moment in history, or would it be God's answer, true for all time? The Bible, of course, records Jesus' reply. Jesus said:

"Thou shalt love. . . ."

What kind of an answer is it, in our world today? A few years ago, a leading American psychiatrist, Karl Menninger, took a walk through his sanitarium in Kansas. Here were men and women whose problems had driven them to this retreat from the world. As he walked through the buildings and the grounds Dr. Menninger asked himself, "Why are they here?" The theory had been that they didn't understand themselves, therefore insight was the answer. But now Menninger had a new idea: What if they were there because they'd never loved or been loved? What if that were the disease?

On this suspicion, he organized the whole sanitarium on a new basis. He told the staff, "We've been giving these people understanding when perhaps what they need is love. From the chief psychiatrist down to the gardener, all our contacts for a while are going to be love contacts. If you go into a patient's room to change a light bulb, go in with an attitude of love."

After six months they took stock to see how the new system was working: They discovered that the average period of hospitalization had been cut in half.

Some years later, a newspaper reporter in Tucson, Arizona, asked Dr. Menninger this question, "Suppose you suspect that you're heading for a nervous breakdown. What should you do?"

You'd have thought that a great psychiatrist would have said, "Go see a psychiatrist." But this is what he did say, "Go straight to your front door, turn the knob, cross the tracks and find somebody who needs you."

In other words, the new finding of psychiatry was that the mind breaks down when love breaks down. Medical doctors were beginning to discover that the body can break down for the same reason. A New York businessman I've known for many years went to his doctor for pains in his neck and shoulders. After examining him the doctor wrote out this prescription, "Go down to Grand Central Station, find someone in trouble and do something for him."

The businessman snorted. But he'd paid money for that advice so he thought he'd better follow it. He went down to Grand Central and there in a corner was a woman sitting on a suitcase and weeping. He went up to her and said, "Madam, may I do something for you?"

At first she was too embarrassed to answer. He was embarrassed too, but he kept at it and finally learned that this was her first trip to New York, her daughter was not there to meet her, and the size of the station had confused and frightened her. He got the daughter's name, went to a telephone book and looked up the address, helped the lady into a cab, bought her some flowers on the way and delivered her to the daughter who had lost her mother's letter and had spent two days waiting in Pennsylvania Station.

My friend went back to his doctor and said, "Say, Doc, that was awfully good medicine. My neck feels better already."

Psychiatry and medicine were revealing a picture of man that was not different from the one Jesus drew. In fact the more science taught us about ourselves, the more we saw His commandment in a new light: not as a difficult assignment for those advanced in the religious life, but as a very condition of life itself.

If this is so, then failure to love should be as fatal as

failure to breathe. And this is just what doctors in New York's Bellevue Hospital found some years ago. The staff on the children's ward made the tragic discovery that they were losing 32 percent of the children under a year old, mostly through minor ailments. The doctors were dumbfounded. They were giving the infants scientific treatment, scientific feeding, sterile surroundings, and the children were dying.

At last someone suggested that what the hospital environment was not supplying was love. So they sent out a call for love-volunteers: women to come and love babies so many hours a day. Hundreds of women responded because they had a need too: the need for someone to love. In most instances they were older women whose own children had grown up and who had no one now to love but themselves or some distant grandchildren. So they volunteered and the death rate began to plunge. After four months the superintendent said, "We could no more do without these love-volunteers than we could do without penicillin."

Now the interesting thing is that love always works as it did with these children in Bellevue Hospital: It is always specific. It is always one woman rocking one particular baby; no one has yet learned how to love people in general. I described the Bellevue experiment in a lecture in Sweden one day and a nurse in the audience came to me afterwards and told me this story.

When she first went to work in a government convalescent home years earlier, she'd been assigned to an elderly patient who had not spoken a single word in three years. The other nurses disliked this patient so much that she always was passed down to the newest member of the staff. But this nurse was a Christian, or at least she'd always thought she was, and she decided that her Christian love was only as good as her love for this particular patient.

The old woman used to sit in a rocking chair all day long. "So I pulled up another rocking chair," the nurse said, "and just rocked alongside her and loved her and loved her and loved her." The third day she opened her eyes and said, "You're so kind."

Those were the first words she had spoken in three years. In two weeks she was out of the home. Now I never saw the patient whose life was transformed by *love*, but I did see the nurse who did the *loving*, and here is another of the unarguable truths about *love*: It makes the lover beautiful.

The great Christian writer and speaker Rufus Moseley used to say, "You are born of the qualities you habitually give out. If you give out hate, you become hateful. If you give out criticism, you become critical. If you give out love, you become lovely. So give out love and only love."

Somebody asked him once, "But Mr. Moseley, suppose they won't take your love?"

His answer: "Increase the dose."

It sounds too simple, put like that. And here is both the glory and the peril of Christ's commandment to love. The glory of it is that we may finally learn enough simplicity to follow it. The peril is that we will try to expand on it. Jesus reduced 3,600 commandments to one; right away the temptation of Christian writers and thinkers was to start putting the others back.

They were tempted, but they didn't give in—not the great ones. It looked for a while as though Paul was making faith as important as love in the new church. But there came a moment when Paul had to select the supreme value and he took the torch from his Master and wrote, "Now abideth faith, hope, and love—but the greatest of these is love."*

There was another perilous moment when John began to write, because it looked as though the most important thing in his theology was going to be knowledge. He was writing for a generation of Gnostics, people who believed you didn't have to have an Incarnation—you could arrive at all truth within yourself. The Gnostics were the Knowers.

John wrote a great deal about knowledge, but he wrote something else, something that had never been written before, and I think all heaven leaned over the battlements to see whether he would write it. And when he did I think heaven broke out cheering, "Oh, they've got it! At last they've got it!" For John had written:

"God is love."

John was in the little group that held their breath to hear the great commandment. And I like to think that afterward he puzzled over it, as we all do when we hear it for the first time.

Is this what God requires of us? Is this the highest thing on earth?

I like to think that later, when Jesus' earthly life was

---

* *I Corinthians 13:13*

over, John woke up in the middle of one cold, starry night and said, "Of course. We are made in the image of God: if we could only see Him we would know what we must be. I have seen Him. I know."

Peace Is Your Job
by Jessie Durlach

A visionary, a humanitarian, a peacemaker, this woman says the answer to world problems lies with you.

Perhaps you have heard the story of the community which decided to present its mayor with a barrel of wine. Each of its residents was asked to bring a pitcherful. One man figured it out this way. Wine would cost him money. He could pour in a pitcher of water and, mixed with the other wine, it would never be noticed.

After the wine barrel had been filled, the wine was tested. The barrel was full of water! Each person had used the same selfish dodge.

I believe this type of thinking is perhaps the main reason for the failure of the world to achieve peace.

Today, 1948, too many of us say, "What difference does it make what I, one person, do?"—forgetting that "a little leaven leaveneth the whole lump." This holds true in voting, in group and community projects, in the whole field of national and international relations.

For years I have worked actively for peace. I was one of those "fighting pacifists" that make up the ranks of the peace movements. Competition, rivalry, and differences of philosophy kept us from accomplishing our major objectives.

It isn't hard to see how political maneuvering, national selfishness and desire for profit keeps countries embroiled. It wasn't nearly as easy to see these things in our organizations, and when we did see them, we were just as helpless in regard to them.

One day I was feeling particularly low—discouraged that the world was spending 1000 times more for armaments than for the then existing League of Nations. I thought we needed more money in the peace movement, but a fellow-worker told me bluntly that it wasn't money that the peace movement needed, it was God.

At the time, I was an agnostic. Yet I was sufficiently sincere in my desire for peace to try anything. So at the invitation of the Oxford Group I set out to find Him.

I went to a Moral Rearmament house party at French Lick. There I made a great discovery. I actually *saw* peace in operation for the first time. I saw progressive education being practiced, not merely preached. I began to gain firsthand experience of the presence of God.

I became convinced that the mess in the world is *our fault*, and not God's.

Until that time, I had sought peace because I feared war. Now my search became rooted in faith in God and love of humanity. I began to see the vital importance of the individual in our search for peace.

One of the most valuable practices I learned from this group is that of "Quiet Time" and "Guidance." It is a variation of the Quaker practice of silence and other religions' meditation. Quieting your own thoughts and seeking to be one with God, you write down what comes to you. It may be a bit of self-revelation; it may include instructions for the day. It's bearing on peace, my own internal peace, peace in my family, in society, in the world, is tremendous.

Take my husband, for example. He is a conservative businessman. My tendencies are radical and idealistic. After one of our all too numerous discussions, I sat down to have "Quiet Time" to see if something might be done about this particular impasse. Guidance came.

I found myself writing substantially this: "The difference between you and him is the way you show your fears. Your common sin is fear. Get rid of that, and you will find little distance between you. Every time you get frightened, you frighten him as well. You rush forward, and he is rooted to the spot or runs backward. This draws you farther apart."

This was a revelation to me. I could see the implications not only for myself and my immediate surroundings, but for the world at large. I saw how this discovery applied not only to my husband and me, but to political parties, to classes and groups of all kinds, to nations. For example, if the U. S. and Russia gave up their mutual fears, we would be free of the danger of atomic warfare and could give our attention to the use of atomic energy for the good of mankind.

Lots of people "work for peace." They work earnestly and with great sacrifice—but they make little or no headway.

WHY?

Because peace will come only as a result of education, education at its best, education which concerns itself with the whole personality—with the body, mind and soul—with the emotions as well as the intellect. Such education has to be communicated to individuals *by individuals,* individuals who themselves have experienced peace in their own lives.

Only faith can overcome fear. Only a confidence in life can overcome the headlong flight to death which our wars, our diseases, our crimes and our mental aberrations of one sort or another represent.

When this conviction came to me, who had so long believed in the use of mass media to influence peoples' doing and thinking, I experienced a great sinking of the heart. Surely it would take hundreds of years before we could begin to make any impression on the world.

Then a forgotten formula from my school days came to mind. What of geometric progression? So I put it down in black and white. If I, who believe I am truly imbued with the desire for peace, can win but two others to a similar dedication—and these in turn do likewise, how many times will we have to repeat the process before we contact the entire population of the world?

To my amazement the answer was merely 31. *World peace can start with me, or you.* It is our responsibility. When you and I have learned the art of peaceful living and have won two other persons who, in turn, will each win two more and so on—when this happens thirty-one times—a total of 2,147,483,648 persons will have been reached, and that is approximately the population of the world.

This was indeed a discovery and made me far more hopeful of peace than I had been in all the previous years of my endeavors. But this still doesn't make the job a simple one. To convince others, you have to be extremely peaceful yourself, peaceful in your own mind and heart, peaceful in your relations with your family, your neighbors, your business associates, your rivals, and all who cross your path.

Peace means that the fate of one's neighbor is just as important if not more important than one's own fate. Peace means that you would rather die than kill.

Our ambition blocks us, our desire to dominate, to lead

rather than serve. The humility needed for such a program is rare, indeed, and most difficult to achieve.

Leadership, let us not forget, is an animal ideal and ultimately leads to such manifestations as Der Fuhrer or Il Duce—the German and Italian equivalents of the English words, The Leader. Service is a human ideal. With true service there is no rivalry, no competition, no jealousy, no desire to dominate or control. With true service fear is at a minimum, security at a maximum. These are the requisites of a peaceful world.

Peace, personal and international, is no longer a mere dream, but is actually within our grasp and is the responsibility and privilege of each one of us. If I, or you, fail to do the job, then not only would we lose out, but the whole world would suffer because of our personal failure, a terrifying thought indeed—one that should arouse us to the greatest effort.

There is nothing new about the idea of chain communication, about passing on information by word of mouth from one person to another. All folklore has spread that way. The Apostles used that method. Political parties use it in their whispering campaigns and we can use it as well. The important thing is not how many people we reach, but how profoundly we affect those whom we contact.

The answer to the world's problems lies with you, and with none but you. You are an essential link in the world chain.

Perhaps this factory hand, or that delegate, this alcoholic or that college professor is the man to whom God wants you to bring this message. Are you ready and willing to *win him*, not fight him?

"May the Lord bless you and keep you. May the Lord let His Countenance shine upon you and be gracious unto you. May the Lord turn His Face toward you and give you peace."

LET ME HOLD YOUR HAND

Let me hold your hand as we go downhill,
We've shared our strength and we share it still.
It hasn't been easy to make the climb,
But the way was eased by your hand in mine.

Like the lake, our life has had ripples too,
Ill-health, and worries, and payments due,
With happy pauses along the way,
A graduation, a raise in pay.

At the foot of the slope, we will stop and rest,
Look back, if you wish; we've been truly blessed,
We've been spared the grief of being torn apart.
By death, or divorce, or a broken heart.

The view ahead is one of the best,
Just a little bit farther, and then we can rest.
We move more slowly, but together still,
Let me hold your hand as

we go
downhill. . . .

PEGGY CAMERON KING

What Every Father Should Know

by Daniel A. Poling

*The memories of a son's growing faith—a faith
that was to give courage to people the world over.*

The telegram had a solemn, urgent tone. I was to meet the
train at Grand Central Station and "say nothing to Mother."
It was from Clark Poling, my youngest son, who was fifteen
years old at the time and away at Oakwood School.

I wondered what kind of a jam my boy might be in. By
the time I had met Clark and we had closeted ourselves in
my office, I was going through one of the most uncertain moments of my life.

"Dad," he began, "what do you know about God?"

That was all. I was relieved, but checked an impulse to
show it. Who can tell what tumultuous emotions, inner uncer-
tainties and fears lie behind such a question?

What *did* I know about God? I'm glad I didn't have
time to prepare my answer. For what I said came from the
heart and not the head.

"Clark," I said, "I know mighty little about God. But
what I do know by test and experience—sickness and health,
sorrow and joy, death and life—controls my whole life."

I told him how temptations and wrong impulses came to
me as they do to everyone . . . in every relationship and decision—that we may make mistakes, yet through faith in God
we can be guided to do the right thing.

For three hours we talked, then we went home where a
surprised mother welcomed us and soon had us seated before
a steaming home cooked meal.

Clark Poling later worked out his own answer to the
question: How can I know God? He wrote:

373

". . . through Jesus Christ! and, of course, through prayer, Bible study and service to men, women and children. God is a Being so great and good that when we are rightly related to Him, we are spiritually prepared for whatever experiences we have to meet."

He was to demonstrate its truth too!

Both as a father, and now as a grandfather, I usually learn more from my children than they do from me. And parents have so much to live up to! What the father does, more than what he says, will determine his son's actions in life.

Clark was four when I took him to have his tonsils removed. His struggles and cries had become so violent in the doctor's office that I had to lift him in my arms and pin his limbs to his sides.

Suddenly he was completely calm.

"Daddy, will you stay all through?" he asked with a searching look. I said I would.

Later the doctor nodded to tell me that he was under the anesthetic, and I could leave. At the door, I remembered my promise. *"He* wouldn't know, Doctor, but I would." So I stayed to the finish.

When the boy's eyes fluttered open, I grinned reassuringly. "Daddy, you did stay through, didn't you?" he said weakly. I was very glad I had the right answer. A small point, some may say, yet now I feel somehow that youngsters see through most small deceits by parents, and little dishonesties can build barriers between parent and child.

Clark played football in college, was outstanding in debates, yet I felt sure he was always irresistibly heading for the ministry. Both my sons were born to a preaching tradition. For six generations, with but one exception, my forebears have been clergymen. Their parishes have ranged from New England to the Pacific Coast. Always, however, the decision to preach came from some inner conviction.

I'll never forget a certain night Clark and I spent in a Detroit hotel in 1931. I was there to make an address and Clark had come down from school to be with me.

It was late when we retired. I was tired, but he wanted to talk. Several times I was on the verge of asking him to turn it off (as you often had to do with him). Then suddenly it occurred to me that he wanted to tell me something, and that it was through such informal, natural moments that father and son best express their love, share confidences and create the type of relationship that transcends all others.

Quietly, but so impressively that as long as I live I shall remember the electriclike shock with which I heard him speak the words, he flung his arm across my bed and I felt his hand over my chest: "Daddy, I'm going to preach. I've *got* to do it!"

I wasn't sleepy or tired then. I knew that this was what I had always wanted. We talked until dawn.

There was much of the unconventional in Clark's ministry. One moment he would be swinging a pick on a road, or helping some of the boys clear away boulders. Minutes later, after slipping on shirt and coat, he would be leading a religious conference with assurance and vigor.

He and his charming wife, Betty, made a perfect team during the five years they spent in Schenectady, tirelessly helping to rebuild their church into one of the most active religious centers in the community.

Shortly after Pearl Harbor, Clark enlisted in the Chaplain's Corps.

After months of training and duty, the day came when Clark was to leave on the troop transport "Dorchester." We had dinner together in Boston—Clark, his wife, Betty, their son, Corky, and myself. I saw him last at the bus station. All fathers of Servicemen know that final glimpse of their boys' faces at such partings . . . Then the bus was gone and it was dark, but Clark's farewell smile stays with me.

Their common love of God brought the four chaplains together during the now well-known night of dark terror on board the torpedoed "Dorchester" back in 1943. The world thrilled to the story. After giving away their own life jackets, the chaplains stood with their arms locked, praying for the safety of the wrecked men to the end. One survivor told of hearing Clark Poling's contagious and calming laugh only minutes before the ship went down.

Mrs. Shallow Goes to School
by Elizabeth Sherrill

A Guideposts family goes to Africa to teach—and learn.

I remember that as I walked for the first time across the cow pasture to the little African school where I was to teach English, the headmaster's voice sailed across the mud walls.

"This are a pencils!"

"This are a pencils!" 50 young voices shouted back, and I knew I had my work cut out for me.

The Uganda government, on reaching independence two months before, had decided that English was to be used in all schools—in place of the dozens of small tribal languages—and it was to help with this that I had volunteered.

I was especially interested in this school, for it had not been built by the government or a foreign mission, but by African Christians in the little community of Salaama. With its thick mud walls, it looked like any other house in Salaama, except that its roof was tin instead of grass and that a bicycle wheel-rim hung in a tree outside, which was banged with a stone at the start and end of the school day.

Now as I got closer, a little girl ran up to me, snatched my pocketbook, and headed back to the school with me at her heels. In the doorway she dropped to her knees and held up the purse to me on both hands.

I learned later that it is considered beneath the dignity of a teacher to carry anything and that children habitually kneel when giving something to an adult, but for the moment I was completely nonplussed.

The headmaster, Mr. Muwanga, came to the door and gave a speech in Luganda which I took to be the official welcome but found later was the daily hello. Then he showed me proudly through the school's three rooms. The floor was earth, spread *weekly*, he stressed, with fresh cow dung to keep down the dust. The walls stopped at about four feet, sticks embedded in them supported the roof. This arrangement, of course, let in rain as well as light, but later I noticed that whereas I would jump at the first drop, the children would work on, oblivious to a floor gradually turning to mud beneath their feet.

And yet I reflected, watching Mr. Muwanga's pride in the school, that this was the first headmaster I'd known who had built his school with his own two hands.

There were 150 children in the three rooms, sitting on long board benches, ranging in age from 6 to 16. Mr. Muwanga introduced me. But alas for Sherrill! The sounds "r" and "l" are difficult for many Africans and in each room the name that came back was "Mrs. Shallow."

I began coming to school three mornings a week and before long I began to fear that the name was only too true. Like the morning when I found the entire school digging frantically in the ground. A particular species of termite had hatched in the night and the children were hoping to find enough for their mothers to make stew. They could not resist nibbling a little of their catch and every now and then an especially juicy bite on one of these insects made me shudder.

I got a glimpse of the fact that this was shallowness in me a few days later. I had been talking about protein, which is lacking in diets here, but when I came to the word "cheese" I drew a blank: no word could be found to translate it.

So I told them I would bring some to school with me. I chose a lovely piece of very mild yellow cheddar, but no sooner had I unwrapped it than every child in the room clapped his hand to his nose. A little offended, I cut off a piece of cheese and ate it. Then I saw in every face the very reaction of horror I had felt at their insect orgy.

Sometimes they picked up attitudes of mine that I myself hardly was aware I had. The school opened each day with prayer and Bible reading in Luganda. One day I asked if anyone knew in what language the Bible had originally been written. Every hand went up; that was easy: English!

So I launched into a description of the great age of the Bible, a difficult idea in a country with a written history only 100 years old. I told them that the Old and New Testaments were written in different languages and I mentioned that the New Testament represented God seen more clearly, salvation achieved, the ultimate truth.

Wondering if they understood, I asked the same question a week later. One little girl sprang up confidently: the *Old* Testament was written in English, the *New* Testament in American.

The thought haunted me. Was I insisting on American ways and values instead of looking for Christ as He shows Himself in Africa?

I remembered an episode during my first month at the school. I had assigned the Beatitudes for memory work, using the Basic English Bible, "Happy are they——" and the room was full of silent concentration when suddenly a tall boy in the rear of the room leaped to his feet and cried out something in Luganda. Another boy began to clap, a third beat out a rhythm on the bench. Soon the whole class was on its feet, Mr. Muwanga as well, shuffling and stamping and swaying.

I was enchanted. But I kept thinking: at this rate we will never learn the Beatitudes.

The dance stopped as suddenly as it had begun and the children settled back to work. "What," I asked Mr. Muwanga, "was that?"

"Oh," he said, "that was a dance for the Beatitudes."

I thought of Sunday schools I had sat in, classes intoning "Happy are they" with faces like doom, and decided these children had learned the Beatitudes better than I knew.

I often brought an ambitious pile of books, maps, lists to school—it seemed to me there was so much information to get across in addition to English. And then one day I received a book I hadn't expected. It was a scrapbook made by a sixth grade Sunday-school class in Racine, Wisconsin, who had read about this trip in Guideposts and sent it "to someone in Africa." One of the things they had pasted in was a picture of children all over the world.

But when I took the scrapbook down to the school every child there seized on something I had not noticed at all. The African child, wonder of wonders, was not beating a drum or throwing a spear. He was reading a book. The children ran from one to another with the amazing page, marveling and proud. Mr. Muwanga said nothing at all for a long time and when he looked up I thought there were tears in his eyes.

"Is that how they think of us in America?" he said softly. "And I never knew." From that day on, it seemed to me, the whole school stood a little straighter.

But it was Mrs. Shallow who gained most from the experience and when I looked back it was odd that I had had to learn it again. It was not facts these people needed from Americans. It never is. It was an experience of being liked.

The student greeting me on the first day of school, Mr. Muwanga's gracious welcoming and good-bye ritual each morning were part of the African's own ability in human relations. For in the art of showing love the African has genius, and this is what I will remember when I have forgotten the muddy floors and sagging walls.

I will remember how the children banded together to keep mosquitos off me, knowing that I was bothered by them.

I will remember the mothers of the children, waiting along the road to school, babies strapped to their backs, voluminous cotton dresses sweeping the ground, holding out to me in both hands an egg or a bunch of bananas. We had no common language between us, but what they could achieve in friendship with a handful of fruit was a school in itself.

And I will remember the party given to honor us. We were all there, Mr. and Mrs. Shallow, Scott, Donn and Elizabeth. They sang the tribal songs, they danced, they gave us food, and then Ssagala, the school's best pupil, put into two sentences the African gift for relationships.

"We do not call you teacher," he said, "because it sounds too far away. We call you our parents and our brothers and our sister, because you have sat down and looked into our hearts."

The Man Who Forgot Himself
by Glenn D. Kittler

Albert Schweitzer was the inspiration for—

The little girl had a temperature of 106°. At her bedside stood the doctor, gently bathing her malaria-ridden body. All around him the night was filled with hospital sounds: the soft cries children make in their sleep, the low groan of a man kept awake by pain, the tight-lipped gasps of a woman awaiting the miracle of birth.

They were familiar sounds to the doctor: He heard them every night as he made his last rounds. They were with him a few minutes later as he walked through the black jungle night down the hill to his house.

He was very tired, but he did not mind. He was a happy man. There in the pits of the Haitian jungles he had found the purpose for himself.

Two dozen years ago, William Larimer Mellon, Jr. was happy in quite a different way. He had everything he wanted: a beautiful wife, four splendid children, a prosperous Arizona ranch, all the money he needed, and a successful background in the U.S. diplomatic corps and various enterprises of the famous and wealthy Mellon family. At 37 he had retired; the rest of his life, he thought, would be spent at what was almost a hobby of breeding cattle.

Then one night he read a magazine article that changed everything. It was about Dr. Albert Schweitzer, the medical missionary who years before, when he was 30, had put aside successful careers in music, writing and teaching to become a doctor and work in Africa.

Mellon recalls:

"Until that night, I didn't know much about Schweitzer.

380

I was deeply impressed by what he had done, but I was even more moved by the reason he did it—'reverence for life.'"

This attitude—Schweitzer has explained—maintains that every living thing has the right to a painless and happy existence, and it is the duty of every man to do what he can to provide it for all others. Larry Mellon felt that, at least in these terms, he hadn't done much with his life.

An idea began to grow in him. He read all he could about and by Schweitzer and eventually wrote to him in Africa.

"I am 37 years old; I have a family and all the responsibilities that go with it. But I want to do what you have done. What do you advise?"

Schweitzer replied: "Many men have asked me the question you have sent, but I have always been reluctant to advise them. The decision is difficult, and there are many hardships. It is the plight of the dogooders in this world that others should throw rocks in their path. But you seem courageous. I urge you to pursue your goal."

Mellon made his decision. There was only one person to be told about it: his wife. Larry Mellon recalls:

"I found Gwen on a ladder, doing housework. I went to her and blurted out: 'I think I'll go to medical school, then settle down somewhere that can use a good country doctor.' She didn't seem too surprised. At least she didn't fall off the ladder!"

But other people were surprised—especially since in his youth he was considered somewhat of a playboy. His friends accused him of suffering a belated attack of adolescent idealism. Medical schools said he was too old, that he would never survive the stiff course of studies. But Tulane University reluctantly accepted him in 1947.

To be sure, the studies were difficult, but by the hardest work he was able to keep up his grades. On Schweitzer's suggestion, he and Gwen spent a summer at Lambarene. He also visited with Schweitzer in Europe, learning more from the man whose principles had become his own.

Mellon's plan was this: When he finished school he would build a hospital wherever he felt it was most needed, he would name it after Albert Schweitzer, and he would spend the rest of his life there. During vacations, he traveled through the world seeking the proper site for the hospital.

For his graduate paper, Mellon had chosen the subject of tropical ulcers, and these were prevalent in Haiti. Accompanied by his family he spent weeks doing research in the island country, and his travels eventually took him into the Artibonite Valley.

One look was all he needed: thousands of people lived in the poorest conditions. Tuberculosis, malaria, malnutrition and tetanus were rampant. Excepting a small obstetrical unit, there were no medical facilities within miles. Surely this was the place for the hospital.

In mid-1956, the hospital was there. It had cost almost $2,000,000, and Larry Mellon paid for this himself. Annual maintenance costs were estimated at $150,000 but have proved to be almost twice that. About a third of it comes from contributors who have learned about the hospital; less than another third is provided by patients' fees (20 cents a visit), and Larry Mellon makes up the difference.

Much more important than giving his money, however, is the fact that Larry Mellon has given himself. Gwen Mellon has done this, too. With her husband, she is at the hospital at dawn, and she remains on duty far into the night.

At all times, Schweitzer's philosophy of reverence for life is keenly evident there. One recent morning two surgeons and five nurses waged a battle to save the life of a child who was already close to death when brought to the hospital. Drastic surgery had been performed to correct the intestinal deformity with which she was born, and for a while it seemed that all would go well.

But in the morning, the four-year-old took a turn for the worse. Her tiny heart stopped. Immediately the surgeons performed a tracheotomy and were thus able to pump oxygen into her lungs. Then they opened her chest and for five desperate hours they alternated massaging her heart. Thin hopes for survival hung on each feeble beat.

The sight of Mellon and his staff tensely huddled over the jungle child, exerting all their knowledge and skills to save her, was a living portrait in reverence for life. And when at last they were forced to step back defeated, there was no sense of failure in the room; there was instead the air of quiet respectfulness of dedicated men and women who had learned to accept the choice of God.

Anyone who has seen both the primitive Schweitzer hospital in Africa and Mellon's modern, well-equipped plant in Haiti quickly recognizes that the differences between them are as great as the ocean which separates them. But these are externals. In what they achieve, the two hospitals are uniquely equal.

Without them, thousands of the world's forgotten people would be living in shocking disease and dying in painful terror. By providing the means for good health, Schweitzer and Mellon are opening doors which can lead the jungle people to every form of a better life. Being healthy, they can work harder, and through working, acquire the higher standards which will unite them with their fellowmen throughout the world.

Specific strides toward that goal are evidenced in the many Haitians Larry Mellon has already sent to the United States for advanced training. Cooperating with Haitian medical authorities, Mellon looks forward to the day when he will have enough skilled Haitians on his staff to turn the hospital over to them and go elsewhere to establish a new one. In a distinct way, this makes Larry Mellon a remarkable missionary.

Yet he says: "I don't think there's anything remarkable in what I'm doing. There is no special virtue in becoming a doctor in an area that needs everything.

"Medical work is simply my personal application of Doctor Schweitzer's philosophy. Each man can find his own way of applying it. The most important thing we have to give to God and our fellowmen is ourselves, and we can do that even when we merely give our time to some community project that needs our help."

It is a truth which Larry Mellon's present life vividly exemplifies.

Our Search for Inner Peace
by Dr. Thomas A. Dooley

Happiness was his goal, and he found it by serving others.

I was waked this morning by a very angry old man. His wife was dying, he said. My medicine had hurt her very badly. I sat up slowly, trying to get fully awake. I'd been up all night, operating on a child whose eye had been ripped out by a tiger; I'd been in bed less than an hour.

I followed the man groggily to where his wife squatted in the little clinic room. The old woman's face was distorted with pain. I remembered her well. Two weeks ago, I'd removed an immense growth from her neck. I'd kept the incision as clean as I could: sterile instruments, scrubbed hands, antiseptics, a sterile dressing, but even in the pale dawn light I could see, all around the bandage, the livid purple lines that said infection had set in.

Anxiously I peeled off the layers of dressing. Last of all, next to the woman's skin, was a putrid black object. I picked it up between thumb and forefinger.

It was a rotting bat's wing.

I looked inquiringly at the husband. "Yes," he said proudly, "I put it there to keep away the pain. And it's a good thing I did! See how purple the neck is!"

With the aid of penicillin and blood plasma, I believe this old woman will survive her husband's well-meant ministrations. But for me, she was only the first of the nearly 100 suffering people I saw during this one day. As I was rebandaging the old woman's neck, a mother carried in a five-year-old boy who could neither sit up nor see. What was his diet? I wanted to know. Why, rice and water! What else should a child eat?

A man showed me a tiny scratch on his wrist, so long-infected I had to tell him he must lose his hand. A sad-eyed

384

woman timidly asked me if I could make her have live babies. Of course, she knew one out of two babies always died—that was only normal. But she had had 11 babies and all had died. Was there something in my magic bottles to make the next one live?

Why have I come half-way round the world to live with heartbreak? I suppose the best answer would be that I was born with a burning desire to help people—it would be the best answer—but it wouldn't be true.

If people can be born with a desire, I guess mine was to have a good time, and good times came easily in our home. There was plenty of money; I had my own horse, went to school abroad, studied to be a concert pianist.

They weren't just surface good times, either. We were genuinely, deep-down happy. I think my father's religion had a lot to do with that. We were the prayingest family you ever saw. We prayed when we got up in the morning, when we sat down to eat, when we finished eating, when we went to bed, and frequently in between. Among my favorite prayers were the Beatitudes.

I loved them, I think, because they talked about what interested me. "Blessed" means "happy"—and that's just what I wanted to be. Here were the rules for happiness.

But now, in retrospect, it is the second Beatitude, *Blessed are they that mourn . . .* that means something special to me. My father must have explained to me many times that to "mourn" as it's used in the Bible, doesn't mean "to be unhappy." It simply means, he used to say, "to be more aware of the sorrow in the world than of the pleasures."

But I couldn't really follow that explanation. How could you think about sorrow and be happy?

Even when I entered med school, it wasn't because I was stricken with the sorrow of sick people. It was more that I wanted to share my own good times with them.

There were some lonely old people at the hospital where I was a student. So I bought a convertible—a long, sleek one—and, weekends, I'd pile the old folks into it and drive them out to the stable. While I jumped my horse, they enjoyed the fresh air. Have fun and share it—that was my formula for happiness.

I might have gotten away with it, too, if it hadn't been for a sizzling morning in July, 1954. I was fresh out of med school with a brand-new "Doctor" in front of my name and a new Navy lieutenancy as well. My ship was assigned to cruise-duty in the western Pacific, and I passed the slow days trying to decide where, in all Missouri, was the very best place to raise horses. I hardly heard the Captain that morning when he announced we'd been ordered briefly to Haiphong, on the coast of North Vietnam, to transport some refugees to Saigon.

In the harbor at Haiphong a small boat approached us from the shore, an open landing-craft, built for less than 100 men. As it came nearer I saw that there were more than 1,000 people on it—and, oh Lord, so many of them were babies!

The waves in the choppy harbor washed over the open boat again and again. In the 115° heat, most of the children fainted. Now they were alongside, and I thought I would be the one to faint. Here were smallpox, terminal tuberculosis, hideous cancers, and some diseases I couldn't even name. It was my first glimpse of Asia.

As they struggled up the ladder to the ship, the stink of long-untended sickness overwhelmed me. I wanted to run, to vomit, to pretend I'd never seen them.

But I was the only doctor on the ship, and so I set out my poor array of bottles and needles and cotton swabs, and blindly, hopelessly attacked the mountain of suffering before me.

But before long, a strange excitement began to grow in me. It was so apparent that a simple plaster cast would take the agony out of this broken arm! A few shots of vitamin C could have this man on his feet! This swollen hand needed only a simple lancing. I was learning that even my inexperienced, fumbling hands could work miracles for people who had never seen even a greenhorn doctor.

Hours later, I stopped for a moment to straighten my shoulders and made another discovery—the biggest of my life. I was happy. Deeply, joyously happy, happier than I had ever been before.

We came back to Haiphong for another boatload of refugees. Now we expected cholera, and whooping cough and leprosy, and rather than simply ferry these highly contagious diseases down to Saigon, I set up a makeshift hospital on shore to treat them before they boarded ship. I volunteered to work ashore for one month. I stayed nine, and processed 610,000 of the most neglected human beings in the world.

Here I was, the guy who loved convertibles and new

clothes, working around the clock in sweat-stained khakis and a two-week growth of beard. Scrubbing patients who—some of them—had never had a bath. Cleaning wounds that had festered for years. Glowing with happiness.

When the evacuation was finished, I went home; but only long enough to get out of the Navy and raise enough money to come back to Indo-China on my own. To come here to the disease-haunted jungles of Laos, to build this little shack of a hospital, to show a Lao greatgrandmother a cake of soap and teach her how to wash her hands.

Recently I had a letter from one of my old professors who knew about my plans for the good life. "What happened, Tom?" he asked. "Why the big change?"

"There wasn't any change," I wrote back. "I'm still the same, egotistical, self-centered guy to whom you tried to teach some medicine. I've never wanted anything except happiness for Tom Dooley—and here I've got it."

You see, when Jesus gave us the Beatitudes, He wasn't describing some dream-world that might someday come to pass. He was talking, simply and matter-of-factly as He always did, about things as they are. If you're extrasensitive to sorrow, He said—and you do something, no matter how small, to make it lighter—you can't help but be happy. That's just the way it is.

I know—and I'm a guy who'd do anything to be happy.

A Voice for God

by Jerome Hines

A remarkable behind-the-scenes story of a famous opera basso who was in Russia during the Cuban crisis.

It was 3 A.M., Moscow time, October 23, 1962, when President Kennedy went on the air to announce the American quarantine of Cuba. My wife, Lucia, and I were asleep in Moscow's Metropole Hotel. Two blocks away lights were ablaze in the Kremlin.

For me it was the last day of a five-week singing tour of the Soviet Union. A final performance of *Boris Godunov* was booked for that evening at the Bolshoi Theater.

At breakfast, Bill Jones, a friend and traveling companion, told us that he had heard a rumor about a new crisis between Russia and America. Four hours later we had lunch with Foy Kohler, the American ambassador. He confirmed to us officially that the United States had established a quarantine of Cuba.

Immediately, we wondered what effect all this would have on our evening performance of *Boris*. Would there be demonstrations against Americans? The ambassador, however, had reassuring words, "The Russian people have not been told about the crisis."

The rest of the day was tension-filled. Back at the hotel, we packed, made a few phone calls and then tried to rest. About 3 P.M., I left the hotel for the half hour's walk I take before each performance.

As I walked past the Kremlin, past St. Basil's Cathedral, I was thinking about the many occasions in my life when I had needed God—but, how the steady flow of His guidance had always been dependent on my obedience. . . .

Ten years before in 1952 I first had learned to listen for His help. At that time there was a great conflict going on in my life. On one hand, I did not want God interfering in my life, upsetting my plans and my desires. On the other, I found myself pulled strongly toward Him.

Meanwhile, it was in this year of 1952 that a performance of *Boris Godunov* was scheduled by the Metropolitan Opera. More than anything else I wanted to play the role of Boris. I felt that I was ready for it. The opera manager did not agree. We argued, and I threatened to quit.

But in the end, I received the role. When self-doubt took over, however, it became a hollow victory. For now that I had won this great responsibility, I was obsessed by the fear of failure. And a failure in this assignment could ruin my career. In desperation I conceived an idea for a publicity stunt. Near the end of the opera Boris, dying, plunges down the stairs. With this fall I would feign a back injury.

"Opera star injured in fall." I could see the headlines. What a boost all this publicity would be to my career.

That night in a hotel room in New York, I wrestled with the still small voice of God in my heart.

Is it honest to fake an injury?

"Honesty hasn't anything to do with it," I countered. "What would You have me do?"

Would you be willing to give up the publicity stunt?

"No!" was my instant reaction.

For long agonizing moments I argued with myself. Finally, I realized that either I had to surrender myself to God or separate myself completely from Him.

"All right," I said, "I'll do what You tell me. I want You before all else in my life."

Then came the inner instruction: *open the Bible and there will be your answer.*

When I had checked into the room I noticed a Gideon Bible on top of the dresser. Obeying the order, I got out of bed, opened the Bible and my eyes fell upon these words:

*Who shall ascend into the hill of the Lord? . . . He that hath clean hands, and a pure heart; who hath not lifted up his soul into vanity nor sworn deceitfully.**

Give up your silly, egocentric publicity scheme and get on with your work. How much clearer can guidance be!

The next morning I began to concentrate on the score. So absorbed did I become with the character of Boris that I wrote a psychoanalysis of him which was later published. The

* Psalm 24:3, 7

total result was that when I did sing *Boris Godunov* at the Met*, newspaper reviews could not have been more generous.

This experience of obedience to God revolutionized not only my career, but also my entire life. And yet spiritual growth was so often blocked by my ego. Time after time I would charge ahead on my own steam, only to fall on my face. On each occasion, I would tell myself once and for all to get out of my own way and let God run my life.

Then came the challenge of a lifetime! An opportunity to sing *Boris Godunov* in Russian with the Bolshoi Opera Company in Moscow.

The trip was planned to begin with an August, 1962, tour of Argentina and then a flight from Buenos Aires to Moscow. A week before Lucia and I were to leave, a revolution threatened in Argentina. My agent insisted that we cancel the South American part of the tour, but I hesitated to do this.

We were vacationing at the time near Seaside Park, New Jersey. One moonlit night several days later I felt impelled to go out for a walk. It was almost as if God wanted to tell me something about the trip and could do so best out under His skies.

Now I realize that guidance comes to different people in different ways. Some people obtain it through meditation and Bible reading. To others it arrives at odd moments in the form of quiet mental nudges.

There are times, to be sure, when I want direction, but all I can hear are my own thoughts clamoring for control. Yet I know it is not real guidance when I keep asking over and over, "Now, God, is this what I am supposed to do?" For if God is trying to tell me something, I feel it so strongly that there is no doubt.

On this night I received instructions so clear that I hardly could believe them:

The important thing for you to do is obey Me. For the next two months there will be such a circle of protection around you that Satan cannot touch you. Do your task joyfully. Believe always and have faith, for I am with you every step of the way.

Six days later Lucia and I were on our way to Argentina. By the time we arrived, the situation had quieted down

---

* *Mr. Hines was the first American-born basso to perform the role of Boris.*

and all performances went smoothly. Our stay was delightful.

On September 19, we flew out of Buenos Aires for Moscow. On the 20th riots broke out in Argentina, jets were bombing Buenos Aires and the airport was closed down immediately. We had got out on one of the last planes. The timing of all this was so remarkable that it further strengthened my conviction that I must obey . . . obey . . . obey.

Lucia and I felt that our trip to Russia involved much more than the fulfillment of my long-time dream of being the first American-born basso to do *Boris* in Russian at the Bolshoi. Here was an opportunity to take a stand for Christ in various ways before the Russian people.

How can you do this in an atheistic country? We had some definite ideas. But our witness would not amount to anything unless my performance of *Boris* was effective.

That is why we both were so upset by what happened to me when we arrived in Moscow. I came down with a throat infection three days before my opening performance of *Boris* at the Bolshoi on Sunday September 23. The Russian doctor said that I could not sing. I took the pills he gave me and went to bed.

But the big question was not what the Russian doctor ordered but what God wanted. I opened my Bible and read this passage:

You then, my son, be strong in the grace that is in Christ Jesus . . . Take your share of suffering as a good soldier of Christ Jesus. *

A soldier is under orders. He must obey if the mission is to be accomplished. I knew then that nothing was to be canceled. I was to go ahead despite the doctor's orders, trusting God to provide the voice and the strength.

But Sunday night when I arrived at the theater, my throat still was a question mark. And by the last act, I had little voice left.

Before the last curtain I went behind some scenery in the wings to wrestle this crisis through in prayer. If my voice fails, I thought, the whole Russian trip is finished. Had I mistaken my guidance? Or was my faith being tested to the limit?

In my extremity, I saw clearly that I was to go on stage in God's strength—not mine. And at the moment I needed it, the promised help came. My tension vanished. An energy

---

* *II Timothy 2:1, 3*

from beyond myself revitalized me. My voice was clear, strong.

Later, Lucia and our associates told me that this was the finest act of *Boris* I ever had performed.

In the weeks that followed, the inflow of energy and help continued. Facing an impossible schedule of 12 performances and 12 rehearsals in a 30-day tour of Russian cities, I felt the Holy Spirit inside me, guiding me, giving me strength and courage.

There were ways to show our faith in God too. Lucia and I long had made it a practice to say a quiet blessing in public restaurants before eating; we did this throughout Russia. To the Russian people assigned to help us during the tour, we found occasions to talk about Jesus Christ. We attended church services when possible and invited our Russian contacts to go with us.

During one performance in Leningrad the chorus applauded me backstage. Impulsively I told them in Russian "Give God the credit, not me." For a moment there was stunned silence, then louder applause than before. . . .

And now we were down to the last day, the final *Boris* back in Moscow with the threat of nuclear war over us all.

At 6:15 I was in my dressing room and nearly finished with my makeup. Curtain time at the Bolshoi is 6:30 P.M. Suddenly there were excited voices outside and the stage director burst in.

"Khrushchev's here."

Bill Jones and I stared at each other. Two weeks before we had both felt an odd premonition that this last *Boris* at the Bolshoi would be surrounded by unusual circumstances. How right we had been!

The first act went well. Between acts Lucia and our interpreter rushed backstage. "Jerry," she said, "are you trying to start an international incident? Khrushchev led a standing ovation for you. But you didn't acknowledge it."

"I didn't see him."

"He's in the right hand box."

I calmed them down and promised them I would find a way to acknowledge him.

The opera is set in czarist times at the turn of the century. Boris has committed murder to gain the throne. In the final scene, guilt-ridden, insane and dying, he cries out to God, "Forgive me," and then dies.

I saw a chance to inject a note of Christian hope, to

show that Boris, after asking forgiveness, finds salvation and peace through Jesus Christ. So, after the words "forgive me," with radiant uplifted head as his plea is answered, Boris—as I interpreted him—cries gratefully "Oh, my God."

At previous *Boris* performances in Moscow, Kiev and Tbilisi, the Russians had responded to this additional emphasis with enthusiasm. How would Khrushchev, an avowed atheist, feel about it?

Everything built up perfectly to this climax. When the final scene came, Boris weakly then exultantly finds repentance and, dying, plunges down the stairs.

Instead of waiting for the postlude before applauding, as is customary, this audience broke all precedent by rising at this point. Pounding his hands together in front of them all was a familiar baldheaded figure.

I walked over in front of Premier Khrushchev's box and bowed.

It was a day later when I realized the significance of Khrushchev's presence at the Bolshoi that night. Papers throughout the world reported that by paying a tribute to an American singer, he was indicating the future conciliatory role his government would follow in the Cuban crisis.

If this is true and God was able to use me in this emergency, I am very grateful. For I know that God wants to reach the Russian people. He does have a plan to bring Christ into our hearts. But that plan needs obedient disciples. This means me—and you.

Hot Dogs for Christmas

Last Christmas Eve a prosperous businessman was hurrying to a butcher shop before closing time.

"Buying your Christmas turkey?" a friend asked.

"No. Hot dogs," he answered.

Then he explained how, in the Depression, a bank failure suddenly wiped out his fortune. He faced Christmas with no job, no money for gifts, and less than a dollar for good.

He and his wife and small daughter said grace before dinner that year and then ate hot dogs—a whole kennel of them in fact. His wife had given each frankfurter toothpicks for legs and broom straws for tails and whiskers. Their child was enchanted and her infectious delight spread merriment among them all. After dinner they gave thanks again for the most loving and festive time they'd ever had.

"Now it's a tradition," the man said. "Hot dogs for Christmas—to remind us of that happy day when we realized we still had one another and our God-given sense of humor."

A Foxhole Promise Kept
by John L. Peters

A story of involvement by the president of World Neighbors.

Many years ago I wrote my wife a letter which to this day Kay keeps in a very special, very safe place. It has become a meaningful treasure to us. Both Kay and I knew at the time I wrote the letter that it radiated a deep spiritual significance, but I myself was not sure of its full meaning—then. Only the passage of years has revealed its true depth.

The year I wrote it was 1945, and I was in a military hospital in Korea trying to recover from a series of malaria attacks. World War II had just ended, and our 40th Infantry Division, in which I was a Protestant chaplain, had been dispatched to Korea to prepare the way for an interim military government in Japan.

The war was over, yes, but memories of what we had been through were still raw. I thought of the way we had slogged our way through the mud and jungle of the Philippines. I thought often of a tall, blond, raw-boned soldier who had come into our company as a replacement. He had been a farm boy in Tennessee, and we laughed when a notice arrived from his draft board declaring that, as the only able-bodied man on his father's farm, he was exempt from service. The boy had enlisted before the board made its decision. And there he had been, only three paces behind me when the shrapnel hit him, and I went back to scoop him into my arms. I could feel the warm geyser of his blood on my hands; I was praying for that Tennessee boy as he died.

My mind was troubled, too, by what I saw in the Philippines and in Korea: the black-market enterprises, the long-endured inequities of a feudal society, the arrogance of the few rich and the helplessness of the many poverty-stricken. I was embarrassed by some of our own officers and soldiers who would return the Koreans' remarkable hospitality by calling them "gooks," as though being different made them something to belittle. Thoughts like those made me feel guilty that I had done so little since the moment when I had lain in a foxhole during battle and had promised God, "If I get out of this thing alive, I'm going to do something, somehow, somewhere. . . ."

One night in the hospital I turned on the radio and listened to a dramatization of A. J. Cronin's *The Keys of the Kingdom*. It was the story of a priest who went out into the world and did the exacting work he thought ought to be done, only to find that neither he nor his accomplishments were appreciated, either by the people who were helped or by his own church.

Wouldn't it be wonderful, I began to think, if each of us could be like that priest, if we could go out and help others, do what needs to be done, and forget about who gets the credit.

From that moment, something strange began happening to me. I became conscious of a warm, glorious power moving through my being. I sat there in the ward; I was relaxed, yet I was surging with energy. The room began to change. It was as though a curtain were being pulled aside, a shutter opened, and I was looking into, no longer merely at, the walls around me. It was as though I saw essence, not just form. I walked around the ward feeling an exhilaration I had not known possible. Now I saw the other men in the ward in a new dimension. I saw how extravagantly precious each of them was in God's eyes. I saw how this inner worth, ennobling each of us, was the common bond relating all of us, everyone on earth. And then, somehow, I knew that I was experiencing the Spirit of God.

When I could, I sat down to write Kay. That was the letter we cherish today, the letter in which I tried to explain what had happened, in which I said, ". . . and in the significant work into which God will surely lead me, there will be no fear of failure. It may not be success as the world counts it, but it will always be the assurance of God's care."

The letter went forth from the hospital in Korea to the States, and eventually the mailman placed it in our Oklahoma mailbox with four other letters. When Kay went to the box that morning and took those letters from it, she flipped through them until she came to mine. She stopped. In just touching the envelope, she was seized by a sense of awe. That was the day she put my letter in a very special, very safe place. I was to forget it for a while, but Kay never forgot.

Good health came back to me immediately after that fateful experience, and I returned home soon after. For six long years we did not know what that letter meant. I finished my doctorate at Yale and went to teach at Oklahoma City University. I enjoyed my work and began to find a groove and comfortably sink into it.

Meanwhile I was preaching temporarily at St. Luke's Methodist Church. On April 18, 1951, with my Sunday sermon already prepared, I turned on the radio and listened to Douglas MacArthur, back from Korea, as he addressed a joint session of Congress. He spoke of the people of Asia, how they now wanted dignity and understanding, a little more food in their stomachs, a little better clothing on their backs, that they now sought friendly guidance, understanding and support, not imperious direction.

It was easy for me to think back to Asia as he spoke— mothers stumbling to our aid stations as they held out starving babies, fathers trying to cling to their dignity as they begged for a chance to earn a few coins.

My foxhole promise began to smite and burn.

I tossed aside my prepared sermon and entered the pulpit on Sunday morning hardly knowing what I was going to say. I spoke of the hungry masses of the world who aspire, dream, love and hope. "If we ignore man's needs while we hand him pious platitudes," I said, "we justify the Communists' contempt of religion as 'the opiate of the people.' Yet if we treat the problem as simply economic, then we join the Communists in their crass materialism."

I proposed that we meet real needs with real solutions—a plan to help men help themselves, a sharing rather than a giving. "And of central importance," I emphasized, "any program we undertake must be shot through with the Spirit of Jesus Christ."

Next evening 300 people met and pinned me down: "What do *you* want to do?"

I was aghast. I had only tried to say *somebody* ought to do something. But there they were, and I couldn't say I didn't mean it. We spent a week thinking and talking, but we could form no plan.

Finally they said, "All right, go to New York, go to Washington and find out." I did. I went to the mission boards, the economic-aid people in Washington, the United Nations.

I learned of vast needs, but of inadequate funds. I conferred with senators and representatives, and received my greatest encouragement from Congressman Walter Judd, who had been calling for this very same kind of project for 20 years.

Back in Oklahoma our churchmen and I worked out a plan. We would not offer relief or charity, but would do something *with* people, not *for* them. We would stay nonsectarian to give us the flexibility to work with all churches. We would avoid government financing (we have even, in fact, turned down financial help from our Federal Government), for such funds have strings attached. The strings would require us to work through governmental channels—not only ours, but the bureaucracies of the countries we'd serve. Instead, we'd wor*k with* governments, not as governments. Our program would emphasize food and medicine, literacy and family planning—needs of the *total* man. And we subscribed to the "percolate up" rather than to the "trickle down" theory of social change.

This was all part of the beginning. Today World Neighbors—the name we chose for our cooperative program—is an international organization sponsoring over 100 different projects, worldwide. We are working with almost 40 different missionary groups and many groups that have no formal connection with religion. We work with Jews and Catholics and Protestants, with Muslims, Buddhists, Hindus. To finance these projects, dedicated men have crisscrossed the country, speaking for World Neighbors, seeking donations. The prime moving force of our work is the concerned men who have taken time out from the demands of their business and professional careers to help.

When I look at the accomplishments of World Neighbors today, the meaning of the letter I wrote to Kay is beautifully clear. It has been a truly "significant work." Even so, World Neighbors has lifted only a few stones from the mountain that must be leveled if mankind is to live in peace. It has only begun to answer His eternal challenge: . . . *whenever you did this for one of the least important of these brothers of mine, you did it for me.**

---

* *Matthew 25:40 (TEV)*

My Mission Behind the Iron Curtain

by Brother Andrew

He smuggles God's word to spiritually hungry people.

Up ahead was a line of cars, pulled off alongside the highway between Smolensk and Kiev. I knew what it meant: a road block. Every vehicle was being stopped. Some would be allowed through, others would be detained for hours while luggage was taken apart piece by piece. And on the back seat of my car I had a carton full of books the discovery of which could mean a prison term. The books were Bibles.

A young officer stepped up to my car. I was praying as he asked for my papers and read them carefully. While I stood by he inspected my luggage in the trunk. Then he came back and leaned inside the car. His eyes lighted on the unmarked cardbox box.

"Lord Jesus," I said to myself, "while You were on earth You made blind eyes see. Now, I pray, make these seeing eyes blind."

I stood where I could see the officer's eyes. They scrutinized the interior of the car inch by inch. But his eyes traveled over that box of Bibles as if they were not there.

All the rest of the way to Moscow—where I was to turn the Bibles over to a Russian Christian—I praised God for once again clearing my path.

For 15 years now I have been a lay missionary behind the Iron and Bamboo Curtains. Until today I, and the little band of four men who work with me, have carried on our work in secrecy. Even now I am using my first name only and omitting all names of other people and exact locales. But the time has come to tell the world, however guardedly, that there are riches of Christian opportunity in Poland, Yugoslavia, Hungary, Czechoslovakia, East Germany, Russia, Bulgaria, Albania and even China.

I have spent many months in each of these countries, and I have seen evidence that the yearning for a knowledge of Christ cannot be stamped out by decree or force. I have seen tears in the eyes of a farmer as I stopped by the roadside and simply mentioned the name of Jesus. I have seen the eloquent bouquet of flowers left morning after morning on the doorstep of a nailed-up church. God's people are here, in their thousands, keeping silent faith with Christians around the world.

I began this missionary work while I was still in my early 20s. As a schoolboy in Western Europe, and then a soldier serving in Indonesia during World War II, I'd had little interest in religion. Then a bullet in my heel sent me to a hospital.

I was in a mood of frustration and futility over life when I discovered in the bottom of my Army bag, slipped in months before by my mother, her well-fingered Bible. Reading it in my hospital bed as the weeks and months passed, I discovered a new reason for living.

When I was discharged from the Army, I entered a seminary with the idea of becoming a minister. Missionaries often visited our school to tell us of the work they were doing, but none of them came from countries behind the Iron Curtain. I learned that our interdenominational mission board would not license a man for those areas. It was too dangerous—and besides, the doors were closed.

Were they really closed? I decided to take a trip, just to see. In part, this trip confirmed what I had been told. In some of these countries, Albania, for example, there was not a single house of worship left open. Russian Christians were permitted to worship but not to seek converts. In most countries to import Bibles was to risk prison.

But this was not the whole picture. In more than half the Iron Curtain countries, churches invited me to preach, and they seemed to have the liberty to do so. I received invitations to conduct pastors' retreats and evangelical campaigns. In East Germany I found Bibles for sale in a public bookstore. Even in countries where I was not allowed to preach I could bring "greetings" from the West, and no one objected when these greetings lasted a sermon-length of time.

I had made a startling discovery. Not only were hearts open but churches and borders were open. I came back and asked my own mission board for permission to represent them in the Communist world. I was told that officially they could not do this—but that nothing prevented an independent missionary from going where he pleased. For 15 years now I, and four Christian friends, have had this privilege.

We have had encouraging results. In East Germany as many as 4,000 people at a time have attended our meetings. Hundreds have given themselves to Christ then and there, while thousands more have had the seed sown in their hearts. In Yugoslavia, churches are often so packed the chairs have to be removed to make more room. Whole villages in Hungary turn out to hear us. Time and again we go into hamlets where there is no church, and when we leave there is an infant church underway.

I do not mean that we always get such a reception. Two of our team already have served jail terms for preaching where it was forbidden. Communist governments keep careful check on these Christians; we just assume that each of our public meetings is infiltrated by agents of the police. Twice, pastors have turned out to be spies. We live in an atmosphere of conspiracy—and how like first-century Christianity it must be!

We have one advantage, though, that the first Christians didn't have: in addition to private homes we have the automobile. What a wonderful meeting place for a Christian cell group is a car moving from place to place away from prying eyes and ears. It's a wonderful spot to get married using the Christian ceremony, to pray for the sick or the conversion of a nation. I think if Christians behind the Iron Curtain were to choose a symbol by which to know one another, it might well, in place of the fish, be the automobile.

But while evangelism that depends upon personal contact is uncertain at best in these countries, the part of our work that has become increasingly important is the distribution of Bibles. I know from personal experience that the Bible all by itself, without preachers, without rallies, even without a place to worship in, is the most powerful of all bearers of the Gospel.

And how hungry these people are for Scripture. Whole churches exist without a single Bible. Others have texts that are incomplete. Because they're in such short supply they are taken apart and distributed book by book. I visited one church in Bulgaria where there was great rejoicing because a Bible had been found that was almost complete!

Because of their rarity, Bibles are expensive. I know a

man who owned two cows—by Russian standards considerable wealth. But when he heard that a Bible was available he gladly sold a cow to possess it.

What can you do to help?

First, pray. Pray for the old and for the new Christian, and for the man who has not yet heard the truth.

If you travel to Communist countries, take along a Bible and "accidentally" leave it behind in a hotel room, on a train seat, at a lunch counter. Don't worry about language; there always are translators. And don't worry that it will be destroyed. As one of our team members put it, "Who's going to destroy a book that's worth a whole cow!"

And finally we can give ourselves. The world today needs men who are willing, like Peter and Paul, to take the Gospel into unfriendly soil.

"Go into all the world," Christ said, "and preach the Gospel."

Message to Earth
by Col. Frank Borman

*The commander of the Apollo 8 spaceship, tells
how the Genesis creation story became part of
man's first flight to the moon.*

On the Sunday before I left my home in Texas to go to
Cape Kennedy for the moonshot December, 1968, I walked
into the rector's study of our little Episcopal church feeling
pretty sure that I was in for a ribbing. Because once again, as
had happened before, I was going to beg off reading the
Scripture lesson at the Christmas Eve service.

"You'll do anything to get out of that reading, won't
you, Frank," said one of the other lay readers. "Even go to
the moon."

"I don't think he ought to get off so easy," said another.
"He ought to read the lesson from the spacecraft."

I looked at Rod Rose, a friend of mine from the
Manned Spaceflight Center. He was interested. "Well, that's
not impossible," he said.

And so an idea was planted. I knew that our rector, Father James Buckner, was going to preach that night on the
subject of peace. What if we were to send a message—a
prayer for peace—to the church to coincide with the end of
his sermon!

But right away we ran into difficulties. There were set
times built into the flight plan for our telecasts from the
moon to the earth. And our Christmas Eve service did not
coincide with any of these telecasts. If all went according to
plan, we would be on the back side of the moon at the time
of the service, out of contact with the earth altogether.

We ended up with a compromise. On one of the early
orbits around the moon I would read a prayer for peace. Rod
would record the message at NASA and take it to the church.

Then Jim Buckner would play the tape at the end of the service.

And so it was left that way. The day came for the departure for Cape Kennedy. We said good-bye to our families and took off.

But as time passed, I began to feel uneasy. The more I thought about it, the more I was afraid the prayer for peace, dedicated to my own church, just wasn't broad enough. What about the thousands of people at the base who did not go to that church? What about Jim Lovell and Bill Anders themselves? Bill was a Roman Catholic, and although Jim was an Episcopalian like me, he attended another church. I began to talk with the other astronauts about my wish for a broader prayer.

"Do you realize," I said to Bill and Jim one night while we were getting ready for bed in the crew quarters at Kennedy, "that more than one *billion* people will be watching us on Christmas Eve! What can we do that's special?"

The question became a preoccupation with me. I wanted to get as many suggestions as possible. Bill Anders, for example, thought we might read the traditional Christmas story. But wouldn't that leave out people who were not Christian? Over the next several evenings I telephoned dozens of friends—men whose opinions I respected. I called people at the launch site, I called Washington, I telephoned home and asked my wife, Susan, and the two boys for their thoughts.

And finally one man—he has asked that his name not be mentioned—came up with an idea which no one else had thought of. Why not read the creation story?

From the first, reading *Genesis* seemed right. Jim and Bill and the members of the backup crew agreed. When I put through my regular evening telephone call to Houston to talk with the family, Susan agreed too.

One of the things I like about working for the National Aeronautics and Space Administration is the almost complete lack of censorship. I have never been told what to say or not to say. Still, as a matter of politeness, I wanted to check out our thinking with NASA heads Dr. George Miller and Dr. Robert Gilruth. The next day at dinner I pulled out the slip of paper on which I had typed the first ten verses of *Genesis* and explained my idea.

"We've been wondering what you might come up with," Doctor Gilruth said. "It's a natural idea."

So we were on our way.

Jim and Bill and I each decided to take along a small Bible. But there was a problem. The Bibles were made of flammable material. They would have to be covered with a special fireproof plastic and they would be a little difficult to get at. Wouldn't it be better if we were to have the selection typed right into the flight plan itself? The paper on which this plan of every detail of the flight is printed was made of flame-resistant paper. It would be easy to schedule the reading of the creation story into one of our regular telecasts.

And so into the official record of the first flight of man around the moon went a transcript of the opening ten verses of *Genesis*. Jim and Bill and I carried the message aboard with us along with the original prayer for peace which I would send to Rod Rose and to the people at St. Christopher's during an earlier orbit.

At 7:01 a.m. on December 21, 1968, the flight began. It was an extraordinarily smooth trip, a brilliant piece of coordinated effort on the part of thousands. Part of that effort was prayer. It is astonishing how many people told me they would be praying.

And then we were at the moon and began our orbit. For about an hour, while we were on the back side of the moon, we were out of contact with the earth. It was an eerie feeling. When we came around into the light again, there was the earth, seeming to rise up out of darkness. The flight plan called for our reading *Genesis* as we were making our last turn into the dark. And precisely on schedule, just as we were going into the silence again, we were able to complete our *Genesis* mission.

At least we thought we had completed that part of our mission. But when we got back, we discovered that not everyone agreed with our reading from *Genesis*.

One woman in particular began a campaign to prohibit astronauts from expressing their views in this way. She did have a certain following, because we received 34 letters of complaint. But it is interesting that there were almost 100,000 other letters, from people who found the *Genesis* reading very meaningful indeed.

One man wrote that he was an exconvict. No one knew of his past. But when he read of the opposition to our reading the Bible from the moon, he wanted to go on record in the most dramatic way possible to state his approval—so he announced his support and at the same time told the world of his secret past.

Another letter came from a bishop in Guatemala who wrote that in five minutes the astronauts had done more to catch the ear of young people than a dozen committees had done in five years.

We heard from many Jews, expressing their thanks that we had chosen a selection from the Old Testament.

And we heard from people who didn't go to church at all, but who wanted us to know the readings were meaningful.

But I think the letters which meant the most to me were those that came from behind the Iron Curtain. We heard from people in Russia and Czechoslovakia and Rumania and Bulgaria and Poland and East Germany and Yugoslavia and Hungary—everywhere, it seemed, but mainland China. Some wrote in stumbling English, some in their own language. Without a single exception, every letter from behind the Iron Curtain was favorable.

And so man's first flight to the moon has become history. The flight plan itself will probably end up in the Smithsonian Institution. I hope so. I would like that document, with the reading from *Genesis,* to be a part of our country's history. I would like the record to hint at the excitement we felt as we rounded the dark side of the moon and saw the earth appear to rise up out of darkness.

To me the timing was perfect. A few minutes later we read the creation story. Perhaps, indeed, the earth is just coming out of darkness into a new kind of creation.

Section Ten—

Faith, Doorway to A New Life

Section Ten—
Introduction

"Life is but a walking shadow, a poor player that struts and frets his hour upon the stage and then is heard no more. . . ." These are memorable lines from one of Shakespeare's plays, but are they true?

Men have been wrestling with the question of immortality since the beginning of time, and probably will always do so. Yet for many the issue has been resolved by an act of faith, a leap of faith, that can be summarized in two words, "I believe."

In this section are some of the most quoted and discussed articles ever to appear in Guideposts. That is because they are about life after death, a subject that intrigues and fascinates believer and unbeliever alike. These stories are by believers, people who have crossed the line from doubt to faith, often dramatically.

For example, Dr. George Ritchie's look at the next life took place after he had prematurely been pronounced dead; Billie Kay Bothwell's experience came one week before her mortal life ended; and Dr. Ralph Harlow's encounter with "the other side" took place as he and his wife strolled beside a little brook.

Other stories in this section may be less astonishing, but their message is no less clear cut: That faith is the necessary bridge to new life, both here and beyond.

Return From Tomorrow
by George C. Ritchie, Jr., M.D.

Is it possible to have a glimpse into the next life? This man says yes, and tells of his "threshold" experience.

When I was sent to the base hospital at Camp Barkeley, Texas, early in December, 1943, I had no idea I was seriously ill. I'd just completed basic training, and my only thought was to get on the train to Richmond, Virginia, to enter medical school as part of the Army's doctor-training program. It was an unheard-of break for a private, and I wasn't going to let a chest cold cheat me out of it.

But days passed and I didn't get better. It was December 19 before I was moved to the recuperation wing, where a Jeep was to pick me up at four A.M. the following morning to drive me to the railroad station.

A few more hours and I'd make it! Then about nine P.M. I began to run a fever. I went to the ward boy and begged some aspirin.

Despite the aspirin, my head throbbed, and I'd cough into the pillow to smother the sounds. Three A.M.—I decided to get up and dress.

The next half-hour is a blur for me. I remember being too weak to finish dressing. I remember a nurse coming to the room, and then a doctor, and then a bell-clanging ambulance ride to the x-ray building. Could I stand, the captain was asking, long enough to get one picture? I struggled unsteadily to my feet.

The whir of the machine is the last thing I remember.

When I opened my eyes, I was lying in a little room I had never seen before. A tiny light burned in a nearby lamp. For a while I lay there, trying to recall where I was. All of a sudden I sat bolt upright. The train! I'd miss the train!

Now I know that what I am about to describe will sound

incredible. I do not understand it any more than I ask you to; all that I can do is relate the events of that night as they occurred. I sprang out of bed and looked around the room for my uniform. Not on the bedrail: I stopped, staring. Someone was lying in the bed I had just left.

I stepped closer in the dim light, then drew back. He was dead. The slack jaw, the gray skin were awful. Then I saw the ring. On his left hand was the Phi Gamma Delta Fraternity ring I had worn for two years.

I ran into the hall, eager to escape the mystery of that room. Richmond, that was the all-important thing—getting to Richmond. I started down the hall for the outside door.

"Look out!" I shouted to an orderly bearing down on me. He seemed not to hear, and a second later he had passed the very spot where I stood as though I had not been there.

It was too strange to think about. I reached the door, went through and found myself in the darkness outside, speeding toward Richmond. Running? Flying? I only know that the dark earth was slipping past while other thoughts occupied my mind, terrifying and unaccountable ones. The orderly had not seen me. What if the people at medical school could not see me either?

In utter confusion I stopped by a telephone pole in a town by a large river and put my hand against the guy wire. At least the wire seemed to be there, but my hand could not make contact with it. One thing was clear: In some unimaginable way I had lost my firmness of flesh, the hand that could grip that wire, the body that other people saw.

I was beginning to know too that the body on that bed was mine, unaccountably separated from me, and that my job was to get back and rejoin it as fast as I could.

Finding the base and the hospital again was no problem. Indeed I seemed to be back there almost as soon as I thought of it. But where was the little room I had left? So began what must have been one of the strangest searches ever to take place: the search for myself. As I ran from one ward to the next, past room after room of sleeping soldiers, all about my age, I realized how unfamiliar we are with our own faces. Several times I stopped by a sleeping figure that was exactly as I imagined myself. But the fraternity ring, the Phi Gam ring, was lacking, and I would speed on.

At last I entered a little room with a single dim light. A sheet had been drawn over the figure on the bed, but the arms lay along the blanket. On the left hand was the ring.

I tried to draw back the sheet, but I could not seize it. And now that I had found myself, how could one join two people who were so completely separate? And there, standing before this problem, I thought suddenly:

"This is death. This is what we human beings call 'death,' this splitting up of one's self." It was the first time I had connected death with what had happened to me.

In that most despairing moment, the little room began to fill with light. I say "light," but there is no word in our language to describe brilliance that intense. I must try to find words, however, because incomprehensible as the experience was to my intellect, it has affected every moment of my life since then.

The light which entered that room was Christ: I knew because a thought was put deep within me, "You are in the presence of the Son of God." I have called Him "light," but I could also have said "love," for that room was flooded, pierced, illuminated, by the most total compassion I have ever felt. It was a presence so comforting, so joyous and all-satisfying, that I wanted to lose myself forever in the wonder of It.

But something else was present in that room. With the presence of Christ (simultaneously, though I must tell it one by one) also had entered every single episode of my entire life. There they were, every event and thought and conversation, as palpable as a series of pictures. There was no first or last, each one was contemporary, each one asked a single question, "What did you do with your time on earth?"

I looked anxiously among the scenes before me: school, home, scouting and the cross-country track team—a fairly typical boyhood, yet in the light of that presence it seemed a trivial and irrelevant existence.

I searched my mind for good deeds.

"Did you tell anyone about Me?" came the question.

"I didn't have time to do much," I answered. "I was planning to, then this happened. I'm too young to die!"

"No one," the thought was inexpressibly gentle, "is too young to die."

And now a new wave of light spread through the room already so incredibly bright and suddenly we were in another world. Or rather, I suddenly perceived all around us a very different world occupying the same place. I followed Christ through ordinary streets and countrysides and everywhere I saw this other existence strangely superimposed on our familiar world.

It was thronged with people. People with the unhappiest faces I ever have seen. Each grief seemed different. I saw businessmen walking the corridors of the places where they had worked, trying vainly to get someone to listen to them. I saw a mother following a 60-year-old man, her son I guessed, cautioning him. He did not seem to be listening.

Suddenly I was remembering myself, that very night, caring about nothing but getting to Richmond. Was it the same for these people; had their hearts and minds been all concerned with earthly things, and now, having lost earth, were they still fixed hopelessly here? I wondered if this was hell. To care most when you are most powerless; this would be hell indeed.

I was permitted to look at two more worlds that night—I cannot say "spirit worlds" for they were too real, too solid. Both were introduced the same way; a new quality of light, a new openness of vision, and suddenly it was apparent what had been there all along. The second world, like the first, occupied this very surface of the earth, but it was a vastly different realm. Here was no absorption with earthly things, but—for want of a better word to sum it up—with truth.

I saw sculptors and philosophers here, composers and inventors. There were universities and great libraries and scientific laboratories that surpass the wildest inventions of science fiction.

Of the final world I had only a glimpse. Now we no longer seemed to be on earth, but immensely far away, out of all relation to it. And there, still at a great distance, I saw a city—but a city, if such a thing is conceivable, constructed out of light. At that time I had not read the Book of Revelation, nor, incidentally, anything on the subject of life after death. But here was a city in which the walls, houses, streets, seemed to give off light, while moving among them were beings as blindingly bright as the One who stood beside me. This was only a moment's vision, for the next instant the walls of the little room closed around me, the dazzling light faded, and a strange sleep stole over me. . . .

To this day, I cannot fully fathom why I was chosen to return to life. All I know is that when I woke up in the hospital bed in that little room, in the familiar world where I'd spent all my life, it was not a homecoming. The cry in my heart that moment has been the cry of my life ever since: Christ, show me Yourself again. It was weeks before I was well enough to leave the hospital and all that time one thought obsessed me: to get a look at my chart. The room was left unattended: there it was in terse medical shorthand: Pvt. George Ritchie, died December 20, 1943, double lobar pneumonia.

Later, I talked to the doctor who had signed the report. He told me there was no doubt in his mind that I had been dead when he examined me, but that nine minutes later the soldier who had been assigned to prepare me for the morgue had come running to him to ask him to give me a shot of adrenalin. The doctor gave me a hypo of adrenalin directly into the heart muscle, all the while disbelieving what his own eyes were seeing. My return to life, he told me, without brain damage or other lasting effect, was the most baffling circumstance of his career.

Today over 25 years later, I feel that I know why I had the chance to return to this life. It was to become a physician so that I could learn about man and then serve God. And every time I have been able to serve our God by helping some broken-hearted adult, treating some injured child or counseling some teen-ager, then deep within I have felt that He was there beside me again.

About Dr. Ritchie

In doing research, Guideposts has come across many fascinating stories similar to this experience described by Dr. Ritchie. Yet we asked him to relate his story because there is documentary evidence available supporting the circumstances surrounding it. Guideposts has in its possession affidavits from both the Army doctor and attending nurse on the case which attest to the fact that Dr. Ritchie was pronounced dead on the morning of December 20, 1943.

Probably as remarkable as the story itself is the transformation it caused in Dr. Ritchie's life—a transformation which changed him from an indifferent Christian into a man whose life is centered in Christ. For 18 years he has been active in youth work in Richmond, Virginia, and in 1957 he founded the *Christian Youth Corps of America* for the purpose of helping to develop Christian character in our young people. Dr. Ritchies' vision is "a world run by men who are run by God."

THE EDITORS

The Rope Held
by Adela Rogers St. Johns

Into my grief, an answer brighter than light . . .

The rope held.

For many years I had held onto that rope as I climbed, sometimes an inch at a time, sometimes slipping back, up the narrow trail with the dark abyss yawning beside me.

The rope, I knew, was faith. Faith in God. Faith in God as Love. Faith as a grain of mustard seed which would move me up this mountain until, at its summit, faith would become sight.

As best I could I had woven the rope of prayer, and of the words and deeds of those who had trod the path before. Sometimes on sunny days, when I could see my way and feel the pathway firm under my feet, I wondered—would the rope hold if the worst happened?

The worst—or so it seemed to me—did happen.

A bent old man brought me that telegram which in war years hung like a suspended sword over the heart of every mother.

. . . regrets to inform you that your son, Pilot Officer William St. Johns . . . killed in action.

That is 25 years ago now. But as though it was this minute I remember how the words looked, hear my voice saying, "No—no—."

I am telling you this, which is so sacred to me, because I want you to know, and Bill would want you to know, that the rope held and how it held. For part of the rope was his. It is not easy to speak of these things, but I have no right not to share them. I am under orders. *Go and show those ye have seen and heard, how that the dead are raised—**

No, no. Not Bill. Not my son.

---

* Luke 7:22

415

Somehow, Bill was the one we were sure would come back. He was so much loved, a big, kindly boy who did unto others as he was sure they would do unto him because he loved them, too. Before we entered World War II, he enlisted in the Royal Canadian Air Force, but even when I knew he was flying missions over Berlin and Nuremberg, in those terrible raids of 1943, I wasn't afraid for Bill.

Nothing *bad* could happen to Bill. I knew it then; I know it now. That is what I have to tell you.

Returning from a Berlin raid his plane was hit. Months later I learned he had held it in the air until back over England and seven of his crew could parachute to safety.

Bill went down with his ship. As the Skipper must. He was my eldest son.

In the hours that followed, it seemed to me I could not bear it. I must plunge downward into that darkness which is loss of faith in God. How could there be a God and this happen to Bill—to me? To the sons of other women as dear to them as Bill was to me?

My house in New York was beside the East River, and I left my daughter, who in her own grief was still trying to comfort me, and went upstairs on shaking knees to look out over the water. But I found no comfort when I was alone. No comfort anywhere.

Bill was *dead*.

He wouldn't come home. I didn't know where he was. My baby—my little boy—my dear young son. I couldn't pray. No tears came. I couldn't even ask that the Christ in the boat of my own driven soul be awakened and still the storm of my hopeless words and anger against heaven.

I don't know how long it lasted . . . Many hours.

But prayer is God speaking to you, the answer, not the plea.

The small voice that stills the wind and the fire and the earthquake, how else could they ever be stilled?

As I swayed above the abyss, I put out my hands. That, too, is prayer. For I found the rope—it slipped and pulled and burned my hands, but it was there, the rope of my faith in His Love, His Wisdom, His *caring* for His children.

And it held, so that I know now it will always hold.

I do not know what it was that touched my hair. I have no explanation. It might have been imagination or a little wind from the river. But I felt what seemed to me a gentle hand upon my head, and the storm quieted into a moment of warm, sweet silence.

In that quiet, I *knew* beyond anything that can ever be, beyond anything I can express, beyond my own poor capacity to know, beyond any doubt that could ever attack as long as I live, with a knowing deeper than breathing, closer than the beating of my sore heart, with a clearness brighter than light, an activity greater than wind or flowing water—I *knew* my son lived.

I had been right. Nothing *bad* could happen to Bill.

I knew he had gone *through* the valley of the shadow called death, and I did not need to know what he had found at the other end. We have not been told that. Only that they are raised up, *this day* they shall be with Him.

The still small voice in my heart said gently, *All is well with the child.*

What more need any mother *know*?

There was a sound, softer than any sound I have ever heard before, as of a door closing. I knew then that he had closed the door behind him, and what was tormenting the human me was that I wanted to see beyond that door. But I knew that though the door was closed to me, The Father was on the other side of it, too, and Bill had to be with Him.

Sorrow I have. Missing my son I have always. But of grief I was healed when The Comforter told me, "All is well with the child." For who am I to say where and how my son shall live and what The Father's business for him may be? Who am I to say that to *live* he must inhabit this little part of God's universe which is all I am familiar with, when I know he inhabits eternity? Who am I to bound his life that is without end by my poor little ideas of time and space? To limit his glory and his service with the chains of my human limitations?

In the 25 years that have passed, moments of sorrow and longing come, but now I miss him as though he had been sent on a mission to some distant place. There has never been a moment when I haven't been as aware of his existence as I am of my own.

Sometimes I try to imagine what is beyond in that other kingdom, and what he is doing there now. I only know that he dwells in one of the many mansions in His Father's Kingdom, and while perhaps he misses me, he, too, is comforted for he has Love itself as his abiding place.

Into my rope of faith has been woven the strongest

strand of all—that *knowing*. Into our daily lives as a family has come the added glory that the rope held in our greatest sorrow. We talk of Bill as we talk of each other, knowing without one doubt that he lives, perhaps more abundantly than we do. He's away, that's all.

We know that he expects that faith of us, and our respect and love for him that would not let us insult his new birth, his immortality, by cowardly despair.

Bill expected the rope to hold. It always had. Once the door was closed between us, he could not come back to comfort me in this as he had in so many other things. I could not fail Bill by allowing him to see or hear anything but the same courage and laughter and love of others that he had when he lived on this side of the door. I could almost hear him say, "Hey, Mom, where's your *faith?*"

Though sometimes it was hard, I did gain from that very effort not to let him down, the deep, abiding sureness that my son is God's son, that He knows more about him than I ever could, and to say "Bon Voyage, Billy, *I'll be seeing you*," as I had every time he went away before.

On my desk is a small snapshot of Bill's navigator, taken in the cemetery at Stratford-on-Avon where men of the RAF are buried. This friend, who had flown that last mission with Bill and parachuted in time, is standing on a little bridge, smiling softly. On the back of the snapshot he wrote, "Do you know why I am smiling? I've just been to the Skipper's grave—*and he isn't there!*"

His friend *knew*, too.

I told you that part of the rope that held was Bill's.

It was the custom for a pilot to write a letter "To be mailed in case of death." At the time of Bill's last flight over Berlin, the average life of a pilot was short—he could count it in weeks. So when Bill wrote that letter, he knew what he was facing. Mine came. Copied in Bill's boyish scrawl was a poem by another pilot. Bill wrote that it said all the things he had no words to say.

> *To My Mother**
> *Weep not, lady, though no more*
> *He shall pass in by your door.*
> *Though the garden gate is wide*

---

* Poem is by: Flight Lieutenant Anthony Richardson, RAF in "These—Our Children." George G. Harrap and Co. Ltd.

And his footprints scarce have dried
Where he trod his merry way
On his last leave's final day!
So he went, as once he came,
Calling you by that dear name,
As a school boy back from class,
Buoyant as the clouds that pass—
He was like a school boy, then
Off to that harsh school of men.
Weep not, lady, you did teach
What the parsons try to preach—
That a man's life only means
What the eager spirit gleans,
That at twenty he may see
What's still hid at eighty-three.
This he knew—it was no end
Suddenly to meet His Friend,
Suddenly to meet those others,
Those, his comrades, those his brothers,
This is Truth! This thing I know—
No such moment merits woe!

Can we do less than know what they know now?

I do not know how people meet such grief without faith. I do not know how people live life at all without faith. I do know you can weave that rope and that—it holds.

Eternity Can Begin Now
by John L. Sherrill

The turning point in my life came when I learned that immortality does not have to wait on death.

I still remember that I whistled as I strode up New York's Park Avenue that spring morning ten years ago. I stepped through the door of my doctor's office and nodded to his receptionist—an old friend by now. I'd been coming here every month since a cancer operation two years previous, and it was always the same: the doctor's skilled fingers running down my neck, a pat on the back, "See you in a month."

But not that day. This time the fingers prodded and worked a long time. When I left I had an appointment at Memorial Hospital for surgery two days later. What a difference in a spring morning!

I walked back down the same street in the same sunshine, but now a cold fear walked with me. All cancer patients know this fear. We try to stay on top of it in various ways. Now I could no longer hold the fear down. It rose up, scattering reason before it: This was the Fear of Death.

I drove into the first church I came to, looking for darkness and privacy. It was St. Thomas Episcopal, on Fifth Avenue. Mechanically, I sat down. A few minutes later a young minister mounted the pulpit to give a noonday meditation. I didn't know it then, but this brief address was to provide the key which would rid me of this most basic of all fears.

At the time it seemed wretchedly irrelevant to my problem. His text was: . . . *Whosoever believeth in Him should not perish, but have everlasting life.** I wasn't ready for everlasting life; it was life here and now I wanted!

---

* John 3:16

The next morning, however, I was to hear these words again. My wife, Tib, and I were having coffee after a sleepless night when the phone rang. It was a neighbor, Catherine Marshall LeSourd.

"John," she said, "could you come over for a few minutes? I've heard the news and there's something I've got to say to you."

Catherine met us at the door wearing neither makeup nor a smile, which said more than words about the concern she felt. She led us into the family room and plunged in without polite talk.

"I know this is presumptuous of me. I'm going to talk to you about your religious life, and I have no right to assume that it lacks anything. After all, you've been writing for Guideposts for ten years. But often the people who are busiest with religion are farthest from the real, lifechanging heart of it."

I looked at Tib. She sat still as a rock.

"John," said Catherine, "do you believe Jesus was God?"

It was the last question in the world I expected. I thought she would say something about God being able to heal—or prayer being effective—something to do with my crisis. But since she had put the question to me, I considered it. Tib and I were Christians in the sense that we wrote "Protestant" on application blanks, attended church with some regularity, sent our children to Sunday school. Still, I knew that these were habits. I never really had come to grips with the question, was Jesus of Nazareth, in fact, God?

"You might ask what difference it makes," said Catherine. "It spells the difference between life and death, John. The Bible tells us that when we believe in Christ we no longer have to die, but are given everlasting life."

There it was again. But it was precisely at this point of belief that I always had my difficulty. I knew what the Bible promised, and I admired and envied people who accepted it unquestioningly. For myself, there were roadblocks of logic which invariably halted me. I started to list them for Catherine, but she stopped me.

"You're trying to approach Christ through your mind, John," she said. "But it's one of the peculiarities of Christianity that you have to experience it *before* you can understand it. And that's just what I'm hoping for you today—that without understanding, without even knowing why, you make the leap of faith—right over all your doubts—to Christ."

There was silence in the room. I had an eternity of reservations and, at the same time, a sudden desire to do exactly what she was suggesting. The biggest reservation, I admitted frankly: It didn't seem right to shy away all these years and then come running when I had cancer and was scared. "I'd feel like a hypocrite," I said.

"John," said Catherine, almost in a whisper, "That's pride. You want to come to God in *your* way. When you will. Where you will. Healthy. Maybe God wants you now, without a shred to recommend you."

When we left, I still had not brought myself to take that step. But halfway home, passing a certain telephone pole on Millwood Road in Chappaqua, a pole which I can point out today, I turned suddenly to Tib and said:

"I'm making that leap, Tib. I believe in Christ."

That's all I said. Yet I believe now that in some mysterious way, in that instant, I died.

I didn't think of it in those terms at the time—but certainly it wrenched like death. It was a cold-blooded laying down of my sense of what was logical, quite without emotional conviction. And with it went something that was essentially "me." All the bundle of self-consciousness that we call our ego, somehow seemed involved in this decision. I was amazed at how much it hurt, how desperately this thing fought for life, so that there was a real slaying required. But when it was dead and quiet finally, and I blurted out my simple statement, there was room in me for something new and altogether mysterious.

The first hint that there was something different about me came rather amusingly at the hospital. Shortly before the operation a snappy young nurse came in to give me an injection. Since Army days I have had a morbid horror of needles. Yet this time it was different.

"All right, over we go," said my nurse efficiently. But when she had finished, her tone changed. "My, you're a relaxed one! You act like you're taking your vacation here."

It wasn't until after she had left that I realized how true and how remarkable this was. I *was* relaxed. Before the operation, during it, and afterwards. As we waited out the report, my attitude was one of a man who had nothing to fear. How was it possible?

Then I had a strange thought: A man who already had died would certainly not be afraid of death. And that was just how I felt—as though death was behind me.

I wondered if there was any Biblical backing for this idea. Back home and still in doubt on the doctor's verdict, I got out a Bible and a concordance. And there it was in Christ's own words:

"In very truth," Christ told His Disciples, "anyone who gives heed to what I say, and puts his trust in Him who sent Me, had hold of eternal life and does not come up for judgment, but already has passed from death to life."*

How can I describe the excitement that leapt to me from that page? Was it possible that when I took that leap of faith a new life began for me, existing parallel to my earthly life but strangely independent of it? A life that was born of the Spirit and which would use my perishable body only temporarily?

If so, then I should see evidence of something new inside me that owed nothing to my earth-bound existence.

And I did.

The first evidence came when the doctor's report arrived. It was a hopeful one: but I found that this had ceased to be of primary importance to me. Something else seemed far more pressing: to discover what this new life was, where it came from, what it meant.

I had a strange new hunger to explore the New Testament, which I read with a sense of excitement and of recognition. Wasn't it likely that this was the new life, recognizing its natural environment of spirit, feeding on a new kind of food which it needed as my body needed food?

The same was true of church. Suddenly, I *wanted* to attend church: It was no longer a habit, but an experience which quenched a deep thirst.

And—perhaps the most important evidence of all—Christ whom I had approached as a problem in logic, became for me a living Person. I feel now that it was Christ I sought and found in the Bible, in the sacraments, and in the company of Christians.

Ten years have passed since the day Tib and I drove past that telephone pole on Millwood Road. They have been fabulous years, filled with meaning and excitement and wonder. I found, as the months passed and I came down from my mountain top, and slipped into old patterns I'd hoped I'd left behind, that the door always was open for my return. I

* *John 5:24*

always was drawn back. It was as if the new life which began that day was not dependent on my faithfulness, but on Christ's.

And it is this which gives me conviction that it is an undying life, a part of the eternity of God.

To Live Each Day
by Betty Bothwell

Billie Kay, 15, wrote her prophetic essay just one week before the accident.

Parents never are prepared for the day that their children become young men and women. But inevitably, faces that once wore smiles of egg yolk and jam come to us washed and serious, bearing news that is startlingly mature.

With our son Bob it was his decision to pay his own way through college. He said his schooling would mean more if he earned his own money. When he told me this, I suddenly realized I wasn't talking to a boy in knee pants any longer. And through a scholarship and a summer job, he already has made it on his own through three years of college.

A similar awareness occurred the spring of 1963 when my only daughter, Billie Kay, a 15-year-old sophomore at Mississinewa High School, surprised my husband and me with her spiritual perceptiveness. This first came through some themes she prepared as English assignments. One was entitled "The Last Week of My Life." Billie Kay wrote:

"Today I live; a week from today I die. If a situation came to me such as this, I would probably weep. As soon as I realized that there were many things to be done, though, I would try to regain my composure.

"The first day of my suddenly shortened life, I would see all my loved ones and assure them that I loved them. I wouldn't hint that anything was wrong because I wouldn't want to remember them sorrowing but as being happy. I would ask God to give me strength to bear the rest of my precious few days and give me His hand to walk with Him.

"On the second day I would awake to see the rising sun in all its beauty that I had so often cast aside for a few extra moments of coveted sleep. I would gather all my possessions and give them to the needy, trying to console them as much as possible and urge them to consult God for courage.

"The third day, I would spend alone in a woods with the presence of God's creation and goodness around me. In the sweetness of nature I would sit and reminisce of my fondest memories.

"On my fourth day I would prepare my will. The small sentimental things I would leave to my family and friends. This being done, I would go to my mother and spend the day with her. We have always been close and I would want to reassure my love to her especially.

"Friday would be spent with my minister; I would speak to him of my spiritual life. I would like to go with him to see those who were ill and silently be thankful that I knew no pain.

"Saturday I would spend seeing the shut-ins I had so often put off until another day. On this night before my death, I would probably remain awake fearing my impending death, and yet also, preparing for it knowing that God was by my side.

"Upon awakening Sunday I would make all of my last preparations. Taking my Bible, I would go to my church to spend my last hours in prayer. I would ask Him for the courage to face the remaining hours that I might die gracefully. I would hope that my life had bearing on someone and had glorified His holy name. My last hours would be spent in perfect harmony with my God. . . ."

This is the end of Billie Kay's theme, "The Last Week of My Life," but it is not the end of the story. Billie Kay's English paper which was dated Friday, March 15, 1963, was finished just seven days before her life was snuffed out in an automobile accident.

She was returning from a movie with three teen-age friends March 22, about 11 o'clock when the car in which she was a passenger was struck from the rear and rolled over two or three times. Then it caught fire.

My daughter's three friends were pulled out of the wreckage with injuries from which they have since recovered. Billie Kay, who died instantly, was pinned inside.

The last time I saw Billie Kay was earlier the evening of the 22nd when my husband and I dropped her off at a church meeting. She joined friends, laughing and talking.

The events which followed in the next few hours still bring on a vertigo. My husband, Joe, was at work. I was lying down reading when I heard the doorbell ring. When I opened the door, I looked into the face of a police officer.

I don't remember much of anything for the next few hours. I never had known a pain so piercing. Over and over we asked ourselves the question which accompanies all tragedy: Why? Why?

At the moment we could not understand how her death could figure in God's plan. Such a waste it seemed: taking a life in its bud. A life which promised to be as productive as Billie Kay's. She was an excellent student, planning to go to college like her brother; a wonderful Christian, active in our church. How could a loving God permit such a thing to happen?

If I told you that now I accept this tragedy with complete resignation, I would not be telling the whole truth. It is so difficult to accept. Yet, now, I am able to praise God for His abiding love; praise Him for understanding when we were ready to desert Him for "failing" us; thank Him for loaning us an angel for the short time He did.

You see, I now know that our children are not ours, but God's. He sends them for us to shepherd, but they do not belong to us.

Too often, I think, we count up our material accumulations and boast about what is ours when really not even the next breath we take is ours without God's grace. Since Billie Kay has gone, I have had time to think a great deal. I have come to realize the importance of listening for God's calling and responding immediately. Time is so precious. None of us know exactly when our personal judgment day will come. Each fleeting moment wasted is one less minute we have to do Christ's biding.

Joe and I know that Billie Kay's life was not a waste, but a great inspiration—to us and to many others. It was a life which fulfilled His purpose. By our standards 15 years does not connote completeness, but our finite minds can't understand God's yardstick. He does not measure life by length alone, I am sure.

Though I doubt that Billie Kay had any premonition of her death as some have suggested, I feel—without reservation—that she was prepared for it. This belief sustained me in the period of torment following her death.

For Billie Kay also wrote another essay in January, entitled "A Visitation," which also reassures me that Billie Kay was in the center of God's will. Here, in part, is what she wrote:

"I am walking in a forest to escape the noise of the city when suddenly the path all about me grows dim, until at last a heavy fog surrounds me. And finally nothing but deep, lasting darkness fills my entire being; yet it is strangely peaceful and I feel as though I am in the presence of someone powerful and great. . . .

"Peace, wonderful peace is now flooding my entire person and I feel no want or pain. . . . Then approaching me on the path are two glowing yet very gentle eyes, drawing closer and closer. . . .

"Within these gentle eyes I find peace beyond understanding. I am no longer driven with wants and duties. I feel content, secure. I fall on my knees and pray—for what I do not know. The eyes tell me to rise. Though he did not speak, suddenly I realized this was death. He seemed to tell me not to be afraid for it was an eternal, lasting place, a part of everything. . . .

"As I walked home I thought of that one phrase over and over in my mind: 'It is a part of everything,' and when one thinks about it, death really is a part of everything. I fear death no longer and I feel I have a purpose in life. The great power I felt and saw must have been the Almighty Himself. I shall not speak of this until the right time, as it was much too wonderful. Yes, I will keep it in my heart until the right time, maybe even until death."

As I re-read Billie Kay's essays, I find a guide for my life. I see clearly that I must live each day, not as if I had seven days remaining, but as if today I die. Whatever comes, I take great solace in Jesus' promise: *Let not your heart be troubled: ye believe in God, believe also in Me. In my Father's house are many mansions: if it were not so, I would have told you. I go to prepare a place for you, and if I go and prepare a place for you, I will come again, and receive you unto Myself; that where I am, there ye may be also.**

I rest assured that Billie Kay has already taken residence in my Father's house.

*** John 14:1-3**

I Tell You They Have Not Died

by Geoffrey O'Hara

The story behind a famous song of faith.

Years ago a concert singer came to me with a deeply moving story. A skeptic would have casually passed off the tale he told, but I listened intently. Music is a strong bond between people. Moreover, his story was about my song, "There Is No Death."

The tale he told concerned his mother. She had married an irresponsible man who immediately left her. After this marriage her father had disowned her, but when he discovered that she was destitute, he let her return—to live in a chicken coop which he had made over with a bed and scattered articles of furniture. In this chicken coop the singer-to-be was born. His mother died in childbirth.

When the young boy grew up, he decided to take up singing as a career. Soon he acquired a fine reputation, toured the country, and always at the close of the program he would sing, "There Is No Death."

At this point the man's voice quickened with excitement as he gripped my arm tensely. "Mr. O'Hara, just before I sing this song the most amazing thing always happens. My mother appears by my side. I can see her as well as I see you now. She smiles at me and places her soft hand on my shoulder. I feel it as surely as you feel my hand on your arm. She stands by my side until I finish the song. Then she is gone. . . ."

It would take a cold-blooded man not to respond to his story. I didn't mention that the words in the song affected me with the same electric effect, that shock waves coursed up and down my body when I wrote the music to these powerful words. This man's experience was similar to many others I have heard, all from people who had either lost their fear of death after listening to the song, or from those who had felt a similar contact with a departed loved one.

The story behind the composition of "There Is No Death" is equally powerful and moving. The words were written by my friend, the late Gordon Johnstone, who penned the lyrics to many of my songs. Four people, including an Army colonel, Gordon Johnstone, myself and the publisher, Walter Eastman, played a prominent part in the story.

In 1919 Gordon Johnstone met a retired Canadian Army colonel whose command had been wiped out in a series of bloody battles. At first, feeling the loss of his men to the marrow of his bones, the colonel was bitterly despondent. Then slowly his attitude of abject despair had changed to one of quiet faith—a faith in God and in eternal life, because, the colonel said, "I began to feel their breath, their hands touched mine as I walked down the trenches. I could hear their voices. I tell you they have not died. . . ."

Something about this hardboiled colonel's faith—his confidence in the "other world" where his men now laughed and talked together—inspired Johnstone. The words "I tell you they have not died" raced through Johnstone's brain as he rode back to his home that same night. He discovered verses forming on his lips. No sooner had he reached his house than he rushed to the telephone and called his publisher. Then without having written a line down on paper, he poured forth the words to "There Is No Death" over the telephone to Walter Eastman.

> *"I tell you they have not died,*
> *They live and breathe with you;*
> *They walk here at your side,*
> *They tell you things are true.*
> *Why dream of poppied sod*
> *When you can feel their breath,*
> *When Flow'r and soul and God*
> *Know there is no death.*
> *"I tell you they have not died,*
> *Their hands clasp yours and mine;*
> *They are but glorified,*
> *They have become divine.*
> *They live! they know! they see!*
> *They shout with every breath:*

> *All is eternal life!*
> *There is no death!"*

Walter Eastman, head of the New York agency of Chappell & Company, London publishers, listened to the words and was also gripped by their great intensity. Having lost his brother in the war, they struck him with the impact of a howitzer. I was then called in, and the three of us agreed that it was a song to be fashioned with "reinforced concrete." The great positive truth in the words had to burst on the listener with a smashing effect. "I tell you they have not died. . . ."

The challenge was powerful, too important to call for any quick tune that I might hammer out. I realized that I must await a proper "inspiration." Day after day I took out the words, read them over, groped, strained. . . . Several times I did compose complete music, but in each case, three times in all, I tore up the results. When the right music came to me, I would know it beyond any possible doubt. (Editor's note—During this period Mr. O'Hara did manage to compose thirty-two other numbers all of which have since been published.)

How many composers have so grappled and struggled with a song! Then quite unexpectedly the solution fairly clouts them between the eyes. And where does it often happen? On a train. Riding over wheels seems to create a steady rhythm that soon dissolves into a sublime silence. While traveling thus from Boston to New York four months after receiving the words to "There Is No Death," I slipped into such a relaxed state. On a hunch I brought out the words again and read them over. Suddenly, like the shock of a plunge into an icy lake, the music came to me, numbing me all over. Feverishly I wrote. By the time I reached New York I had the framework of the song finished.

That same evening I retired at 9 P.M. in order to be fresh in the morning when I planned to finish the piano accompaniment and do the final inking job. The hours ticked away—ten, eleven, twelve, one o'clock—but I could not sleep. The summons was too strong to deny. I arose and went to work. As I toiled on through the night, I felt that a battery was attached to my chair and was sending a steady current coursing through my body. Never have I experienced such a strong spiritual force driving me on. Never before or after did I do my composing at such an unusual hour. At three o'clock in the morning I finished the song, and not a note was changed from that moment on. The next morning I took the music without delay to Walter Eastman, the publisher, and played it for him. His reaction was unusual as had been all the experiences connected with "There Is No Death." He listened to it quietly, then without a word picked up the song, put it in the safe, turned the lock and walked out of the building. Such eloquent silence meant more to me than any words.

My strong religious faith dates back to my boyhood. My father and mother, and their families before them, believed in "the Fatherhood of God and the fellowship of man" principle, and they lived their religion. My father was the most truly democratic man I ever knew. I have yet to meet his equal.

At an early age I discovered that there were many people who accepted blindly but one isolated interpretation of God and the Bible. Once their narrow opinion took possession of their equally narrow minds, all further thought or ideas were shut out. Like moles they moved through life in a sort of darkness, distorting Biblical passages to conform with and reinforce their own dogmatic ideas, and never accepting the possibility that interpretations of life other than their own could be right.

As a result I determined to keep an open mind toward religion and God. Indeed, I have often wished that I could organize a movement to re-study the Bible translations in the light of scientific knowledge to help people out of the rut in which they have mired themselves.

God was good to me when He gave me talent to compose music. Perhaps I can pay off some of my debt to Him through my songs. I believe that a song should say something, and if the message has a useful effect on people, then may I not feel that I have made a contribution to the world? In many cases I have discovered that it is not the serious songs that do the most good. Sometimes a quiet humor or expression of a simple sentiment in a song can be of great stimulus. "K-K-K-Katy" which I composed in 1917 proved popular with the soldiers, and I like to think it did much for their morale.

"There Is No Death" and "K-K-K-Katy" are contrasts in

songs, but each made its contribution. So, too, may contrasting views of religion offer a contribution to all mankind, for by understanding different viewpoints we can come to a really great understanding of God.

Parable Of A Water Beetle

by Norman Vincent Peale

---

*A famous movie producer gets an object lesson
from Nature on immortality.*

Cecil B. DeMille, the famous motion picture producer, was
a man of great talents and keen insights.

He liked to get off by himself at times to think out a
problem. One such time when he was faced with some vexing
personal problems, he went out in a canoe on a lake in
Maine.

After a while, the canoe floated inshore to a place where
the water was only a few inches deep. Looking down he saw
that the bottom was crowded with beetlelike bugs. As he
watched, one of the water beetles came to the surface and
slowly crawled up the side of the canoe. Finally reaching the
top, it grasped fast to the wood and died.

DeMille soon forgot the beetle and his thoughts went
back to his own problems. Several hours later, he happened
to notice the beetle again and saw that, in the hot sun, its
shell had become very dry and brittle. As he watched, it
slowly split open and there emerged from it a new form, a
dragonfly, which took to the air, its scintillating colors flashing in the sunlight.

That winged insect flew farther in an instant than the
water beetle had crawled in days. Then it circled back and
swooped down to the surface of the water. DeMille noticed
its shadow on the water. The water beetles below might have
seen it, too, but now their erstwhile companion was in a
world beyond their comprehension. They were still living in
their limited world while their winged cousin had gained for
himself all the freedom between earth and sky.

Later when DeMille told of this experience, he concluded with a very penetrating question.

"Would the great Creator of the universe," he asked, "do that for a water beetle and not for a human being?"

My Best Singer

When Johnny first came to my classroom, he was several years older than the other students at 13, untidy, undernourished, and a slow reader. Sympathy overpowered me and I decided to do all I could to give him a sense of belonging to the group. But how?

Since man is created in God's image, then there is something good in each individual. Looking at Johnny, I had to search for something to praise. He stumbled through the third reader, faltered through the third arithmetic and labored with the second speller. He did not get along well with the other children.

Then, one day, I discovered that he had a rather sweet and pleasing voice. Immediately, I complimented him on it and the effect was almost miraculous. His behavior improved. He started combing his hair. He became one of the group.

For our Christmas program, Johnny was chosen to sing the only solo. Some weeks later when the school superintendent visited our class, she stopped in front of Johnny's desk. Johnny was embarrassed; he realized he should have been working in a much higher grade. Suddenly, he looked up and announced with great pride, "I'm Mrs. Spray's *best* singer."

In the years since, I have had other "Johnnys" in my classes—all with something to praise. But I'll never forget "my best singer" because he made me realize that every person has at least one talent and the right compliment can help him find it.

PAULINE E. SPRAY
Benton Harbor, Michigan

The Host of Heaven
by Dr. S. Ralph Harlow

Could it really have happened? Two people—
husband and wife—substantiate a "vision."

It was not Christmas, it was not even wintertime, when the
event occurred that for me threw sudden new light on the ancient angel tale. It was a glorious spring morning and we
were walking, my wife and I, through the newly budded
birches and maples near Ballardvale, Massachusetts.

Now I realize that this, like any account of personal experience, is only as valid as the good sense and honesty of the
person relating it. What can I say about myself? That I am a
scholar who shuns guesswork and admires scientific investigation? That I have an A.B. from Harvard, an M.A. from
Columbia, a Ph.D. from Hartford Theological Seminary?
That I have never been subject to hallucinations? That attor-
neys have solicited my testimony, and I have testified in the
courts, regarded by judge and jury as a faithful, reliable
witness? All this is true and yet I doubt that any amount of
such credentials can influence the belief or disbelief of another.

In the long run, each of us must sift what comes to us
from others through his own life experience, his view of the
universe, his understanding. And so I will simply tell my
story.

The little path on which Marion and I walked that
morning was spongy to our steps and we held hands with the
sheer delight of life as we strolled near a lovely brook. It was
May, and because it was the examination reading period for
students at Smith College where I was a professor, we were
able to get away for a few days to visit Marion's parents.

We frequently took walks in the country, and we especially loved the spring after a hard New England winter,
for it is then that the fields and the woods are radiant and

436

calm yet show new life bursting from the earth. This day we were especially happy and peaceful; we chatted sporadically, with great gaps of satisfying silence between our sentences.

Then from behind us we heard the murmur of muted voices in the distance, and I said to Marion, "We have company in the woods this morning."

Marion nodded and turned to look. We saw nothing, but the voices were coming nearer—at a faster pace than we were walking, and we knew that the strangers would soon overtake us. Then we perceived that the sounds were not only behind us but above us, and we looked up.

How can I describe what we felt? Is it possible to tell of the surge of exaltation that ran through us? Is it possible to record this phenomenon objectively and yet be credible?

For about ten feet above us, and slightly to our left, was a floating group of glorious, beautiful creatures that glowed with spiritual beauty. We stopped and stared as they passed above us.

There were six of them, young beautiful women dressed in flowing white garments and engaged in earnest conversation. If they were aware of our existence they gave no indication of it. Their faces were perfectly clear to us, and one woman, slightly older than the rest, was especially beautiful. Her dark hair was pulled back in what today we would call a ponytail, and although I cannot say it was bound at the back of her head, it appeared to be. She was talking intently to a younger spirit whose back was toward us and who looked up into the face of the woman who was talking.

Neither Marion nor I could understand their words although their voices were clearly heard. The sound was somewhat like hearing but being unable to understand a group of people talking outside a house with all the windows and doors shut.

They seemed to float past us, and their graceful motion seemed natural—as gentle and peaceful as the morning itself. As they passed, their conversation grew fainter and fainter until it faded out entirely, and we stood transfixed on the spot, still holding hands with the vision before us.

It would be an understatement to say that we were astounded. Then we looked at each other, each wondering if the other also had seen.

There was a fallen birch tree just there beside the path. We sat down on it and I said, "Marion, what did you see?

Tell me exactly, in precise detail. And tell me what you heard."

She knew my intent—to test my own eyes and ears; to see if I had been the victim of hallucination or imagination. And her reply was identical in every respect to what my own senses had reported to me.

I have related this story with the same faithfulness and respect for truth and accuracy as I would tell it on the witness stand. But even as I record it I know how incredible it sounds.

Perhaps I can claim no more for it than that it has had a deep effect on our own lives. For this experience of more than 35 years ago greatly altered our thinking. Once both Marion and I were somewhat skeptical about the absolute accuracy of the details at the birth of Christ. The story, as recorded by St. Luke, tells of an angel appearing to *shepherds abiding in the field* and after the shepherds had been told of the Birth, *suddenly there was with the angel a multitude of the heavenly host praising God, and saying, Glory to God in the highest.**

As a child I accepted the multitude seen by the shepherds as literal heavenly personages. Then I went through a period when I felt that they were merely symbols injected into a fantasy or legend. Today, after the experience at Ballardvale, Marion and I are no longer skeptical. We believe that in back of that story recorded by St. Luke lies a genuine objective experience told in wonder by those who had the experience.

Once, too, we puzzled greatly over the Christian insistence that we have "bodies" other than our normal flesh and blood ones. We were like the doubter of whom St. Paul wrote:

*But some man will say, How are the dead raised up? and with what body do they come?***

In the 35 years since that bright May morning, his answer has rung for us with joyous conviction.

There are also celestial bodies, and bodies terrestrial: but the glory of the celestial is one, and the glory of the terrestrial is another. . . . So also is the resurrection of the dead. . . . It is sown a natural body; it is raised a spiritual body. There is a natural body, and there is a spiritual

---

* *Luke 2:8-14*
** *I Corinthians 15:35*

*body. . . . And as we have borne the image of the earthly, we shall also bear the image of the heavenly. . . . For this corruptible must put on incorruption, and this mortal must put on immortality.**

All of us, I think, hear the angels for a little while at Christmastime. We let the heavenly host come close once in the year. But we reject the very possibility that what the shepherds saw 2,000 years ago was part of the reality that presses close every day of our lives.

And yet there is no reason for us to shrink from this knowledge. Since Marion and I began to be aware of the host of heaven all about us, our lives have been filled with a wonderful hope. Phillips Brooks, the great Episcopal bishop, expressed the cause of this hope more beautifully than I can do:

"This is what you are to hold fast to yourself—*the sympathy and companionship of the unseen worlds.* No doubt it is best for us now that they should be unseen. It cultivates in us that higher perception that we call 'faith.' But who can say that the time will not come when, even to those who live here upon earth, the unseen worlds shall no longer be unseen?"

The experience at Ballardvale, added to the convictions of my Christian faith, gives me not only a feeling of assurance about the future, but a sense of adventure toward it too.

---

* *1 Corinthians 15:40-53*

Message To The Bereaved
by Natalie Kalmus

"Never again will death frighten me. That was my sister's inheritance to me."

Don't worry, but come to me as soon as you can," my sister, Eleanor Smith, wired. At the time I was in London working out Technicolor problems with one of the British motion-picture companies.

I felt a deep, numbing pang. I knew Eleanor had been ill some time. Surely this was her gentle way of telling me the end was coming.

I could not picture—or accept it. Always radiating charm, friendliness and an inner happiness, my sister had been a wonderful inspiration to those close to her. She had that rare trait of always giving others a pat on the back, lifting their spirits and sending them off with a fresh outlook on life.

When first stricken by the most fearsome of medical enemies, the doctors had told her that her days were numbered. Knowing this had not made the slightest difference in her warm interest in people—nor in her deep abiding faith.

But now she needed me. I returned to the States and hurried to Eleanor, expecting to find her in bed in great pain. Instead she was in the living room perched jauntily on the sofa, looking more like a school girl of 17 than an incurably ill woman.

"Natalie," she held out her arms joyously, "I'm so happy now that you're here. We have so much to talk over." To anyone listening I might have dropped in for a casual call.

After Eleanor had later retired for the night, the doctor drew me aside. "Mrs. Kalmus," he said, "I think that it will be a most trying experience for you if you stay here through to the end. I'm afraid that your sister's last hours will be an agony of pain."

Medically I knew he was right. Yet the exquisite radiance I noticed in my sister's face seemed somehow to refute his statement. The strange feeling swept over me that the strength of my sister's spirit could well triumph over her pain.

During the next few days I discovered that Eleanor was doing many things to baffle the doctors. They were preparing her for some very grim final moments. She was ignoring their solemn suggestions and remedies. One night she had me sit down on the side of her bed.

"Natalie, promise me that you won't let them give me any drugs. I realize that they are trying to help relieve my pain, but I want to be fully aware of every sensation. *I am convinced that death will be a beautiful experience.*"

I promised. Alone later, I wept, thinking of her courage. Then as I tossed in bed on through the night, I realized that what I looked to be a calamity, my sister intended to be a triumph.

One afternoon Eleanor, in the most airy and lighthearted manner, asked several friends to a dinner party which she, on the spur of the moment, decided to hold. I was stunned. But Eleanor grinned at me impishly in high spirits. The sight of the happiness in her face checked my objections.

On the night of the party Eleanor dressed meticulously, concealing the pain I knew she felt. We helped her downstairs before the guests were to arrive. Sitting in a turquoise chair in her yellow evening gown, she sparkled with life and gaiety. Again I noticed the school girl look on her face.

The party was a grand success; the guests were never once aware of the illness which my sister concealed so expertly. That night, however, when she was carried to bed, her deep physical weariness appeared on the surface. Then I realized that my sister knew this was her final social fling. She had planned it that way.

Ten days later the final hour drew near. I had been at her bedside for hours. We had talked about many things, and always I marveled at her quiet, sincere confidence in eternal life. Not once did the physical torture inside overcome her spiritual strength. This was something that the doctors simply hadn't taken into account.

"Dear kind God, keep my mind clear and give me peace," she had murmured over and over again during those last days.

We had talked so long that I noticed she was drifting off to sleep. I left her quietly with the nurse and retired to get some rest. A few minutes later I heard my sister's voice calling for me. Quickly I returned to her room. She was dying.

I sat on her bed and took her hand. It was on fire. Then she seemed to rise up in bed almost to a sitting position.

"Natalie," she said, "there are so many of them. There's Fred . . . and Ruth—what's she doing here? Oh, I know!"

An electric shock went through me. She had said Ruth! Ruth was her cousin who had died suddenly the week before. *But Eleanor had not been told of Ruth's sudden death.*

Chill after chill shot up and down my spine. I felt on the verge of some powerful, almost frightening knowledge. She *had* murmured Ruth's name.

Her voice was surprisingly clear. "It's so confusing. So many of them!" Suddenly her arms stretched out as happily as when she had welcomed me! "I'm going up," she murmered.

Then she dropped her arms around my neck—and relaxed in my arms. *The will of her spirit had turned final agony into rapture.*

As I lay her head back on the pillow, there was a warm, peaceful smile on her face. Her golden brown hair lay carelessly on the pillow. I took a white flower from the vase and placed it in her hair. With her petite, trim figure, her wavy hair, the white flower and the soft smile, she looked once more—and permanently—just like a school girl.

Never again will death frighten me in any way. This was my sister's inheritance to me—her final, beautiful gift. I had seen for myself how thin was the curtain between life and death. I had glimpsed part of the wonderful truth about everlasting life.

In the weeks that followed, however, there was a tremendous vacuum inside me which I could not fill. Then, as though heaven-sent, a famous authoress came to visit me and brought me a prayer by Rudolph Steinert, written to comfort those grief-stricken by the death of loved-ones.

I read the words slowly, letting them settle deep inside me. Soon many facts became clear. Without realizing it, I had been desperately trying to hold on to my sister, which was fair to neither of us. It might well be handicapping Eleanor in her efforts to adjust to her new life. It was upsetting my own normal life. With this realization a new peace and tranquillity began to fill the emotional vacuum inside me.

A perfect relationship now exists between my sister and me. Frequently, I feel her comforting presence. At the same time I am again able to draw full satisfaction and enjoyment from both my business and social life. Whenever the opportunity arises, I am happy to share the remarkable story of my sister's passing with others for the help and comfort it can give them. And always I have the feeling that it is Eleanor herself who is passing on this beautiful understanding of death—*through me.*

As for those occasions when loneliness assails me, I say the words of this prayer over and over to myself as I remember them:

Into thy new surroundings let my love be woven.
Warming thy coolness, cooling thy warmness,
Live upward bourne by love, illuminated by light.
The beautiful love me found
I shall now send into the realms of the spirit
To link soul with soul when, from the spirits' illuminous lands,
Thou wilt turn in search of what thou seekest in me
Thou wilt find my love in thinking.

Man Is Not Alone
by Everett McKinley Dirksen

A moving testimony from a senator no one will forget.

Several years ago, I made a recording about the faith of
America in response to the "God-is-dead" idea that became
current for a while. The recording began with Genesis and
included a brief poem which carried the title, *Man Is Not
Alone*. That poem, in part, went like this:

> *Not alone as we reach for a star in the sky,*
> *Not alone as we live, not alone as we die,*
> *Let us never despair in whatever we do,*
> *Someone is there who will help us come through,*
> *We are left on our honor, but not on our own,*
> *Always remember—Man is not alone.**

I believe in these words, because I have felt God's
presence in my life for as long as I can remember. One of
my earliest recollections is of our family gathered in the parlor with Mother reading from a huge Bible, which always
rested on a table in the center of the room.

Father died when I was five, leaving Mother with three
young boys and two stepsons to rear. But the loss did not
shake her great faith. Life went on about as it did before, except for the fact that there was much more responsibility on
us boys. All of us had to pitch in with the chores, and even
on a small farm like ours those chores were there seven days
a week.

There was one thing which took priority over work.
That was church. Every Sunday morning we went early to
Sunday school and then to church. In the evening I attended

---

the Christian Endeavor meeting for young people and after that, the Sunday-evening church service.

With such indoctrination, I learned to include God in all my plans and dreams. I talk to Him about my aspirations every day. Most people call it prayer. I have thought of it as conversation with Him.

I remember one night when I was a senior in high school. We had organized a minstrel show and traveled to a neighboring town to give a performance. In those early days I thought I might become an actor, but Mother exacted a promise that I not go on the stage, because she felt it was a wicked place. The town where we performed was about ten miles from Pekin, Illinois, my birthplace and home town.

I had scarcely been away from my home town overnight and always felt the urge to get back there no matter how late it might be. It was suggested that the minstrel troupe stay with some of the townspeople, but I demurred at the idea. I said, "I have chores to do at five o'clock in the morning," and I walked home.

It was one of those moonless nights when you could see little ahead of you. The night was rent with strange noises, or perhaps they were imagined. In any event, it was frightening, but I knew I wasn't alone. It took several hours to traverse that ten miles' distance, but in those hours I had a steady conversation with God.

There have been many other times when I have sensed His presence. One of them was during World War I when I was a balloonist in the United States Army in France. The job of the observer was to sit in a balloon basket 3,000 feet in the air and watch field artillery, or howitzers, fire on an enemy target. And then, by telephone, direct the battery by letting them know if they were to the right or left of the target.

The Balloon Corps was referred to in many quarters as the "suicide squad." I cannot honestly say that I was devoid of fear because of the presence of the Almighty. I knew He was there as He was in the presence of Job, and with Him I could say, *Though He slay me yet will I trust Him.**

There was another time when I realized that I was not alone. It happened in 1948 when, for the first time, the Congress was trying to prepare a legislative budget. This work required long hours of reading fine print and small fig-

---

* *Job 13:15*

ures, and after five or six weeks, I began to experience a
strange blur in both eyes. An eye specialist diagnosed it as
chorioretinitis. He didn't think the condition was too serious,
but when other doctors were added to the list of consultants,
I learned that some were afraid there might be a malignancy.

I was advised to go to Johns Hopkins Hospital in Baltimore and condition myself for an enucleation. (It is a polite
term for the removal of an eye.) After a conference call involving all the doctors—and there was a difference of opinion
among them—I boarded a train for Baltimore.

Enroute, I began a conversation with God. It was very
simple, very practical, and perhaps I should confess it was a
little tearful. I simply told Him I hoped I would not have to
yield an eye, but if it was His way, I would accept it. What I
really wanted to know was whether to permit them to
proceed with the operation. On my knees in that train, I got
the answer.

When the great eye surgeon—no longer living—suggested we prepare for the removal of the right eye, I said, "Doctor, I have decided not to have the operation."

His answer was, "Why did you come here?"

I said, "I came because other doctors, including one who
is a graduate of the clinic in this very hospital, suggested that
I should come and see you, but I found another doctor."

He looked at me rather quizzically and said, "You
couldn't have."

"But," I said, "I did find another doctor. He is the Big
Doctor way upstairs."

The surgeon looked at me with disbelief in his eyes and
said, "So you are one of those guys are you?"

I kept the eye. It is my better eye.

This adventure, however, caused me to quit my political
career and return home to convalesce. There was the comfort
of having Mrs. Dirksen read to me so many appealing passages from so many books in the Scriptures and particularly
Psalms and Proverbs. I developed the urge to work in the
soil, where one can see the whole miracle of creation—the
miracle of a tiny seed nurtured by sunlight and water,
sprouting in due course and providing a majestic flower or a
succulent vegetable.

Gradually my sight improved, and I began to think seriously of going back to practicing law. There are those who
look at me in a state of disbelief when I mention this healing

experience, but I account for it in no other way. I knew I was not alone.

Before I could think too seriously about returning to a law practice, the delegations came to my home to urge me to be a candidate for the Senate in 1950. Two years before, my party had been roundly defeated at the polls. What interested me most about the delegations who came to make this appeal was that almost invariably they would say, "Of course you can't win, but somebody must make the race."

My answer usually was, "If I do make the race, I shall not do so with the idea of going through the agony of a hard campaign and losing. I would expect to win." And I did win.

I have found the nation's capital to be an incredibly interesting place. It is the seat of government of the greatest free democracy on earth. It is where history unfolds and discloses a divine pattern if we will only look for it. I believe it must be in accordance with His plan. For if there is a creative hand behind this universe, there must be that same creative hand to give direction to this good land.

Today we are astounded by the exploits of our astronauts, but there are so many other things which are not exploits. They are fixed patterns. The earth moves around the sun every 365 days. We call it a year. If the earth were any closer to the sun, we might all be burned to a crisp, so would our subsistence. If we were farther away, we might freeze. There is a moon. It has an attractive power upon the waters of the earth. If the moon were much closer, we would be engulfed by unbelievable tides. If it were much farther away, vast land surfaces would be exposed. There is a strangely measured distance between the planets.

The whole pattern of this universe is an amazing piece of adjustment, and all of it rises to testify that there is a creative force at work. God not only operates in meticulous detail to shape our world; He is also concerned about the destiny of each one of His children. Man is not alone.

If He Came To Your House

When you saw Him coming, would you meet Him at the door
With arms outstretched in welcome to your heavenly Visitor?
Or would you have to change your clothes before you let Him
*   in?*

Or hide some magazines, and put the Bible where they'd been?
Would you hide your worldly music and put some hymn books
out?
Could you let Jesus walk right in, or would you rush about?
And I wonder—if the Saviour spent a day or two with you,
Would you go right on doing the things you always do?
Would you go right on saying the things you always say?
Would life for you continue as it does from day to day?
Would you take Jesus with you everywhere you'd planned
to go?
Or would you maybe change your plans for just a day or so?
Would you be glad to have Him meet your very closest
friends?
Or would you hope they stay away until His visit ends?
Would you be glad to have Him stay forever on and on?
Or would you sigh with great relief when He at last was
gone?
It might be interesting to know the things that you would do,
If Jesus came in person to spend some time with you.

LOIS BLANCHARD EADES

The Blessed Assurance
by Norman Vincent Peale

"Darkness is powerless before the onslaught of light. And so it is with death."

All members of the human race have two things in common: Each of us was born, and each of us must die. Most of us are not too concerned with the circumstances of our birth; we don't remember it; it lies far behind us. But the thought of dying is another matter. The knowledge that our days on this earth will come to an end is an inescapable part of our existence—somber, mysterious and sometimes frightening.

Quite often people come to me and confess that they are haunted by a fear of death which they try to conceal from other people, and even from themselves. These people are not necessarily old or ill. Often they are in the prime of life, with many useful years ahead of them. But sometimes, it seems, the more they love life, the more they dread death.

What I usually do with such people is admit that I, too, have moments when I flinch from the thought of dying. I suggest that this is perfectly natural, that in my opinion the good Lord planted a certain amount of this fear in all of us so that we would not be tempted to relinquish the trials and responsibilities of this life too easily. But, I add, I'm sure the Lord didn't intend us to be panicky about it. Finally, I try to reassure these troubled souls by outlining the thoughts that have helped me rise above the fear of death, or at least keep it under control.

Take, for example, the inevitability of dying. This seems to appall some people, but it always has struck me as a merciful thing. Suppose there were loopholes in this universal law; suppose that somehow there was a one percent chance of avoiding death. Consider how frantically we'd search for that loophole, how wretched we'd be not to find it.

But consider how wretched we'd be if we did find it! No

449

one would be happy trying to live forever. It's a little like being at a wonderful play. During the performance, one hopes that it will go on and on, but one wouldn't really like to stay in the theater all night, or until boredom set in.

Another thing I tell the worried ones is this: You may be frightened in advance, but it is almost certain that when the time comes you will not fear death at all. I have talked to doctors and nurses who have seen hundreds of people die, and they all tell me that at the end, unless they are tormented by a guilty conscience, people go peacefully and thankfully. The truth is, death has been miscast as a grim reaper. To almost everyone, when it finally comes, it comes as a friend.

"That may be true," say some of the fearful ones. "The moment of death may be less terrifying than we thought. But then what? Is there a life after death? Is there any proof?"

To these I reply, "It depends on what you mean by proof. To me the evidence is overwhelming, whether you consult your reason or your instincts. Look at the vast Universe that surrounds us, the laws that govern the spinning solar systems and the whirling electrons, the balance and economy of a stupendous Reality that uses everything and wastes nothing. Does it seem reasonable that the Intelligence behind such a Reality would create a being as complex and sensitive as man just to snuff him out forever like the flame of a candle? Of course it doesn't!"

What is death, then? It is a change into some new form of existence. We are not permitted to know exactly what this new existence is like, but I believe that sometimes we are given glimpses. Time and again it has been reported of people on the brink of death that they seem to become aware of a great radiance, or hear beautiful music, or see the faces of departed loved ones who are apparently waiting for them across the line. Are these just hallucinations? I don't think so. Several of them have happened within my own family.

My father, who died at 85 after a distinguished career as both physician and minister, struggled against a very real fear of death. But not long after he died, my stepmother dreamed that he came to her and told her that his fears had been groundless.

"Don't ever worry about dying," he said to her. "There's nothing to it!" The dream was so vivid that she woke up, astounded. And I believe that my father did come to reassure her, because that is precisely the phrase I have heard him use a thousand times to dismiss something as unimportant or trivial.

In 1939 when news reached me that my mother had died unexpectedly in another town, I was alone in my office, numb with grief and loss. There was a Bible on my desk, and I put my hand on it, staring blindly out of the window. As I did so, I felt a pair of hands touch my head, gently, lovingly, unmistakably. The pressure lasted only an instant; then it was gone. An illusion? An hallucination caused by grief? I don't think so. I think my mother was permitted to reach across the gulf of death to touch and reassure me.

And eight years ago, when I was preaching at a Methodist gathering in Georgia, I had the most startling experience of all. At the end of the final session, the presiding Bishop asked all the ministers in the audience to come forward, form a choir and sing an old, familiar hymn.

I was sitting on the speakers' platform, watching them come down the aisles. And suddenly, among them, I saw my father. I saw him as plainly as I ever saw him when he was alive. He seemed about forty, vital and handsome. He was singing with the others. When he smiled at me, and put up his hand in the old familiar gesture, for several unforgettable seconds it was as if my father and I were alone in that big auditorium. Then he was gone, but in my heart the certainty of his presence was indisputable. He was *there,* and I know that some day, somewhere, I'll meet him again.

We don't try to prove immortality so that we can believe in it; we try to prove it because we cannot help believing in it. Instinct whispers to us that death is not the end; reason supports it; psychic phenomena uphold it. Even science, in its own way, now insists that the universe is more spiritual than material. Einstein's great equation indicates that matter and energy are interchangeable. Where does that leave us, if not in an immaterial universe? The great psychologist, William James, said, "Apparently there is one great universal mind, and since man enters into this universal mind, he is a fragment of it."

This intangible in all of us, this fragment of the universal mind, is what religion calls the soul, and it is indestructible because—as James said—it is at one with God. The Founder of Christianity said specifically that there is a life beyond the grave. Not only that, Jesus proved it by rising from the dead Himself. If you believe that it happened, death should hold little terror for you. If you don't believe it, you are not a completely fulfilled Christian.

The Easter message is one of such hope and joy that even unbelievers are thrilled by it. Several years ago a reporter I know covered the sunrise service that is held each Easter on the rim of the Grand Canyon. It was cold—below freezing, actually—and he had not worn an overcoat. Not a particularly religious man, he stood there shivering dolefully and wishing himself back in bed.

"But then," he told me, "when the sun cleared the canyon rim, and light poured into that stupendous chasm, I forgot all about being cold. One moment everything was gray, formless. Then came torrents of light plunging down the canyon walls, making them blaze with color, dissolving the blackness into purple shadows that eddied like smoke. Standing there, I had a most indescribable feeling, a conviction that the darkness that had filled the great gorge was an illusion, that only the light was real, and that we silent watchers on the canyon rim were somehow a part of the light. . . ."

Strange words, coming from a hard-boiled reporter, but close to a profound truth. Darkness *is* powerless before the onslaught of light. And so it is with death. We have allowed ourselves to think of it as a dark door, when actually it is a rainbow bridge spanning the gulf between two worlds.

That is the Easter message. Yet there are people, even good Christians, who accept it with their minds but really never feel it in their hearts. I know this from personal experience: the message never got through fully to me until I went to the Holy Land and saw with my own eyes the hills and fields and roads where Jesus actually walked. One day we visited the beautiful little village of Bethany.

This was the home of Mary and Martha and Lazarus. And there is still a tomb there, said to be the tomb of Lazarus. We went into that tomb, down 22 steps, and saw the place where the body of Lazarus is presumed to have lain until the voice of Jesus wakened him from the dead. I was so deeply moved that when we came up out of the tomb I turned to my wife and said, "We are standing where the greatest statement ever uttered was made, 'I am the resurrection and the life: he that believeth in Me, though he were dead, yet shall he live.'"

At that moment, for the first time in my life, Easter really happened to me, and I shall never be the same again. For the rest of my days I shall preach, out of a conviction so deep that it can never be shaken, that if people will accept Jesus Christ they will have eternal life.

Recently, I was at Mount Holyoke College in New England, visiting my daughter Elizabeth, a student there. Walking around the campus, we came upon a sundial. On it was an inscription: *To larger sight, the rim of shadow is the line of light.*

There you have it in just 12 words. Believe me, death is only a momentary rim of shadow. Beyond it, waiting for all of us who deserve it, is the radiance of eternal life.

Heartwarming Books
of
Faith and Inspiration

INSPIRATIONAL FAVORITES

EUGENIA PRICE

St. Simon's Trilogy

☐	13682 Beloved Invader	$2.25
☐	14089 Maria	$2.50
☐	14406 New Moon Rising	$2.50
☐	14195 Lighthouse	$2.50
	and	
☐	6485 Don Juan McQueen	$1.75

HAL LINDSEY

☐	14096 The Late Great Planet Earth	$2.50
☐	14286 The Liberation of Planet Earth	$2.50
☐	14374 Satan Is Alive And Well On Planet Earth	$2.75
☐	14571 The Terminal Generation	$2.50
☐	14108 There's A New World Coming	$2.50

Bantam Book Catalog

Here's your up-to-the-minute listing of over 1,400 titles by your favorite authors.

This illustrated, large format catalog gives a description of each title. For your convenience, it is divided into categories in fiction and non-fiction—gothics, science fiction, westerns, mysteries, cookbooks, mysticism and occult, biographies, history, family living, health, psychology, art.

So don't delay—take advantage of this special opportunity to increase your reading pleasure.

Just send us your name and address and 50¢ (to help defray postage and handling costs).